The Penn Commentary on Piers Plowman
Volume 5

The Penn Commentary on Piers Plowman

VOLUME 5

C Passūs 20–22; B Passūs 18–20

Stephen A. Barney

PENN

University of Pennsylvania Press
Philadelphia

Published by
University of Pennsylvania Press
Philadelphia, Pennsylvania 19104-4112

A cataloging-in-publication record is available from the Library of Congress

For

David Marshall Barney

and

Beverly Garrett Barney

Contents

Note to the Reader

The text of *Piers* quoted here is that of the Athlone edition, under the general editorship of George Kane. The commentary is keyed first of all to the C Version of the poem, then in reverse chronology to the B and A versions. Latin quotations in the poem are cited by adding the letter "a" to the end of the line number. In passūs 21 and 22, the line numbers of the C and B Versions are identical, and the B lineation is consequently not recorded. In C Passus 20 the differing line numbers of B.18 are recorded with the lemma. The editions of Schmidt and Pearsall differ little in their lineation from the Athlone edition, and the quotation of the beginning and ending words of each passage commented upon will make reference to those editions easy. Skeat's line-numbering differs somewhat more; in the C Version, add one to the Athlone passus number to arrive at Skeat's passus number. References to lines of the A and B versions are specifically labeled with the letters A and B; references to C lines are generally not labeled. When reference is made to lines that fall in parallel passages of the versions, the references to parallel passages are enclosed within parentheses. Hence the notation "see 11.116–33 (B.10.176–221, A.11.128–64)" refers to passages that are closely parallel in the three versions; a notation like "see 1.146–58 (B.1.148–62; cp. A.1.135–38)" indicates a substantive difference in the version prefaced by "cp."

Each passus of the poem in this installment is supplied with an introductory "Headnote," which summarizes the main features of the passus and treats matters relevant to the passus (or group of passūs) as a whole. We have been careful to provide divisions of the text as we understand the movement of the poem. These are usually preceded by a more general, summary note; such *summulae* are followed by notes on particular passages. The discussion repeatedly encompasses larger units first, then devolves to smaller ones, in a nested structure.

Translations from the Vulgate Bible are taken from the Douay-Rheims text (Challoner revision) in modernized spelling (New York: P.J. Kenedy & Sons, 1914), with slight adjustments when necessary. Douay references to I and II Kings correspond to I and II Samuel in the Authorized Version, III and IV Kings to AV's I and II Kings, and Psalms 10–145 correspond to AV's Psalms

11–146. Quotations from the Latin Vulgate generally follow the modern (Clementine) text, as represented in the edition printed by Typis Societatis S. Joannis Evangelistae (Rome, 1956). When biblical passages are parallel in the synoptic Gospels—Matthew, Mark, and Luke—we cite a single Gospel's chapter and verse and add the notation "et synop."

Occasionally we refer to the "Duggan/Cable" principles concerning the metrics of *Piers*. This refers to rules concerning the syllabification of the *b*-verse (off-verse; second half-line) of the long lines. Duggan and Cable hypothesized that the alliterative poets of the second half of the fourteenth century generally require two metrically stressed syllables in the *b*-verse. Before each of these staves is a dip: one of the two dips must be of zero or one syllable, and the other must correspondingly contain two syllables or more. Cable adds (and A. V. C. Schmidt agrees) that the last syllable of the line must be unstressed. Duggan and Cable independently arrived at this conclusion in 1985. For representative studies see Thomas Cable, *The English Alliterative Tradition* (Philadelphia: University of Pennsylvania Press, 1991) and Hoyt N. Duggan, "The Shape of the B-Verse in Middle English Alliterative Poetry," *Speculum* 61 (1986): 564–92. See also Stephen A. Barney's "Langland's Prosody: The State of Study," listed in the List of Works Cited.

Except where otherwise noted, translations are our own.

The following special abbreviations are used:

Alford, *Gloss.*: John Alford, *Piers Plowman: A Glossary of Legal Diction*. Cambridge: D. S. Brewer, 1988.

Alford, *Quot.*: John Alford, *Piers Plowman: A Guide to the Quotations*. Binghamton, N.Y.: Medieval and Renaissance Texts and Studies, 1992.

A-ND: *The Anglo-Norman Dictionary*. Ed. William Rothwell, et al. London: Modern Humanities Association, 1981–92.

Brev.: *Breviarium ad usum insignis ecclesiæ Sarum*. Ed. F. Proctor and C. Wordsworth. 3 vols. Cambridge: Cambridge University Press, 1882–86.

Gloss: *Glossa ordinaria. Biblia latina cum Glossa ordinaria*. Facsimile Reprint of the Editio Princeps. Adolph Rusch of Strassburg 1480/81. Intro. by Karlfried Froelich and Margaret T. Gibson. 4 vols. Turnhout: Brepols, 1992.

L: Langland

MED: *The Middle English Dictionary*. Ed. Hans Kurath et al. Ann Arbor: University of Michigan Press, 1956–2001.

MWME: *Manual of Writings in Middle English*. Ed. Albert E. Hartung. New Haven, Conn.: Connecticut Academy of Arts and Sciences, 1967, continuing.

Nicodemus: The Gospel of Nicodemus. Ed. Hack Chin Kim. Toronto: Pontifical Institute of Mediaeval Studies, 1973.

OED: *The Oxford English Dictionary*. 2nd ed. Oxford and New York: Oxford University Press, 1989.

PL: *Patrologiae Cursus Completus . . . Series Latina.* Ed. J.-P. Migne et al. 221 vols. Paris,
  1844–64.
PP: *Piers Plowman*
Prol.: Prologue (to versions of PP)
Rot. Parl.: *Rotuli Parliamentorum.* Ed. J. Strachey et al. 6 vols. London: Stationery
  Office, 1767–77.
SR: *The statutes of the realm. Printed by command of His Majesty King George the Third.
  In pursuance of an address of the House of Commons of Great Britain. From original
  records and authentic manuscripts.* 11 vols. London: George Eyre and Andrew Stra-
  han, 1810–1828.

Citations of primary works are indicated by editor and year of publication, and so listed in the List of Works Cited. All citations of Chaucer are from
Larry D. Benson, gen. ed., *The Riverside Chaucer*, Boston: Houghton Mifflin,
1987. Citations from *Le Roman de la Rose* are from the edition by Daniel Poir-
ion, Paris: Garnier-Flammarion, 1974.

The major editions of *Piers Plowman*, with their prefaces and notes, are
abbreviated as follows:

K-A: George Kane, ed. *Piers Plowman: The A Version: Will's Visions of Piers Plowman
  and Do-Well.* London: Athlone, 1960. Cited is the Revised Edition (London: Athlone, 1988), with only slight revisions.
KD-B: Kane and E. Talbot Donaldson, ed. *Piers Plowman: The B Version: Will's Visions
  of Piers Plowman, Do-Well, Do-Better and Do-Best.* London: Athlone, 1975. Similarly, Revised Edition, 1988.
RK-C: George Russell and Kane, ed. *Piers Plowman: The C Version: Will's Visions of
  Piers Plowman, Do-Well, Do-Better and Do-Best.* London: Athlone, 1997.
Bnt: J. A. W. Bennett, ed. *Langland: Piers Plowman: The Prologue and Passus I-VII of
  the B Text as found in Bodleian MS. Laud 581.* London: Oxford University Press,
  1972.
Prsl: Derek Pearsall, ed. *William Langland: Piers Plowman, The C-Text.* London;
  Edward Arnold, 1978. Cited is the Corrected Edition, Exeter: Exeter University
  Press, 1994.
Schm: A. V. C. Schmidt, ed. Text cited from *Piers Plowman: A Parallel-Text Edition of
  the A, B, C and Z Versions.* Volume I, Text. London: Longman, 1995. Schmidt's
  comments are cited from *William Langland: The Vision of Piers Plowman: A Criti-
  cal Edition of the B-Text* (whose text is identical to the B text in the *Parallel Text
  Edition*). 2nd ed., Everyman, London: Dent, 1995.
Skt: Walter W. Skeat, ed. *The Vision of William concerning Piers the Plowman in Three
  Parallel Texts.* 2 Vols. London: Oxford University Press, 1886; with addition of
  Bibliography, 1954. Other editions or works by Skeat are cited by their year of
  publication and included in the List of Works Cited.

Preface

In 1986 four friends agreed to join with me in the preparation of a commentary on *Piers Plowman*. We decided to divide the poem into five portions, with each of us primarily responsible for one stint, but with all of us fully collaborating in the work of all. One of us, John Alford, was unable to continue with his work, though he has graciously reviewed our draft efforts; Andrew Galloway consented to take his place. This segment of the commentary, the fifth part but the first completed, will be followed in due course by installments from my colleagues, all professors of English: part one by Andrew Galloway (Cornell); part two by Ralph Hanna (Keble College, Oxford); part three by Anne Middleton (California, Berkeley); part four by Traugott Lawler (Yale).

The time seemed right for a general commentary on the poem. The notes to Skeat's edition of *Piers Plowman*, fine as they are, have long been outdated by the progress of scholarship, particularly in the last generation. By 1988 the B Version of the poem in the Athlone edition (1975) had been stimulating a burst of new scholarship, and the C Version (1997) was on its way. We were very grateful in the early stages of our work to be able to use the hitherto unpublished text of the C Version, as prepared by George Russell and George Kane. This, and other advice and encouragement, were very kindly supplied to us, eight years before their publication, by the editors.

Our goals are several. Although the form of this commentary has obviously the look, and some of the character, of explanatory notes to the poem, keyed to sequential lemmas of the text, we aim to take seriously the etymological base of the term "commentary," and to apply thought to the poem, that is, to perform literary criticism. It is our conviction that *Piers Plowman*, more than most poems, yields its riches to close examination of its individual passages and lines, and correspondingly less in its larger movements. First of all, then, we claim to have been attentive to the detail of the poem.

Although we hope to have explored all the previous scholarship and criticism of the poem, we have referred only to that work of other students of the poem that furthers understanding. This is not, then, a Variorum commentary. Nor does it provide preliminary information of the kind found in editions of the poem designed for beginning students. For such guidance we recommend first of all Pearsall's excellent edition of the C-Text, or Schmidt's Everyman Library edition of B. Further, we have, against the usual preference, keyed and focused our commentary on the C Version, as representing the author's latest thoughts, and by no means, in our view, inferior. A special feature of this commentary, not attempted by Skeat, is its thorough explication of the development of the poem through its (primarily) three Versions, A, B, and C. This effort will not be as evident in this fifth installment, which treats the least revised segment of the poem, the last three passūs. We have everywhere attempted, as well, to provide context, literary and historical, sufficient to catch the tone of the poem, to configure the arena of discourse in which the poem, moment by moment, resides.

Our work has been generously aided by our universities, in the form of research support funds, leaves of absence from other duties, and other help, and by granting agencies. We are grateful to the University of California Humanities Research Institute, located at the University of California, Irvine, for substantial funding and for allowing us to gather at the Institute's offices at the Irvine campus in 1990 and again in 1994. We wish especially to thank the exceptionally helpful staff of the Institute, and its first directors, Murray Krieger and Mark Rose. The late Professor Krieger guided us and a distinguished group of colleagues through a preliminary conference in 1988 on the topic of "Annotation and Its Texts," the result of which was a collection of essays with that title which I edited (New York: Oxford University Press, 1991). Professor Rose guided and encouraged us further, and made our 1994 stay at the Institute possible.

We were further given major support for this project by way of a five-year Interpretive Research Grant (1992–97) from the National Endowment for the Humanities. Our grant number is RO-22392-92. It goes without saying that without the Endowment's support this work would be much feebler and much slower to appear.

I must individually thank the University of California, Irvine, and a succession of Deans of Humanities there, for many leaves of absence, small research grants, and professional encouragement of various kinds. The University of California granted me a UC President's Research Fellowship in the Humanities, relieving me of other duties for several months; I am indeed grateful.

A number of colleagues have encouraged this work and provided help and information of various kinds: my thanks to them all. I particularly wish to thank Max Byrd, Walter Cahn, Glen Davis, the late E. Talbot Donaldson, Henry A. Kelly, Wendy Lewis, George Russell, Paul Schaffer, A. C. Spearing,

Linda Voigts, and Joseph Wittig. My sons Thomas and Peter compiled for us a spreadsheet of texts and prior editors' annotations. Peter also made an index to the elaborate Prefaces of the Athlone editions (now published in *YLS* 7 [1993]: 97–114 and *YLS* 12 [1998]: 159–73), and Kathleen Hewett-Smith made a concordance to the poem; these aids were invaluable to us—much thanks to you three.

I owe great thanks as well to five excellent scholars who read this commentary in detail and contributed greatly to its improvement: John Alford, Lee Patterson, Derek Pearsall, James Simpson, and Robert N. Swanson. Most of all I thank my collaborators in this work, who set high standards, gave generous and demanding critiques, provided a great many ideas, and drove me to do better work than I would have on my own. To my wife Cherry, who endured this labor with benign patience, much thanks and love.

C Passus 20; B Passus 18

Headnote

The last three passūs of PP consist of the last three dreams with their waking intervals, the sixth through the eighth, or the eighth through tenth if the dreams-within-dreams are counted (see Alford 1988a:31; Frank 1951; Bowers 1986:129–64). According to some of the erratic and perhaps not authorial manuscript rubrics (Adams 1985a vs. Clopper 1988; further Adams 1994, Clopper 1995), Passus 20 presents the second dream of Dobet (see Headnote to C.18), and C.21 and 22 (B.19 and 20) the two dreams of Dobest.

The action of the three dreams, each neatly bounded within its passus, is relatively firm in outline; the passus divisions manifest increasingly transparent orderliness toward the poem's end. L began his "Life of Jesus" in 18.123 (B.16.90), and sketched the betrayal of Jesus in 18.163–77 (B.16.137–61), in B taking the action through the jousting with the devil and the fordoing of death (B.16.162–66). He then turned with a new dream from the Gospel sequence and the sequence of the Church calendar back to "myddelenton sonenday (C.18.181 [B.16.172]), renewing Will's characteristic visionary mode as participant in and interrogator of the action.

With Passus 20, L seems to pick up his thread from the mid-Lent episode (see 13n below) as he returns to the last events in the life of Jesus, the traditional Passion narrative from Palm Sunday to the Resurrection on Easter Sunday (see 7.129–40 [B.5.487–500]). The last two passūs continue the narrative of salvation history with the Pentecostal founding of the Church and the apocalyptic coming of Antichrist.

The sixth dream (C.20, B.18) comprises three sequences: first the actions of Holy Week, from the triumphant entry of Jesus into Jerusalem on Palm Sunday through the Crucifixion, presented as a bachelor-knight's festive dubbing-joust blending into a judicial trial by combat, a *bataile* or "jugement of Armes" (18.128 [B.16.95]) in 6–112 (B.18.7–109); second the descent to hell, with a debate between the Four Daughters of God, including the speech of Book, in 113–270 (B.18.110–262); third, the Harrowing of Hell, with the argument of the devils and the reconciliation of the Daughters, in 271–466

(B.18.263–423). Surrounding this dream are representations of Will awake (1–5, 467–75 [B.18.1–6, 424–31]). See the notes to these passages for further divisions of the text and comment.

Skeat correctly identified three main (not necessarily proximate) sources of this passus: the Gospels (and one should add, their abundant presence in the liturgy); for the Harrowing, the apocryphal but commonly known Latin prose *Gospel of Nicodemus* (ed. Kim 1973, Tischendorf 1876; see 259n below); and for the debate between the Four Daughters of God, Robert Grosseteste's Anglo-Norman poem, the *Château d'Amour* (ed. Murray 1918). *Nicodemus* was often translated into Middle English (MWME 2:448–49; Hulme 1907:vii–lxx; Izydorczyk 1985:85–93; Marx 1995:80–91), but no specific influence of English versions on Langland has been identified. A summary of *Nicodemus* appears in the section "De resurrectione domini" in the *Legenda aurea* (ed. Graesse 1846: 242–44; trans. Ryan 1941, 1993).

Together with these major sources, L drew upon several traditions of Passion narratives widely circulated in his time (surveyed by Marrow 1979:7–27; Bestul 1996). It should be added that among these, no writer was so innovative as L. He focuses on matters of law, chivalry, and struggle, and omits both the elaborate allegoresis of the older narratives, which would moralize the palm branches and the vinegar, and the affective meditations on Jesus' suffering characteristic of newer accounts drawn largely from Aelred, Bernard, and pseudo-Bonaventure (but see 403–7n below).

Grosseteste's *Château* was likewise several times translated or redacted into Middle English (MWME 7:2337–39; Sajavaara 1967, with full and excellent Introduction, pp. 25–258; Marx 1995: 74, 160–68; Creek 1941; for a review of the tradition of the Daughters' debate see Traver 1907, and further Traver 1925, Hunt 1982). Perhaps because Traver's influential study disclaimed any specific resemblance of PP to the *Château* (1907:49), its obviously detailed and direct influence has been little examined (but see Coghill 1962: 209–14, Waldron 1986:78–80, Green 1999:347, 360–63): see especially notes to 8–12, 21, 34, 102–3, 168, 298–311, 309, 330–31, 417–41 below. Most important is Grosseteste's "feudalizing" and legalistic presentation of the Four Daughters' debate, although he may draw this slant from earlier treatments that promoted legalism (see Alford 1977:943–44, Hunt 1982:294, Traver 1925).

A close and good translation of Grosseteste's French is Sajavaara's "Version A" (p. 101), the *Castle of Love*, preserved in three manuscripts of which the earliest demonstrates transmission of the poem in England's Southwest, the Vernon Manuscript (Bodleian Manuscript Eng. poet. a.1., ed. Sajavaara and also Horstmann 1892:355–406), written toward 1390 or a little later. This manuscript also contains the copy of the A Version of PP that Skeat used as the base text of his edition (Manuscript V of A). Sajavaara also edits another English version of the *Château*, the *Myrour of Lewed Men* (British Library, Manuscript Egerton 927). Because the *Castle* translation is close, and the particular diction that L seems to adopt is nearly equivalent in French and English, whether L used the original French version or an English translation cannot be determined. Several apparent echoes in PP of *Cursor mundi* (ed. Morris, 1874–92, Fowler 1990, vol. 2, lines 9517–975), which contains another, less closely translated version of the *Château* (lines 9375–10222), may well reflect common sources (evidence of *Cursor's* circulation in the south of England is not apparent until ca. 1400), but that immense and baggy poem, like PP, contains in English versions of the Debate of the Four Daughters and the Nicodemean Harrowing of Hell, as well as a siege allegory. Three manuscripts of the *Château* contain copies of French translations of *Nicodemus* (Marx 1995:80); clearly the two texts were taken as linked.

To these sources should be added the abundant quotation of the liturgy in this passus (see esp. Vaughan 1980; St-Jacques 1967, 1977; Barr 1986; Furrow 1995:36–37). Specific references to the liturgy of Holy Week, from Palm Sunday to Easter, may be found below in the notes: Palm Sunday, notes 1, 6–34, 6–7, 8–12, 13–14, 15, 21, 22–23, 34, 141–44, 270; Tenebræ, note 59–62; Maundy Thursday, notes 34, 467–68; Good Friday, notes 1, 115–467, 141–44, 185–92, 469–75; Holy Saturday, notes 185–92, 270, 424; Easter Sunday, notes 8–34, 28–34, 52–53, 184a, 225, 259, 270, 271, 362, 465, 467–68, 469–75. The sixth vision enacts, in the person of Will, a Christian's commemorative experience of the Passion and Redemption, and L persistently marks the course of that experience with wording from Mass and Office, more densely quoted in this passus than elsewhere in the poem.

A number of notes below refer to medieval French drama. Mazouer's survey (1998:172–79) gives these dates for the plays: E. Mercadé, *La Passion d'Arras*, before 1440; *La Passion du Palatinus*, ca. 1300; the *Passion des jongleurs*, 1243; J. Michel, *Le Mystère de la Passion*, before 1452; *Le Mystère de la Passion Notre Seigneur*, ca. 1350. Whether L had direct access to the earlier French plays is not known—whether copies circulated in England, whether any of these plays were performed there, or whether L traveled in France. They show at least the penetration into a vernacular of doctrinal commonplaces relevant to PP.

The various topics, allusions, contexts, and subtexts of this passus are noted below as they emerge, but one particular thematic strand, now a rhetorical figure, now an authoritative citation, now a narrative form, now a theological principle, so governs the movement of this passus that it should be noted at the outset. It is the idea of reciprocal justice, in law called commutative justice, the iron principle of retaliation (*lex talionis*) and equipollent forces, associated with the Old Law (381 [B.18.338]), an idea that L adopts and finally converts into the idea of love associated with the New Law (see Birnes 1975; Stokes 1984:1–54; Georgianna 1990; 11.193n above). This theme seems to emerge out of the Samaritan's repeated use of "contrary," verb and noun, at the end of his speech (19.315, 324, 329 [B.17.335, 344, 349]). The religion of tit for tat is not "destroyed" but "fulfilled" (Matt. 5:17, quoted in 395a [B.18.349a]) by the religion of "kindness" in senses of the word developed in PP (see 417–41n below). The passus is organized around figures of debate, conflict, echoing, and answering.

Briefly to review this pattern: the larger narratives of the passus are set up as three parallel conflicts between apparent equals: Jesus versus Satan/Lucifer, in joust and in debate, figured as Life and Death; the happy sisters Peace and Mercy versus the severe Justice and Truth, in debate; the devils' pathetic squabble among themselves (on such debate literature in Middle English see Conlee 1991 with bibliography). By inserting the Harrowing within the debate of the Four Daughters, L brings the several actions to a climax simultaneously at the conclusion of the long speech of Jesus which discomfits the demons, reconciles the Daughters, and provides for the return of peace and love, the latter personified at last as if she too were a Daughter of God (see 361–466 and n; references to C lines and notes in the next paragraphs can be located in B by way of the notes).

These larger conflicts are replicated in a number of more local figures and persons in the passus who are set in opposition. The calendar and other processes of time too have their contraries: Lent and Easter (5, 468) or Palm Sunday and Good Friday (6, 51); daylight and dark (60, etc.); and after Jesus' transforming, showers and sun, war and love, etc. (452–58).

Further, the authoritative Latin citations embedded in the text often take the form of parallel contraries that ground and echo the principle of justice as satisfactory requital, tit for tat: first what "þe olde lawe . . . asketh" (387), as voiced in the Ur-text *oculum pro oculo* (385) and kindred pairs: *osanna* vs. *crucifige, tolle* (7, 46–47); *humana natura* vs. (and united with, in anticipation of the resolution of this theme) *consummatus deus* (22–23); *O mors ero mors tua* (34); *Ars ut artem falleret* (165, 392); *fletus* vs. *leticia* (184); *nullum malum* vs. *nullum bonum* (433); *Caro . . . Caro . . . Caro* (450). The passus marks a transition in salvation history, and this transition, the basis of typology in historical interpretation, finds rhetorical expression in the transformed significance of terms, often in schemes of repetition with a difference. After Quintilian we may call this form of paranomasia *regressio* or *antanaklasis* (*Inst.* 3.3.35–36, 66–68, ed. Butler 3:464–67, 484–85).

These Latin reciprocations and *regressiones* have English counterparts: that man will save man, tree win what tree lost, death relieve death (142–44); that venom fordoes venom (155); that the guiler is beguiled (163, etc.); the oppositions of weal and woe, hunger and repletion, etc. (210–38); lie set against lie (345–48); life requiting life (387); "maistrie" countered by right and reason (394–95); and then with Jesus' transformation of such terms, guile into grace (396), law into grace (428), blood's response to bleeding (438), and king as kin (441). Such locutions sum up the rhetorical as well as narrative and theological form of this passus.

Given the naturally litigious and hence juridical work of reciprocal action, L inevitably represents the two major histories of this passus, the Crucifixion and Harrowing, as matters under law. Forms of the word "law," in English and Latin, occur about once every 46 lines in PP, but in C.20/B.18, following Grosseteste, L emphasizes legal diction, best approached by way of Alford's glossary (*Gloss.* 1988b). From the beginning of the poem (Prol.158–64), and especially in the Mede episode, L has persistently challenged the corrupt contemporary practice of law, and expressed the hope that a perfected law will become, not a source of money, but "a laborer" in concert with love, peace, and truth (3.453 [B.3.300, A.3.276], 4.144 [B.4.147, A.4.130]).

With Passus 20/B.18 the poet explores foundational principles of law in biblical history and *sub specie æternitatis*; our justice is set against the Judgment. Here Jesus' joust develops into a judicial combat, a civil duel of law in terms of a Writ of Right dispute between Death and Life over ownership of property, namely humankind (see esp. notes at 8–34, 18, 28–34, 36, 102–3, 298–311). The Passion events focus on the trial before the justice, Pilate (notes at 35–79), and on the land tenure of Jews and Longeus (notes at 93, 95–112, 106–10). Although L does not cast the debate between the sister virtues in one of its traditional forms, as a trial before God in the court of heaven, it has touches of legal as well as scholastic disputation (115–270n), including the argument of the eldest sister, Justice (Rihtwisnesse) herself (169n), and it temporarily concludes, as many a trial would, by introducing a letter patent from a high authority (185–92n, 191–92n).

The Devils' Parliament is a web of pettifoggery in which the "Devil's Rights" over humankind are at issue, and it addresses questions of property rights, "true title" and prior seisin (dominion), force vs. justice, and the Writ of Deceit (notes at 20, 274–360, 298–311, 303–40, 309, 324, 349). Jesus treats these same issues systematically, assimilating the devils' claims to the Old Law that he even now "fulfills" with the New Law of mercy and grace, an overcoming of the deadly law of retaliation by redress consistent with royal prerogative (notes at 360–446, 370–72, 379–92, 386–87, 393–94, 395, 413–46, 417–41, 420a,

421–29, 428). The grandest instance of the law of love, turning the other cheek, is the Crucifixion itself. Finally, though commutative justice still applies in hell (445–46n), we find that in the Christian dispensation justice and mercy are the same (431n, 432–36n). It is not hard to imagine the passus, even as it answers to and brings to a head many of the themes of the poem, as also a separable set piece of heightened brilliance, relatively self-contained, and showing signs of particular address to such an audience of clerks and lawyers as might be found in London and Westminster (see 350–58n, Kerby-Fulton and Justice 1997).

Issues of law continue in the next passus, especially with regard to a king's administration of justice (notes at C.21/B.19.15–62, 186–87, 297–308, 465–76). In the last passus, with pointed and terrible anticlimax, we seem to return to the bad law of the world of Mede (notes at C.22/B.20.7–11, 90–92, 136–37, 138–39, 156–64, 274, 276, 279a, 285–89, 290–93).

Another theme of special moment runs through this most visionary of L's visions, the activity of seeing (see 438an). Faith, the first presiding figure of the passus, is "the substance of things to be hoped for, the evidence of things that appear not" (Heb. 11:1, and see John 20:29, quoted at C.21/B.19.181); this passus makes visible for Will the prime objects of faith and dwells on aspects of witnessing, blindness, "looking" as tending and protecting and acknowledging. Our quality of seeing as readers parallels the quality of the doings of the actors. See 16n below, and especially lines 10, 19, 29, 45, 59, 60, 81, 88, 115, 140, 213, 223, 239, 241, 246–53, 258, 284, 292, 333, 341, 344, 358, 368, 379, 425, 428, 448. For a preliminary survey of ocular sensation in this passus in connection with L's idea of "imagination" see Gallagher 1991; on the complex of imagery of light in this passus see Norton-Smith 1983:85–86.

Will awake

1–5 (B.18.1–6) Wollewaerd and watschoed . . . y slepte: The dreamer has awakened from a dream whose conclusion is disturbing: the answer to the question he addresses to the Samaritan—suppose I were to sin against the Holy Ghost, "myhte y nat be saued?" (19.282 [B.17.302])—is affirmative (so thow myhtest repente) but not encouraging (Ac hit is bote selde yseyen). The imperfectly amended Will seems to return, in one of those recursive movements so characteristic of the poem, to his state at the outset, when he asked Holy Church "How y may saue my soule" (C.1.80). The terms of the Samaritan's last speech, the possibility that mercy might overcome righteousness, invoke the leading terms of Passus 20 (B.18), from Ps. 84:11, artfully not quoted until it is accomplished at the end of the passus: "*Misericordia & veritas obui-auerunt sibi; Iusticia & pax osculate sunt*" (20.464a [B.18.421a]; see 20.115–467n). Three of these terms—in English "mercy" or "reuthe," "rihtwisnesse" or "iustice," and "sothnesse"—occur conjoined at the outset of the Samaritan's response (19.284–86 [B.17.304–6]).

This waking interval, however, presents a Will scarcely attentive to what he has dreamed, and perfectly ambivalent, as often. His self-presentation here should be compared with that of the opening lines of PP, and, for a striking difference, with the closing lines of this passus and opening of the next (see 469–75n). As usual Will's social identity, state of mind, and appearance are richly multivalent and seem to be in a state of flux (see Prol.1–13n). Complicating the picture is the possibility of a historical allegory, in which the perplexed Will, having met Abraham and Moses, represents "the state of man before the Crucifixion had re-opened the way to salvation" (Frank 1957:92).

In representing Will L exploits, as he had in the second and third lines of PP (see Prol.2–3n) and often elsewhere, the ambiguity of the words "as" and "like" (either "in my actual character as" or "in my [merely apparent] similarity to"), here **As a recheles renk** and **ylike a lorel**. Will is like typical characters, but we have trouble knowing what he is. Four portraits, none reconciled with the others, emerge here: first, an impoverished and bohemian wandering misfit taken with an [affected?] anomic lassitude, a sort of lunatic loller; second, a disciplined abstinent penitent on a pilgrimage expressing contempt for the world and a Christ-like absence of solicitude for earthly concerns; third, a despairing sinner suffering from acedia, roving in regret; fourth, a moonsick lover of the pastourelle convention (see 5n below). The second and third of these four characters embody the distinction, commonly cited in treatments of *acedia* and *tristitia*, between "the sorrow that is according to God" that "worketh penance" and the "sorrow of the world" that "worketh death" (2 Cor. 7:10). Each character, willy-nilly, has his corresponding readiness to receive this vision as a gift.

1 (B.18.1) Wollewaerd and watschoed: garbed with (rough) wool rather than linen next to the skin and with wet shoes or barefoot. Will regularly describes himself as garbed in wool (see Prol.2–3n). The dress prima facie bespeaks poverty: the "Peres" of *Pierce the Ploughman's Crede* (after 1393) says friars should "werchen and wolward gon as we wrecches vsen" (line 788, ed. Barr 1993:94), and Patience spoke of beggars as wetshod (16.14 [B.14.161])—but the terms also suggest a penitential mortification of the flesh (see OED s.v. *woolward*, Skeat 1896:31, Whiting 1968: W573, Vaughan 1980:125), or an apostolic simplicity adopted by religious, especially Franciscans (Matt. 10:10, Luke 10:4, *Monu-*

menta Franciscana, ed. Howlett, 1:28, 572; 2:67; Szittya 1986:43–44; Leff 1967:113, 149; see also the rules for hermits treated in Hanna 1997:34–35, and the Middle English *Brut* 99/16–18 [ed. Brie 1906]). The Franciscan depicted in the illustrated PP manuscript Douce 104 is barefoot (facsimile ed. Pearsall and Scott 1992: color plate 46r).

Franciscans were criticized for fudging the rule that they go barefoot: see *Pierce the Ploughman's Creed* 298–300, *Mum and the Sothsegger* 426–27 (ed. Barr 1993). Wyclif chastises friars for their foolish quarrel—they "contend inanely"—about whether Jesus went barefoot (the Franciscan position) or shod (the Dominican—*Sermones*, ed. Loserth 1886, 1:53, and see 1:24 and 1890, 4:139–40; see Hinnebusch 1951:239–40, 245–46, and see 12n below). As Skeat noted, the chronicler Walsingham contemptuously described Lollards as going about barefoot and robed in russet (see 10.1 [B.8.1]) "in sign of their greater perfection" (Skt C.6.2n [= RK-C 5.2]; Walsingham ed. Riley 1863, 1:324–25). Walsingham may have drawn his phrase, "incedentes nudis pedibus" (going about barefoot) from similar wording, "Nudis incedunt pedibus," in an anti-Lollard poem (ed. Wright 1859, 1:233).

Whether "wetshod" means simply the opposite of dryshod, with shoes drenched in bad weather (as it now means in Lancashire [Burgess 1992:183] and Oxfordshire [Skeat 1896:395]), or perhaps, in a witty colloquialism, "barefoot," is disputed (Schm, Prsl; MED defines it as "having wet feet or shoes"). In the fifteenth century it could mean "drunk" (see Orme 1989:106). If the (more obvious?—see 16.14 [B.14.161]) former, compare the depiction in the Douce manuscript of Activa-Vita (Haukyn) with shoes distinctly out at toe and heel (ed. Pearsall and Scott 1992:69r). Sixteen lines above, the Samaritan interpreted "rayne" as "seeknesse and oþere sorwes" (19.320 [B.17.340]); this may be the rain that wets Will's feet.

Vaughan suggests that L refers by antithesis to the Hebrews' dryshod crossing of the Jordan, an event associated with Palm Sunday, the day on which Will begins his dream, and with Baptism (1980:124–25; see the York and Sarum Manuals, ed. Henderson 1875:111 and ed. Collins 1960:23; Trevisa's translation of Bartholomaeus, Lib. 9, cap. 31, ed. Seymour et al. 1975:547; and Durandus, *Rationale* 6.67, ed. 1568, fol. 215^r, 215^v). If the word means "barefoot," along with the possible reference to Fransciscans noted above, see the illustrations of the barefoot beggar and the lunatic loller in the Douce manuscript—the loller is clad in a rag, presumably of wool (51r, 42r). Like Will, the lunatic lollers are wanderers, careless of the elements, and minstrels of heaven, and the text says they are barefoot (9.105–33, not in B). At the service of Adoration of the Cross on Good Friday in some rites the custom was to go barefoot

(Rupert, ed. Haacke 1967: 6.3., lines 174–75); at the end of this passus Will participates in such a rite (see 469–75n). See also 8–12n below.

2–3 (B.18.2–3) recheles . . . ylike a lorel: Recklessness is a sufficiently complex idea in PP; Scase's observation that the figure Rechelesnesse "is in a kind of gyrovague state" associated with poverty but not religious commitment, and with the poet's self-conception, is relevant here (1989:167–68). Clopper argues that Will here conforms to a Franciscan behavior type (1997b, Ch. 8). One form of recklessness issues from sloth: the instructional manual *Memoriale credencium* (early fifteenth century) for example, under "Sleuth" describes a person "nouʒt recchyng" how he performs his religious offices—"Sleuth . . . makiþ him dredful for to suffre for god. ne fastyng oþer *wolward* goyng . . ." (ed. Kengen 1979:116). On the connection between Will and sloth see Bowers 1986:152–54 et passim.

In B.15.5 the waking Will says some took him for a "lorel."

5 (B.18.5) lened me to lenten (to a lenten B): lay down, tarried until (or: during) Lent (MED *to* prep. 8.(a) and (e)-(i)). Possibly L plays on the sense "have a tendency toward" (MED *lenen* v.(1), 2.(b)), as Will should, in light of the Samaritan's warnings, incline himself to the penitential season—finally to "creep" at the end of the passus (see Davlin 1989:90, Martin 2001:87). Bowers treats the term **lene**, which repeatedly describes the dreamer's posture as he falls asleep, as a sign of sloth (1986:145–46).

L plays on the expected word, in a common alliterative collocation, *lynde* (MED *lind(e* 4.); see 10.64 (B.8.65), "vnder lynde vpon a launde lened y," and the alliterative *Morte Arthure* 454, "Lugge þi selfe vndyre lynde" (ed. Brock, 1961, line 454; see also Robbins 1959:98, line 8, and 99, line 2). The lyric "A Bird of Bishopswood"—of the 1390s?—seems to imitate PP here. It begins, "In a sesone of somere þat souerayne ys of alle," and continues (line 12–13, 17): "And I had lenyd me long al a Lenten tyme . . . In vnlust of my lyf and lost al my joye; . . . And as I welk þus and wandryd, wery of myself . . ." (ed. Kennedy 1987:83). The situation recalls the conventions of pastourelle, like that at the opening of PP.

6–112a (B.18.7–109a) Of gurles and of *gloria* . . . *cessabit &c*: L represents the events of Holy Week in four sequences, each commented on as a coherent pericope in the notes below: the Entry into Jerusalem (6–34), the Passion (35–79), the story of Longeus (80–94), and Faith's harangue (95–112).

The entry into Jerusalem (Palm Sunday)

6–34a (B.18.7–35a) Of gurles and of *gloria . . . ero mors tua*: The representation of Jesus' triumphal Entry into Jerusalem is imagined in part as taking place during the liturgical commemoration of that Entry in churches on Palm Sunday, one week before Easter, and in part as a joust (see 8–34n). This oneiric condensation of the liturgical procession and the historical event makes literal what instructional literature encourages the pious to do in spirit (e.g., in Aelred of Rievaulx's *De institutione inclusarum*, ed. Ayto and Barratt 1984:20, 45). A similar condensation is made by Margery Kempe: when she would see the Palm Sunday procession in England, "it semed to hir gostly syght as þei sche had ben þat tyme in Ierusalem & seen owre Lord in hys manhood recevyd of þe pepil as he was whil he went her in erth" (ed. Meech and Allen 1940:184). Hence here the singing *osanna* as in the Gospel (Matt. 21:9, Mark 11:10; also in the Palm Sunday liturgy—see 13–14n below), but also *gloria laus* ("Glory, laud"), not in the Gospel narrative (although Luke 19:38 has *gloria in excelsis*) but the name of a hymn sung repeatedly in the processions around churches on Palm Sunday, that is, *Dominica in ramis palmarum* (B.18.6). The Palm Sunday procession was in fact the most elaborate of the Church year, including the unique singing of two hymns, *Gloria laus* and *En rex venit*, whose content L seems to echo (Bailey 1971:72, 115–17, 175; Feasey 1897: 53–83; Hughes 1982:256; Duffy 1992:23–27; see 8–12n and 21.5–14n below).

Jesus' Entry here recalls the king's entry in the B and C Prologue, itself recalling Richard II's triumphal procession at his coronation (Donaldson 1949:116–18). Mann argues that the Entry likewise foreshadows the royal breaking-in imagery of the Harrowing itself, as in 360–65 (B.18.316–22) below. The presence of such civic typology is reinforced by Walsingham's account, cited by Mann, of "Peter de la Mare's triumphant return to London [in July 1377] after Richard on his accession had released him from prison: he was greeted by crowds of citizens crying 'Benedictus qui venit in nomine Domini'" (ed. Riley 1864, 2.384; see line 15a [B.18.17a] below, Mann 1994:204–6, 210, also Kipling 1998, Index, s.v. Benedictus, a number of comparisons of royal entries to the Entry into Jerusalem).

Jesus is introduced as a bachelor about to be dubbed and participate in a joust, but under Faith's tutelage Will slowly becomes aware of the stakes of this duel, which turns from joyous celebration to bitter suffering, and becomes a judicial trial by combat whose issue is whether death shall have dominion.

B.18.6 Reste me þere and rutte faste: The collocation of resting and rutting (snoring) likewise describes those rich people who slept though the Nativity while the shepherds kept watch (14.95 [B.12.151]). Sloth himself snores in 7.7 (B.5.391). The implication of indolence is expunged from C, perhaps merely from confusion of the text (see B.18.9n), or perhaps to maintain the ambivalence of Will's condition as not so undignified.

6–7 (B.18.7–8) gurles . . . oelde folk: The pattern of reciprocation in this passus begins here with the liturgical responses of the children's *gloria laus* and the adults' *osanna* in the hymn (where the latter word occurs also). In the Sarum use the hymn, which itself refers to children's singing, was in fact sung responsively by the boys' and men's choirs (Tyrer 1932:59); the custom is reflected in the N-Town and Chester plays on this story (ed. Spector 1991:263, Lumiansky and Mills 1974:259). The presence of children (**gurles**), but not of old people, is made explicit in Matt. 21:15–16; in the *Cursor mundi* those who sing at the Entry into Jerusalem "Wit harp and pipe and horn and trump" are "Ald and yong" (ed. Morris 1876, lines 15011–13). The distinction of ages may point to the transition from Old to New Testaments; compare our symbols of the New Year.

This joyous *osanna* contrasts with the terrible answering *Crucifige! Tolle, tolle!* below (46–47 [B 46–47]; see 13–14n below). The antithesis, two public cries in response to Jesus, was commonplace: the *Summa virtutum* sets it among a number of instances of Jesus' turn from weal to woe and his exemplification of patience (ed. Wenzel 1984:200–203); see also Ludolph of Saxony's comprehensive *Vita Jesu Christi*, well known in England, quoting Bernard (Sermon 2 on Palm Sunday, ed. Leclercq and Rochais 1968:48): "O how unlike is *Tolle, tolle, crucifige eum* from *Benedictus qui venit in nomine Domini, hosanna in excelsis*" (ed. Bolard et al. 1865:493–94). The same antithesis is drawn in *Memoriale credencium* (ed. Kengen 1979:99) and the *Golden Legend* (ed. Graesse 1846:927–29, cap. 217), and Rupert of Deutz in his treatise on the liturgy says Jesus entered Jerusalem "with glory, which soon malice would follow" (ed. Haacke 1967:6.1, line 2). These antitheses derive from the fact that on Palm Sunday were read both the account of Jesus' Entry into Jerusalem and Matthew's Passion narrative.

by orgene: whether "accompanied by instruments" (so Schm and MED *organe* 1.(a), *organie*, and see the quotation from *Cursor Mundi* above in this note) or "homophonically" (so Prsl, Vaughan 1980:127) cannot be determined, although the latter sense was more common in late medieval Latin usage (Sadie 2001, 18:671–72, s.v. "Organum"). If the latter, this may be the first recorded use in English (MED *organ(e* and *organie*; whether L would distinguish these two words is also unclear). Supporting the latter interpretation is the notion that only the adults sing **by orgene**; the children would not be trained in complex part-singing (but see Orme 1973:246 on *organum* used in the 1380s for homophony in which boys participated). In an English Wycliffite text of uncertain date (ca. 1400?) we find the collocation "deschaunt, countre note, and orgon," pretty clearly the additions of parts above and below the melody, as the note ad loc. says (ed. Winn 1929:90, 166). The London *Liber albus*, compiled in 1419, refers in Latin to a processional singing of *Veni creator Spiritus* sung alternately by vicars and *organa*, clearly by monophony (plainchant) alternating with homophony (ed. Riley 1859:29). The encyclopedists were careful to note that the Latin *organum* could mean any instrument, or particularly the organ (Trevisa's translation of Bartholomaeus, Bk. 19, cap. 130, ed. Seymour 1975:1388), or the harmony (*modulatio*) made in singing (Johannes Balbus, *Catholicon*, s.v.). *Organum* could even mean "psalter" or other service book (Williams 1993 passim). If L means the pipe organ specifically, he may refer to the "portative" organ that could be used in processions (Hickman 1936:39–42), but evidence for such a use is doubtful (Williams 1993:74–81).

B.18.9 And of cristes passion and penaunce, þe peple þat ofrauȝte: Skeat thought that this line "almost certainly" belongs here rather than where the manuscripts have it, after line 5, where it seems to be nonsense (see KD-B.176, Schm; Wittig argues for conserving the archetypal reading, 1975:71–72), and Skeat translates it [And I dreamed] " 'of Christ's passion and penance ["suffering"; see C.18.41 for this sense] that extended to the people'; with reference to the *effects* of the Passion." Kane, more persuasively, would translate **ofrauȝte** as "got possession of" (1993:141). Elaborating, he finds a clear instance of this meaning in another text, and glosses **þe peple** as those held in Limbo (2000:50).

Jesus' joust

8–34 (B.18.10–35) Oen semblable . . . *ero mors tua*: In 18.128–29 (B.16.95–96) Will had learned that Jesus would "iouste" for Piers' fruit (see 18n below) "by iugement of armes" against "the fende," and further in B.16.163–65 (omitted from C as too distantly proleptic?) that he "iusted in Iherusalem . . . On cros" in a "bataille / Ayeins deeþ and þe deuel." From the terms "jugement" and "bataille" (the common word in Anglo-Norman legalese for a trial by combat) Will should anticipate a judicial duel, a grim *duellum* or *gaige de bataille*, a practice regularly censured by the Church but practiced in L's time, rather than a festival tourney, *armes de plaisance* (for the terms, see Prost 1872:23;

Thorne 1954:95–96; Whittaker 1895:109–12; see 102–3n below). But in spite of what he has learned, and of Jesus' appearance here, the excited Palm Sunday crowds make Will think that this will be a tournament of the kind often held in celebration of a dubbing—for the practice see Barker 1986:114, 62–63. The event disabuses him, although L continues to use some of the terms of the festival tourney (e.g. **auntrous** 14n, "gre"—"prize"—101 [B.18.98]).

Abundant biblical, liturgical, and literary traditions present the "Christ-knight" (see Waldron 1986; Bennett 1982:62–84; Woolf 1962; Gaffney 1931; Le May 1932; St.-Jacques 1967; Warner 1996); a number of instances are noted below as relevant. Psalm 23:8, "the Lord mighty in battle," quoted below (361 [B.18.318]) suffices to motivate the idea; for other proof-texts see Isa. 59:17, Ps. 90:13, and generally Harnack 1905. In the Harrowing Jesus is obviously a conqueror; in a familiar antiphon of Easter, *Cum rex gloriae*, Christ at the Harrowing is king of glory and *debellaturus*, warring conqueror (Young 1933, 1:151, etc.; see also Bourquin 1978, 1:501–2; Henderson 1875: 180).

The Anglo-Norman "Tretys de la passion" attributed to the early fourteenth-century Franciscan poet Nicolas Bozon, a work L may have known (see Bourquin 1978:702–7), presents a knight, patently Jesus, who regains his lady (evidently the soul, as in the analogues—cp. 10.128–34 [B.9.1–7 and 50–55]) on Friday from the tyrant Belial (paraphrased by Gaffney 1931; ed. Wright 1868, append. to Langtoft's *Chronicle*, 426–34; see further 330–31n below).

8–12 (B.18.10–14) Oen semblable . . . galoches ycouped: Like Will, Jesus is first presented ambivalently—even paradoxically—with focus on what he is *like*—**semblable to þe samaritaen and somdeel to Pers þe plouhman** (see B.15.212) and **he lokede / As is the kynde of a knyhte**. The theological import is the need to see the two-in-one identity of the God-man.

Will's inability to recognize Jesus parallels the blindness of others who witness the Passion (see 16n, 70n, 88n), and reflects two further ideas: that knights in tourneys (but of course not in judgments of arms, where the combatants had to be known and were formally identified—see Rickert 1948:152) in romance and in life were often disguised, and that Jesus' divinity was "hid" in flesh at the Incarnation, in part to deceive the devil (see 12.122–28 [B.11.233–39]; Rivière 1934:57–58; and 22–23n, above, 298–31n, 330–31n below). On the chivalric disguised knight see Gaffney 1931:156, Waldron 1986, Clifton 1993, and most suggestively Crane 1997, making the point that the incognito first *concealed* the combatant, but finally *revealed* the combatant as the valiant fighter he was apart from his noble lineage. Edward III was among those who actually appeared at tournaments in disguise (Barker 1986:86–87, Crane 1997:66). On delayed identifications generally see 1.68–71n.

L likens Jesus to the Samaritan in that they both enact charity. Further, they both ride beasts of burden—Will's first observation about the Samaritan is that he is "sittynge on a muyle" (19.49 [B.17.51])—and the Samaritan was regularly identified with Jesus in medieval interpretation (Wailes 1987:45–46, 209–214). Jesus is specifically **semblable** to the Samaritan—he is the Samaritan's meaning—but only **somdeel** so to Piers, as is explained in 19–25 below.

Jesus' **sp(r)akeliche** (line 10 [B.18.12]), "lively, vigorous," *looking* (see Headnote; the first instance of this theme in the passus), too, makes him seem a bachelor knight on the way to a festive dubbing joust (Barker 1986:114, 61–63; Barber and Barker 1989:168), but otherwise he has anything but the look of the "ful bold bacheler" whom Abraham saw (B.16.179). In at least one version of the Christ-knight allegory Jesus is called *baccalarius* (cited Bennett 1982:65). But this is the Jesus of the Entry into Jerusalem, barefoot, astride an ass, without boots, spurs, or spear. Broadly, in this passage L plays the language of chivalry off against the events of the Passion.

Liturgical commentators regularly compare church processions with imperial progresses: "a procession is as it were the progress of an emperor and his army to war" (Honorius Augustodunensis, *Gemma animae*, PL 172.566). And so, ultimately, is this, but L emphasizes the paradoxical humility of Jesus, in keeping with Zacharias, "thy king will come to thee . . . he is poor, and riding upon an ass" (9:9, quoted in John 12:15). The Palm Sunday hymn *En rex venit* speaks of Jesus progressing "beautiful in virtues, not in bellicose horses and high chariots" (ed. Henderson 1875:50). Ludolph's *Vita*, citing Chrysostom, elaborates: "he did not sit on a golden chariot, shining with precious purple . . . but on the ass of tranquillity. . . . You see around him not splendid swords or other ornaments of terrible weapons. But what? Leafy branches, the testimony of piety and peace" (ed. Boland et al. 1865:489). In the *Gospel of Nicodemus* the devils see Christ and ask, "Who are you so great and little, humble and exalted, soldier and emperor, wonderful warrior in the form of a slave . . . ?" (cap. 22).

So here Jesus is paradoxically **Barfoet on an asse back boetles**. L seems to draw his wording from *The Southern Passion*: "Wiþ such prute [pride, pomp] com he þuder nouȝt as ffel a kyng to do, / *Barffot vp-on an asse* yhaltert and open the heued [bareheaded] al-so" (lines 69–70, ed. Brown 1927:3). Schm suggests a pun on bootless as "helpless, unavailing," with irony; see 207 below—a crime was bootless if the accused had no right to a defense (Plucknett 1956:426; compare Adam's bootlessness as a "thrall" in *The Castle of Love*, ed. Sajavaara 1967, passim). L may allude to the legal custom that a combatant in a Writ of Right trial was to appear barefoot at the "wager of battle" (Baldwin 1981a:68); Neilson reports a barefoot champion in a duel of 1329 (1890:148).

Jesus is a **prikiare** (24 [B.18.25] below) like a gentle knight, even though **Withouten spores oþer spere**—to prick is "to ride" in general, but the verb derives from the idea of spurring. A bachelor would **geten hym gult spores** at the dubbing ceremony (Keen 1984:64–82). In a lyric in John Grimestone's commonplace book (before 1372) Jesus says he has come to fight "with-outen seld [shield] and spere" and brings a "blisful bote [remedy] of bale" (ed. Brown 1924:82, no. 63); see Woolf 1968:53–56 on representations of Christ's arms in the English lyrics. Cp. the *Meditations on the Life and Passion of Jesus*, perhaps contemporary with L: "The hors þat þou onne rydest / Þou þorlest not with spores his sydes. / Bryȝt armure hast þou non; / In þis bataile þou fyȝtest alon. / Þou ridest vp-on a sely asse" (ed. d'Evelyn 1921: lines 1591–95).

Jesus rides **As is þe kynde of a knyhte**. The metrical emphasis thrown on **kynde** may point to the persistent theme of *kynde* in the poem, and here the hard question, who is this **oen**? On **kynde** see 417–41n below. The diction evokes (for contrast) chivalric values like those of *Sir Gawain and the Green Knight* 2379–81: "cowardyse me taȝt / To acorde me with couetyse, my kynde to forsake: / Þat is larges and lewté, þat longez to knyȝtez" (ed. Andrew and Waldron 1978). L speaks of firm courtesy and readiness to die in defence of the commune as the **kynde** of a knight or king (8.161 [B.6.164, A.7.149]; C.17.287). In the course of this passus Jesus progresses, figuratively or actually, from bachelor to knight to champion to king to conqueror: "knyht, kyng, conquer-our may be o persone" (C.21/B.19.27). By "conqueror" L means specifically a ruler who dominates another realm by conquest (see e.g. C.3.251–55, 21. 32–40n).

12 (B.18.14) galoches ycouped: Jesus is not described as wearing the **galoches ycouped**—he is barefoot—and the vigorous knight with whom he is compared is on his way to get them at a dubbing ceremony in simile only. Yet L's linking of Jesus with **galoches** alludes to contemporary controversy. Galoches are sandals or clogs (MED; Fairholt 1885, 2:177; *Promptorium parvulorum*, ed. Way 1843:184 with confusion of the meaning of *ycouped* that led Way and Skeat astray; see also Thomas 1932:221). Their value is distinctly indicated by uses in Chaucer, alluding to John the Baptist's unworthiness to unbuckle Jesus' sandal, *galoche* (SqT 555), and in *Dives and Pauper*, as noted by Prsl: Pauper explains with reference to Mark that the apostles are commonly depicted as barefoot "in tokene of innocence and of penaunce," even though they were not entirely barefoot but "þey vsedyn gallochis, a soole benethyn wyt a festyng abouyn þe foot" (ed. Barnum 1976:93). On apostolic footwear, Ludolph's *Vita* reconciles Matt. 10:10 with Mark 6:9 by observing that the apostles were instructed not to wear *whole* shoes, *calceamenta*, but only *sandalia*.

Dominicans argued that Jesus went shod, and Franciscans, that he went barefoot, or at least bare on the top of the foot (see 1n above). Conventual Franciscans went shod; Carmelites were of two kinds, "discalced" (barefoot) and "calced" (Mayo 1989:37–38). The tradition of satirizing such squabbles was old by L's time; see for example "L'ordre de bel ayse" from the Harley Lyrics, lines 195–96 (ed. Astin 1953:137). The writer of a Lollard sermon, impatient with the friars' arguing over whether Jesus went with "hyȝe schon" or "barefoot," says "we supposen of owre Jesus þat he took ful lytel hede of seche maner of wendynge" (ed. Hudson 1983, 1:343). In *Winner and Waster* the friars' mandate to go barefoot or at least wearing galoches only is satirized, as the Franciscans carry a banner depicting fur-lined *galegs* (galoches) with a pair of buckles each (ed. Conlee 1991, lines 156–59; see 1n above). The writer of Manuscript Bodley 851 (the "Z-Text") has Mede attack friars: "That weren woned to wade in wynteres ful colde, / Now beth they boted . . ." (Z 3.157–58, ed. Schmidt 1995). L plays off, then, current satire on the pretentiously humble (or less than humble) footwear of those counterfeiting apostolic simplicity.

In keeping with this satiric note, the galoches are **ycouped**, fashionably slashed in a way resembling the tracery of church windows, like "Poules wyndow corven" worn "fetisly" by the delicate Absolon in the Miller's Tale (lines 3318–19). A shoe so slashed, remarkably preserved from L's time, is depicted in Newton 1980:37; see also Fairholt 1885, 2:65. The knightly connotation of such slashing is established by the citations in MED (s.v. *coupen*), as in the romance *Degare*, "He was iclothed wel ariȝt, / His sschon icouped as a kniȝt" (ed. French and Hale 1930, lines 789–90; and see the English *Romaunt of the Rose* [in the Riverside Chaucer] 842–43). Of course it is ridiculous to speak of thongs or sandals as slashed.

The image has further meaning. Psalm 59:10 says, "Into Edom will I stretch out my shoe (*extendam calceamentum meum*)." We know who it is "that cometh from Edom" (Isa. 63:1; see C.21/B.19.5–14n below)—Jesus. Commentators on the Psalm interpreted this shoe as emblematic of the Incarnation, in which divinity donned humanity as a human would don clothing (see 21–25 [B.18.22–26] below). The *Speculum Christiani* of the late fourteenth or early fifteenth century concludes its account of a priest's vestments: "The couerynge of feete representez incarnacion of Cryste," glossing *calciamentum* as *humana natura*, and concludes that "the preste, when he representez Criste, he awe not to do messe bare-fette" (ed. Holmstedt 1933:180). Compare the Samaritan's riding a horse named "*caro*" (B.17.110). In his treatise on liturgy Rupert of Deutz says the shoes of a pontifex signify the shoes of the Lord, and specifically that the shoes are the Incarnation, stretched out as in Ps. 59:10, *extendam* (*De divinis officiis* I.23, lines 498–502, ed. Haacke 1967). The Gloss on Ps. 59:10 cites Augustine to the effect that the *calceamentum* is "humanity in which deity hid (*latuit*)." In his *Distinctiones*, Peter the Chanter likewise cites this psalm in defining *Calceamenta* as "the union of divinity and human-ity" (Reims, Bibl. mun. Manuscript 508, s.v.). This interpretation probably derives from the notion that God is the head of Christ, and his feet the human-ity he assumed (so the reading from Augustine in the Breviary, ed. Proctor 1882, I.mcccxlv). See for a vernacular example the Last Supper play of the N-Town cycle: "Be þe hed ȝe xal vndyrstand my Godhed, / And be þe feet ȝe xal take myn humanyté" (ed. Spector 1991:279), practically quoting the *Golden Legend*, "the head of that lamb is his divinity—whence I Cor. 11:3 'his [Christ's] head is God'—the foot his humanity (*pes ejus humanitas*)" (ed. Graesse 1846:929).

In this compressed simile, then, L both satirizes a mendicant misappro-priation of an emblem of apostolic simplicity and alludes to an exegetical image of the Incarnation.

13–14 (B.18.15–16) faith . . . an heraud of Armes: The figure of Faith, identified (B.16.176) or associated (C.18.184, but see 18.198) with Abraham, was said to be a herald of arms at C.18.185, though here (in keeping with the equivocal representations of Will and Jesus) he only acts **As** a herald. Hence he is able to identify from their coats of arms, according to the office of heraldry, knights in combat: "Herowdys of armes in justyng or in turnaments wayten who doth best and his name thei crye" (*Jacob's Well* ed. Brandeis 1900:134; see Rickert 1948:155; Wagner 1956:25–40; 1967:2; Barber 1970:30–31, 172; Keen 1984:134–42; Alford *Gloss.* s.v. *Haraud of Armes*). In 22/B.20.94 we learn that "heroudes of Armes" were to have "descreued lordes" at the outset of a battle.

Abraham had seen the triune God (18.241 [B.16.225]; see n) and is appro-priately herald (in the early sense of *praeco*, forerunning announcer) of Jesus. In the *Gospel of Nicodemus*, a major source for this passus, the Jews are irri-tated that Pilate sent for Jesus with a runner rather than a *preco*—a herald in his office of crier (1.2); possibly the scene suggested the figure to L. Of course Abraham was in the Limbo of the Fathers at the time of the Crucifixion (see 146 [B.18.143] below); the potential inconsistency may have induced L to settle on the name "Faith" for this figure.

in a fenestre: The French term for "window" suggests the elegant lan-guage of chivalry. "Fenestration" is the term for display of arms, the "helm-show" or *mis en fenêtre* at a tournament site, for pomp and so that a herald could check the identity of combatants for eligibility (Keen 1984:210–11; Barber and Barker 1989:9, 111, 180, 184; Stanesco 1985). The word also suggests a church window (see 16.41 [B.14.200]), and of course Abraham often appears in stained glass—it is as if he watched the procession from his depiction in a window. In portrayals of tournaments in painting and romance, and doubtless in reality as well, spectators look on from windows or the window-like openings of scaffolding booths (see e.g. Barber and Barker 1989:22, 26, 52, 59, 64, etc.). In *Cursor mundi* children watch Jesus' Entry into Jerusalem from walls and windows (ed. Morris 1876, lines 15035–37). L continues the conflation of the biblical action with its commemoration in the church processional and with jousting proceedings.

'**a!** *fili dauid!*': from Matt.21:9, *Hosanna filio David* (with *filio* altered to the vocative *fili*). The Gospel of Matthew begins, "Liber generationis Jesu Christi, filii David, filii Abraham," pointing to the connection of Faith/Abraham with Jesus (see also Matt. 9:27, Isaiah 11:1–10, and C.21/B.19.133, 136n). The antiphon *Osanna filio David* initiates the Palm Sunday procession in the Sarum rite (Hughes 1982:256). After L's time, heralds of arms had to know (and were commissioned to register) noble genealogies in order to deal with hereditary coats of arms; presumably more local offices of this sort were performed by heralds of arms well before the establishment of the formal College of Arms in the late fifteenth century. Abraham as herald and witness of the Trinity (Gen. 18:2) immediately knows Jesus' nature, begotten of the Father, and puts it in somewhat Abrahamic (Hebraic) terms, son of David.

William Durandus, noting that Palm Sunday is the "heralding of the Passion" (*praeconium passionis*), found in the peoples' two cries on that day, quoted here and in line 7 (B.18.8) above, reference to the two natures of Christ: his deity (*Osanna*) and his humanity (*Fili David*): *Rationale* 6.67, ed. 1568, fol. 214r, 215r—see 22–23n below.

The **Auntrous** are the venturesome, especially knights errant seeking adventure or, like modern adventurers, tournament prizes (Barker 1986:152; see 231 [B.18.222] below for the fulfillment of this figure). L continues to use the diction of chivalry. See 22/B.20.165–200n.

15 (B.18.17) Olde iewes: With a glance at the Pauline topic of "old" (pre-Christian) humanity, Abraham's race about to be superseded (see 95–112n and 106–10n below), L settles the action for a time in Jesus' Jerusalem rather than a church procession, and the quotation from Matt. 21:9, "Blessed is he that cometh in the name of the Lord," is drawn from the words of Jews of old in Ps. 117:26. The *Benedictus* is thoroughly familiar as part of the Sanctus at Mass, as well as among the antiphons for Palm Sunday (Alford, *Quot.*).

16 (B.18.18) y fraynede: Will's question echoes that of Isaiah 63:1, "Who is this that cometh?" (see 12n above), and Matt. 21:10, "the whole city was moved, saying, 'Who is this?'"—in the next verse after the one just quoted. Will also raises a question that might be asked of a herald at an actual tournament, "qui sont cil qui ont jousté?" (*Le Tournoi de Chauvency*, ed. Delbouille 1932, line 1019). From Will's early curiosity about Holy Church, "Thenne hadde y wonder in my wit what woman he were . . . What she were wytterly" (1.68–71 [B.1.71–74, A.1.69–72]), he persistently asks about the mere identity of the figures he sees. We readers share in this wonder, and much of the action of the allegory of PP is simply exposition of the meaning of such terms as Mede, Imaynatif, Anima, Hope. Here the concealed identity has theological as well as narrative force: see 22–23n below.

A number of figures in this passus share this inability to recognize what they see: the Jews cannot see Jesus for what he is until "Somme saide he was godes sone" (70 [B.18.68]); blind Longinus is at first doubly unseeing; the Four Daughters wonder at the light in hell—Truth herself especially is "wendynge to wyte what þis wonder meneth" (129 [B.18.126]); the devils are utterly confused—"'What lord artow,' quod lucifer" (360 [B.18.316–17], which adds the essential text from Ps. 23, *Quis est iste rex gloriae?*—see 270n below)—and they accuse God of deliberate obfuscation (327); the protoparents did not recognize the demon in the lizard (B.18.335–38; cp. C.20.378–80).

18 (B.18.20) feche þat þe fende claymeth, pers fruyt þe plouhman: See 32n below. In 18.110–16 (B.16.79–85) the devil has seized the fruit of the Tree of Charity—there specified as the righteous patriarchs and prophets, "holy men" from Adam to John the Baptist, the fruit of the tree of Adam (18.68)—and carried it to the limbo of hell. *Libera voluntas dei* then attacks the devil with the tree-prop that symbolizes *filius*. In B, Piers is owner of the tree and attacks the devil; L neglected to revise C here and in line 32 below (see Godden 1990:200 and 20n below). Here the agricultural metaphor folds into the chivalric action, as before a jousting metaphor emerges from the arboreal symbol (18.127–29 [B.16.94–96]) with similar wording, "iesus sholde iouste" and "fecche this fruyt." In somewhat similar language the Vernon "Dispute between Mary and the Cross" has the cross bear the fruit Jesus who goes "To fecche folk from hellewaerd" (line 496, ed. Morris 1871:148).

claymeth: a legal term, "demands by right" (Alford, *Gloss.* s.v. *claimen, right*); Jesus disputes this claim below (372 [B.18.329], 343). The joust now appears to be a trial by combat—see 8–34n, 36n, 102n.

19 (B.18.21) 'Is Peres in this place?': As always, Will is excited to hear of Piers. His question imitates the formal question put by a herald in a judicial trial by combat (see 16n above). In B, the dreamer was looking for Piers when he met Abraham/Faith (16.171); in C, until Piers was named in 20.8, he had not been mentioned since 16.340. **Place** may have here its specific sense "field of combat" (*platea*; MED *place* 2.(c)). Faith **printe**, looked significantly at the dreamer, to quiet him (cp. B.13.86, C.15.120 [B.13.113]; see Burrow 2001:81–82), or, as the modernizing scribe of manuscript HM 114 takes it, reading *nodded* for **printe**, to assent. See 16n, 26n.

20 *Liberum dei Arbitrium* (not in B): "The Free Choice (or Will) of God" has not appeared by this name heretofore in the poem, although in the C version *libera voluntas dei*, surely the same figure, occurs as the agent of the attack on the devil (18.118; see 18n above), and he is perhaps the same as the *liberum Arbitrium* who taught Jesus leechcraft (18.138, not in B) and more surely the same as the figure who wielded the third plank in B.16.50. The added reference to this figure here in C may be a partial correction of its line 18 (see note above) in light of earlier C revision, and an indication of L's consciousness, having written B, of the prominence of this theme later in the passus.

The reference here to God's free will points to an important issue in this passus and in contemporary theology: how free God or Christ is to break, from the devil's point of view, his own law, to be in a technical way unjust, in order to save sinners. The contested question regards whether God's power is enacted as absolute (purely willed) or *ordinata* (ordered, ordained: rational, consistent, covenanted, revealed), a question applied to soteriology as early as Peter Lombard and Alexander of Hales and treated by Duns Scotus and Ockham (see Franks 1962:178, Marilyn Adams 1987:1257–97, Coleman 1981, Colish 1994:85, 298). The issue is addressed explicitly in the debate between the Four Daughters below. See 12.113n, 20.299–311n, and 393 (B.18.348) below. The phrase **for loue** here anticipates the resolution of the debate (see 443–44 [B.18.400–401] below).

21 (B.18.22) of his gentrice: literally, "in accordance with his nobility," his gentle birth (or, here, begetting) or his gracious and courteous manner. Of course Jesus, *filius David* and conceived of the Holy Spirit, is of gentle birth; Bennett cites a Middle English "that gentilman Jhesus" (1982:101; see also B.10.35 [A.11.27], and 441n below). His mother, too, was a "gentil womman" (B.11.248). Wyclif spells out why Jesus is *nobilissimus homo* (ed. Loserth 1888:28). Jesus jousts in Piers's arms **of his gentrice** also because he is of the human family, one of our "blody bretherne" (12.110–12 [B.11.202–4], etc.). The issue of Jesus' gentility vs. his poverty was lively especially in mendicant controversy (see 22/B.20.40–50n). Compare L's play with the idea in B.14.181, his puns on "gentle" and "gentile" in B.19.48., etc., and most strikingly 12.108–11 (B.11.199–203). See 22.242–45n.

Further, a noble human (a God-man) is required to be a sufficient advocate and champion for the joust (see 78–79n, 102n). This idea is developed at length in the *Castle of Love*, which L knew (see Headnote to this passus). Adam is a thrall; an advocate "iboren fre" and "wiþouten synne," Jesus, is required to bring to law his case for "riht" and "heritage" (ed. Sajavaara 1967, lines 241–70).

in Pers Armes, probably "clad in Piers's heraldic coat-of-arms" (see 18.186–87 [B.16.179–81]) as well as simply "with Piers's weapons and armor." The former is the meaning of C.21/B.19.12, which echoes this passage; the latter is suggested by what follows. On a knight's wearing the arms of another knight to a tournament see Barker 1986:86–87 and 8–12n above. Piers's arms are incarnate humankind, "oure sekte" (7.140) or, in the earlier version of the same line, "oure armes" (B.5.500). In earlier allegories these are the arms of Adam (Bennett 1982:67, 70). In the *Castle of Love* Jesus says, "Nimen ichulle þe þralles [Adam's] weden" (line 547), translating Grosseteste's *Château*, "Del serf prendrai la vesteüre," namely, "la vostre humanité" (ed. Murray 1918, lines 449, 561). In one of the Middle English Charters of Christ, Jesus has a "cote armure" of the "lyuere" [livery] of humanity, powdered with the "fyn roses red" of his wounds (Spalding 1914:40, and see 76–79). In Bozon's shorter Passion poem Jesus takes the arms (the incarnate body) of "son bachelor Adam" as part of his cunning deception of the devil (lines 37–38, ed. Jeffrey and Levy 1990:187; see next note). The widespread notion that the instruments of the Passion—cross, nails, sponge, spear, etc.—are the *arma Christi*, sometimes depicted on heraldic shields, is amply documented in Berliner 1955.

The allegory of Piers at this point best reads him as the ideal potential of humankind. Schm aptly cites Philipp. 2:7, "But [Jesus] emptied himself, taking the form of a servant (*formam servi*), being made in the likeness of men, and in habit found as a man (*habitus inventus ut homo*)." This lesson was read on Palm Sunday (Sarum *Missale*, ed. Dickenson 1861–83: col. 263; see 21.15–62n below). See B.18.356n below. On Piers as Christ's human nature see generally Overstreet 1989–90:304–9.

22–23 (B.18.23–24) haberion, *humana natura . . . consummatus*: From the *Meditations on the Life and Passion of Christ* Schm cites the line, "þis haberion is þy body fre" (ed. d'Evelyn 1921, line 1603). That Jesus deliberately concealed his consummate, thaumaturgic divinity while incarnate in human nature is a theme found in the Gospels and Paul (e.g., Matt. 9:30; I Cor. 2:7–8); see 8–12n above. The deception here is part of the strategem by which God beguiles

Satan in the redemption, as the remainder of this passus makes clear; see 330–31n below. The precise source, if any need be sought, of the Latin phrases here is unidentified; the terms generally recall Hebrews 5:9 and 2:9–10. The distinction between the names **iesus** (21) and **Crist** (23) will be developed in the next passus; see 21.15–62n.

That themes of the Incarnation emerge here, as it were on Palm Sunday, is apt. The Gospels narrating the Entry into Jerusalem were regularly read on both Palm Sunday and the first Sunday in Advent, and preachers regularly compared the events of the Entry with the Incarnation (Spencer 1993:27–28). See the Headnote for a list of further allusions to the Palm Sunday liturgy in this passus.

25 (B.18.26) as *in deitate patris*: "as in the godhead of the Father," that is, in his substantial (but not necessarily incarnate) identification with the godhead. The construction with **as** is difficult; for other instances of this use (see MED *as* 7.?) see B.15.580 and Mustanoja 1960:332—or it may simply be pleonastic, as often in Chaucer. L refers to one explanation for the Incarnation and Passion of Jesus, that God is "impassible," incapable of suffering, whereas human salvation required a divine sacrifice, and hence a God-man. For this doctrine see Bennett 1982:92–95, Overstreet 1989–90:312–13, the survey by Mozley 1926:104–19, and 208–38n below. Jesus will joust in mere flesh, being unable to be hurt in substance—**no dynt shal hym dere.**

L further refers to the question of Jesus' nature at his death; a common conception was that his soul was united with the godhead, *deitas*, for the Harrowing, whereas others (e.g. Wyclif) held that he was man until the Resurrection (Izydorczyk 1985:34; Bloomfield 1961a:217, n75; 370n below). A common view was that of the *Mirour of Mans Saluacioun*, "And thogh it ware that Cristis sawle fro the body departid, / The Godhede fro the body nor from the sawle no tyme was disseueryd" (ed. Henry 1987, lines 3051–52). The *Northern Passion* speaks of Jesus' "godhede" as descending to hell (line 1810, ed. Foster 1913:213; Rawlinson Manuscript line 3032, ed. Heuser and Foster 1930:128). Mirk says Jesus despoiled hell "In soule and godhede with-owte nay, / Whyle the body in towmbe lay" (lines 510–11, ed. Kristensson 1974:95). L worries with the issue as he revises B.5.489 to C.7.130. See also 271n below.

26 (B.18.27) iewes or scribʒ: Will seems to think that these unwarlike people are an unlikely class from which to draw jousters. Although in the Gospels Jesus often singled out the scribes and Pharisees as his particular enemies, the earthly adversaries of Jesus are not the main question in the theology of the Passion. The dreamer mistakes the cosmic mission of Christ for the historical conflict with citizens of Jerusalem. With this question Will, having been silenced (19n above), ceases speaking as an interlocutor until line 470 (B.18.427) below (but see 350–58n).

27 (B.18.28) 'Nay,' quod faith: So the writer of Ephesians, having instructed his brothers to "Put you on the armour of God" against the "deceits of the devil," says "For our wrestling is not against flesh and blood; but against the principalities and powers, against the rulers of the world of this darkness, against the spirits of wickedness in the high places" (Eph. 6:11–12)—that is, the fiend. That the Crucifixion is a combat between death and life is a commonplace. In *Cursor mundi* the figure Hell speaks in similar terms of the unredeemed "Done bi dome to deþ so dym" (line 18071, ed. Morris 1876:1037).

and fals doem to deye: As punctuated by the Athlone editors and Schm, an ambiguous construction—the meaning is either that the fiend will joust with Jesus "and false judgment will die" (with a "testamentary" absolute infinitive **to deye**; see notes to 31, 264–68, 389 below, and with a full account, Wittig 1986) or, as if with hyphens (as in Prsl's ed. and Donaldson's trans.), that a figure named False-judgment-to-die will joust with Jesus. Prsl (and in effect Schm) glosses **fals doem to deye** "the false judgment of death upon mankind." The latter interpretation, in addition to being consistent with B.16.165 (not in C), "Ayeins deeþ and þe deuel," has easier grammar, seems more sprightly, and leads into the elaboration of the following lines; it is echoed in 427 (B.18.385) below, "doem to þe deth." In an earlier study Kane preferred for the B text the (archetypal?) B reading *fals dome and deþ* (1948:16). If this reading is right, the root of the variation may have been *y/þ* confusion (**deþ(e)/dey(e)**) and consequent smoothing. Except with the preposition "to," however, the stressed monosyllable *deth* never appears at line end elsewhere in PP (on this metrical phenomenon see Barney 1995:82–85, following Cable 1991).

The **fals doem** at any rate is specifically the idea that the patriarchs and prophets are damned for good, an idea that Treuthe will espouse below (145–52 [B.18.142–49]), and that Rihtwisnesse will call the "doem" that God himself gave at the Fall (196 [B.18.191]).

Life challenges Death

28–34 (B.18.29–35) Deth saith ... *mors tua*: These lines constitute the formal challenge or wager of combat (*gaige de bataille*) in a judicial duel, in which the opponents publicly give one another the lie. In this reported debate **Lyf** prom-

ises to perform actions elsewhere performed by the "lord of lyf," Jesus: fetch-
ing the fruit of Piers (18 above), giving the lie (to Lucifer), and binding him
(445–46 below). In the next passus Conscience echoes this passage, saying of
Jesus that "Myhte no deth hym fordo ne adown brynge" (C.21/B.19.51); in B,
the Samaritan has predicted that the devil will be fettered "er þis day þre daies"
(and see 41 below) and has quoted *O mors ero mors tua* (B.17.112–14).

Here then **Lyf** is the eternal life granted humans, and specifically it is
Jesus, the resurrection and the life (John 11:25) and the way, the truth, and the
life (John 14:6) who will, in the Pauline martial imagery, destroy death and
bring victory (1 Cor. 15:26, 54–57; 2 Tim. 1:10). The epistle to the Hebrews again
(see 22–23n above) echoes Paul's imagery and can be read so as to furnish an
authority for the linkage of the Harrowing with the idea of human brotherhood in Christ (see 419n below): Jesus called us brothers (*fratres*) and hence
shared our flesh "that, through death, he might destroy him who had the
empire of death, that is to say, the devil: and might deliver them . . . For no
where doth he take hold of angels: but of the seed of Abraham he taketh hold.
Wherefore it behoved him in all things to be made like unto his brethren
(*Unde debuit per omnia fratribus similari*)" (Heb. 2:11–17).

The debate of Death and Life forms the theme of the alliterative poem
Death and Liffe, probably of the fifteenth century (ed. Hanford and Steadman
1918; Donatelli 1989; Conlee 1991). Its editors trace the theme in literature and
art from the Easter sequence *Victimæ paschali laudes*, which includes the line
Mors et vita duello conflixere mirando ("Death and life fought a wondrous
duel"—Hanford 241–45, Donatelli 23–26; see also Le May 1932:31–34). *Death
and Liffe* concludes with a joust between Jesus and Death, and an account of
the Harrowing of Hell (lines 368–44). Whether it draws on PP is uncertain
(Hudson in Alford 1988a:254; Donatelli 1989:26–29); its lines 238, 260, 345–47
seem to reflect wording from this passus, but many of the two poems' common materials were widely repeated. An analogue of interest because it
includes the term "maystre" (cp. "maistrye," 298–99, 393–94 and n below) is
from a lyric attributed to Richard Rolle: "Dede & lyf bigan to stryf wheþer
myght be maystre mare" (ed. Brown 1924, no. 83, line 43; see also Rolle, ed.
Allen 1931:43). The motif is of course ancient (see e.g. Kroll 1932:50).

29 (B.18.30) loketh: Again in 21.175 looking, that is, being possessed of one's
senses, is collocated with living; see Headnote to this passus.

30 (B.18.31) leyeth his lyf to wedde: stakes his life as a pledge (tenders his gage
in a duel) for the proposition that Deth lies, fulfilling 18.283–84 (B.16.267–68).
The common collocation "lay one's life" (3.259, 4.191, 20.161, and B/A counter-

parts) puts into alliteration a common asseveration (2.36), here charged with the witty notion of Lyf staking his life—like Contrition leaving contrition (C.22/B.20.371), Need in need (C.22/B.20.20, 37), Truth knowing the truth (20.150 [B.18.147], A.2.86, etc.), reasoning with Reason (C.13.183, etc.), or Wit who would "wisse" (10.111) or be "ywyte" (10.125). Kane calls such figures "double allegorization" (1989:97). Of course Lyf does wager his life: if Deth is not lying, death will *not* be dead, and life will cease. Similarly Boek stakes its existence on the sequence of events in 264 (B.18.255) below.

31 (B.18.32) to walke: "he will walk abroad, live" (MED *walken* 7.(a), but see 2b., citing this line); an absolute infinitive (see 27n above), as are *feche, legge, bynde, forbete, brynge* below.

33 (B.18.34) þere hym liketh: presumably heaven, where Christ would bring the redeemed.

34 (B.18.35) And forbete . . . *O mors ero mors tua*: The line forcefully answers the shrewd lawyer's advice, "Betere is þat bote bale adoun brynge" (4.88 [B.4.92, A.4.79]). L may recall a line, "Þou bete al my bale with bote of þi blood," from a Passion lyric well enough known to have been quoted by Richard Rolle in his *Meditations on the Passion* (line 172, ed. Allen 1931:172, 133). See 262 (B.18.253) below. Schm reads *forbite* from Manuscript R of B and many manuscripts of C, and glosses "bite through," thinking of the full quotation from Osee (Hosea) 13:14: "O death, I will be thy death; O hell, I will be thy bite" (*morsus*, with play in the Latin on *mors*, death). This fuller (and well known) Latin quotation appears in Manuscript R's ally, Manuscript F. See B.16.35 for the word "forbiteþ," and the parallel variant at C.18.39.

To speak of Jesus as biting hell is not uncommon: the *Castle of Love* says of Jesus at the Harrowing, "A gret bite he bot of helle anon" (ed. Sajavaara 1967, line 1345) from Grosseteste's *Château*, "A enfers fist un grant mors" (ed. Murray 1918, line 1323). These uses reflect the Sarum Palm Sunday processional, where Jesus is called *inferni morsus*, biter of hell (ed. Henderson 1882:51; Tyrer 1932:59), as in Venantius Fortunatus's commentary on the creed, "In part he bit (*momordit*) hell" (quoted Waterland 1870), following Augustine's treatise on the creed, *De symbolo*, "In part he bit (*momordit*) hell, with regard to those whom he freed; in part he let it go, with regard to those who, in their original sin, remained in torment" (PL 40.1194). See 207 (B.18.202) below.

One use of the familiar antiphon *O mors ero mors tua* (see B.17.114a) is at the service of Tenebræ, commonly Matins and Lauds of the three days before Easter Sunday, in which the church's candles are extinguished, and then one candle reintroduced (Brev. I.dcclxxxii), an effect resembling the light effects of this passus (see 59–62n below).

The Passion

35–112 (B.18.36–109) Thenne cam Pilatus . . . sanctus sanctorum cessabit: The story of the Passion draws from the Gospel accounts, especially Matthew, from the liturgy, especially of Holy Week, and from a variety of familiar apocryphal and legendary materials, *vitæ* of Jesus, and meditations on the Passion. It intersperses sacred narrative with boisterous and vivid speeches, "al þat fare" (16 [B.18.18]), in a way that recalls the French Passion plays and the emergent English drama of the mystery plays. On the use of comic and grotesque actions in holy settings and their background in popular English writings see Kolve 1966, chs. 6–8. The action picks up where it is left off at C.18.177, and where the detailed narrative stops at B.16.159; see C.18.161–62n and B.16.160–66n.

The action falls into three parts (see notes): 35–79, the Trial, Crucifixion, and death of Jesus—the Passion proper; 80–94, the Longinus (**Longeus**) episode; and 95–112, Faith's harangue.

The trial, crucifixion, and death of Jesus

35–79 (B.18.36–77) Thenne cam Pilatus . . . to touche in deynge: In the account of the Passion legal terms abound, as befits a trial (before Pilate) that increasingly incorporates elements of a trial by combat. Remarkable is L's foreshortening of the account of the Crucifixion; both the literature of the Passion and the liturgy itself, especially in the elaborate homilies on the Seven Words of the Cross on Good Friday, tended to dwell on every detail of Jesus' suffering and speech (Aers and Staley 1996:15–76, esp. 70–71). L concentrates instead on the themes of importance for the passus as a whole, including the working of the law, conquest, God's hidden power. As Harbert observes, "Langland is unusual for his period in the way in which he represents the Passion, having more of the heroic early medieval spirit than most of his contemporaries: the liturgy was one of the sources from which he imbibed this" (1990:57).

35 (B.18.36) with moche peple: In Matthew 27:15–19 the *populus* have, *congregatis . . . illis*, gathered before Pilate *seden[s] . . . pro tribunali*, seated in the judgment seat. In this and the following lines legalisms like "iustice," "court," "pelour" emphasize the theme of judgment (with a general suspiciousness of petty lawyering) that dominates this passus (see 413–42n below), and should be read in light of Alford's handbook on legal diction (*Gloss.*).

36 (B.18.37) douhtyliche . . . do: The phrase, of distinctively chivalric connotation (see MED *doughti*), recalls the jousting metaphor. Hence Pilate would **demen her beyre rihte,** "render judgment as to the right of the two of them, adjudicate their claim" (MED *right* 4.(a); Alford, *Gloss.*). The language suggests a trial by combat, specifically a "civil duel of law" of the kind that could be engaged under the terms of a Writ of Right, a legal proceeding usually concerning property rights (or, an extension of the same idea—with regard to the king's property—treason and matters of royal succession and dominion). For the "manner of conducting judicial duels" according to Thomas, Duke of Gloucester, Constable under Richard II, see Rickert 1948:151–56. In fact Writ of Right disputes were rarely settled by combat in the fourteenth century (Palmer 1984:156), although the chronicler Knighton reports one in 1384 (ed. Martin 1995:334–35). The property in question is Piers's fruit—those in limbo and all humanity; the dominion in question is Christ's or Satan's, Life's or Death's. See Baldwin 1981a; Neilson 1890; Headnote and 8–34n, 18n above, and 371n below.

37 (B.18.38) aʒeyns iesus: The **iustice** is surely Pilate if the word is indeed singular (see variants); he shows no sign of the neutrality he affects in the Gospels, or of his later conversion as told in some legends. Contemporary satire made Pilate the type of the false judge (Owst 1961:344).

39 (B.18.40) a pelour: an "appealer" or accuser (see 46–47n below), standing for the multitude of chief priests and elders, the *falsi testes*. An appeal of treason (*appelacio de prodicione*) might precede a judicial duel (Hector 1982:105–6). In Matt. 26:60, two such witnesses specifically accuse Jesus of claiming the power to destroy and rebuild the Temple, though they do so before the high priest, not Pilate. As noted in 18.161–62, and conforming with many medieval retellings of the Passion, L conflates the separate appearances before the high priest and Pilate into one.

42 (B.18.43) Edefien hit eft newe: The phrase reflects the Latin *reædificare* of Matt. 26:61. For Jesus' claim to re-edify see 18.159–62 (B.16.131–34), where (C only) L avoids misunderstanding: "Ac þe ouerturnynge of the temple bitokened his resureccioun," the usual gloss from John 2:21.

46–47 (B.18.46–47) *Crucifige . . . Tolle, tolle*: "Away with him; away with him; crucify him," John 19:15; see 6–7n above. A **cachepol** (see 75 [B.18.73] below)

is a minor official, like a policeman or process-server, or the *magistrates* of
Luke 22:4, in its original use a tax gatherer (Alford, *Gloss.*); in Anglo-Norman,
a sheriff's officer (*A-ND*). The *Promptorium parvulorum* glosses it "pety-
seriawnte," and under *Pilowre* [confusedly for *Pelowre*; see 39n above] adds
that a "catchepol" is "he þat pelythe [appeals in prosecution] oþer menne"
(ed. Way 1843:58, 391, 399).

The accusation of **wycchecrafte** may simply respond to the claim of
miraculous Temple-rebuilding, but more generally to the accusation by the
Jews that "with soercerye" (B.16.120, "þoruȝ wichecraft") "he wrouhte"
(17.304 [B.15.596]; 18.149 [B.16.120]) in his miracles, especially the recent raising
of Lazarus (John 11, esp. verse 47; and 71 [B.18.69] below). The Gospel account
of the raising of Lazarus was read on Friday before Passion Sunday, two weeks
before Good Friday. The *Gospel of Nicodemus* has the accusers before Pilate
call Jesus *maleficus*, an evil magician (1.1, 2.1, etc.), perhaps half-remembering
the Gospel term *malefactor* (John 18:30). The accusation is commonplace in
accounts of the Trial, e.g. in the N-Town cycle (ed. Spector 1991:307, 311) and
the Towneley Buffeting, 103 (ed. Stevens and Cawley 1994:255), as well as the
(earlier) French Passion plays (e.g., ed. Jodogne 1965, lines 19512–14; ed. Runnalls 1974, lines 509, 1748, 1896, etc.; see also Goodman 1944:100–101). The
accusation may also reflect the fear of and proscriptions against magical aids—
virtuous stones, written charms, and the like—in trials by combat (Neilson
1890:119, 152, 162–63, 174; Prost 1872:36); see Arthur 1901:64 for an ordinance
on this point under Richard II, and Rickert 1948:153.

49–50 (B.18.49–50) saide in Enuye: "spoke with malice"; see 18.163 "Enuye
and euel wil" in a similar context . As punctuated by the Athlone editors, **saide**
is intransitive (MED *seien* 6.), avoiding redundancy with **quod** in the next line;
Schm punctuates otherwise, taking **quod** as pleonastic.

50 (B.18.50) 'Aue, raby': "Hail, master," quoting Matt. 26:49, spoken by Judas
at the betrayal, and reflecting Matt. 27:29 et synop., *Ave, rex Judæorum*, spoken
by the mocking soldiers at the Crucifixion. The first half-line repeats 18.168
(B.16.151), where Judas is the **ribaude**.

redes shotte vp to his yes. The next sentence in Matthew et synop. says
the soldiers struck Jesus' head with a reed, not that they shot reeds (darts?—
MED *red* 2.(f)) up to his eyes or (B) **þrew reedes at hym**—does L refer to the
joust? or is he thinking of some buffoonish stage action in a mystery play?

51–59 (B.18.51–59) Thei nayled hym . . . his eyes togederes: The account of
the Crucifixion emphasizes the passivity rather than the triumph of the "com-

bat" until its startling last line, "The lord of lyf and of liht tho leyde his eyes togederes" (cp. C.21.142 and n). The word **lord** has not before been used in this passus; it occurs seventeen times (15 in B) hereafter. Jesus is **naked**, mocked, and pitiful and pale like a prisoner who dies.

52–53 (B.18.52–53) poysen . . . And beden him drynke his deth to lette and his dayes lenghe: That the drink, vinegar in the Gospels, is (alliterating) "poison" and not merely any potion (Latin *potio*) seems to follow from Matthew, Mark, and John, in which Jesus dies immediately after drinking it (although many accounts represent Jesus as refusing to drink)—MED evidence for any other sense is weak, though A-ND attests a French sense "medicinal potion," a sense found in the *Torneiment Anticrist* (ed. Bender 1976, lines 1386, 2661, etc.). In PP **poysen** is venom (17.223–32 [B.15.560–67]). A fifteenth-century poem on the "Symbols of the Passion" presents the usual idea, that the vinegar (and gall; medieval accounts conflated the drinks offered Jesus at various points in the Passion) were "venym" by which one would be "poysynd" (ed. Morris 1871:186–87, lines 107–8). Similarly the *Mirour of Mans Saluacioun* says that the myrrhed wine, vinegar, and gall were proffered "þat thow shuld dye with more peyne" (ed. Henry 1987, line 4696). *Cursor mundi* compares the gall given to Jesus with the "appul þat adam eet" (ed. Stauffenberg 1985:131, lines 16943–44). Skeat's proposal that it may be an anodyne has no support in the tradition (see below in this note), and Schmidt rightly rejects it (1983:177).

In archetypal B (adopted in Schm; emended to C by KD-B, see their p. 91 and RK-C, p. 75) the reading of line 53 is *And beden hym drynken his deeyvel—his dayes were ydone.* This yields obvious sense, and may represent scribal mistaking of the irony; the C version (so Prsl) reflects the mocking that becomes more overt in the next line, and is typical of Passion presentations. In *Le Mystère de la Passion*, for instance, the soldiers sarcastically offer Jesus "buvraige riche et chier"—vinegar, gall, and myrrh (ed. Jodogne 1965, line 25791); the N-Town Crucifixion play has the mocking (*illudentes:* Mark 15:31) chief priests and soldiers say, "Is not þis drynk of good tast?" (ed. Spector 1991:333).

It has been suggested (Prsl's alternate interpretation; Ruffing 1991) that the C version revises B with the idea that the devils actually wanted to prolong Jesus' life as they belatedly discovered who he was, an interpretation supported by 334–35 (B.18.300–303) below in which Satan ("goblin") says he wished to lengthen Jesus' life and (B only) sent a dream to Pilate's wife in an effort to call off the Crucifixion. C. W. Marx cites some earlier versions of the story in which the devil both plots and fears Jesus' death (1993:104). On the widespread legend of Pilate's wife's dream in European Passion plays see Goodman

1944:31–35. The terms **lette** and **lenghe** occur in both passages. But the drink here is poison; the devils are not stupid about material things. Although Peter the Comestor had said that the devil strove that Christ *not* die, he also said that the soldiers' motive in offering the drink was to have their job done more quickly: *ut citius possent liberari a custodia* "so that they might be freed more quickly from their guard duty" (*Historia scholastica*, PL 198:1628, 1632). This represents the common tradition: see the *Golden Legend*: *dicitur enim crucifixos citius mori, acetum si bibant*, "for it is said that those crucified die more quickly if they drink vinegar" (cap. 53, ed. Graesse 1846:226). The *Golden Legend* presents another tradition as well (p. 243), in which Satan brags to Inferus that he effected the death of Jesus, providing the lance and mixing the gall and vinegar, an idea probably drawn from homilies attributed to Eusebius and read in some rites on Easter or Easter Eve (MacCullogh 1930:177; see Young 1910:934–35, Rand 1904:261–78). See too the Middle English *Evangelie* (lines 1568–73, ed. Campbell 1915:603) and *Complaint of Our Lady* (ed. Marx and Drennan 1987:105); Rolle's "Meditation B" (ed. Ogilvie-Thomson 1988:465–68); the *Pèlerinage Jhesucrist* (line 9439, ed. Stürzinger 1897); and a French version of the *Gospel of Nicodemus*, where Satan admits having foolishly tried to hasten Jesus' death with the drink (lines 610–11, ed. Ford 1973:54). See Schmidt 1983:176–82 for further references.

This issue would be trivial but for the actual resonance of this passage with 400–12 (B.18.362–70) below, where the counter-drink of love is named, and (in C only) the word of Jesus in John's gospel, *Sicio*, is finally quoted.

54 (B.18.54) sotil: "guileful" (cp. 12.240) or "of magical power" (cp. B.15.12), referring to the mockers who said that if Jesus could rebuild the Temple in three days he should save himself (Matt. 27:40 et synop.), not seeing that in his death the guiler was beguiled (165 [B.18.162] below).

55 (B.18.55) yf thow be Crist and kynges sone: conflating Luke 23:35; Matt. 27:40, 42; Mark 15:32.

57 (B.18.57) *Consummatum est*: John 19:30. See 22–23n above.

59–62 (B.18.59–60) The lord of lyf . . . derk nyht hit semede: With these lines L introduces the imagery of Christ as light that pervades this passus, imagery deriving from the *tenebrae* that covered the earth at Jesus' death in Luke 23:44, and from liturgical uses of light and dark during Holy Week—see for instance Rupert of Deutz, *De divinis officiis* 5.26–28 (ed. Haacke 1967) on the symbolism of extinguishing and relighting candles, and see 34n above—but especially from the first chapter of John and the *Gospel of Nicodemus*, 18ff., with its concordance of scriptural texts on Christ as light. Compare 7.131 (B.5.491). When Jesus closed his eyes, shut out the light, he became *deus consummatus* represented as the harrowing light among the shades. Earlier the figure Kynde is called "Lord of lyf and of lyht" (10.155 [B.9.29, A.10.30]).

leyde his eyes togederes: The phrasing of line 59 echoes *Cursor mundi*: at Jesus' death "To-geder fell his eghen" (ed. Morris 1876:958, line 75); *The Southern Passion* also speaks of Jesus' eyes: "and þo closed his eye, / And his heued heng a-doun" (ed. Brown 1927:58, line 1581; see Pickering 1984:179, line 2535). See on this passage Schmidt 1983:185–88: the closing of the eyes of the Sun of Righteousness (see 271n below) "*causes* the light to be extinguished." For God, who should "loke on" ("protect"—see 428 below) us, to close his eyes is terrible: it is we who should close our eyes at the spectacle of the hanging Lord (see next note). That Jesus closed his eyes on the cross and grew pale (often with physiological explanations) are commonplaces (e.g. Ludolph, *Vita*, ed. Bolard et al. 1865:670).

60 (B.18.60) The daye for drede withdrouh and derke bicam þe sonne: Luke 23:44–45, "et tenebræ facta sunt in universam terram usque in horam nonam. Et obscuratus est sol" (and there was darkness over all the earth until the ninth hour. And the sun was darkened); cp. 7.131 (B.5.491). Transferring the fear from the witnesses to the daylight, L anticipates the fuller allegory that follows, in which the fiends people the darkness and the day-star Jesus descends to hell (126 [B.18.123] below). In a similar way the Gloss says the sun withdrew (*retraxit*) its rays that it might not see the hanging Lord (at Luke 23:44; see also Marx 1993:104–5). So the sun is active while Jesus is passive. The Vernon Manuscript "Dispute between Mary and the Cross" has a similarly vivid account of the darkness at the Crucifixion: "Þe lyht leop of the sunne" (line 385, ed. Morris 1871:144); in *Cursor mundi* the "son withdrogh his light," unwilling to shine on those who harmed the Lord (Cotton version, line 35, ed. Morris 1876:958). See also the *South English Ministry and Passion*, line 2535 (ed. Pickering 1984:179). The language of the *Myrour of Lewed Men*, one of the fourteenth-century translations of Grosseteste's *Château*, is close to PP: "The sunne sone withdrogh his liȝt and the erthe whoke, / And the vail of the temple euen brast in two, / And the harde stones swiftly cleue also; / Many a man rose than that were before dede, / And al bare thei wittenes of his godhede" (ed. Sajavaara 1967, lines 668–72). On the theme of witness see the Headnote to this passus.

61–62 The wal of the temple tocleyef . . . hard roch (B.18.61 The wal waggede and cleef): Matt. 27:51, "velum templi scissum est in duas partes a summo

usque deorsum" (the veil of the temple was rent in two from the top even to
the bottom). The veil, not the wall of the temple, was cleft in two (so Mark
15:38, Luke 23:45). Foster suggests, of a similar use of "wall" for "veil" in *The
Northern Passion* (line 1774), that "wall" is probably corrupted from *wayll*,
"veil" (1913, 1.208, 2:192), and MED reports that *wal* is simply a spelling of *veil*,
recording two other spellings of the Temple veil as "wayle, wale" (*veil* n. (1),
2.(c)), to which may be added *Cursor mundi*, lines 16786 and 24420 (ed. Morris
1876, 1878). It is unlikely that L confused wall and veil, but scribes may have
misinterpreted his spelling; the Athlone editors report no scribal spelling with
v. The B reading, not mentioning the temple (in an effort to correct?), refers
to the earthquake generally, and continues **and al þe world quaued**: *et terra
mota est, et petræ scissæ sunt* ("and the earth quaked, and the rocks were
rent"—Matt. 27:51). In C the line continues **euene a to peces**, "entirely (or,
cleanly) into two pieces," as the Gospels said of the veil. The rending of the veil
of the Temple was commonly associated with Moses' breaking of the tablets of
the law, which L calls "a pece of an hard roche" (19.12 [B.17.11]), echoed in the
hard roch of line 62.

62–63 The hard roch . . . as hit quyk were: These lines, added in C perhaps
from the suggestion of B.18.247–48 (where the earth is fully animated; see
256–57 below), emphasize the sympathy of nature, a commonplace, and invert
the usual attributes of quick humans and dead earth. Ludolph quotes Pope
Leo as saying *universa creatura congemuit* ("all creation lamented") at the Crucifixion (*Vita*, ed. Bolard et al. 1865:672)—cp. "The Dream of the Rood," *weop
eal gesceaft*. The *Meditations on the Life and Passion* says "Creatures mornedon
alle" at Jesus' death (ed. d'Evelyn 1921, line 923). The *Lignum vitae* attributed
to Bonaventure proposes that at the Crucifixion "hard rocks are split as it were
with natural compassion" (*quasi naturali compassione*) (ed. Peltier 1868:12,
77–78).

64–69 dede men: The rising of the dead from their graves and their appearing
to many people is found only in Matthew's Gospel (27:52–53). Ludolph carefully observes that these dead rose "not then" when the graves were opened,
but at Jesus' Resurrection, as Matthew (27:53) specified (ed. Bolard et al.
1865:672). Wyclif agrees rather with the tradition that L seems to follow:
acknowledging that Christ was the first-born from the dead, he still finds that
bodies were raised before the Resurrection to bear witness to the efficacy of
Jesus' death—but they rose not to life (*ad vitam*); their souls were only
mechanically joined to their bodies *ut motrices*, zombie-like (ed. Loserth 1890,
4:182).

In the *Gospel of Nicodemus* two of these risen, Karinus and Leucius, are discovered, write down their account of the Harrowing of Hell which they witnessed, and then are transfigured and disappear—they do not sink back into the earth (17, 27.3). See 259n below. On the confused traditions regarding this resurrection see MacCullogh 1930:288–99.

One of these dead reports on the engagement in battle of Life and Death (see 28–34 above); he emerges from his tomb with a dantesque mysteriousness and special knowledge. L seems to imagine that the earthquake and other signs of nature's distress, the **tempest**, are the impact on the surface of the earth of the battle in hell, but that the battle's outcome will not be revealed until Jesus rises on Easter Sunday. The precise timing of events from the Crucifixion to the Resurrection varied in the traditions. The terms **derkenesse** and **maistry** are picked up in Faith's response in lines 104–5 (B.18.101–2). **no wyht** here can refer only to living humans. L puns with **sonne rysynge**; see MED *sonne* 8.(b) for more obvious examples.

70–73 Somme saide . . . somme saide: The distributive grammar can suggest popular speculation about the uncertainties of an exciting event, like the predictions about the tournament in Chaucer's Knight's Tale (2513–22). We are now in universal salvation history, but the folk at the Crucifixion—excepting the centurion—are at a hanging spectacle. The quotation is of Matt. 27:54, the centurion's response to the death of Jesus: "Indeed this was the Son of God."

Those who think Jesus **can of soercerie** (see 46–47n above) or (B) **was a wicche** seem to fear that he will harm them if they take him down alive; cp. 85–86 (B.18.83–84). Similarly in Guillaume de Deguileville's *Pèlerinage Jhesucrist* Judas kissed Jesus, "un enchanteur," fearing that he would change shape (ed. Stürzinger 1897, line 8175).

73–76 (B.18.71–74) Two theues . . . tho theues: As the Athlone text is punctuated, L means that according to law thieves would be crucified in those days (but not now). Barnes (1989:22) proposes that the second half of line 74 rather goes with what follows: those crucified should be killed by having their legs broken so as not to violate the Jews' **comune law** concerning the sabbath that was to begin at sunset on the Friday, as is clear from John 19:31. (John does not say that their arms were broken.) Ludolph of Saxony explains the law: a Jewish feast was not to be polluted, and the period after sundown on Good Friday was especially solemn as a double feast, sabbath and Passover (*Vita*, ed. Bolard et al. 1865:674). The law was in fact both **comune** (in Judaism) and statutory: a hanged man was to be "buried the same day: for he is accursed of God that hangeth on a tree: and thou shalt not defile thy land" (Deut. 21:22–

23). The same idea is found in pseudo-Bonaventure's *Meditationes*, cap. 80 (ed. Peltier 1868:608) and in *La Passion des jongleurs* (ed. Perry 1981, lines 3073–80).

The disposition of the syntax in the meter—beginning a sentence in mid-line and running it on (see lines 70–71 [B.18.69–70] above, and 21/B.19.148–49, 22/B.20.85 below)—is unusual in PP and tells against Barnes's idea, as does the proleptic use of **so**, but his argument is corroborated by contemporary English analogues. The *Southern Passion* specifies, following John, that it was "hare lawe," the Jews' law, that a body had to be removed from a cross at the time of the feast (ed. Brown 1927:60, lines 1629–31); similarly the *South English Ministry and Passion*, with the wording "here lawe" (ed. Pickering 1984:180, lines 2563–65).

78–79 (B.18.76–77) kynde forȝaf . . . hardynesse: usually (Skt, Prsl) translated as "God granted at that time (most manuscripts have easier *tyme* in BC) that no knave would have the audacity . . . ," but **kynde** here more likely means "natural decency" than "God" (MED *kinde* n. 5b.(a)). Chivalric comportment required combatants of equal status; the motive here is analogous but different: L reflects a doctrine of atonement in which the economy of redemption requires an (apparent) equation of the just and unjust—see Headnote to this passus and 102–3n below. Fowler (1961:141) compares Pilate in the N-Town "Second Trial Before Pilate" charging "Þat þer be no man xal towch ȝoure kyng / But yf he be knyght or jentylman born" (ed. Spector 1991:322).

Longeus (Longinus)

80–94 (B.18.78–91) Ac þer cam forth . . . with þat a wepte: The legend of Longeus, more commonly Longinus, developed early from the account of the centurion who was converted at the Crucifixion (70–73n above) and John's statement (19:31–34) that, seeing that Jesus was dead, the soldiers did not break his legs, but one of them pierced his side with a lance (Gk. *longché*, perhaps hence "Longinus"). Peebles (1911) traces the story from the early appearance of the name in the *Gospel of Nicodemus* to the fully developed account in the *Golden Legend* and beyond (Ludolph attributes the legend to Chrysostom, ed. Bolard et al. 1865:674–76). In the *Golden Legend* we learn that Longinus was a centurion who, when he pierced Jesus' side, was healed of his blindness by the blood flowing down the lance, and was converted and led thereafter a monastic life until, his tongue and teeth having been cut out, he was beheaded by pagan persecutors (ed. Graesse 1846:202–3).

The ideas that Longeus was forced to pierce Jesus by the Jews (themselves unwilling, perhaps fearful—see 70–73n), that in his blindness he did not know what he was doing, that he was a knight (in some versions even a Jewish knight), that he was unwilling to do it, and that he knelt, pleaded ignorance, and begged forgiveness as he realized what he had done, are all found in various versions of the legend (Peebles 1911:29, 51, 77–78, 89, 92, 94, 98–99, 110, 124, 132–33; see also Weldon 1989:50–55, and on Longinus as a Jew in medieval charms Peebles 1911:93 and Ebermann 1903:43, 48–50). In *Cursor mundi*, for example, Jews break the thieves' legs and make Longeus, a blind knight, use his spear (ed. Morris 1876, lines 16829–37). The idea is that the Jews would avoid bloodshed—"We [Jews] may not kill anyone" (*Nicodemus*, cap. 3). In short the legend as it developed emphasized Longinus's innocence and the Jews' complicity, and it disregarded the facts of the Gospel narrative.

As L recasts the story his emphasis is on the proper conduct of a joust, chivalric motives developing from Abraham as herald, the lance of the Gospels, and the royal birth of Jesus. The action is still in a **place** (see 19n above); the bystanders **hoved** (as Prsl notes, a term used of knights waiting for battle or tourney: MED *hoven* v. (1) 2.(a)); Jesus gets the **gre**, the prize for victory. The "natural" chivalric ethos, here **kynde**, granted that no **boie**, common fellow, might touch Jesus, a knight and king's son; hence Longeus, a Jewish knight and therefore a combatant of appropriately gentle birth, is produced as the Jews' **chaumpion Chivaler, chief knyht** (see 102–3n below). In making Longeus a Jew, a rare idea in the tradition, L can make nice, and important, distinctions between individual and racial guilt.

Because Jesus is dead during this "joust," the question of the chivalric demeanor of the combatants is on the face of it absurd, "a boyes conseille" as Faith observes (98 [B.18.95]; see 102–3n)—the real battle is going on in hell. But the irony redoubles: in fact Longeus is saved. The question of the Jews' nobility has, too, theological significance that will emerge in Faith's harangue: see 95–112n.

80 (B.18.78) a knyhte: Longeus's knightly estate, a common feature of the legend, probably originated in the Latin term (out of John's Gospel) *miles*, "soldier," a term later used for the feudal class "knight." The legend versions show none of L's interest in Longeus's nobility.

81 (B.18.79) as þe lettre telleth: At first blush a formula of the type "as the bok tellith" in the alliterative tradition, but here the locution may register L's sense that he needs special authority for this extra-biblical legend (see 17.6n, 21.71n). Compare his citation of Scripture again when he undertakes to render the post-biblical traditions of the Harrowing and the debate of the Four Daughters (115 [B.18.112] and 113–15n below; Kane (1982) 1989:98).

83 (B.18.81) Maugre his mony teth: that is, in spite of himself; the proverbial expression (Whiting 1968:T406) may reflect, as Schm suggests, the legend's account of Longeus's later career, in which persecutors smashed out his teeth (ed. Graesse 1846:202).

B.18.82 Iew Longeus: KD-B suggest (p. 94) that the archetypal (and unmetrical) B reading, **To take þe spere in his hond and Iustin wiþ Iesus**, is a scribal rewriting to "exclude the notion that Longinus was a Jew," and they (and Schm) restore from C. If so, the corruption testifies to L's eccentricity here (see 80–94n above), under pressure of his emphasis on the supersession of Judaism (see 106–10n below).

88 (B.18.86) vnspered his yes: The unblinding of Longeus follows the closing of Jesus' eyes and precedes the unlocking of hell ("vnspere þe ʒates," 270 [B.18.262] below), and recalls such unblindings as those of the travelers to Emmaus who, when they took bread with Jesus, recognized him as he vanished (Luke 24:31). The recognition continues the motif of the "disguised duel" (Clifton 1993:125–26; see 8–12n above). Longeus is willy-nilly the champion of "death and the devil"; when he is unblinded, Jesus will by his light blind Lucifer ("ablende," 140 [B.18.137] below), continuing the project of equipoised reciprocation (see Headnote to this passus). Such paradoxes of seeing are here pointed by the play on "unspering" by way of a spear.

89 (B.18.87) vppon knees: So Longeus is often depicted, e.g. in the *Prose Complaint of Our Lady* (ed. Marx and Drennan 1987:108). Peebles (1911:51) draws attention to a painting in a Cambridge manuscript book of hours (Trinity Coll. B.11.17) that depicts a Crucifixion scene in which Longinus kneels with his spear, the word *amor* written on his robe, and the background is filled by the words of Ps. 84:11 (see 464a [B.18.421a] below), a collocation of texts and images that underlie much of this passus.

93 Bothe my lond: The line, added in C, presents the figure of the knight yielding in combat and acknowledging his loss in a Writ of Right duel (see 102–3n below). That Longeus is landed accentuates his distance from those Jews who, Faith foresees, will be landless (see 106–110n below). In the *Passion des jongleurs* Longis is a 200-year-old propertied inhabitant of Jerusalem; whether he is Jewish is not made explicit (ed. Perry 1981, line 1673).

94 (B.18.91) reuthe, riȝtfol: Continuing the formal, judicial character of Longeus's yielding, the juxtaposition of these terms also anticipates the debate of mercy and justice to follow.

Faith's harangue

95–112 (B.18.92–109) Thenne gan faith . . . *sanctorum cessabit*: Faith as herald announces the outcome of the joust. The vehemence of this attack on those who would order a blind man to stab a dead man may in part be motivated by Faith's identification with Abraham, who seems especially offended that his descendants fail to see Christ in Jesus; hence their unction ceased (112a [B.18.109a]; see 106–10n below). The historical detail of the curse on Jews in any case mouths common medieval opinion that runs against the spirit of lines 26–27 (B.18.27–28) above, which assign the role of adversary not to Jews but to the devil. In 18.258–59 (B.16.241–42) Abraham says his issue would have mercy if they asked for it; only Longeus does.

If a note of pitying regret as well as despite and aristocratic contempt can be heard in this passage, it would evoke Jesus' laments for Jerusalem at Luke 13:34, 23:28–31; see 106–10n and 107n below. The occasion is epic-elegaic: the death of a nation. Generally on medieval representations of Jews in Latin Passion accounts see Bestul 1996, ch. 3, and for a review of anti-Jewish elements in PP see Davlin 1996:107–11. Narin van Court makes a persuasive argument that between the B and C Versions, L changed his view of Christianity's form of supersession of Judaism from fulfillment to replacement (1996).

Continuing the large analogy of chivalric honor and religious righteousness, Faith berates the Jews with a batch of terms belittling their class as less than "gentle" (see 21n above)—they are caitiffs, villains, boys, recreants, lurdans, unhardy, thralls, churls: **knyhthoed was hit neuere.**

98 (B.18.95) boyes: "churls"; see Prol.78 (B.Prol.80, A.Prol.77), and *Winner and Waster* 15–16, "And eke boyes of no blode, with boste and with pryde, / Shal wedde ladyes in londe . . ." (ed. Conlee 1991:67). For a full account of the word's etymology and meaning see Dobson 1940.

102–3 (B.18.99–100) chaumpioun Chiualer . . . recreaunt remyng: hence the loser in a trial by combat (see Alford, *Gloss.* s.v. *Recreaunt*) **riht at iesus wille**—he yielded himself as a knight to the pleasure of Jesus, and yielded himself according to the (divine) will of Jesus, and is now in the pun re-creant, believing in return. The sense of **recreaunt** is "coward, vanquished one," but its etymology (unbeliever, apostate) encourages the apt pun, as Schm and Alford observe. The speaker here, Faith, is *creaunce* personified. See 80–94n, and compare 14.132, 153 (B.12.193, 214) where the penitent thief "ȝeld hym creaunt" and was, like Longinus in the legendary tradition, saved. A number of manuscripts read *creaunt* here. Skeat notes similar language (but to the opposite effect) in Chaucer's Parson's Tale, "he that despeirith hym is lyk the coward champioun recreant, that saith 'creant' [uncle!] withoute nede" (698). To be recreant was, according to Blackstone, to be deprived of the right to hold property (Baldwin 1981a:70)—see 106–11n below. In civil cases tried by combat the parties were required to present champions, who were to be equals, *parigals* (Whittaker 1895:109–11; Neilson 1890:47; Prost 1872:51–53). Baldwin observes that only in civil Writ of Right (land possession) duels would a **chaumpion** be used (1981a:66—see 18n, 36n above, and Alford, *Gloss.* s.v. *Champion*). In criminal duels, e.g. for treason, the parties themselves fought (Plucknett 1956:117). Hence primarily at issue in this representation is a matter of seisin—who owns Piers's fruit? See 299–311n below. Baldwin further holds that the champions here are Death and Lyf, whereas they seem to be Longinus and (incarnate) Jesus, who is of course Life itself.

MED records L's as the first use of the common noun **chiualer** in English. A document about judicial combats in a Writ of Right from 1469 assumes that the *champyons* will be *chevalers* (Thorne 1954:95–96). Elsewhere Jesus is commonly spoken of as **chaumpion** and **chivaler** in accounts of the Passion: *Meditations on the Life*, "þat champioun in þis batayle" (ed. d'Evelyn 1921, line 643); in an early French version of the *Gospel of Nicodemus* the souls in limbo call Christ "chevalere e combatere" (ed. Le May 1932:44); in the *Passion des jongleurs* the devils call Jesus "beaus chevaliers cortois" (ed. Perry 1981, line 2743); and in Bozon's Passion poem he is "un noble chivaler" (ed. Jeffrey and Levy 1990:186, line 2). *Cursor mundi*'s Passion narrative speaks of "ihesu oure champioun / Þo he lay deed for oure raunsoun" (ed. Morris 1876:1069, lines 18651–52). In B.8.45 (A.9.41) "charite" is "champion, chief help ayein synne," clearly an advocate.

But closest in its collocation of terms to this passus is *Castle of Love* (see Headnote to this passus): Jesus says "Ichulle þe *batayle* nyme for þe. / To *ple* ichulle þis princes hauen / And þi *rihte* ichulle crauen, / For icham of þi *lynage*, / I may crauen þin heritage; / And icham of *freo* nacion, / Me ["one"] ouȝte ihere my *reson* . . ." (ed. Sajavaara 1967:964–70, emphasis added). The same terms occur in the original *Château*, ed. Murray 1918:940–46: bataile, enpleider, dreit, lignage, franche, reson. Both Grosseteste and L draw the analogy between the requirement in law that appellants had to be of suitable status (especially in combats; see 80–94n above), and the requirement of Anselmian soteriology that only a God-man could redeem original sin.

recreaunt remyng: "shouting 'I surrender!'" Skt and Schm accept the B archetype's (and several C manuscripts') *rennyng*, "riding a course" (or running away?), in B.18.100 where C.20.103 has (all editors) **remyng**, "crying out" or "weeping." Manuscript W of C, perhaps modernizing, reads *wepyng*. Possible also is *reniynge*, "renouncing his (wrongheaded Jewish) belief" (with minim confusion); cp. Manuscript Hm of B *renegat*, MED *reneien* v. (1), *reni-ant, reneiing(e*; see also 12.60–61 (B.11.125–26) and 12.64–65 (B.11.129–30). In this last passage both verbs *rennen* and *reneien* occur with "caytif," and some manuscripts read *renne*, etc., for "reneyed." None of these alternatives is smooth in context.

106–10 (B.18.103–7) And ȝoure franchise . . . lawes defendeth: The Jews, then, have forfeited not only knighthood but their status as freemen and landholders. L refers to the common notion, derived from Daniel (see 112n below), that Jewish political independence ended shortly after and in retaliation for the Crucifixion, especially with the destruction of Jerusalem in 70 C.E (see 17.305–6 [B.15.597–98]). The key text is John 11:48, in which the Jewish leaders worry that if they leave Jesus alone "the Romans will come, and take away our place and nation (*locum et gentem*)." Perhaps too L recalls John 8:33–40, where Jesus says, to Jews who believe in him but nevertheless insist that they are of the seed of Abraham and therefore free, that in fact they are slaves of sin. Further in Matt. 23:38, Luke 13:35, Jesus' lament for Jerusalem, he says "Behold, your house shall be left to you, desolate (*domus vestra deserta*)." The Gloss to Luke 13:35 comments, "The Romans . . . took away [the Jews'] land and nationhood (*locum et gentem*)." This phrasing reflects John and other early sources: Augustine has "For by killing Christ they lost both land and nationhood (*et locum et gentem*)" (*Enarr. in Psalmos* 52.9, CCSL 39:644); Bede associates the same phrase with Jewish barrenness like the sterile fig tree (*In Lucam* 4.13, ed. Hurst 1960:266, lines 1407–15).

Aside from this scriptural tradition, L may point to the contemporary status of Jews. Before their expulsion from England in 1290, Jews in England did "hold" land, at least by lease (in forfeit for unredeemed mortgages) and probably by real freehold "of the king," at least in 1201 under King John and in early 1271. See Richardson for the complex situation of Jewish land tenure in England (1960:83–108). Later in 1271 this right was taken away by statute (although Picciotto observes that Jews still held land), and in 1275 they were forbidden by statute to lend money at interest (Rigg 1902:l-lv, 1.70; Roth 1941:66, 70; Chazan 1980:77–78; Picciotto 1918–20:67–84; Moore 1987:39–40).

In consequence of course they were bereft of livelihood, and of no further use to their royal protectors as sources of revenue; hence they were expelled.

So the Jews have lost **lordschipe in londe** in contemporary England as well as in ancient Judea (see 93n above, 347n below). Abraham had been blessed with "lond and lordschip ynow" (18.256 [B.16.240]); the term in Grosseteste's *Château* is *seignurie* (ed. Murray 1918, line 89 etc.). Moreover, L may allude to the doctrine, espoused by FitzRalph and, following him, Wyclif, that only those in a state of grace could have lordship, dominion (see 22.1–51n, toward the end). The doctrine derives from the Austin friars' chief theologian, Giles of Rome, who held that infidels could have no possession, lordship, or power (Gwynn 1940:37–38, 59–73).

The accusation that Jews were spiritually **bareyne** (see 107n below) and hence lived by **vsure**, the seeking of fruit from a fruitless thing, money, was common (Noonan 1957, Index, s.v. "Usury, sterility of money").

107 (B.18.104) ȝoure childerne, cherles: echoing Jesus' warning, "Daughters of Jerusalem . . . weep for yourselves, and for your children. For behold, the days shall come, wherein they will say: Blessed are the barren" (Luke 23:28–29). See B.16.121 for similar language, and 95–112n, 106–10n above.

110 (B.18.107) all lawes: probably referring to the oft-cited texts against usury in the two testaments: Luke 6:35, Lev. 25:35–37, and others (see 18.264 and Noonan 1957:16 and Index s.v. "Bible"), and to the canon and civil laws (see 13.80n). Possibly the reference is to the natural (Edenic) and positive (Sinaitic) law, as in the *Castle of Love*: Jesus knew "alle þe lawen" (ed. Sajavaara 1967, line 1475; see lines 167–70).

112 (B.18.109) tocleue: *Cum veniat:* Daniel 9:24–27 prophesied the time when *ungatur Sanctus sanctorum* (the saint of saints may be anointed), but the wording here, as Ames notes, appears in a pseudo-Augustinian sermon *Contra Judæos* (PL 42.1124), used in a lesson for the fourth Sunday in Advent (Brev. I.cxxxvii): "When the holy of holies comes, [your unction will] cease," that is, the anointed royal line from David is removed from the Jews with Jesus' advent, and their "lordschipe" is therewith lost (Ames 1970:125–27). The sentence is quoted and explicitly attributed to Daniel in B.15.600. Henry has traced the sentence to Tertullian, and the Daniel attribution to the anonymous *Tractatus adversus Iudaeum*, and speaks of it as "a stock prophecy of the Nativity" (1990:52–53).

The verb **tocleue** specifically suggests the destruction of the Temple (61n above). B's *b*-verse reads **þe crowne sholde lese**, recalling the common depiction, based on Lam. 5:16–17, of the Synagogue as a woman whose royal crown is toppling as the unction ceases (Weldon 1989:52); here Jesus is crowned—with thorns—and king (C.21/B.19.27).

The vision of Hell

113–449 What for fere . . . leue which hym likede: The account of human redemption from sin falls into two passages: the debate between the four virtues commonly called the Four Daughters of God (see 115–270n) and the Harrowing of Hell (see 271–449n).

113–15 (B.18.110–12) What for fere . . . *secundum scripturas*: Like the Jews, and like Truth a few lines later (128 [B.18.125]), Will reacts to the **ferly** (the expected content of a dream; see A/B.Prol.6 and n) with fear, as he repeats the locution **false iewes** (see 95 [B.18.92]). He goes, **I drow me**, into the locale of hell, in a rare instance of Will's steering his own visionary course (cp. 13.134): the reflexive verb can be taken actively or, in mysterious transport, passively. The locale is characterized only by its **derkenesse**—as is typical of the Passion-Harrowing narratives deriving from the *Gospel of Nicodemus* and before (see Kroll 1932:87–88)—its crossroads, and its gates with the light before them.

As the converse and reciprocation of Will's action (as the sun had withdrawn, 60n above), the saints in limbo "shal fro merkenesse be ydrawe" (139 [B.18.136]). L's hell is strikingly remote from the exotic site of torments of medieval legend (e.g., in *The Pricke of Conscience*), partly because he describes only the "Limbo of the Fathers" and not the lower regions of punishment. As compared with the earlier tradition of the vision of hell (see Owen 1971), the passus notably lacks sensational visual description; it is an intellectual hell.

In this carefully marked transition the dreamer imitates the way of Jesus, and "he descended into hell" in the phrase from the Apostles' (and Athanasian) Creed (in later use *inferos* replaced *inferna*), where his experience is authenticated as seeing **sothly** in the formula from the other, Nicene Creed, "in accordance with the Scriptures." The Nicene Creed attaches the phrase immediately to the Resurrection rather than the Descent. (A remote analogue is the "Vision of Anellus Scholasticus," whose narrator dreamed that he went with Christ in the Harrowing ["In Salomonis ferculo," ed. du Méril 1843:200–17].) L's emphasis on scriptural and credal authority here authenticates his hell and the largely apocryphal events that follow (see 81n above). For traditions about the Descent, see Young 1910, MacCullogh 1930, Kroll 1932, Izydorczyk 1985. These quotations begin an extensive reference, filling the rest of the passus, to the liturgical representation of the Descent (see in general Cabrol 1920, Vaughan 1980).

It is as if Will were in church, as he will be at the end of the passus (see 6–7n above), as he dreams, and as if he were drawn not into a nether space, but into the credal words. The grammar makes **descendit ad inferna** a place name, and **secundum scripturas** can be construed as another reification, what Will sees. This reading would require adjustment of the punctuation and deletion from B.18.113 (not in C) of **Where**, editorially added *metri causa* but syntactically otiose if a new sentence begins here (cp. KD-B, p. 199). Perhaps Will is also "following the scriptures," constantly quoted in the succeeding vision, as it were "suynde my teme" (see 358n). For parallel reification of a credal phrase see 412n below; see also *Redde quod debes* (21/B.19.186–87n), *Fiat voluntas dei* (C.5.88), and 225n below. Simpson notes here a nice conflation of experience (I saw) and reading (the credal phrases)—1996:215–17. At the outset of the next vision Will falls asleep at the offering, which follows the creed at Mass (C.21/B.19.4).

The Four Daughters of God

115–270 (B.18.112–262) And there y seyh sothly . . . Attollite portas &c: The credal formula specifies that Jesus rose on the third day **secundum scripturas** (but see 8n, 113–15n above); the **wenche** who comes from the west and her sisters are therefore a non-biblical surprise, whose basis in *scripturis* is the wording of Ps. 84:11, "Mercy and truth have met each other; justice and peace have kissed," quoted in 464 (B.18.421) below (as well as Isa. 43:6—see below in this note). The explanatory quotation is withheld until the end of the action (when the kissing occurs), as it were a commentary preceding its text, in many other versions of the story of the Four Daughters as well, e.g., pseudo-Bonaventure's *Meditationes vitae Christi* (ed. Peltier 1868:511, cap. 1), the N-Town cycle's "Parliament of Heaven" (ed. Spector 1991:118), and *Rex et Famulus* (ed. Hunt 1981:307–10). L had anticipated in the preceding passus the terms of the debate: see 1–5n above.

The best account of this legend, especially as related to the version in the *Castle of Love*, is Sajavaara 1967:62–90; see also Traver 1907, 1925; Owst 1933:90–92; Rivière 1934, App. II; Mäder 1971; Izydorczyk 1985:53–63, and Hunt 1981. L refers to the four "virtues" as sisters, but not as daughters of God.

The debate in its typical form responds to a problem in soteriology: if humans are sinful, they are justly damned. In the allegorical versions God is represented as a king, and the debate takes place in a (heavenly) court. The sisters Justice and Truth take this severe side of the argument; like Abraham they argue that if God is a just judge, he must judge justly (Gen. 18:25). Mercy argues in reply that God's nature is to be merciful; if he refuses to grant mercy to humans, he contradicts himself. The argument hinges, then, on the identity of God. With this unpeaceful strife between the daughters, Peace leaves the country. Reconciliation among the daughters results from God's son's offering of himself as satisfaction of justice, and therewith God can justly be merciful—the Son is both identical and not identical with God. Apart from the bare bones of this argument, L's version is largely unique.

L's connection of the debate story with the Crucifixion and Harrowing also seems to be unique; it usually occurs either at the story of the Fall, where the pseudo-Bonaventuran *Meditationes* has it, or, where Bernard's influential version has it, in association with the Annunciation, the first event of the Incarnation, whose purpose is explained by the story (*Sermones* 2, *Opera*, ed Leclercq and Rochais, 5, 1968:13–29, and quoted in Ludolph, ed. Bolard et al. 1865:10–11). *The Castle of Perseverance* (early fifteenth century) concludes with the debate, set at the time of Mankind's death and individual judgment. As Vaughan observes (1980:138–39) all these events—Fall, Annunciation, and the original Good Friday—were assigned the same date, March 25, as in the calendar mnemonic that accompanies the Sarum *Manuale* (ed. Collins 1960:181; also Augustine, *De trin.* 4.5).

The Advent, Descent into Hell, and Last Judgment (see 412–44 [B.18.370–401] below) were often set in parallel as three condescensions of God to earth (so Ambrose, PL 17.929; see Izydorczyk 1985:53–62). Wyclif speaks of Jesus' *quadruplex descensus*: the Incarnation, the Harrowing, the descent into holy souls, and Doomsday (ed. Loserth 4:436); a Lollard Advent sermon speaks of "þre aduentis" of Jesus at the Incarnation, Passion, and Judgment (ed. Hudson 1983, 1, serm 26). Certainly holding the debate just before the Harrowing heightens the narrative suspense (Frank 1957:93). Cassiodorus associated the Four Daughters with the Incarnation, and like Langland linked the two pairs with the two testaments, law and grace, now joined (*Expos. in Ps. 84,11*, CSEL 98.728; see Mäder 1971:15, n25).

L probably knew, at least indirectly, Huon de Meri's *Torneiment Anticrist* (see 21/B.19.335–480n); a brief reference to the four figures presents Mercy and Truth as daughters of Charity, and has Justice and Peace kiss as in the Psalm verse (ed. Bender 1976, lines 1931–34).

The shift from the male-dominated events of the Passion to the sprightly narrative of these bickering sisters (see 459–64n below) is leavening, and anticipates what will become the great leavening event of redemption. Coghill judged that the Daughters in the *Castle of Love* and elsewhere are prigs, in contrast with the "homely naturalism" of L's portrayal of "God's wenches" (1962:213–14). The sisters are witnesses—their responses imitate those of the redeemed from limbo—and their argument exposes the significance of Jesus' doings. The representation of the opposed figures in a debate as on the one hand grumpy and saturnine, on the other buoyant and mercurial, recalls such debate poems as *The Owl and the Nightingale* and *Winner and Waster*.

The four positions held by the Sisters—here represented as their compass orientation—tend in all these treatments of the sisters' debate to merge into a single binary opposition of Justice and Mercy. The compass orientation, not present in other treatments of the Four Daughters of God, derives from Isa. 43:6: "I will say to the north: Give up (*Dicam aquiloni: Da*): and to the south: Keep not back: bring my sons from afar, and my daughters from the ends of the earth" (so Prsl, Schm; see also 167–70n below). Linking this text with the Harrowing is the understanding represented in the Gloss of the phrase *Dicam aquiloni: Da* as *diabolo redde quos captivasti*, "[I will say] to the devil, 'Hand over those whom you have captured.'"

131–32 (B.18.128–29) moder withouten velynge Of eny kynnes creature: usually taken as "without the sensation of carnal intercourse" (Schm, Prsl, Donaldson 1990), and so "withouten wommane wem" (134 [B.18.131]). For **velynge** as sexual touching see 22.195. An alternative would take **velynge** not as "feeling" but (in south-England spelling) "defiling" (see MED *filen* v. (2), *filing(e* ger. (2)). Three manuscripts of C read *fylyng*.

conceyued thorw speche: as it were a mental conception (see Augustine, *De trinitate* 9.7–9, ed. Mountain 1968:303–6, and Galloway 1998:120–27, 142 et passim) and an allusion to Gabriel's "Ave, Maria." The common depiction of the Word made flesh as a speaking by the Holy Spirit of the Logos into Mary's womb by way of her ear occurs as in *The Siege of Jerusalem*, line 108 (ed. Hanna and Lawton 2003) and the hymn *Gaude virgo mater*. Compare the account of the Annunciation at 18.123 (B.16.90). Hence, the Annunciation is the Conception.

135 (B.18.132) tale . . . y take god to witnesse: Mercy witnesses to God by God to verify her tale before Verity. Cp. 81n above, and see 150n below. In this context **tale** means "the plaintiff's account in a legal suit" as Alford notes (*Gloss.*).

141–44 (B.18.138–41) For patriarkes . . . deth shal releue: The trio of *regressiones* (see Headnote)—playing on slightly shifted meanings of **man, tre,** and **deth**—derives from the famous hymn *Pange lingua gloriosi proelium certaminis* of Venantius Fortunatus (ed. Dreves 1909, 1:37; ed. Blume and Dreves 1907,

50:71–73), sung on Passion and Palm Sundays and at the Veneration of the Cross ceremony on Good Friday (Tyrer 1932:131; Vaughan 1980:130; Brev. I.dcc-xviii, dccl). A stanza sometimes appended to the hymn has *Te prophetæ cecinerunt redemptorem omnium* (prophets sang of you as redeemer of all), seconding L's attribution to **prophetes**. In the hymn a number of commonplaces of this passage, and this passus, converge: the cross-tree redeeming the tree of the Fall; the crucifixion as a victorious battle; the defeat of guile by guile, *arte* (var. *ars*) *ut artem falleret* (see 163–65n below, and pseudo-Cato's distich, *sic ars deluditur arte*, "so guile is deluded by guile" quoted at B.10.196 (A.11.148)—see Galloway 1987:11). The contrasting of the two trees is common; see e.g. the opening of a poem on the Invention of the Holy Cross, "Þorwh a treo we weore for-lore . . . Þorwh a treo seþþe to liue i-brouȝt" (ed. Morris 1871:18–19, lines 3–4). Davlin notes that this conceit may be found in the Sarum preface to the Mass in Holy Week (1989:96): "the one who conquered on a tree also was conquered on a tree." The rhetorical elegance of Mercy's lines, characteristic of Latin hymnody, may evoke the plainspoken irritation of Truth's rejoinder.

141 (B.18.138) patriarkes and prophetes: L's and others' usual way of speaking of the Old Testament righteous, the inhabitants of the "Limbo of the Fathers" saved at the Harrowing (see e.g. 147, 227, 366 below and some ten uses of the formula elsewhere in C: see Izydorczyk 1985:24; *Nicodemus* 18.1; Luke 13.28). L calls this place *limbo inferni* at 18.115 (B.16.84), and equates it with Abraham's bosom (18.270–72 [B.16.254–56]; see Luke 16.:22). Traditionally required of pre-Christians for salvation were acknowledgement of the Trinity and charity (see 414n, 443–44n). In *De civili dominio*, cap. 39, Wyclif, citing Heb. 11:6, generalizes: the minimum necessary requirement for salvation is belief "that God exists and rewards his servants" (ed. Poole 1885:437).

145–50 (B.18.142–7) a tale of walterot . . . y, treuthe, woet þe sothe: Treuthe denies Mercy's truth as **walterot**, "balderdash" (a word unrecorded elsewhere; could it be a proper noun?) and in wordplay answering 135 above (see n) as it were claims her being as her authority. Apparently Truth has only seen the **patriarkes and prophetes** in limbo, whereas Mercy has understood what they preached. Truth's response to Mercy is something like the Doctor's, who called the words of Patience and Love a **dido** (15.170 [B.13.172]). L often repeats the phrase "truth knows the truth"; see 30n above.

152 (B.18.149) parfit patriarke . . . *nulla est redempcio*: Job was righteous (*rectus*, Job 1:1). The quotation, "For in hell there is no redemption," may draw from Job 7:9, "so he that shall go down to hell shall not come up." The Latin wording here, from the Office of the Dead and penitential literature (Gray 1986:58), is widely quoted in vernacular literature (Alford *Quot.*, Whiting 1968:H333): for example, twice in *The Pricke of Conscience* (ed. Morris 1863: 2832–33, 7248–51), and in the *Parliament of the Three Ages* (ed. Conlee 1991, line 642). Truth is right if purgatory and limbo are taken as distinct from hell, as in *Pricke* 2785–819 (see 274–360n below on the quadripartite hell, and Matsuda 1997); L seems to suppress this common idea.

154–60 (B.18.151–57) Thorw experiense ... vertu of hymsulue: Mercy's appeal to **experiense** and **euydence** distracts from her actual reasoning, which is by analogy rather than (what is actually taking place at the Harrowing) *demonstratio ad oculos*. But note that "an euydence" *is* an analogy, a "*simile*," at 19.164 (B.17.198). Archetypal B, accepted by Schmidt, has **and that I preue by reson** for **þer fecche I euydence** (see KD-B, p. 92). The antithesis of **experiense** with "reson" was common (see MED *experience* 1a.). (Or could Mercy mean, "I think they ought to be saved by way of the experience of venomous death"?) L may have thought the reasoning here too quick or subtle, or he may have forgotten his reasoning, and revised for clarity. The terms suggest the familiar (Chaucerian) opposition of experience and authority—Mercy's putatively hard science (experience as experiment, putting to the test) over against Truth's reliance on patriarchal and prophetic *auctoritas*. On the interplay of these terms in late medieval thought see Burlin 1977:5–22. A fifteenth-century lyric has Jesus saying from the cross, "ffor mercy to give I am redy, / Thus shewith experience by expresse ['explicitly']" (ed. Brown 1939, no. 105, lines 75–76).

Venym fordoth venym: In Bartholomæus Anglicus's encyclopedia a potion of scorpion's ashes in wine, or a poultice of scorpions in oil, is a remedy for scorpion bite (trans. Trevisa, ed. Seymour 1975:434, 1249–50), a remedy that was proverbial (Whiting 1968:V20). Mercy's insistence that *only* a scorpion can cure a scorpion's bite recalls the equivalency doctrine of the atonement—only the blood of a child born of a virgin can save the wounded man (19.85–88 [B.17.95–100]). The basis for the idea, homeopathic medicine, is common (e.g. Isidore, *Etym.* 4.9.5–8, ed. Lindsay 1911:1.175–76) and appears in instructional literature in texts like Chaucer's *Melibee* (1276–92) that inveigh against vengeance, "harm for harm" (Rom. 12:17)—see Headnote.

Mercy's analogy has its point in the need for death in either remedy, scorpion or Jesus—a man's death heals man's first wound—and its theological source in the Bible, "O death, where is thy sting" (1 Cor. 15:55) and "O death, I will be thy death" (Hos. 13:14, quoted at line 34 above) and "that, through death, he might destroy him who had the empire of death, that is to say, the devil" (Heb. 2:14). Jesus as antidote through his **vertu** for Adam's snakebite recalls Holycherche's idea, "loue ys triacle for synne"; see 1.146 (B.1.146) and note, Smith 1966:21–23 (Christ as *tyriaca in veneni remedium*, "the tryacle of our sauvacyon" as Caxton puts it), and Bourquin 1978:510–11. Isidore uses *tyriaca* as an example of an antidote by similars: "*Tyriaca* is a serpentine antidote by which venom is expelled, in order that the disease may be cured by the disease (*ut pestis peste salvatur*)" (*Etym.* 4.9.8, ed. Lindsay 1911:1.176). In a sermon attributed to Wyclif, with reference to John 3:14—Moses lifting up the serpent—a similar comparison is drawn between Jesus crucified "in forme of addris of venym" with the serpent of Eden, "þe first addre" (ed. Winn 1929:58).

160 (B.18.157) ferste venemouste: that is, the poisonousness, *venemosité*, of the scorpion's original bite, in apposition with "yuel" (159).

163–65a (B.18.160–62a) gylour thorw gyle . . . vt Artem falleret: The proverbial wordplay on the **gylour . . . bigiled** (Whiting 1968:G491) is emphasized by the three-line alliteration on *g*. The diction is repeated at length in 377–92 (B.18.334–63) below. That grace, God, who began all will **maken a goed ende** concludes a series of references to beginnings and ends, the Fall and the Redemption, in a common phrase that often means "to end a story well," a matter of *ars* (cp. C.Prol.29 and n, etc.). The Latin means "in order that craftiness may deceive craftiness"; see 141–44n above. Peter the Chanter cites a principle of civil law: "All laws and rights permit one to fend off force by force (*vim vi*) and to weigh guile against guile (*dolo dolum*)"—Couvrer 1961:305.

The particular form of God's guile is letting the devil think that Jesus is merely human (see 331n below; Izydorczyk 1985:151–68 with many references; Nelson 1972). In a passage excised from C, Study had warned Will not to be curious about why "god wolde / Suffre Sathan his seed to bigile (B.10.121–22, 129–30); the issue mattered in the controversies about the devil's rights (see 299–311n below; Marx 1995).

167–70 (B.18.164–67) north . . . southe: the orientation here may allude to the common layout of churches wherein Old Testament figures appear to the north, New to the south (Mâle 1958:5–6; see end of 115–270n above). North is Lucifer's seat (see 1.111n; Russell 1984:69–71), east is Truth's (Prol.14).

168 (B.18.165) Rihtwisnesse: the most common Middle English rendering of *justicia* (see MED), as in the Wyclifite translation of Ps. 84:11 and the *Myrour of Lewed Men*, translating Grosseteste's *Château* (ed. Sajavaara 1967, line 213, etc.). Like "ryhtfulnesse" (5.32, not in B), a quasi-personified figure perhaps drawn from **ryhtwisnesse** here, this justice leaves little room for "a gobet of his grace" (5.100); her stern judgment accords with that of *The Pricke of Conscience*, where to sinners at Doomsday "Sal noght be shewed bot rightwysnes . . . with-outen mercy" (ed. Morris 1863:6090–91). See 439n below.

169 (B.18.166) ar we bothe: It has not been satisfactorily explained why justice should precede mercy and truth: the commonplace holds that "merci passeþ strengþe & riȝt" (ed. Brown 1924:126; Whiting 1968:M508) in accordance with James 2:13, "And mercy exalteth itself above judgment." L may have in mind the Psalm verse following the verse that names the four virtues, in which *justitia* is *de caelo* and truth *de terra*: the heavenly virtue would be prior (Ps. 84:12; see Jerome's comment cited in Mäder 1971:16, n27). In the chronology of salvation history justice (the age of Law) precedes mercy (the age of Grace), but it does not precede truth in any obvious way. For an aggrieved person a sense of justice and truth, irritated self-righteousness and desire for vengeance, might well precede a sense of mercy, forgiveness. In the *Castle of Love, Cursor mundi,* and *Rex et famulus,* Merci is explicitly "alre eldest" of the daughters, probably because she is first mentioned in Ps. 84:11 (ed. Sajavaara 1967, line 347; ed. Morris 1875, line 9585; ed. Hunt 1981:308).

Only in the version of the Four Daughters story found in the *Gesta Romanorum* has L's order been identified: Justice is *Soror senior,* Veritas is *secunda,* Misericordia *tercia,* and Pax *quarta* (ed. Oesterley 1872:351–52, cap. 55). Perhaps Trinitarian analogies of Father with Justice, Son with Truth, and Holy Spirit with Mercy underlie this conception—the common triad is Power, Wisdom, Goodness (or Grace: see 18.34–52 [B.16.30–52], Clopper 1979). Conscience says the *spiritus Iusticie* is foremost of the cardinal virtues (C.21/B.19.406).

171–78 (B.18.168–75) pees pleiynge . . . she gladie thouhte: Pees's playfulness anticipates the joy at the end of the passus, when the sisters are reconciled. She seems already to be wearing her Easter dress; for her **rich clothyng** compare the "riche robes" of Charity (16.353 [B.15.228]). Pees's garb of patience means to **gladie** others, not flatter herself. Pees is **in pacience yclothed** (171, 175) because the early Church was exhorted to "Put ye on (*Induite vos*) therefore . . . the bowels of mercy, benignity, humility, modesty, patience (*patientiam*) . . . And let the peace (*pax*) of Christ rejoice in your hearts" (Colossians 3:12, 15): the epistle reifies patience as clothing. Peace, patience, and love are associated—Love is Patience's lemman (B.13.139; "Charity is patient," I Cor. 13:4) and Love is Pees's lemman (185 [B.18.182] below); see also 454–58 (B.18.411–15) below. Broadly love, peace, mercy, and patience go together and, as light-hearted and childlike, are eligible for the kingdom of heaven. For such blessed **pleiynge** see 18.271–72 (B.16.255–56), Will's glimpse of the Leper and patriarchs and prophets "pleynge togyderes" in Abraham's bosom. Tavormina suggests that Pees resembles a "much-indulged, much-loved youngest child" (1995b: 201). On L's characteristic imagery in such "gracious imaginings" see Lawler 1979. This Peace is very unlike the Peace of the Mede episode; see Headnote to C.4.

173 (B.18.170) som lettre: See 185–92n below.

182 (B.18.179) Mer[y] shal synge: The C archetype reads *mercy shal synge* and the B archetype *mercy shul haue*. Adams (1991:13–14) persuasively argues that archetypal C is L's original, and that Moses and the rest sing the response *Misericordia* ("Mercy") as recorded in the Sarum Breviary (ed. Proctor and Wordsworth 1882: 1.ccccxxxi), "Thy mercy, Lord, is great upon me. And thou hast liberated my soul from the lower hell." The response is from Ps. 85:13.

184a (B.18.181a) *Ad vesperum*: "In the evening weeping shall have place, and in the morning gladness" (Ps. 29:6). The coincidence of joy and morning in the Psalm—as if **ioy bigynnethe dawe**—associates it with Easter weekend, as the Gloss, quoting Augustine, Jerome, and Cassiodorus, confirms. Moreover its fourth verse seems to prophesy the Harrowing: "Thou hast brought forth, O Lord, my soul from hell."

185–92 (B.18.182–87) such lettres . . . *dormiam & requiescam*: In a passage echoing 19.1–17 (B.17.1–22) Pees points, as *Spes* had, to the Redemption's conversion of the law from justice and truth to mercy and peace, a conversion of course initially offensive to Rihtwisnesse and Treuthe. For the meaning of the legal jargon L wittily invokes here in treating the law, see Alford, *Gloss.* s.v. *foryeven, given and graunten, graunten, lettre, mainpernour, mainprisen, patente, dede,* and Birnes 1975. Pees can offer a salvific legal document that opposes the blindly literalist legalisms of the devils.

Broadly the sense is that God, as love and Christ, has gone bail for humankind through mercy, peace, and grace to deliver them from the prison of hell, and has provided a public royal document (or indulgence: see B.7.200) to that effect, namely Psalm 4 (see next note), the answer to the "hard roche" (19.11 [B.17.12]), also called a "patente" (see also B.14.192), the Mosaic law now overwritten with the law of love. L puns on **forgyue**: "grant, enfeoff" and "forgive, have mercy." The parallel with Fals's "feffament" (2.75 [B.2.73]; see next

n) and especially with the pardon from Truth (9.1–3 [B.7.1–3]), which also
turned out to be a bit of authoritative language (there the lines from the Athanasian Creed) is inescapable. Christ has converted the very nature of righteousness (the terms are made more explicit by C's addition of 189–90), who,
personified, responds like Truth above (145) with contemptuous disbelief,
"Rauest thow?" (193 [B.18.188]).

191–92 (B.18.186–87) Loo! here þe patente: Pees authenticates herself with a
document about peace. The deictic formula replicates that of the display of the
"feffament" of Fals, "loo! here a Chartre" (2.71 [B.2.69]), and another letter
patent, the Ten Commandments, "Lo, here the lettre" (C.19.4); cp. 370 and n
below. The notion of divine ordinance as legal, written documents informs
much of PP, e.g the "patente" of B.14.192. In the Passion context L alludes
especially to common conceits of Jesus as parchment charter on the cross, his
wounds as seals, the blood as ink, etc.: see 19.7–8 (B.17.7–8) and (in the context
of the Four Daughters) Mäder 1971:16n and Woolf 1969:57–60; also Bennett
1982:47 and 214n41; Swanson 1998:21; MWME 7.2343–44; Birnes 1975:79; *Fasciculus morum*, ed. Wenzel 1989:212–13; Rubin 1991:306–8; Spalding 1914. With
reference to its source in Paul, Ludolph of Saxony in the *Vita Jesu Christi*
explains the link between the charter of the Fall and the charter of the cross:
"For because the first man, by extending his hand to the tree of prevarication,
had composed the document (*chirographum*) of our damnation in the devil,
therefore our Savior, in order to blot out that document, was willing to be
fixed by hands and feet to the wood of the saving cross by nails of invincible
charity, 'Blotting out' through this 'handwriting of the decree (*chirographum
decreti*) that was against us, and he hath taken the same out of the way, fasten-
ing it to the cross' (Col. 2:14)" (ed. Bolard et al. 1865:653).
    The **patente** itself is the first four words of Ps. 4:9, quoted also at B.15.254,
In pace in idipsum, "In peace in the selfsame" together with the assurance
that the **dede**—a pun on two senses of the word, "documentary warrant" and
the saving "action" for which Pees (*In pace*) is mainpernor (personal surety)—
will endure in perpetuity: *dormiam & requiescam*, "I will sleep, and I will
rest." The inspired words of the Psalm are the assurance, as Pees says, that we
may finally rely on God's mercy. These are the last words of Bernard's Annunciation sermon, in which he tells of the Four Daughters of God (ed. Leclercq
and Rochais 1968:29). The antecedent of *idipsum* in the Psalm is unclear, but
probably "the light of [the Lord's] countenance," something like "ȝone lihte
(194 [B.18.189]); in C it is **Crist** or **Loue**, in B, **Loue**. The Psalm was sung at
prime on Holy Saturday—the day on which this debate would have taken
place, and the right time of day, the dawning (so 184 [B.18.181] above)—and

as Prsl notes the verse is divided in the Breviary as versicle and response just as L divides it (Brev. I.dccxcv). In the Sarum and York liturgies and the *Regularis concordia* the verse is also used in the Good Friday "burial of the cross" ceremony associated with the Creeping to the Cross (Young 1933, 1:146, 164, etc.; ed. Henderson 1875:111, 159; Sheingorn 1987:19, 348, 365; see 469–75n below).

The brief Psalm 4 refers to justice, mercy, and peace; it further says "The light of thy countenance, O Lord, is signed (*signatum*, "sealed") upon us," linking the imagery of "ȝone lihte" (194) with the figure of letter and seal (cp. 19.7 [B.17.7] where the seal is cross, christendom, and Christ). The Psalm says "the Lord hath made his holy one wonderful" (4.4); the inevitable Christian reading makes Jesus the bringer of the Psalm's peace. The patriarchs and prophets in limbo can now say "I will sleep and I will rest."

193–207 (B.18.188–202) Rauest thow? . . . that they eten: Rihtwisnesse largely repeats Treuthe's argument above, as she acknowledges: **y . . . recorde þus with treuthe** (204), as the four figures in the Psalm inevitably are reduced to a binary opposition. On the legal term *recorden* see 373–75n below.

193 (B.18.188) riht dronke: So in their ecstasy at Pentecost the apostles were accused of drunkenness (Acts 2:13); see 411–12n below.

196–99 (B.18.191–94) At the bigynnynge . . . fruyt eten: See 373–75n below.

206–7 (B.18.200–202) let hem chewe . . . that they eten: let (present tense) Adam's issue now **chewe** as humankind then (past tense) **chose** (the forbidden fruit), reflecting the proverbial idea that one must choke down one's own bad food (see 401–2n), reap what one has sown. L repeats the collocation **chewe/ chose** with a similar dismissive tone at C.22/B.20.237. Their suffering is **boteles bale**, a punishment without the right of legal recourse (see 8–12n above); Rihtwisnesse knows no idea of Purgatory, where "preyer" can "hem helpe" (205)—Purgatory could not exist before the Resurrection.

208–38 (B.18.203–29) And y shal preue . . . welaway hym teche: Pees tests and proves (see 234a, not in B), setting forth her thesis like a challenge, a legal brief or a scholastic disputation. Her argument resembles Mercy's idea of homeopathy in resorting again to the idea of the reciprocation of contraries, but it adopts the opposite strategy—Mercy has two similars (two applications of scorpion poison, two deaths) bring about dissimilars (health from disease, life from death), whereas Pees has dissimilars (**wo** and **wele**) bring about a similar (experiential knowledge of both contraries). Roughly comparable is the

notion in *The Mirour of Mans Saluacioun* that "als the matiers be thaire contraries in sekenesse has curacioun," so Christ's defeat of the devil teaches us to
defeat vice with virtue (ed. Henry 1987, lines 3190–94). The medical idea is that
the elemental qualities—hot, cold, wet, or dry—can be brought into balance,
temperance, in the body by means of specifics of opposite quality.

Pees's idea resembles that of the *felix culpa*, which L cites (7.125a
[B.5.483a]) in a passage that also emphasizes the kinship and similitude of
Jesus and humankind. Both passages suppose a theodicy like that of Hebrews
2, which treats the brotherhood of humanity and Jesus ("to be made like unto
his brethren"), Jesus' tasting death "for all" (*gustaret mortem*—Heb. 2:9; cp.
**Ne hadde god ysoffred . . . He hadde nat wist witterly where deth were sour
or swete**, lines 217–18, not in B, and Whiting 1968:S943). The chapter concludes with a story like the narrative of this passus: "Therefore because the
children are partakers of flesh and blood, he himself in like manner hath been
partaker of the same: that, through death, he might destroy him who had the
empire of death, that is to say, the devil: And might deliver them . . ." (Heb.
2:14–15). See 22–23n, 154–60n above.

Bourquin (1978:516–17) finds a close analogue to L's reasoning here in
Bernard's *De gradibus humilitatis* (PL 182.945, 948), of our savior "who wished
to suffer, that he might be compassionate, to become wretched (*miser*), that
he might learn to have pity (*misereri*) . . . . he wished to experience (*experire*)
for himself what they deservedly suffered for working against him . . ." (see
also Burch 1950:136–37). See also Anselm, *Proslogion*, 8; Murtaugh 1978:119–21;
Harwood 1992:142; Goldsmith 1985:325; 25n above; but cp. Augustine, 231–34n
below. The *Gesta Romanorum* has an analogous if cruder account, that Jesus
refused his father's command to kill the human soul because "I took on
human flesh from my mother, and therefore will not be able to kill man" (cap.
100, ed. Oesterley 1872:426; see 417–41n below). See further 231–34n below.

The idea that a thing can be known only if its contrary is known is widespread (see B.10.434n); Prsl cites places in Boethius (*De cons.* 3.m1 and 4.pr2),
the main medieval source of the idea, and *Le Roman de la Rose*, Chaucer's
Troilus, Lydgate's *Temple of Glass* (lines 391–416, etc.; see Norton-Smith
1966:177–78, 185); see also Alanus de Insulis, *Liber parabolum* (PL 210.581–82),
quoted to similar effect below—see 451n. But the passage in the *Rose* (ed. Poir-
ion 1974, lines 21550–74) provides so close a parallel as to seem a direct source:
see C.1.78–79n, and generally on PP and the *Rose* see the Headnote to the Prologue. In *Troilus* 3.1212–21 the ideas of homeopathic medicine and knowledge
by contraries (applied, of course, to human love) are joined as they are here
by the Mercy-Pees argument. Like Mercy above, Pees argues that "experiense,"
here literally the sensations of hunger, color, daylight, taste, rest, well-being in

general, must qualify our understanding of the authority of biblical narrative adduced by Treuthe and Rihtwisnesse. But as if acknowledging that the argument—the mere witness of the senses—is not conclusive, Boek itself will appear to support Pees's proofs.

209–11, 234 (B.18.204–6, 225) wo into wele, wo . . . ioye: The familiar and proverbial opposition (*Troilus* 1.4; Whiting 1968:W132–40) begins and concludes the set of contraries, which here emphasize poverty and hunger; cp. 451n below and 12.207–9.

211 (B.18.206) soffrede: The repetition of this word four more times in Pees's speech registers L's manipulation, in this context of sense perception, of medieval psychological terminology—for example in the Latin versions of Aristotle's *De anima* and the many commentaries on it—in which "to suffer" and "to be the recipient of an action, to perceive, experience" are expressed by the same Latin verb, *patior*. A sense organ "suffers" a sensation—the verb has nearly this sense in 12.145 (B.11.259), in another passage on contraries; see also MED *sufferen* 2. One might imagine the godhead suffering experience but not pain—it is "impassible" (see 25n above)—while the God-man does both. Hilary of Poitiers, however, said that Jesus too "felt the force of suffering, but not its pain" (quoted in Hallman 1991:104). Compare L's play on senses of "suffer" as "permit" and "endure pain" with similar repetition in 13.194–204 (B.11.376–86).

225 (B.18.216) modicum: RK-C(p. 98) reject as an easier reading C archetype's reading *moreyne* ("pestilence"), accepted by Schm and Prsl. The use of Latin suggests a scriptural reference; the allusion may be to Psalm 36:16, "Better is a little (*modicum*) to the just, than the great riches of the wicked." For the type of personification see e.g. 4.140 (B.4.142–43) and C.21/B.19.187, 295, as well as 113–15n above, B.18.393 below.

A possible further allusion, to John 16:16–19, may have come into L's mind in the context of the Redemption and by association with the contraries, the **wo into wele,** of the following verse in John, "You shall lament and weep, but the world shall rejoice; and you shall be made sorrowful, but your sorrow shall be turned to joy" (John 16:20). Repeated through this passage, in which Jesus enigmatically announces his death and resurrection, is the word *modicum*, translated as "a little while": "A little while, and now you shall not see me; and again a little while, and you shall see me, because I go to the Father . . ." to which the puzzled apostles respond, "What is this that he saith, A little while?" In this context, **til *modicum* mete with vs** would assume additional meaning: "until 'in a little while,' the time of the Resurrection, may come to us [no one knows what 'enough,' the sufficient redemption, means]." John 16:16 and 16:18 are antiphons at Lauds and Second Vespers of the third Sunday after Easter (Brev. I:dccccxii).

231–34a (B.18.222–25) And aftur god auntred . . . *est tenete*: "And afterwards God ventured forth [see 13–14n above] himself and became incarnate to know [B: see] what Adam has suffered in three different places—in heaven and earth, and now he who knows all joy means to go to hell to know what all woe is." Similarly B.16.215, not in C: God became human "to knowe what was boþe," divinity and humanity. See also 18.202 (B.16.193), Hebrews 2:18, 208–38n above, and Hebrews 5:8, "he learned obedience by the things which he suffered." On God as learning through experience see Aers 1975:107–9 and 208–38n above.

Augustine held that to imagine that something could be added to God's knowledge is *absurdissimum atque falsissimum* (quoted in Hallman 1991:105); so also Thomas Aquinas, *Summa theol.* I, qu. 14, art. 15. For the traditional view, espoused for instance by Peter Lombard, that God is immutable in knowledge (as in everything), see Colish 1994:288. In his commentary on the *Sentences* Thomas Aquinas with fine discrimination held that Christ descended to the "hell of the holy fathers with respect to place, but not with respect to the experience of darkness (*tenebrarum experientiam*)" (quoted in Marx 1993:107). Murtaugh (1978:120) documents the idea of a distinction between Christ's omniscience (*notitia habitualis*) and his need to acquire experiential knowledge (*notitia experimentalis*). See further Pelikan 1978:149, Overstreet 1989–90:311; Davlin 1971:13.

Omnia probate: the quotation, added in C, adds authority to the appeal to experience, "prove [= try] all things; hold fast that which is good" (I Thess. 5:21); cp. 3.491 (B.3.339) and n.

232 To wyte (B.18.223 To se): RK-C (p. 93) and Schmidt B and C accept the defective alliterative pattern of the B archetype and C, which KD-B conjecturally emends (see pp. 113, 206). The sequence of **To wyte**'s in B.18.221–25 drew a scribe into error.

240–68 (B.18.231–60) Boek . . . lyf and soule: Treuthe and Rihtwisnesse having relied on scriptural "authority" for their argument, and Mercy and Pees having relied mainly on "experience," **Boek**, who is prima facie sacred Scripture itself, now speaks, attesting of himself (**y wol bere witnesse**—one swears on the Book; MED *bok* 3a.(d)) and "by God's body" that a savior was born in

Bethlehem, as the book tells. But as if bound to provide a surfeit of other proofs, Book adduces the testimony of the nativity star (or comet), in whose meaning all the wise accorded, and (having thought of the star) of the systematic **witnesse** of the four elements, and the *Gospel of Nicodemus*, and finally— what might even convince the utterly materialist Lucifer—the actual physical presence of Jesus the giant (see 261and n below), the light at the gates of hell. (On the theme of witness see the Headnote) As if still conscious that no authority can supplant faith, Boek, now the book of nature (experience) as well as of written *auctoritas*, concludes that he will come to nothing unless Jesus rise to life and his people honor and believe in him.

    with two brode eyes: usually interpreted as the two testaments, or as the literal and spiritual senses of Scripture (with many parallels, none exact, see Kaske 1959), or as the past and future (Kaske 1960:40). For a contextual interpretation see 259n below. Since a **wihte** usually has two eyes, perhaps the emphasis is on **brode**—of large scope, hugely witnessing?—seeing more broadly than the sisters Truth and Righteousness.

    Why Book is specifically a **beaupere**, according to MED usually a father-confessor, is not obvious, nor is his characterization as **a bolde man of speche**, perhaps "well-spoken" (MED *bold* adj. 6.(a)) but more likely "forward" (*bold* 4.), as his first words, like Piers's first words, are an oath. On L's use of oaths and his explicit condemnations of idle swearing see Chadwick 1922:89–90).

242 (B.18.233) blased: In Middle English a comet was called a "blazing star" (MED *comete*). See 248n below.

246 (B.18.237) elementis: namely the air (**welkene**), earth (**erthe**, 250 and 256), fire and light (*stella*, **torche**, **lihte**, **sonne**), and water (**watur**, **se**). The association of the witnessing elements with the time of the Crucifixion may derive broadly from the interpretation of the earthquake (Matt. 27:51) reported in the Gloss: "All the elements demonstrate (*omnia elementa . . . demonstrant*) that the crucified one is their Lord: the earth quakes, not enduring to carry its Lord hanging." Kaske (1959:119) located the source of the particulars here, as the *elementa* testify to Jesus as their creator, in a homily of Gregory read at Matins on Epiphany: "the heavens acknowledged that he was God, for at the outset they sent the star. [See 261n below.] The sea knew him, for it made itself fit for walking under his feet. The earth recognized him, for it trembled at his death. The sun knew him, for it hid (*abscondit*) the rays of its light. The stones and walls knew him, for at the time of his death they were split. Hell (*infernus*) acknowledged him, because it gave back those whom it was keeping in death." See also Psalm 18:1 and 261n below.

The appeal to the redoubled authority of nature and book is paralleled in a fourteenth-century English paraphrase of this homily also cited by Kaske (pp. 120–21). As Kaske notes, the homily repeats the common English author-ity-formula, "as the book says," and may hence have prompted L's personifi-cation (see also 21.71n). **Boek** may include, along with the Bible, such authorities as the *Gospel of Nicodemus*, the *Golden Legend*, the writings of Gregory, and other readings, *legenda*, in the Divine Office: see 17.6n.

248 (B.18.239) *stella comata*: See Alford, *Quot.* 111 on the nativity star as a comet. Acknowledging while contradicting this notion, Bartholomæus Angli-canus cites John Chrysostom to the effect that "þe sterre þat was iseye in þe burþe of Crist was not *cometa*" because its westerly movement was the con-trary of a comet's (trans. Trevisa, ed. Seymour 1975:497).

250 (B.18.241) **lowe erthe**: The nativity star as torch bows down to the low earth (see Matt. 2:9), in evocation of John 1:8, 14, "He was not the light, but was to give testimony of the light . . . And the Word was made flesh, and dwelt among us." Boek's account recalls the equally brilliant account of the preter-natural Incarnation at 1.148–54 (B.1.152–58). The elements seem to interchange their natures, such that fire descends to the earth, water solidifies, and (to invoke more modern terms) the sun becomes a black hole and the earth lique-fies; further hell no longer does the thing it properly does, hold. Citing "Denys," (pseudo-Dionysius the Areopagite, in an unidentified passage) a fif-teenth-century lyric observes that at the Crucifixion "Al vr kuyndes haþ lost vr kende," nature is denatured (ed. Morris 1871:145, line 405). Adso's treatise on Antichrist has him make *naturas in diuersis figuris mutari* (natures change into different forms—ed. Verhelst 1976:24). A "testimony of the elements" passage not cited by Kaske (246n above) in the pseudo-Augustine *Sermo contra Judæos, paganos et Arianos* says the sea gave witness "when having forgotten in some way its nature as the liquid humor" it bore Christ's footsteps (PL 42.1127).

254–57 (B.18.245–48) **sonne gan louke . . . Quakid as quyk thyng**: see 60–64 (B.18.60–62) and notes above.

259 (B.18.250) **symondes sones**: the sons of Simeon (Luke 2:25–35), briefly res-urrected as witnesses to the Crucifixion, had witnessed the Harrowing, as recounted in the *Gospel of Nicodemus*, the main medieval source of the account of the Harrowing in the rest of this passus. Much of the material found in *Nicodemus* was widely and independently dispersed, some of it antedating the apocryphal *Gospel* (Campbell 1982; Izydorczyk 1985:268), but the *Gospel* itself was thoroughly well known in many redactions available in England in Latin, French, and English, including a version in the *Golden Legend* (cap. 54, ed. Graesse 1846:242–45; see Headnote). Traditionally the sons of Simeon were resurrected with, not before, Jesus (e.g., B Version, ed. Tischendorf 1876:418).

Simeon was the first material witness to Christ among the Jewish leaders (as Nicodemus was a later one), and he was reckoned by Christians as, like John the Baptist, among the last prophets. In the account of the Harrowing in *Nicodemus* Simeon is among those who first recognize the light in hell as Jesus; he is twice a witness (18.2). No parallel has been identified with L's idea that Simeon's sons, special witnesses like their father, were witnesses of the Crucifixion; that any of the resurrected were such witnesses is a rare tradition in any case (see MacCullogh 1930:288–99). In the *Gospel of Nicodemus* and its derivatives they are reporters of the Harrowing.

Non visurum se mortem: Simeon "should not see death, [before he had seen the Christ of the Lord]" (Luke 2:26). The emphasis on his visual witness extends into the wording of Simeon's familiar canticle, the *Nunc dimittis*: "mine eyes (*oculi mei*) have seen thy salvation," (Luke 2:30, quoted in *Nicodemus* 18.2). This canticle is sung frequently in the Office, and is the last song of the Easter vigil (Brev. I.dccciii). The glossators' interest in these eyes may account for Book's two broad eyes (see 240n above). Paraphrasing Bede's remark that Simeon's *oculi* are now "both of the flesh and of the heart" (*et carnis et cordis*; PL 92.345), the Gloss on Luke 2:30 specifies that when Simeon sees the Lord's salvation he sees the man with his fleshly eyes, and God with the eyes of his heart (*et carnis hominem et cordis deum*). In his comment on Simeon Bede further adduces the essential text of witness and faith: "blessed are they that have not seen, and have believed" (John 20:29, quoted in C.21/B.19.181).

The quotation *Non visurum* here, added in C, has otherwise unobvious relevance besides merely identifying **symond** as him of the *Nunc dimittis*, and not the **Symondes sones**, simoniacs, of 5.79 . The verse can be read with reference to the sons, too, who in a way did not finally "see death" before seeing Christ, both crucified and harrowing.

260 (B.18.251) now shal lucifer leue hit: Even the devil requires authoritative witness, and will receive it *now*, in the Harrowing. That the devils came to believe at the time of the Harrowing was a common tradition. Lucifer is not a figure in *Nicodemus*; see 274–360n below.

261 (B.18.252) iesus as a geaunt: The B archetype's *gigas* ("giant") *þe geaunt* for **iesus as a geaunt** seems the more likely original reading (adopted by

Schm), made explicit in the C tradition by L or a scribe. Kaske (1957) locates the source of the conception in Ps. 18:6, *Exsultavit ut gigas ad currendam viam* "[he] hath rejoiced as a giant to run the way." The commentators regularly gloss *gigas* as the Son hastening to become flesh (e.g., *Meditationes*, ed. Peltier 1868:516, cap. 4; Aelred, *De Jesu puero*, ed. Hoste and Talbot 1971:251). The whole Psalm emphasizes nature's witness of God: "The heavens show forth the glory of God" (Ps. 18:1, quoted in C.18.213a); cp. 247 (B.18.238) above, "That he was god þat al wrouhte the welkene furste shewede." Psalm 18 immediately precedes Psalm 23 (see 271n below) in the first Matins service of the feast of the Annunciation (March 25; Vaughan 1980:140).

Kaske (pp. 180–81) shows that the *gigas* as man and superman (Gen. 6:4) was understood as a figure of the dual substance, human and divine, of Jesus (see 22–23 [B.18.23–24] above), and further that in some hymns Jesus was called the "true Samson," a *gigas fortis* who snatched away the gates of death, in the Harrowing, as his type Samson had carried off the gates of Gaza (Judges 16:1–3; see e.g. Gregory, *XL homiliarum* 2.21, PL 76.1173C). The Vernon Manuscript "Hail, Mary!" speaks of Jesus as *"gigas manu fortis . . . Þe geaunt of hond so strong,"* in connection with his Harrowing of hell (ed. Horstmann 1892:98–99, lines 1126c, 1128), and later: *"gigas . . . gemine nature . . .* Geaunt . . . Þat is of double kynde" (103, lines 1214d, 1217–18). The same conceptions are found in the late thirteenth-century poems of John of Hoveden (ed. Raby 1939:6, 46, 65, 135). See further Kantorowicz 1957:50–51.

gyn nicely translates *ars* (165a [B.18.162a]), and means "ingenuity," "strategy," and (here apt) "siege machine" (MED *gin(ne* 1., 2., 4.).

264–68 (B.18.255–60) And y, boek . . . ylost, lyf and soule: "And I, Book, will (or: am willing to) be burnt [cp. B.15.83] unless he arise to live [in all the powers of man, and to gladden his mother: inexplicably omitted in all manuscripts of C], and to comfort and bring out of care all his kin, and to take apart and unlock [cp. B.18.264 below] all the joy of the Jews; and unless they do reverence to his Resurrection and honor the rood and believe in a new law, [they] are to be lost, body and soul." See 30n above.

Wittig (1986) has persuasively untangled the grammar of these lines against Kaske (1959), Hoffman (1964), and Donaldson (1966): **bote** (264, 267) means (as usual in this construction) "unless," not "but"; **aryse** is naturally subjunctive (not infinitive with **wol** understood); **lyue** is an infinitive expressive of purpose (somewhat unusual but not unheard of for this phrase); **gladie** (in B only), **comforte, brynge, vnioynen,** and **vnlouken** are infinitives parallel with **lyue**; and **be ylost** has for its subject **they** (the Jews) from the preceding line, and is subjunctive, or infinitive with **wol** from 264, or conceivably present indicative: "they are (to be) lost."

As Blythe noted, line 264 echoes Paul, 1 Cor. 15:14, "And if Christ be not risen again, then is our preaching vain . . ." (1995:139). The reference to the conversion of the Jews reflects, as Hoffman (pp. 63–65) shows, a widespread notion derived from Malachias 4:5–6, developed in Augustine (*De civ.* 20.29) and Gregory (*Moralia*, PL 76.921–22), and repeated in Adso (see C.21.219–26n below) that Elias and Enoch would convert the Jews before Doomsday (see 3.480 [B.3.327] and Lerner 1976b). In this familial context (**his kyn; his moder** in B; see 414n, 417–41n below) the refusal of the Jews—with such important exceptions as Simeon and his sons and Abraham—to join in the witnessing is especially pointed, seeing that they are notably "kynde" (see B.9.84–90).

269 (B.18.261) y here and se bothe: The daughters of God at last do not require arguments from natural process or bookish authority to accept the Redemption; presumably this ocular proof finally makes believers out of Truth and Righteousness. Alford notes that "to hear and see" is a legal formula used of first-hand witnesses (*Gloss.* s.v. *Heren and Sen*). John of Patmos wrote the visions he had "heard and seen" (Apoc. 22:8). At this point the four sisters become, with Will, witnesses to the Harrowing, and their contention is now supplanted by the wonderfully arrogant, pathetic, and comic "Devils' Parliament"; see 274–360n below.

270 (B.18.262) vnspere . . . *Attollite portas &c*: The famous lines from Psalm 23, like Psalm 4 (191n above) sung at Matins on Holy Saturday, are more fully translated in 360–63 (B.18.316–20) below—in B, more of the Latin is quoted and more of it translated. The repetition of the phrases ("Lift up your gates, O ye princes, and be ye lifted up, O eternal gates: and the King of Glory shall enter in. Who is this King of Glory? the Lord who is strong and mighty") imitates their repetition in the Psalm, as if repeated knocking were needed to arouse the dwellers within. The Psalm asks the question that the sisters have been wrestling with, and that Satan tried to figure out (330–31 [B.18.297–98] below)—who is this?—the same question Will had asked (line 18 above). Answering now, in the function of herald (see 13–14n above), is the "vois" (271), Jesus himself (see 360–446n below). The interchange of speakers in the Psalm provoked the dramatization that developed in medieval tradition. In the Palm Sunday and Easter liturgies of some rites, and in rites for the dedication of a church, a priest would knock on the church door with a cross, and a voice from within would ask "Who is this," etc. (Young 1933, 1:163–65; Maskell 1882, 1:204–206; Chambers 1903:4–5). Margery Kempe alludes to the ceremony (ed.

Meech and Allen 1940:186–87). The inevitable glossing of this Psalm as referring to the Harrowing is reflected in its likewise repeated use in *Nicodemus*,
where it also brackets part of the Devils' Parliament (21.1, 3).

On **vnspere** see 88n above. In the paraphrase of *Nicodemus* in *Cursor
mundi* the figure Hell casts out Satan at this point and bids his minions "Spers
your yates" (ed. Morris 1876, line 18086).

The Harrowing of Hell

271–449 (B.18.263–406) A vois loude . . . leue which hym likede: L's account
of the Harrowing of Hell contains two larger sequences (see notes): the Devils'
Parliament (274–360 [B.18.266–317]) and Jesus' response to the devils (360–
446 [B.18.317–403]). In C (but not B) L marks these divisions distinctly: both
sequences begin with a **vois** speaking.

271 (B.18.263) vois loude in þat liht: The editors differ as to whether this line
with the quoted discourse that follows in the next two lines is spoken by Treuthe. Schm and the Athlone editors assign B.18.263–65 to Treuthe and
C.20.271–73 (with Prsl) to the narrator, presumably in view of the alteration of
verb tense, **crieþ** vs. **saide**. The **vois** is the utterance of Psalm 23 (Vulgate),
merging with the voice of Jesus.

The depiction of the harrowing Christ as light derives from Isa. 9:2, a
common proof-text of the Harrowing quoted in 7.133 (B.5.493), in 366
(B.18.323) below, and in *Nicodemus* 18.1: "The people that walked in darkness,
have seen a great light: to them that dwelt in the shadow of death, light is
risen." In the *Nunc dimittis* (see 259n above) Simeon had called Jesus "a light
(*lumen*) to the revelation of the Gentiles" (Luke 2:32, quoted in *Nicodemus*
16.1, 18.2). Christ was the "Sun of Righteousness" of Malachias 4:2 (Dölger
1972) especially when he descended into hell (Ludolph, *Vita*, ed. Bolard et al.
1865:692). The agent of the Harrowing was regularly taken to be the soul of
Christ (so 341 [B.18.307]; see 25n above and 370n below), the figure *Anima
Christi*, for instance, in the N-Town play of the Harrowing. The *Speculum
Christiani* says that Christ descended "in soule" (ed. Holmstedt 1933:10). On
the theological question see Colish 1994:411, 436–37 and Brantley 1999:52.

Just as hell is only the voices of its inhabitants, so the Harrowing (like the
Conception, 132n above) is a matter of voice and light (see 364n below). Similarly emphatic on the *eterna nox inferorum* are the lections from Eusebius to
be read on Easter eve in some rites (Young 1910:937).

272 *Principes*; B.18.264 Prynces: the term from Psalm 23:7, 9, translated in B. See 362 (B.18.319) below. In this passus C omits a handful of B's Latin quotations, and adds a double handful.

The Devils' Parliament

274–360 (B.18.266–317) Thenne syhed satoun . . . 'What lord artow?' quod lucifer: The Devils' Parliament begins and ends pathetically, opening with Satan sighing and closing with Lucifer asking who this light-spirit might be (see 16n above). For the Devils' Parliament, from a common tradition with the "Processus Belial" and "trials of Satan" in the English play cycles and elsewhere, see Traver 1907:49–69, 127–33; Traver 1925; Marx 1995, Index s.v. "*Conflictus, Devils' Parliament*, Hugh of St. Victor, trials of Satan"; Marx 1993; Vinogradoff 1929:128–30; Rand 1904; Alford and Seniff 1984, Index s.v. "trial of Satan." The tradition culminates in the fully juridical *Processus Belial* of Theramo. Broadly on medieval devil-lore see *Le Diable au moyen âge* (1977) and Russell, esp. *Lucifer* (1984). The idea of associating a debate between Christ and the devil with the Harrowing of Hell first appears in a Middle English adaptation of *Nicodemus* (Marx 1995:86).

In the main source of this passage, the *Gospel of Nicodemus* (sects. 20–23), the participants are Satan (also called Beelzebub) and *omnes sancti*, who speak, and Hell (Inferus) and Death (Mors) with their officers and ministers, who speak with one voice. Lucifer does not appear. Broadly, in *Nicodemus* the debate is between Satan and Hell; in PP, between Satan and Lucifer. The devils' roles were not kept neatly distinct in the tradition. In some accounts, for example, Lucifer's name changed to Satan when he fell from heaven (*Cursor mundi*, ed. Morris 1874, lines 479–80; Chaucer, Monk's Tale 2004–5). For a typical account of the late medieval quadripartite hell (Purgatory, Nether Hell, and the Limbos of the Unbaptized and of the Fathers) see Le Goff 1984:264–65. The *Mirour of Mans Saluacioun* calls the fourth part the hell "of seintes of the Olde Lawe" and the "Lymbus of Abrahams bosme" (ed. Henry 1987, lines 3010, 3044). See 141n above.

The figure **helle** appears only once in PP, unspeaking and barely personified if at all, as the recipient of Jesus' and Satan's speeches in 270, 274 (B.18.262, 266)—but L may mean that Lucifer and hell are the same, as the sequence in 271–95 (B 263–73) can suggest. The assignment of speeches in L's debate in hell is vexed. Clearly Satan speaks 275–294 (B 267–72). Lucifer, surely a distinct figure (addressed in the second person by Satan), speaks 295–311 (B 273–85). Satan speaks 312–21 (B 286–91) at least. At that point speeches are attributed to **gobelyne** and **þe deuel** and **the fende** (322–49 [B 292–315]). Finally Lucifer's last speech occurs at 360 (B 317).

It seems best to take the speech assigned to **þe deuel** (325–27 [B 295 continuing through 315, with a possible change of speaker, accepted by no editor, around B 309]) as simply a continuation of **gobelyne**'s speech with a superfluous speech-marker included for clarity and alliteration (so Prsl, and Schm for C but not B, against the Athlone editors), and further to take the speech of **the fende** in 341–49 (B 307–15) (marked as such in C and emended B; B archetype has speaker-continuing **he**) as merely continuing this same speech (with the Athlone editors and Schm-B, and against Prsl, Schm-C, and Skeat). For other instances of superfluous speech-markers see 21/B.19.419, 451; 22/ B.20.322, 356–58, etc.

Finally, against all the editors, one best takes **gobelyne**'s speech, now unified (322–49 [B 292–315]), as itself merely a continuation of Satan's speech, clearly marked as such at its end, 350 **Sethe þat satan myssaide thus** (not in B; C attempts to untangle the confusion). Each of the names of the four figures within this passage—**gobelyne, þe deuel, the fende,** and **Satan**—fills an alliterative pattern, and all are best taken simply as by-names for Satan, whose name in any case is legion. Wyclif says the same devil is Satan or Belial or Leviathan, "as he is named with diverse names" (ed. Loserth 1889, 3:477). The supposed speeches assigned to these figures contain no adversary positions. Finally we have biblical warrant that some of **gobelyne**'s speech (in C 330–31) is Satan's: he tempted Jesus and asked if he were God's son, and Jesus names him Satan (Matt. 4:3–11, esp. 10).

Hence in both B and C the only speakers in the Devils' Parliament are Satan and Lucifer. As Russell observes, Satan is typically the name for the devil in the postlapsarian period, and he is sometimes figured as Lucifer's lieutenant, sometimes as his equal or as identical with him (1984:24–48).

275 (B.18.267) lazar hit fette: that is, it fetched Lazarus, with pleonastic **hit** and the word order *causa metri.*

276 (B.18.268) Care and combraunce: a formula; **combraunce** was often used of the devil's destructive power (MED *combraunce* 3.(a)); the tables are turned.

278 (B.18.270) þer lazar is: Pearsall notes Satan's confusion: Lazarus of Bethany was brought from Satan's domain to life on earth (traditionally, some two weeks before these events), not to heaven (John 11:1–44). Satan has no experience as yet of people brought from hell to heaven—Elias and Enoch ascended from earth—and hence he has no idea where those saved are going. In some traditions Lazarus lived for fifteen years after his resurrection (*Pricke of Conscience*, ed. Morris 1863:6521). It is unlikely that L confuses Lazarus of Bethany with the Lazarus who rests in Abraham's bosom in the parable (Luke 16:19–31; see 8.278–81, 17.302–4 [B.15.593–95], and 18.271 [B.16.255]), or that L refers to the two Lazaruses within a few lines in so confusing a way (cp. Fowler 1980:278). In *Nicodemus*, Hell remembers Jesus' snatching away of Lazarus as evidence of his power over death (20.3).

    lihtliche: punning, "easily, by means of light."

279 (B.18.271) parled: This first recorded use in English of the verb may point to the genre of the following speeches, a "Devils' Parliament" (see 274–360n above). Doomsday could be spoken of as a "parlement": see the "Dispute Between Mary and the Cross," lines 297, 304 (ed. Morris 1871:207) and other references in MED s.v. *parlement* 2.(a). The citations in MED of *parlen* suggest that the word, from law French, was used in legal and administrative contexts—a parliamentary term.

281–435 (B.18.273–392) Ac rise vp, Ragamoffyn . . . *in furore tuo Arguas me*: The latest (in the narrative, probably not in the sequence of L's composition) extensive signs of the poet revising his B version occur in this passage: the additions of C 281–94, 350–58, 405–10 (with revised matter from B.18.367–78 retained), and thorough revision at C 304–40 (B 281–306), 379–92 (B 336–47), and 434–35 (B 391–92). These revisions, examined at their occurrences below, seem local in motivation, although a desire for clarity, even legalistic clarity about important theological matters, is apparent. Two of the revisions reemphasize L's insistence on love as the solution to the problem of salvation. Some of the alterations excise apocryphal and legendary matter. Perhaps L returned to this passage with special care because it contains the speech of Jesus.

281–94 (not in B) Ac rise vp, Ragamoffyn . . . acloye we hem vchone: In the B version **belialles barres** had been mentioned (321, C 364). This boisterous addition might at first have been L's explanation of them, gotten delightfully out of hand. Does it embody L's response to a viewing of some Corpus Christi play, or reading a French Passion play, after he issued the B version? Alternatively, the passage may simply have been scribally omitted in the B archetype, through confusion of homoioarchic lines 280, 296 (B.18.272, 274).

    The comic names of the devils derive from a tradition, developed in French drama, that may take its first impulse from such exotic-sounding biblical names of pagan deities and devils as Belial, Baal, Beelzebub, Astaroth (Astarte, Ishtar; see 447n below), etc. One reckoning has Astarot as a devil-character in fourteen French mystery plays (of 68 surveyed), and Belial in ten, together with a batch of other farcical names like Buffomet, Crochart, Gorgarant (Wieck 1887:7–9; e.g. the *Mystère de la Passion*, ed. Jodogne 1965:55, etc.). On such names and buffoonery see Dustoor 1930, McAlindon 1963, Lazar 1978.

Elsewhere in the passus we have "Gobelyne," **Belial**, and **Astarot**; here with **Belial** and **Astarot** we have **Ragamoffyn, Coltyng**, and **Mahond**. The Towneley plays have a devil called Ribald along with Belzabub, Astarot, Bellyal, Satan, Lucifer and others (ed. Stevens and Cawley 1994:326). The name **Ragamoffyn** is recorded only here of a devil in Middle English, but it was used as a proper name in a document of 1344 (MED *raga-muffin*, "a ragged lout"). "Ruffin" is more common as a devil's name (MED *ruffin*, citing instances from the Katherine Group and the mystery plays, e.g. the Chester *Lucifer*, line 260, ed. Lumiansky and Mills 1974:11), probably connected with Lat. *rufo*, red. Surprisingly, the only recorded use of **Mahond** (Mohammed) as a devil's name in Middle English is in PP (MED *Mahoun*; see also C.18.150 and B.13.83); it is common as the name of a false god, but of course "all the gods of the Gentiles are devils (*dæmonia*)"—Ps. 95:5. "Gobelyne" (323, 328; B.18.293) is common (MED *gobelin*), as in *Fasciculus morum* which speaks of "a certain demon (*demon*) which is commonly called *Gobelyn*" (ed. Wenzel 1989:699); it may also have come to L by way of French drama (e.g. *La Nativité*, ed. Whittredge 1944). A Wycliffite sermon speaks of goblins as minor devils, who "haue not but litil power to tempte men in harme of soule" (ed. Hudson 1983, I:686; see Green 2003:35–36).

Here the action is energized by farcical domestic strife (compare the Noah's Wife material in the mystery plays); the absurd blacking out of hell so the light won't **lepe** in like a catapulted bomb; and, in what Prsl notices is evidence of Satan's "incurably literal way of thinking," a comic effort at siege defense, as the Adversary supposes that Jesus comes with squadrons of cavalry. Imagining hell with its gates as a castle or stronghold and the Harrowing as a siege is commonplace in literature (Izydorczyk 1985:134–35; e.g. pseudo-Juvencus, PL 19.385) and in plastic art. In Huon's *Le Torneiment Anticrist* hell (the city of Broken Faith) is depicted as well defended against a siege (ed. Bender 1976, lines 3438–63; see 21.335–480n below). The B version has no reference to the Harrowing as a siege, whereas C underscores the chivalric figuration begun early in the passus.

Satan's intention to use stagy burning sulfur and brazen guns foreshadows an evaluation, with some biblical basis (Apoc. 14:10, etc.), of gunpowder as devilish already emergent in the fourteenth century and much developed in *Paradise Lost*. In *The Siege of Jerusalem* the Jews defend their town by casting from the walls "Brennande leed and brynston many barel fulle" (ed. Hanna and Lawton 2003, line 675). For the demonic use of gunpowder on stage (in *Mercadé*) see Lazar 1978:56. MED *gonne* 2.(a) cites a mostly Latin text from 1390, Mirfeld's *Sinonoma*: "that warlike or diabolic instrument which commonly is called *gunne*" (see also Vale 1981:137).

In the last six lines Satan deploys a pounding, bombastic battle-alliteration of the kind Chaucer likewise parodies (KnT 2605–16, LGW 635–48, TC 4.39–42). Both poets seem to take noisy alliteration on *b* and *sh* as a special mark of war poetry. Satan is carried away with his generalship; he seems to represent deviltry as it works in human history, with its usual backfiring effect—the devils are agents of God (cp. Chaucer's Friar's Tale). Lucifer, who seems to be a deeper devil, the principle of turning from God (1.107–29 [B.1.106–27]), has to shut him up: "Lustneth!" (295).

288 the car to saue: The verse as printed in RK-C is metrically defective in the Duggan/Cable hypothesis—another syllable is needed before either **car** or **saue**. A reading *carre*, "cart, chariot" (MED) would do. But no chariot seems to be in question, although depictions of the devil with some sort of vehicle for hauling away souls are not uncommon (for literary versions see Wieck 1887:22; MED s.v. *char* 3.(c) does cite "sathanas chaar" from a Wycliffite chariot-allegory, and Kellogg treats the topic of the devil's *currus* or *quadriga*, 1958:390–97). The word troubled scribes here.

The simplest emendation of **the car** would be **care** (so five mauscripts), metrically unexceptional, the name of Satan's castle in the dale of hell, **þe castel of care** (1.57 [B.1.61, A.1.59]). But naming it **the care** (with 6 manuscripts of C), with the definite article, seems inexplicable; taking its sense as "what is in our charge" (vaguely like MED *care* n. 6.) seems strained. A confused scribe may have added the article before **car[e]**. Prsl conjectures **castel**, suggested by the reading "oure catel" in 12 manuscripts of C. (The reading **catel**, which Skt adopted, is possible; Satan's chattel, he thinks, would be the patriarchs and prophets.) Most likely L wrote **carnel** (so Schmidt 1980:107 and Schm-C) or **carnel(e)s**, "crenellation(s)" (see 7.235 [B.5.588], a line also including both **carneles** and the verb **to saue**), an opening (like "chyne," "louer," or "loupe" of the preceding lines) liable to siege attack (see citations in MED). In *Sir Gawain and the Green Knight* the term "loupe" (loophole for archers), is used together with "carnelez" to describe Bertilak's elaborate and stylish late fourteenth-century castle (792, 801, ed. Andrew and Waldron 1978; see 794n). L may poke fun, from a Londoner's point of view, at fantastic, newfangled, perhaps pretentious provincial architecture and ("gonnes"—291) weaponry.

296 (B.18.274) ys longe ygo y knewe hym: At least for a moment Lucifer sounds like a regretful, remembering elder (to Satan's youthful brashness), a

Hrothgar (see *Beowulf* 372–76): what he remembers is his knowledge of God before the Fall recounted in 1.107–29 (B.1.111–27). Both devils, ignorant of the future, have recourse for knowledge to the past, and, like the people in Dante's hell, can scarcely see the present—hence their interest in time as marked in years—309, 329, 332; B.18.284, 296, 299.

298–311 (B.18.277–85) ac waer hym of þe perelles . . . witnesse is of treuthe: Lucifer's legalism matches Satan's bombast, but the latter knows that an appeal to justice will not help. Lucifer in fact takes the position of Treuthe and Riht-wisnesse above, and trusts in the *ordinata potentia* of God to be reasonable and truthful, as opposed to God's *absoluta potentia* to exert his will in any way (see 20n above). Lucifer argues that God ordained humankind's damnation, and that the devils had established dominion over them in part by prior tenure, their 7000-year uncontested possession, legally "from time immemorial" (in English legal convention, from before 1189 C.E.); he takes the damned as his property. The legal issue concerns which party had the older title (Alford 1977:944–45; Baldwin 1981a:66–67). Satan has to point out that the granting of the devils' seisin was based on fraud, and hence without legal basis according to the ancient principle of civil law, *exceptio doli*, as recorded in Justinian's *Institutes* (see Thomas 1975:314 and below, 324n).

For Lucifer's legalisms see Alford, *Gloss.* s.v. *Reven of Right, Right, Right and Resoun, Seisin, Witness*, and Alford 1977:943–44, Birnes 1975. The legal diction here and in the rest of this passus reflects Grosseteste's *Château* (see Headnote). In the *Castle of Love* the narrator, speaking of Adam's losing his "seysyne" by "wone" (default, here simply "sin"), says, "In the kynges court ʒit vche day / Me vseþ þulke selue lay (that same law)" (ed. Sajavaara 1967, lines 239–40)—Grosseteste's persona is a civil lawyer and knows the jargon. The feeble Satan is obsessed with might, the arch-criminal Lucifer with right; between them, the devils are incompetent at warfare and at law.

The term **rihte** points to the medieval topic of the "devils' rights," their divinely sanctioned dominion over the damned (see 395n below). In this theory humans could be saved only by satisfaction of these rights, commutative justice. The means of satisfaction might be (blood-) ransom (the sacrifice of Jesus), or a claim of the devils' abuse of power (their killing an innocent), or an appeal to the fraud of the original title. For good surveys of the topic see de Clerck 1946 and 1947; Marx 1995; Pelikan 1978:127–39; also Rivière 1934:7–13; Sajavaara 1967:57–58; Woolf 1958; Russell 1984:104–7; Colish 1994:218–20, 459–70. A seminal essay by Timothy Fry treats the abuse-of-power and deception-of-the-devil theories from the patristic period through Peter Lombard, and its emergence in the N-Town plays (1951). For the key concepts of medieval satisfaction and atonement theory in general see Aulén 1961; Rashdall 1920; Burns 1975 (a handy survey); Franks 1962; Fairweather 1959.

In earlier thought, the sacrifice of Christ was a stratagem by which God overcame, by the ruse of a man-God, the just rights of the devil over sinful humankind. Anselm and Abelard pointed out the absurdity of this Augustinian position and demolished it, but see 330–31n below. As Green observes, the "devils' rights" idea persisted in England as late as Mirk in the early fifteenth century. (1999:344). This passus seems to record a movement that took place in eleventh- and twelfth-century theology, from the "war in heaven" style of soteriology in the Augustinian tradition—a tradition apt for heroic narrative—to the position of Abelard, that the outpouring and example of God's love in the Passion was the instrument of salvation (see 399–400 [B.18.362–63] below for the abrupt turn from **gyle** to **grace**, and 400–12n).

Lucifer warns Jesus, **ac waer hym of the perelles: / Yf he reue me my rihte A robbeth me by maistrie** (see 393–94n below). Jesus, then, would behave like the overbearing neighbor Wrong (4.45–63 [A.4.34–47, B.4.47–60]). Possibly L plays on two senses of **maistrie**, the more obvious "by authority alone, by violent force" (MED 1.(a), 2.(a)), but also "with cunning deceit" (MED 4.(d)). The latter sense is evident in Bozon's Passion poem, which has Jesus conquering "Partye par poer e partie par mestrye (partly by force and partly by strategy)" (ed. Jeffrey and Levy 1990:186, line 15).

L adopts the issue from the *Castle of Love*, where Jesus tells the devil he will ransom humankind, and the price is "good reson. / Ne kep I nouȝt toȝeynes riht, / Þorw maystrie binyme þe no wiht" (ed. Sajavaara 1967, lines 1098–1100). Grosseteste's Anglo-Norman has, "Encontre dreit me voil je mie / Tolir tei rien par mestrie (I wish to take nothing at all from you by force [or: strategy] against right)" (ed. Murray 1918, lines 1071–72).

The theologians addressed the issue. Augustine says, "It pleased God that, in order to pluck mankind from the power of the devil, the devil would be vanquished not by power (*potentia*), but by justice . . . not that power was to be avoided as something evil, but order was to be preserved, in which justice is prior" and "in order that humans, imitating Christ, might seek to vanquish the devil by justice and not by power" (*De Trin.* 13.13.17, ed. Mountain 1968:404 and cited in Fairweather 1959:329). Bernard of Clairvaux says that God showed mercy toward humankind, and justice toward the devil (Franks 1962:151). In his treatise on law, Bracton draws out an analogy between God and an earthly monarch (cp. 423–43 [B.18.381–400] below); God "would not deploy the force of his power but the reason of justice (*justitiae ratione*). And He wished to be under the law (*sub lege*) . . . . He did not wish to use force, but justice" (*De legibus*, Woodbine 1915, 2:33, cited in Izydorczyk 1985:285). See, with parallel materials, Rivière's quotation of Alcuin, "the devil was compelled to spew forth his booty, constrained by reason rather than by domination, by justice rather than by power" (1934:14–15). At about the time L was composing the B text, Gower in *Miroir de l'Omme* (ca. 1376–79) wrote that "God does not will to snatch the devil's prey by rapine, but rather He paid the ransom" (trans. Wilson 1992:380).

303–40 (B.18.281–306) That Adam and Eue . . . down bryngen vs all: The revisions and expansions here make C more explicit and legalistic, and reinforce the mandate to love. RK-C find a motive for revision in C, lines 303–11, in L's corrupt B exemplar (p. 73). Towards clarity, B's **alle** (281) becomes **all his issue** (C 303), and adding **Eue** emphasizes the "family" theme otherwise generally less prominent in C (Tavormina 1995:220). B 285 **I leeue þat lawe** is less than clear, and its *b*-verse, **nyl noȝt lete hym þe leeste**, is probably unmetrical by the Duggan/Cable rules for *b*-verses: "I believe that (or, that that) law will not grant him the least [part of the damned souls]" (so Donaldson 1990), or perhaps better "will not permit him [to overcome by sheer strength] the least bit" (so Schm). This is recast to specify that God's original ordination was **lawe** (C 306) rather than a mere **þretynge** (B 282), that the issue is one of **riht** and **resoun** (308; see 299–311n above), and that the very word of God is in question.

B's **in semblaunce of a serpent** (288) becomes C's **Not in fourme of a fende bote in fourme of an Addre** (315), pointing with its parallelism the nature of the fraud, the *ars* to which Jesus' *ars* responds. C clarifies B's chronology of the Fall (Eve first), and corrects the implication that Eve alone was at fault, while adding the biblical authority for the danger of striking out on one's own—***Ve soli!*** (316; Eccles. 4:10)—people alone cannot love. C augments the devil's **tale** to assert the amplitude of the fraud, that the fiend offered the protoparents deification and knowledge of good and evil (317–18; Gen. 3:5). Most important, C adds that the devil worked **Aȝeyne his loue** (314), the love that will finally resolve the matter in mercy and peace.

The addition of C 326–27 continues the notices of duplicity of form: Adam and Eve were **godes ymage**, not gods, and as Lucifer took on the form of an adder, so Jesus walked **in gome liknesse**, that is, Piers's arms, incarnate *humana natura*. C adds (334) the idea that Jesus was martyred, perhaps responding to the repeated references to Jesus' **lyf** and Jesus as a **lyf** (living being, person, body) through this passage, as if it were a martyr's *vita*.

C 336 emends B 304 by omitting the confusing possibility that Jesus would never countenance sin anywhere after his death: the souls Jesus saves are themselves sinful. B 304 in fact records Satan's comically misguided fear that Jesus dead and in hell would annihilate the devils as Jesus alive and on earth busily saved souls and cast out devils. Finally the replacement of B 306 by C 338–40 brings the argument to a sharper climax by reasserting that the new **lawe** is **to louye oþer**: this is the operant law, as even Satan sees.

309 (B.18.284) ben sesed: Satan in the *Castle of Love* complains to Jesus, "Maiȝt þou not vnderstonde / Þat icham prince and lord of þis londe, / And in þe seisyne habbe longe ibe . . ." (ed. Sajavaara 1967, lines 1047–49), closely translating Grosseteste's *Château*, line 1023, "Long tens ai eü la seisine" (ed. Murray 1918). See Headnote.

    seuene thousand: The figure varies in the traditions, often 5000 or 5500, the latter the figure in a Middle English *Nicodemus* (B. Hill 1987:168). Does the lying Lucifer exaggerate? By some reckonings (e.g., the Byzantine calendar), the time from Creation to 1400 would be about 7000 years. The *Golden Legend* gives typical figures: some say Jesus was born 5228 years after Adam (who lived 930 years), some say 6000 years, Eusebius of Caesarea says 5199 years (in "Dec. 25," trans. Ryan 1941:46–47). Other authorities calculate the years from Adam to the time of Jesus as ranging from 3852 (Bede) to 5330 (Hrabanus Maurus)— Dean 1997:46. The Jewish era from Creation to the birth of Jesus is 3761 years.

312 (B.18.286) 'That is soeth,' saide satoun: The Father of Lies accidentally acknowledges the truth of Lucifer's acknowledgement that God "witnesse is of treuthe" (311), or in B, "Sooþnesse" itself (283), and later calls Jesus simply "treuthe" (325 [B.18.295]). But Lucifer lies in saying that Adam's issue will "here" (in hell) "dwelle euere" (304) or "dwelle wiþ vs deueles (B.18.282). Jesus corrects this lie explicitly in 375 (B.18.332), "Y behihte hem nat here helle for euere." L's revision at C 304 may record his sense that the B lie was in fact temporarily true: (nearly) all the dead dwelt with the devils before the Redemption. The revised line draws its wording from its denial at B.18.332.

313 (B.18.287) broke: here and in 380 below, committed the crime of forced entry, breach, into the fenced garden, "palays" (378 [B.18.335] and n) of Eden (Alford, *Gloss.* s.v. *Breken*).

314 (not in B) Aȝeyne his loue and his leue: a legal formula, "without his permission and leave" (Alford, *Gloss.* s.v. *Love and Leve*; MED *love* 1d.(b)); so 381 below.

317–18 (not in B) to knowe / As two godes: see Gen. 3:5.

323 god wol nat be . . . byiaped: nearly translating Gal. 6:7, "Be not deceived, God is not mocked (*irridetur*)."

324 (B.18.294) trewe title: another legalism, *titulus juris* (Alford, *Gloss.* s.v. *Title*). The Writ of Deceit in 1367 permitted recovery of damages in transactions in which fraud or deceit was used (Birnes 1975:82; Alford 1977, n23). See 299–311n above.

326–27 in goynge . . . in goynge: C's addition here nicely replicates, in the parallel goings of serpent and human, **adder** and **weye**, the parallel stratagems, tit for tat, of Satan and Jesus. See 303–40n above.

330–31 (B.18.297–98) Y haue assayled hym . . . short answere: In the Temptation of Jesus Satan says, "If thou be the Son of God (*Si Filius Dei es*)" (Matt. 4:3, 6; Luke 4:3, 9). In the *Castle of Love* Satan asks, "What artou? / Wher þou be Godes son . . ." (ed. Sajavaara 1967, lines 1041–42). Satan seems confused about the nature of the Trinity. Wee (1974) shows that the Gospel words, "If thou be the Son of God," were regularly misconstrued as an unreal (it may be doubted that thou art) rather than real (seeing that thou art) condition. See 16n above.

On the topic of God's deception of the devil see Wee, pp. 3–6, Russell 1984:265–68, and 8–12n, 22–23n above. The idea is old: Izydorczyk (1985:162) cites Ambrose, "In the guise (*specie*) of infirmity [Jesus] laid down the arms of divinity, and assumed the garb (*tegmen*) of humanity" (*Ennar. in Psa. XL*, PL 14.1124–25). Bozon (see 8–34n above) in "Coment le fiz Deu fu armé en la croyz" represents Jesus as a knight disguised in battle, part of the machinery of God's counter-deception of the devil, who "ne sout de veyr qy esteyt cely" (didn't rightly know who this man was) because Jesus "se degwisa" (disguised himself—ed. Jeffrey and Levy 1990:186). In scholastic theology the idea had withered: Franks (1962:171) notes that the idea of the deceptive Incarnation and the Augustinian "cross as mousetrap" theme are adduced "almost for the last time in the history of theology" in Peter Lombard's *Sentences* 3, dist. 19 (see Marx 1995, Index s.v. "bait"; Colish 1994:464); it certainly continued, however, in the other arts, and the *Sentences* themselves kept the topic present in the schools.

The **short answere**, Matt. 4:10, is "Begone, Satan (*Vade Satana*)," or as the *Castle of Love* puts it, "Go awei, Sathan, go!" (ed. Sajavaara 1967, line 1045). Both the devil and Will have trouble recognizing Christ.

B.18.301 Pilates wif: see 52–53n and 303–40n above; Matt. 27:19. The dream of Pilate's wife played a prominent role in the English mystery cycles.

335 (B.18.303) lenghed his lyf: see 52–53n above.

341 (B.18.307) sylinge: KD-B emends B archetype's **seillynge** to the form **sylinge**, "passing, gliding, moving down," a word most attested in alliterative poems (MED *silen*) and found in manuscripts of C (although 16 manuscripts of C read **seylynge**). Schm-B accepts B's **seillynge**, but thinks it may be a variant spelling of **sylinge**. The textual discrimination is right (*difficilior lectio*), but we may regret losing the basis for Skeat's effusion: "This is a beautiful conception, and well expressed: the bright soul of Christ is seen sailing towards the dark abode of the demons, with even and majestic motion."

B.18.313 we lopen out alle: echoing the poem's first description of Lucifer's fall, "Lopen out wiþ Lucifer" (B.1.117; cp. C.1.110, 113).

349 (cf. B.18.315) ylost oure lordschipe: like the Jews—see 106–10n above. *Nunc princeps huius mundi*, "now [shall] the prince of this world [be cast out]" (John 12:31, originally spoken by Jesus, as Schm observes, and here perhaps a "marginal gloss" rather than a part of Satan's speech—see 438an below); with Jesus the dominion of death ends. The Gloss names the *princeps* "*diabolus*." See 10.135 (A.10.8, B.9.8). Both the devils and the Jewish rulers whose unction ceased were often called *principes* in biblical commentary.

350–58 Sethe þat satan myssaide . . . suynde my teme (not in B): A sarcastic little homily on lying with its scriptural text (356a) from Psalm 5:7, "Thou hatest all workers of iniquity: thou wilt destroy all that speak a lie," with a remarkable acknowledgement that the passage is a digression ("A litel y ouerleep," 357), implying that Will's task in this vision is merely to report, not to interrogate or instruct. (In fact we may hear in these lines a larger digression, L's own voice breaking into the narration; cp. 22.277–93.) A similar return from a digression at 21.69 (B.19.69) is less pointedly marked. Elsewhere Will (or L) admits that, out of moral passion, he sometimes cannot restrain himself from digression: in B.11.232, "Why I meue þis matere is moost for þe pouere" and in B.11.318, "This lokynge on lewed preestes haþ doon me lepe from pouerte."

This is Will's only speech, apart from stage directions, from line 26 above (see 26n) until his waking at the end of the passus. The term *ouerlepen* usually means to skip over something (MED; cp. "ouerskipped" 13.119 [B.11.305] and "ouerhuppen," B.13.68, C.17.118 [B.15.386]), as when a priest at Mass omits words, rather than to digress or interpolate, but parallels the use of "lepe" at

B.11.318. What Will skips from is his proper theme, which is *only* what he "seyh sothly" (115 [B.18.112]), his account **as y syhe** (358), as it runs in B, to which he will return. Comparing 5.124 (B.5.22, A.5.22), "Ac y shal sey as y sayh," Burrow remarks that the seen has higher authority than digressive chatter (1993:58; see also 269n above). Likewise Augustine is commended because "he vs saide as he sey" (C.11.150). Will is witness or interlocutor, and only secondarily commentator.

The "overleaping" seems to address an audience that might remember the continuous text of B here without the C addition. Those addressed, such professionals as clerks and lawyers, were doubtless among L's real audience, workers in words whose lying, *trahison des clercs*, would do most harm, especially to **thise lewed men**. Authority for castigation of precisely these groups derives from Jesus' attacks on the scribes and Pharisees. In the B version, of some twenty-two direct addresses (by Will and other speakers) to a specific audience, lawyers are singled out only once (7.57–60), but clerks and the learned in general are addressed five times (10.418, 11.83, 15.332–43, 15.551–56, 17.262), together with addresses to church legates (13.421–26), learned friars (15.70–116), and regular religious (5.315–17). "Ye rich" are counseled seven times: 1.175–99, 7.187–200, 10.83, 13.441–48, 14.140–48, and with the learned, 15.332–43 and 17.262. Advice is offered to "you lords" five times: 3.69–75, 11.154–59, 13.421–26 (with church legates), 15.322, 15.564. Finally warnings are given to beggars (probably friars—7.82–88), "lewed men" (15.128), and all Christians (7.201–6, 15.344). Eight of these addresses are marked by "Forþi" and "Forþi I rede/conseille/lere," and four are marked with a "(Right) so" of confident instruction. In sum, such addresses lend PP largely the character of a work of monitory counsel to the rich, the clerical, and the powerful.

352 at þe laste lyares he rebuketh: The phrase **at þe laste** here and in line 355 means "eventually, finally," as in 12.66 (B.11.131), likewise in a context of rebuke. The particular rebuke L had in mind may be John 8:14, 44, 55, apparently addressed to such scribes and Pharisees as the clerks and lawyers addressed here, or it may be a confused recollection of Matt. 7:23, where Jesus quotes part of Psalm 5:7 (see 350–58n above), but not the words *loquuntur mendacium*.

358 suynde my teme: pursuing my theme, possibly playing on "following my (plow-) team": see 8.20 (B.6.22) and C.21/B.19.261 and notes . The *thema* of this homily is the text Will quotes, Ps. 5:7. For a similar wordplay (with some Langlandian diction) see *Patience*, lines 35–37 (ed. Andrew and Waldron 1978:187):

Bot syn I am put to a poynt that pouerté hatte,
I schal me puruay pacyence and play me with boþe,
For in þe tyxte þere þyse two arn in teme layde . . . .

359 (B.18.316) efte: emphasizing the insistent repetition of the command (see 270n above). C (or its scribal tradition) omits the Latin quotations from Psalm 23 (B.18.316–18), with other small revisions.

360 (B.18.317) 'What lord artow?': see 16n, 270n above.

Jesus' response to the devils

360–446 (B.18.317–403) voys aloude saide . . . Thow shalt abuye bittere!: The **voys**, revised from B.18.317's more specific **light**, is both the words of Scripture (Ps. 23) speaking of **Crist** in the third person (363) and Jesus' voice (see 271 and n above). For Jesus to speak at length extrabiblically has precedent in the French drama. Evidently L took special care with such a representation, "the finest speech in *Piers Plowman*" (Alford 1972:323), and made many small revisions. The speech has two large movements: a compacted reiteration of the themes of commutative justice that have occupied this passus, directed to the devils and echoing many of the locutions used earlier in the passus (361–98 [B.18.318–60]), followed by a fulfillment and surpassing, in light of the Gospel warrant quoted in 395a (B.18.349a), of this *lex talionis* (see 379–92n) for the sake of humankind, an outpouring of mercy and grace that, representing Jesus' tremendous **kynde**-ness in all its senses, strains orthodoxy (399–446 [B.18.361–403]). We had learned from Imaginatyf that even the just man will not be saved at the Judgment "bote *vix* helpe" (15.22 [B.13.19]; cp. 14.203 [B.12.281]); here we see the help.

For Jesus and a devil to debate in hell is an ancient motif (Izydorczyk 1985:146–49); Grosseteste's *Château* is the prime source here. More generally, Jesus' preaching in hell, traditionally to the unredeemed there, was a notion from Origen and before, derived from 1 Peter 3:19–20, a passage adopted as the main proof-text for the Harrowing (see MacCullogh 1930:56–66).

361 (B.18.318) The lord of myhte and of mayne: C translates *Dominus virtutum* from Psalm 23:10, whose Latin phrases are supplied in B—or perhaps more precisely C translates verse 8 of the Psalm, *Dominus fortis et potens*. B fills the second half-line with a closer (or alternate) translation of *Dominus virtutum*: **and [of] alle manere vertues**. See 270n above.

362 (B.18.319) Dukes of this demme place: compare "*Principes* (B Prynces) of this place," 272 (B.18.264); Jesus resumes speaking with a similar address. Middle English translations of the *Gospel of Nicodemus* have the devils address Satan as "þou duke of dethe" (ed. Hulme 1907:115, line 1415) or as Trevisa translates, "Prince and Duk of dethe" (MED *duk* 2.(a)), drawing from the Latin *Nicodemus: princeps et dux mortis* (20.1). Cp. "doctour of deth," 402 (B.18.364) below, and "deþ . . . oure duk" (imitating Langland?) in the spurious A.12.87, as A.12.104 seems to imitate C.22/B.20.100, 105. Christ is *Dux vitæ* in the Easter liturgy, the sequence *Victimæ paschali laudes* (see 28–34n above).

364 (B.18.321) with þat breth helle braek: The breaking of hell answers Lucifer's breaking into the Garden of Eden (313, 380 [B.18.287] above; see B.11.164, and 378n below). Jesus harrows as God creates, not with machinery but with voice and breath alone: "þat lihte bade vnlouke" (359 [B.18.316] above). In *Nicodemus*, Hell complains, "Who is that Jesus who through his word (*per verbum suum*) drew the dead from me without prayers?" (20.3). See 271n above, and for other instances of this conception see B.5.494–95 (and Hill 1973, Kaske 1988), the light blowing the saints to heaven; also B.9.32–46 (A.10.33–34), C.21/B.19.122, and (probably spurious) 5.34–40 of Manuscript Z of A: "Helle yatus hit [God's word] tobarst ant hadde out Adam.".

366–67 (B.18.323–24) *populus . . . . agnus dei*: Two crucial testimonies, from the two testaments, of the act of witnessing itself: Isa. 9:2, Matt. 4:16. See 271n above. **Iohannes songe** is John the Baptist's utterance, quoted by John the Evangelist (John 1:29, 36) and marks the concord of testaments at the moment of redemption. The **songe** may also be the song the "four and twenty ancients" sang in praise of the Lamb in the Apocalypse attributed to John (Apoc. 5:9–12), again linking the Harrowing to the Second Coming, as Mann suggests (1994:207).

370 Lo! . . . lyf and soule bothe (B.18.327 my soule to amendes): John the Baptist's "*Ecce*" modulates into Jesus' vernacular self-witness, **Lo!** Cp. 191 and n above. The revision emphasizes Jesus' role as the Vita who is champion of Lyf (28–34 [B.18.29–35] above), and emphasizes his living form. Jesus makes a formal legal "clayme" (372 [B.18.329]) appropriately *in person* (**Lo! me here**). The common tradition had it that Jesus descended in soul only (Izydorczyk 1985:19; cp. Norton-Smith 1983:66 on Wyclif's departure from this tradition and L's adherence to it); see 25n, and 271n above. The phrase *lyf and soule* usually means "body and soul, entirely" (e.g. line 268 above), but here **lyf** and

soule are not ontologically distinct. Both words may be translated *anima*; see B.9.55 (A.10.43–44) and MED *lif* 1a.(b) and 7.

371 to saue oure bothe rihte (B.18.328 to saue þo þat ben worþi): C echoes 36 (B.18.37) above, where the "rights of the two of them" referred to Deth and Lyf—their champions now confront one another directly. The revision augments the legalisms of the ensuing argument, and may register L's ambivalence about the limits of salvation (see 420–44n below). **Bothe** is ambiguous: either (addressing Lucifer) Jesus preserves both his own and Lucifer's rights in law, which Lucifer misunderstands (see 299–311n above), or, more likely, he preserves both his and the sinful souls' ancient and newly reacquired rights. Jesus will go on to fulfill these legalisms by a divine right that he compares with a king's power to pardon at will.

372 (B.18.339) Myne they be and of me: they are my property; indeed, I created them.

373–75 (B.18.330–32) Althouh resoun recorde . . . helle for euere: Jesus contradicts Rihtwisnesse (196–99 [B.18.191–94] above) and Lucifer (302–5 [B.18.280–82] above; see 312n above). Alford glosses the legal term **recorde**, "to testify on recollection what had previously passed in court," and observes that here "the image is that of God as judge and reason as his *recordeur*" (*Gloss.* s.v. *Recorden*).

378 (B.18.335) palays: i.e., *palys*, a fenced (paled) enclosure. Eden was often called the *hortus conclusus*, from the phrase in Cant. 4:12; see 313n above, 11.294 (B.10.468).

379–92 (B.18.336–47) Falsliche thow fettest . . . vt Artem falleret: The passage echoes 303–21 (B.18.281–91) above. In a number of small revisions L avoids two distractions and reemphasizes the *lex talionis*. RK-C find motive for C's revisions in corruption in L's B exemplar (p. 73). C omits B's reference to Lucifer in Eden as **a Lusard wiþ a lady visage** (337), perhaps again to avoid, especially in Jesus' mouth, a comforting antifeminism and legendary material (see 303–40n above). The conception of Satan as lizard seems to be unparalleled; we have Milton's toad and "cocodrille" in *Le Mystère de la Passion* (ed. Jodogne 1965, line 26242). In an English version of Grosseteste's *Château*, the *Myrour of Lewed Men*, the fiend comes "in neddir liknesse to Eue with a wommans face" (ed. Sajavaara 1967, line 53)—ultimately from Peter the Comestor, and a common depiction in art, as was the legged adder (see Kelly 1971). See also Chaucer, MLT 360–61 and the Riverside edition's note ad loc.

C also omits B's potentially confusing assertion that **Adam and al his issue** would be **at my wille herafter** (B 344), as if Jesus would redeem all humanity—even though B merely asserts Jesus' power to save all, not his will to do it. See 414n, 420–44n below. Further C paraphrases the classic proof-text of the *lex talionis*, "an eye for an eye," before quoting it (from Exod. 21:24, etc.), and C quotes again (superfluously) *Ars vt Artem falleret* (see 165 [B.18.162] above). In the Sermon on the Mount Jesus specifically rebukes the doctrine of eye for eye, commanding rather turning the cheek (Matt. 5:38–39). The passage broadly asserts the requital or ransom theory of the Redemption.

381 (not in B) my loue and my leue: see 314n above.

386–87 So lyf shal lyf lete . . . hit asketh (cf. B.18.343 And lif for lif also): C expands B's phrase in emphasis of the principle of equity. "So must a (living) man lose his life, whenever that (living) man has destroyed the life of another, so that life may pay for life, as the old law demands."

388 (B.18.340) *Ergo*: Alford collects such "disputational language" in PP as *ergo, contra, quodlibet* (*Quot.* 58). Here the valence is rather juridical than scholastic.

 synne to synne wende: another *regressio*, perhaps "sin (the Crucifixion) [shall] turn (in requital) against sin (the Fall)," or as Kane and Prsl suggest, shall "offset, go to balance" sin (Kane 1993:141). Schmidt (more clearly in his 1995 edition of B than in his translation; see note ad loc.) and Donaldson (1990) suggest that it means "sin shall revert to sin" (see 209 [B.18.204] above), "only the unjust will henceforth go to hell, the abode of sin," that is, the sinful (the unjust? the devils?) must (henceforth?) forego their apparent rights and return to the condition of sin (as in B 304 above), namely hell. The former interpretation seems more natural in context, as it continues the series of requitals. None of these senses is recognized by MED, s.v. *wenden*; OED, s.v. *wend*.

 Further, L may have in mind the *regressio* Romans 8:34, "For what the law could not do, in that it was weak through the flesh; God sending his own Son, in the likeness of sinful flesh and *of sin, hath condemned sin* (*et de peccato damnavit peccatum*) in the flesh." The italicized phrase, regularly taken as a grammatical unit in early commentary, was read by Augustine and others to mean that "by sin he condemned sin," that the incarnate flesh, "sin" in a limited sense (= "sacrifice for sin"; the Gloss has *hostia pro peccato*), destroyed sin (Lyonnet 1970:211–14). Hugh of St. Cher, in the passage cited by Smith about snakeskins expelling poison (1966:23; see 154–60n above), cites this place in Romans, explaining that Christ is called *peccatum pro similitudine* whereas the devil is *peccatum veritate.*

Hence, in a logic as complex as Paul's, sin turned toward, responded to sin, or as L puts it again in 390 (B.18.345), Jesus' death will relieve what death (the devil, death in sin) destroyed. The sets of repetitions put in antitheses resembles a nearby place in Romans, 8:12–21.

389 And al þat man mysdede: The line, added in C, introduces plays on **mysdede** with "fordede" in parallel position in the following line, and a new *regressio* on **man.**

y man to amenden hit (B.18.341 I man wole amende): the B original suggests that C's **to amenden,** and **to releue** in the next line, are absolute infinitives (see 27n above). They may however be infinitives dependent on **shal** in line 388—such infinitives with *to* are permitted in Middle English if remote from their auxiliary verbs (Mustanoja 1960:528; Wittig 1986:223–24).

390 þat deth fordede: alluding to Osee (Hosea) 13:14 (see 34n above). Reviewing the ransom theology of commutative justice, Rivière speaks of the death-undoing-death commonplace as "cette magnifique antithèse" (1934:34, see 30–40). L may have written "dede" for **deth** (as read several manuscripts at B.3.267—see variants in KD-B), sharpening the point.

393–94 aȝeyne þe lawe . . . souereynliche by maistrie (cp. B.18.348): answering Lucifer's complaint above, 298–99 (B.18.276–77). Jesus' emphasis on the justice of his redemption, **nat . . . aȝeyne þe lawe,** responds to the issue whether God could properly, by absolute power, redeem humans contrary to human perceptions of justice. See 298–311n above.

B.18.347, 350–52 And þat grace gile destruye . . . Thow fettest . . . no reson ellis: C omits these largely redundant lines, but omits therewith the repeated assertion that Jesus offers ransom by guile according to **good feith;** Alford sees in this phrase allusion to the canon law "principle of bona fides," or freedom from fraud in a transaction (1977:945).

395 (B.18.349) by riht and by resoun: a legalistic collocation suggestive of equity, repeated thrice in this legalistic passus (see 298–311 [B.18.277–85] and n above, and 21.459–64n below). So **raunsome** (bail from prison; ultimately from Latin *redemptio*) and **leges** are legalisms (Alford, *Gloss.*; 1988c). B's insistent repetition of **resoun** and **ransoun** in the following lines is omitted in C; for the terms see C.19.287.

Non veni soluere: "I am not come to destroy the law, but to fulfill." The quotation paraphrases Matt. 5:17, supplying as often a word (*legem*) for clarity or remembering the precise phrase from non-biblical sources (Alford, *Quot.*). Birnes (1975) argues that L parallels Jesus' fulfilling of the law with the development of the law of equity in Chancery, law based on reason and conscience rather than mere precedent.

B.18.356 I in liknesse of a leode: quoting Philippians 2:7, "being made in the likeness of men" (*in similitudinem hominum factus*). See 21n above and C.7.130.

397–98 (B.18.358–59) thorwe a tre . . . thorw a tre: see 143 (B.18.140) and 141–44n above. **Lyue** may be a noun (dative of "lyf") or an infinitive (Wittig 1986:239).

B.18.360a Et cecidit: "and he is fallen into the hole he made" (Ps. 7:16), providing another proof-text of the *lex talionis*. The Psalm continues, "His sorrow shall be turned on his own head: and his iniquity shall come down upon his crown." See note to 420a below.

400–12 (B.18.362–70) And my grace to growe . . . resureccio mortuorum: The persistent repetitions of the preceding passage, echoing the devils' complaints and exploiting the theologizing rhetoric of *regressio* and antithesis, have come to seem clotted, and with this passage Jesus and L freshen the poetic movement as they take a liberating new direction. The opposition of **gyle** and **grace** is witty; wittier in its development is the idea that grace grows.

   At this point the poem's theology of redemption turns from the old "ransom theory" and passes beyond Anselm's "satisfaction theory" (Hort 1938:122–29) to the idea of "subjective atonement" associated with Abelard, the idea of human participation in the redemption by way of God's love and the responding, imitative love of humans for God (see 299–311n and 3.401–3). In his commentary on Romans 3:26 Abelard discarded several earlier conceptions of the Redemption, including the idea that Jesus' death liberated us from the power of the devil. There he gave his most succinct statement of his theory (*Comm. Rom.* 2.242–70, readily available in L's time in England—Luscombe 1969:92), whose terms are relevant here:

   It seems to me that we are justified in the blood of Christ and reconciled to God through this, that—through the singular grace made manifest to us, that His own Son,

in order to instruct us as much by word as by example, took on our nature and perse-
vered in the same even unto death—He bound us to Himself more tightly, so that, we
being inflamed with so great a benefit of divine grace, true charity now does not recoil
from enduring anything for the sake of that benefit. Nor do I doubt indeed that this
benefit inflamed in the highest love of God even the ancient fathers, awaiting it
through faith, as much as people of the age of grace, because it is written: "And they
that went before, and they that followed, cried out, saying: *Hosanna to the son of
David*," etc. Anyone is made still more just, that is more fully loving God, after the
passion of Christ than before, because the fulfilled benefit inflames more fully in love
than the hoped for. And so our redemption is that highest love in us through the passion of Christ. This love not only frees us from the servitude of sin, but also obtains
for us the true liberty of the children of God . . . (ed. Buytaert 1969, 1:117–18; see also
the trans. with fuller context in Fairweather 1956)

Here L's Jesus seems most Abelardian; see also 21.63–68 and n. In the next
passus Conscience explains that Jesus' "doing best" was his granting of pardon
to humankind—with its attendant obligation of humans to do penance—
rather than the Passion itself (21/B.19.182–87), suggesting a subjective soteriology (humans participate) rather than an objective one (Christ's conquest of
the devil). Bernard, returning to the ransom theory, attacks Abelard's subjec-
tivist and exemplarist view and emphasizes that Christ's blood mysteriously
did the work of salvation. Bernard says, "This is the justification of a human,
in the blood of the Redeemer," and "Why . . . ? I am permitted to know that
it is so, but not why it is so" (PL 182.1062–65, 1067–72, esp. 1067, 1069). Abelard's position was condemned at the Council of Sens in 1140, but exemplarism
continued to be promulgated by Abelard's followers, and a version of the doctrine found its way into Peter Lombard's *Sentences* (Luscombe 1969:148–49,
156–57, 227, 239, 250, 256, 275, 294). For a clear review of the issues see Pelikan
1978:127–39.

The Abelardian passage quoted above in fact contains traces of a fusion
of different ideas about salvation, not pure exemplarism, and such a fusion
doubtless persists in common thinking about the work of Jesus. A Latin sermon quoted by Warner (1996), itself linked with L's jousting metaphor of the
Passion, is typical in having it every way: "so that a fit satisfaction might be
made, and that He might vigorously inflame us to love of Him, and through
this completely dissolve sins and the works of the devil."

In its inspired condensation of vivid, often agricultural and alimentary
images and its rapid, cascading shifts of metaphors this passage resembles and
answers (as the Crucifixion answers the Incarnation) another lyrical effusion
in the poem, the "loue ys triacle" passage in Holy Church's sermon (1.146–54
[B.1.148–58]), and should be closely compared with it. C's addition of Jesus'
word on the cross, **Sicio**, confirms the link with the drink of 53 (B.18.53) above

(see note, and Ruffing 1991). Jesus says that, having drunk the bitter drink of death ("Father, if this chalice may not pass away, but I must drink it, *fiat voluntas tua*": Matt. 26:42, 39 et synop.), he will drink its opposite, the drink of life. The drink reflects John 4:13–14 (the Samaritan woman by the well), the drink Jesus offers of everlasting life.

400 (B.18.362) my grace to growe: L often deploys the metaphor of plant growth to describe the surge of grace (e.g., C.14.24 [B.12.60], C.13.23, B.15.424, C.17.48), with ultimate reference to the parable of the Mustard Seed (Matt. 13:31–32 et synop.), and to Jesus' speaking of himself as the "true vine" (John 15:1–8), and with expansive allusion to the agricultural imagery of PP. The topic is thoroughly examined in Tavormina 1994; see also Lawler 1979, esp. p. 207, and on "green love," Hill 2003:72–82. The metaphor begins the chain of associations leading to the vintage of line 411 (B.18.369).

401–2 (B.18.363–64) The bitternesse . . . doctour of deth: reflecting a commonplace of proverbial lore, that one suffers the consequences of one's doing, reaps what one sows, "let hem chewe as they chose" (205–7n above); see Whiting 1968:B529, MED *drinken* 3., *breuen* 3. But compare the new dispensation: Christ bade us "drynke bote for bale, brouke hit hoso myhte" (12.57 [B.11.122]); see Salter 1962:49–52. L plays on a common meaning of "brew," to "incite" (strife) or "cause" (trouble, death), as in "brew bale"; see MED *breuen* 2.

   Specifically Jesus refers to the bitter gall and vinegar offered to him in the Passion, and again to his deception of Satan; the devil's encouraging of Jesus' death caused his own ruin. If grace is an herbal (grassy) remedy (14.23 [B.12.59]), provided by Christus Medicus, the "leche of lif" (B.16.118), its counterpart is the lethal nostrum offered by the **doctour** (of medicine) **of deth**, Satan (on the Christus Medicus in PP see St-Jacques 1991). L alludes to the *poculum mortis*, "cup of death," a phrase from the hymn *Rex æterne Domine* and widespread in Latin and English (Russom 1988, Brown 1940, Smithers 1951–52:67–75), in contrast to the drink of love which is life. It recalls the chalice of the Passion that Jesus knows he must drink (Matt. 26:42). The wording of 401 is recalled at 446 (B.18.403) below.

403–8 (B.18.365–67) loue is my drynke . . . soule sake: *Sicio*: *Sicio*, "I thirst" (John 19:28). From easy allusion to love as plant of peace and "triacle," which Jesus would *give* in his shedding of blood, we move to the surprising image, a counter-eucharist, of the love of (for? from?) human souls as the drink for which Jesus thirsts, a thirst that will only be slaked at the resurrection of the dead in the vale of Josaphat at Doomsday. Depictions of the Crucifixion commonly show the blood and water issuing from Jesus' side being received in a eucharistic chalice. A Middle English sermon urges us to "drynke of þe copp of loue" (ed. Ross 1940: 232). Jesus thirsts because of the fight, the joust, on the cross. The conception inverts that of 7.133 (B.5.493), where Jesus' blood feeds the patriarchs in hell.

A similar coupling of Jesus' thirst on the cross with his thirst to die for love of humankind appears in a fifteenth-century lyric: "His þrist was to seyȝe ["say," i.e. "signify"], / ffor loue of manys soule / Hym longede for to deyȝe" (ed. Brown 1939:141, lines 29–31). Burrow (1993:118 n 19) suggests that L recalls Jesus' *soif . . . de salut humain* (thirst for human salvation) on the cross, from Guillaume de Deguileville's *Pèlerinage Jhesucrist* (ed. Stürzinger 1897, line 9433). But the idea is common: in the influential *Passion des jongleurs* we hear that "sa soif estoit de nous sauver [his thirst was for saving us]" (ed. Perry 1981, line 2316); Rupert of Deutz speaks of Jesus "on the cross thirsting for our salvation" (ed. Haacke 1967: 7.16, line 706); a lyric by Richard Rolle, "'A' quod þou 'me þursteth sore': / Hit was for hom þat dampned wore" (ed. Ogilvie-Thomson 1988:57, lines 207–8; see also p. 80, lines 465–71, and Hudson 1990, 3:184); the *Northern Passion* says, "His meneing was no drink to taste, / Bot to help man saul had he haste" (ed. Foster [Heuser and Foster] 1930:207); Bonaventure wrote, "It is not very credible that he spoke of thirst as if he wanted a fleshly drink, when he knew that he would die in an instant; rather we believe that he thirsted of his most ardent desire for our salvation" (*Vitis mystica*, formerly attributed to Bernard, PL 184.662). See further Wyclif, ed. Loserth 1890, 4:338; Bennett 1982:43 and 110–11; Bestul 1996:206, n64; Watson 1997b:91–93.

In a nice display of the difference between (and combining of) the meditative tradition of affective piety and the older tradition that emphasized Jesus' glory as champion and conqueror and that delighted in allegory, the *Meditationes vitæ Christi* seems to respond to [pseudo-] Bernard (i.e. Bonaventure): "For þouh it so be þat it may be vndirstande þat worde *I þriste*, gostly to þat entent, þat he þrestede þanne þe hele of soules. Neuerles also in soþenes (*in veritate*) he þristede bodily bycause of the grete passing out of blode . . ." (the original Latin ed. Peltier 1868:607, cap. 79; trans. Nicholas Love, ed. Sargent 1992:179, lines 37–40).

Jesus **deyede as hit semede** (404); B 366 has **deide vpon erþe**: the revision may register discomfort with the blunt assertion that Jesus, who had "comsed for to swoene" (57 [B.18.57] above), merely died. After all a living Jesus, the very *anima Christi*, is speaking. Similarly C.7.129 with nearly the same phrase tones down B.5.487.

Ac y wol drynke of no dische . . . depe helle thy bolle. Complicating the figure, C adds three lines (405–7) about the cup that will hold the drink—not a literal dish (with a pun on nearly homophonic *disce*, "learn"?) or the cup of deep learning (an irresistible C version topic; see MED s.v. *drinken* for parallels), but **comune coppes**: not those of a special class (the clergy, although only the clergy were given wine at the Eucharist); universal cups; the familiar cups shared by ordinary people; cheap cups inappropriate for **preciouse** (in one sense) **drynkes**; the cups of the Holy *Commun*ion service. Jesus had said, "Drink ye all (*omnes*) of this" at the Last Supper (Matt. 26:27 et synop.); the cup is common.

In his widely used treatise on the liturgy Johannes Beleth wrote (ca. 1160) that "in the primitive Church the sacrifice [of the Mass] was made in wooden vessels and common vestments. For then there were wooden chalices and golden priests; now indeed it is the converse" (ed. Douteil 1976:76, cap. 42). See likewise "On the Feast of Corpus Christi" in the Vernon manuscript: "And in vessels of treo—Non oþur chalys hadden heo" (ed. Horstmann 1892:187). Compare the silver cups with which Mede corrupts justices (3.23 [B.3.22, A.3.21]; see Kane's *Revised* ed. of A, 1988, p. 461 for the reading "coppes"). For a very similar association of the bitter sponge with a cup of true wine in the Latin poetry of John of Hoveden see Schmidt 1983:179–82, who treats this passage in detail.

As at first the drink of love would seem to be what Jesus offers, not wants, so here **alle cristene soules** would at first be richly construed as in apposition with **coppes**, whereas more familiarly the body would be the vessel of the soul. So the Wife of Bath speaks of herself as a humble vessel, not of gold but of "tree," following Jerome quoting II Tim. 2:20, "In a great house there are not only vessels of gold and silver, but also of wood and earth" (ed. Bryan and Dempster 1941:210).

More striking still, the **soules** may rather be the object of **y wol drynke**, with a shift of metaphor, since the souls are not identifiable with love. Compare again Bonaventure's *Vitis mystica*: "And he drinks the most undiluted blood of grapes, namely the souls of saints squeezed out and separated from the seeds in the wine-press of the cross . . ." (quoted in Schmidt 1983:183). See 34n above. Satan's drink, then, is the unresurrected souls, held in the bowl of hell (407), a bowl that, considering the common depiction of the entrance to hell as a (Leviathan-) mouth, would be its stomach (see Jonah 2:2, Ecclus. 51:7, and Friedman 1981:99–129).

409 pyement . . . ne pomade (not in B): **Pyement** in English is usually a medicinal drink (in Anglo-Norman, merely "spiced wine": A-ND), and **preciouse** often means (of medicine) "efficacious" (MED, 1.f.) as in 1.148 (B.1.152), used of the same medicine, love. The word *piment* is used, probably ironically, of the drink given Jesus in *La Passion des jongleurs* (ed. Perry 1981, line 2327). The word **pomade** is here first recorded in English, and here is its only use in the sense "drink made from apples" (MED, OED; in Anglo-Norman, *pomadre* is apple cider: A-ND). Later uses of *pomade*, taken by OED as a different word, refer to a medicinal ointment, and the medical context here implies that L's **pomade** is medicinal, but probably a drink rather than a salve. The force of the line then contains the twin metaphors of drink and medicine: no costly drinks can slake my thirst; no efficacious specifics can heal me. The **pomade** calls to mind the lethal fruit (*pome*) in Eden. Jesus seems to say that no apple-drink medicine will satisfy his thirst until, at the final resurrection, he can consume the heartier potion of "pers fruyt þe plouhman" (line 18 above), namely, humankind.

411–12 (B.18.369–70) Til þe ventage valle . . . *mortuorum*: On the **rype most** as newly matured and hence best quality wine see Wirtjes 1987; on the **vale of Iosophat** (Josaphat, Authorized Version Jehoshaphat; see Joel 3:2, 12–13) as the site of the final resurrection of the dead, see Lunz 1972. Wirtjes (1987:142) points out that Jesus had said at the Last Supper, "I will not drink from henceforth of this fruit of the vine, until that day when I shall drink it with you *new* in the kingdom of my Father" (Matt. 26:29 et synop.). The emphasis on the wine as *novum* in Matthew and Mark accounts for its designation as must, new wine, here.

The Gloss on Joel 3:12–13, interpreting the valley of Josaphat as *iudicium domini*, speaks of *mustum* as the *malicia* that will be squeezed out by the wine-press, the redeeming Christ. The references to the harvest and the winepress, a common emblem of the Cross, in the passage from Joel reinforced links between the Judgment and the Passion in medieval commentary (Lunz 1972:608; on the winepress see Marrow 1979:83–94).

The phrase ***resureccio mortuorum***, from the Nicene Creed, is reified as the **most**, just as credal phrases were reified in 114–15 (B.18.111–12) above (see n), and as food and drinks are specified as Latin phrases in the banquet scene. Must is especially intoxicating (Acts 2:13); in the hymn *Beata nobis gaudia*, sung on Pentecost, the crowds seeing the apostles filled with the spirit *Musto madere deputant*, "thought them besotted with must" (as also in the hymn *Impleta gaudent viscera* sung earlier on Pentecost): see 193n above.

413–46 (B.18.371–403) And thenne shal y come . . . shalt abuye bittere: Jesus concludes his address to the fiends by asserting the grounds of his mercy in kinship, divine privilege (in which mercy and righteousness are identical), the precepts of English law, kingship, and the distinction between humans and devils, who are judged by their own law of seisin. L includes here several versions of the "escape clause" that tempers severe judgment (see 7.282, 288–91 [B.5.629, 635–38, A.6.114, 120–23]; B.10.376 [A.11.257]; C.21/B.19.404; and Evans 1969:272–73). With one exception (see 432–36n), the minute differences between B and C in this passage suggest either fastidious revision or scribal variance.

Here Jesus, following on his thought of Josaphat, speaks of the Last Judgment, and returns to the present, the Harrowing, in 443 (B.18.400), as marked by a resuming **quod oure lord**. The association of the Harrowing and Doomsday was inevitable (see 115–467n above).

With the argument here Jesus resolves the debate among the Daughters, reconciles the testaments (and all such witnesses), and conquers Satan by enacting the reasoning that law and love are the same, a move anticipated most pointedly at B.11.167–70 (see note), as well as C.12.109–41 (see note), 19.11–18, B.15.584, and B.17.10–12.

413 (B.18.371) as a kynge: Jesus will be Christ in Majesty at Doomsday, recalling Satan's acknowledgement already (277 [B.18.269] above) and anticipating the discussion of him as knight, king, and conqueror in C.21/B.19.26–28. This "prophecy" constitutes the climax of this passus of redemption.

414 (B.18.372) alle mennes soules: that is, all humans will be drawn from hell to face the Last Judgment (and some may return): see John 5:28–29, Apoc. 20:15. The statement is thoroughly orthodox: the Athanasian Creed says, "At his (Jesus') coming, *all* (*omnes*) people must rise with their bodies, and must give an account of their own deeds." The Creed continues with the lines on Truth's pardon. For the faulty inference that the (heretical) notion of "universal salvation" of all, even the unbaptized, emerges here see Hill 1991, with many references (see also Evans 1969, Russell 1984:107, Kane 1982:88, Hort 1938:118–29, Benson 2002:10–11, and Watson 1997b). See below 420–42n, 436n, 449n. The question arose in response to the crucial but enigmatic Greek Testament proof-texts of the Descent, 1 Peter 3:18 and 4:6 (see 361–446n above). Origen had thought that Jesus preached to the damned at the Harrowing, and offered to save all—and, heretically, that after a period of purgation all were indeed saved.

Precise definition of who was salvageable was contested in L's time. See for instance Archbishop Simon Langham's condemnations in 1368, many of which concerned heretical opinions as to who could be saved (ed. Wilkins 1737, 3:75–76). *The Pricke of Conscience* has the usual view, that at Doomsday sinners "Sal noght be shewed bot rightwysnes, / And grete reddure [severity], withouten mercy" (ed. Morris 1863:6090–91). Turner provides a thorough review of the question in medieval thought (1966; see also Sullivan 1992), and Coleman surveys the opinions of the *moderni* (1981:126–46). Vitto examines the issue in PP (1989:5–35), sensibly concluding that Jesus did not lead all the souls from hell at the Harrowing, and that L in this passage leaves the question of who was saved at Doomsday ambiguous. Certainly L often presents ortho-dox restrictions on salvation, for instance in the mouth of Scripture (B.10.349–76) and the Samaritan (19.283–300 [B.17.303–20]). In B.11.80–82 Will asserts that baptism is necessary for salvation, citing John 3:5, and in B.15.456–58 Anima agrees.

Clearly, though, L was moved in this passage to represent the most inclu-sive salvation possible within orthodoxy—Jesus yearns for the salvation of all (see 1 Tim. 2:4–6), and reminds us of God's capacity to grant it if he will. The Holy Ghost "melteth myhte into mercy" (19.196 [B.17.230]). Compare *Quare placuit? Quia voluit* (14.155a [B.12.216a]). The poet is torn.

415 (B.18.373) fendekynes: The word, recorded only here in Middle English, is probably a coinage (perhaps also "baudekyn" at B.3.41 [A.3.40], and "fauntek-yns" used at B.13.213—see OED *–kyn*, MED *–kin*) modelled on Perkyn, Mal-kyn, etc. The word may in context (see 417–41n below) exploit the homophony of *kin* (family) with the (here contemptuous) diminutive suffix: the family of Jesus and the family of Satan are distinguished.

416 at blisse or at payne (B.18.374 wherso best me likeþ): Ultimately C means what B says more directly, "whether they like it or not." The revision may simply reflect C's emendation of B archetype's **wherso euere me likeþ** (accepted by Schm) which lacks a head-stave (so KD-B, pp. 125, 196).

417–41 (B.18.375–98) my kynde . . . my kyn (B: my kynde): The iteration in this passage of the concepts of kinship and kind-ness (in at least three of its senses: natural character, affiliation, graciousness; see Galloway 1994) draws into its ambit an idea of **kyng**-ship as a supreme recognition of the blood-brotherhood of humanity, as if L were conscious of the etymology of *king* (OE *cyn-ing*) as the patronymic of *cynn*: "scion of *the* (royal) family." Compare generally 19.283–300 (B.17.303–20), and C.3.374–412. Among the causes of the Incarnation is not merely God's daring to take Adam's **kynde** in order to know human suffering (see 208–38n above), but also simply his establishing, in Piers's arms, *humana natura*, full kinship with human kind. On **kynde** gener-ally in PP see White 1988, esp. 108–11, Tavormina 1995b passim, and the end of 8–12n above, 21.475–76n below. The *Gospel of Nicodemus* has Jesus call from hell "all my saints, who have my image and likeness (*imaginem et similitudinem meam*)" (24.1), drawing from a doctrine of Augustine, "Whom he wished to make his brothers, them he freed and made his fellow heirs" (*Tract. in Joan.* 2.13, ed. Willems 1954; cp. Rom. 8:15–17). The *Castle of Love* says Jesus "vnder vre wede vre kynde nom (under our clothing took on our kind/nature)" (ed. Sajavaara 1967, line 657).

The conception here of kingship as the centralized cognition of kinship vastly outreaches the disputations of the earlier visions in PP, starting with Prol.136–56 (B.Prol.112–38), vexed as they are by questions of constitutional prerogative and potentially abusive power. Jesus as king resembles the earthly king in his special legal role as rueful agent of mercy by a mere look—a recognition of common humanity (see 421–29n below). The next passus continues the examination of kingship human and divine, carrying over from this passus the idea that a king should be both just and merciful.

419, 436 (B.18.377, 393) hole brethrene . . . haluebretherne: Those both human and baptized are Jesus' whole brothers; unbaptized humans are half-brothers. Archetypal B reads simply **breþeren** for the latter; Schmidt accepts this, arguing that C's **haluebretherne** is a revision for clarity (the Athlone editions have no comment on the line, but Donaldson wrestles with the issue in connection with Uthred de Boldon's theory of the *clara visio*—1982:71–72; Fowler agrees with Schmidt, 1980:223, 264–65). The distinction alludes to the legal question of whether stepchildren had full rights of inheritance (Plucknett 1956:719–22)—generally they were excluded. In the analogy, human paternity and Christian baptism are the two parents that beget whole blood. Humans are Jesus' brothers in blood further by the blood he shed on the cross. On kinship in redemption theology see Franks 1962:136–37 and 21n, 28–34n above. The issue reverts to the problem of the salvation of the heathen (12.75ff. [B.11.140ff.], Trajan, etc.; see 414n above), obviously of great moment to L (see Russell 1966 and esp. Whatley 1984). *Cursor mundi* speaks of the Redemption: "his grace it was and nothing oþer / Þat he wald bicom our broþer" (ed. Morris 1874, lines 854–55).

Blood united God and humanity by the Incarnation, which made God our brother of blood (see 28–34n above). The emphasis here, on genetics rather than sacrifice, parallels the emphasis on mercy over justice, and calls, as 8.215–16 puts it, for an answering "fiale loue" ("trustworthy love," or as several manuscripts and Schm read, *filial*—see R-KC, p. 151), as Piers said to Hunger, "And hit are my blody bretherne for god bouhte vs alle" (see 21n above and A.7.193 [B.6.207]). Thomas Hill makes a persuasive case for the reading *filial* (2003:67–72). Jesus' invocation of the blood brotherhood of humanity (***we***

beth brethrene) inverts a consequence of the Fall. Humankind had been made in God's image (Gen. 1:27, 5:1; see 7.123, 128 [B.5.481, 486], and 10.157–58 [B.9.31–49, 65–67a]) and yet by eating of the tree had become, in God's words, dangerously "as one of us, knowing good and evil" (Gen. 3:22), and was condemned to die. Through the Incarnation, God in the person of Jesus conversely became fully a member of the human family, "in oure secte" (B, "sute"), even unto death, and hence we are brought to life. The idea is expressed in Repentance's speech, 7.120–57 (B.5.478–512), a passage that anticipates and glosses much of this passus and was probably composed after this passus—see 364n above, 451n below, 21.200–12n, and Headnote to C.21.

As Rivière notes, the Daughter Mercy's first appeal on humanity's behalf, in various versions of the story, is to the divine image in humanity (1934:317), a notion less compelling than kinship. There may be reference as well to the chivalric brotherhood in arms; sealing such friendships by commingling or mutually drinking blood was at least known if not practiced (Keen 1962; see also Baldwin 1981a).

420–42 (B.18.378–99) Shal neuere in helle eft come (B: Shul noʒt be dampned to þe deeþ) . . . *cum seruo tuo*: Once Jesus' whole brothers are drawn from hell, at the Last Judgment, they will not return; further, **monye** (436 [B.18.393]) of the unbaptized, **haluebretherne,** will also receive mercy then. See Ps. 85:13, "For thy mercy is great towards me: and thou hast delivered my soul out of the lower hell." C's radically inclusive salvation of all the baptized seems to go beyond B, especially if **breþeren** is L's word at B.18.393 (see B.10.349–76 [A.11.232–57]). But finally the two versions are the same in any case: first, *not* to be damned forever must mean that the baptized do not return to hell after the Last Judgment; and second, if therefore no baptized are eternally damned, then the **(halue-) breþeren** of B 393 must refer to the unbaptized. But the conditional **if lawe wol** in 428 (B.18.386) still limits the universality of salvation. If L had Jesus here assert universal salvation, the distinction of full and half bretheren would be pointless. As Lawler says, "These lines go overboard to emphasize divine freedom, and yet the semi-Pelagianism is there: the mercy depends on repentance, as four places make clear," i.e. 430 (B.18.388), B.18.392, 438 (B.18.395), and 442 (B.18.399) (2001:151). See further 414n above, and 436n, 449n below.

In parallel fashion Paul in Romans seems to extend salvation to all, then to limit the extension carefully to the baptized (5:18, 6:1–4). Jesus, then, can but may not **loke** on the unbaptized at Doomsday (see 421–29n below). For authoritative scholastic opinion on the necessity of baptism for salvation see Dunning 1943, Colish 1994:533–39. The following lines, with their exploitation of the volitive force of **wol** (432 [B.18.390]), corroborate the obligatory force of **shal** here. Even so, at 440 (B.18.398) we hear that mercy will rule **al man-kynde** at the Last Judgment. Aquinas quotes John of Damascus' effort to solve this dilemma (*ST* Ia., Q. 19, a. 6 and 1): "God wills with an antecedent or abso-lute will that all men be saved; and with a consequent or conditional will that some are damned" (cited in Coleman 1981:113; see Sullivan 1992:45). Augustine wrote that Christ released the souls of those whom he chose (*quos voluit*) from hell (PL 33.715; see Turner 1966:177 and C.14.155a [B.12.216a]).

420a (B.18.378a) *Tibi soli*: "To thee only have I sinned, and have done evil before thee," Ps. 50:6. If we have sinned before God *only*, then God has exclu-sive power of penalty or remission—no other party being wronged, no other party could make a legal appeal. Thomas Aquinas argues that mercy granted to an offender by a judge who has no superior, a prince, can be just—no higher power or principle is involved, hence a sovereign is free to forgive (*ST* 3., Q. 46, a. 2). Such aggressive exploitation of biblical authority by pressing the meaning of one word (*soli*) is paralleled by the use of *vix* (14.203 [B.12.281], etc.) and warranted by Jesus' pharasaical hermeneutic practice in Matt. 22:41–46 et synop. Medieval logicians treated at length the force of such "syn-categorematic" terms as *solus*. Alford (1972:325) notes that this text, along with the Psalm texts quoted in B 360a above (not in C), B.18.392 (not in C; see n below), 435a (not in B), and 442a (B.18.399a), all occur as lections in the *Dirige*, the office of the dead for Matins, an office Will claims to sing for his "lyflode" (C.5.46). At this high moment of the poem, Will seems to display the particu-lar instruments of his craft, the dirge Psalms.

421–29 (B.18.379–87) to hangen a felone . . . deye or dey nat: Jesus adduces in analogy two principles of law. The first holds that for even a most serious crime (as of a **tretour**) one cannot, by customary law (**Hit is nat vsed**), be hanged twice; the second, that the king, when *present* (line 425, **and he loked on hym**) at an execution, may pardon the criminal. **Loke on** in this passage, especially in its second use in line 428, may mean "care for, regard with favor" (MED *loken* 8b. and 8c.; see 425n below). Alford, *Gloss.* s.v. *Hangen*, cites docu-ments concerning both principles. A late thirteenth-century writ tells of a woman who was hanged but survived overnight and was pardoned *diuine cari-tatis intuitu*, "in consideration of [literally, "by the *look* of"] divine charity" (ed. de Haas and Hall 1970:101; see also Hurnard 1969:176, Baldwin 1981b:74 and n39). In another case in 1397 a condemned thief was spared hanging by King Richard *superveniens per viam*, "happening to pass by" (ed. Sayles

1971:90). In 1392 Richard Maidstone wrote of a condemned homicide who, at an unspecified date, threw himself in front of the king's horse and received pardon (ed. Wright 1859, vol. 1, lines 185–90).

The first principle refers to the idea above that those baptized who have suffered in hell should not return there after the Judgment. The second principle refers below, to the idea that Christ, the supreme king, may surely, in the presence of his blood brothers at the Last Judgment, retain the power and exhibit the mercy of an English king. The two ideas are conflated, with some confusion, in Skeat's note alluding to a case in 1363 reported by Henry Knighton, in which Edward III pardoned a man who survived hanging (ed. Martin 1995:188–91). In that case a clergyman guarded the man lest he be hanged again, and there is no indication that the king was present at the hanging, or that he pardoned him merely because he was present; rather "God gave you life and we will give you a charter of pardon"—the king pardoned him in respect of God's permitting him to survive. The two legal ideas are distinct— the former acknowledges God's miraculous intervention in the survival of a hanged person, the latter acknowledges the power of the king's presence and prerogative—and only the former is in question in Knighton's story. In *Cur Deus Homo* Anselm likewise posed the analogy of a king's pardon to salvation (2, cap. 16, ed. Schmitt 1968, vol. 1).

424 thief (B.18.382 feloun): KD-B accept alliteration of þ and ƒ (p. 132; cp. B.18.367 above). C's revision may draw attention specifically to the thief (*latro*) Dismas, amazingly saved on his cross by Jesus: "*this day* [before the Harrowing, usually thought to have taken place on the Saturday] thou shalt be with me in paradise" (Luke 23:39–43). See B.5.464–66, in Roberd the Robber's speech, and C.11.252–60 (B.10.420–26), where Dismas is called "feloun" and "robbere," and is said to have preceded the harrowed saints into paradise (see Allen 1989). In *Nicodemus* the redeemed saints are surprised to find the *latro* already on the right side of paradise (26).

425, 428, 448 (B.18.383, 386, 405) he loked . . . y loke . . . dorste nat loke: The theme in this passus of looking as witnessing and guarding (see Headnote) modulates into a theme of looking as extending grace; the devils dare not even begin to accept it. "Regard" and "reward" are etymologically identical words in Middle English, derived from two dialects of French. With the king's wondrous power compare Matt. 9:20–22: a woman touches Jesus' garment and he, "turning, and seeing her (*videns eam*)," says that her faith has healed her (whereas in Mark and Luke it is the mere touch of his garment that heals her).

428 (B.18.386) if lawe wol y loke on hem: that is, seeing that Jesus is required, at the Last Judgment, to review human cases—or does L represent Jesus as saying he can extend grace conditional upon the will of law?

429–30 (B.18.387–88) Where they deye . . . boldenesse of here synnes: On the issue of whether one's behavior on earth affects one's final reward see Allen 1989. This passage specifically responds to the issue and imagery of 19.279–87 (B.17.299–307).

430 (B.18.388) Be hit eny thyng abouhte: "If it (the audacity of their sins) be in any way paid for" (MED *anithing*). The sense is "redeemed the least bit." Schmidt argues that the payment would be any virtuous acts the sinners may have performed (1980:103; so Lawler 2001:151, clarifying that the virtuous act would be contrition), whereas Skt and Prsl take the phrase to refer to Christ's sacrifice and the Redemption. The former (perhaps semi-Pelagian) interpretation makes better sense of the conditional **Be hit**, and avoids a kind of tautology: "I may be merciful to them if I have redeemed them at all." Alternatively, Jesus may refer to Purgatory; see 432–36n, B.18.392n below.

431 (B.18.389) mercy . . . rihtwysnesse . . . trewe: Jesus summarizes with reference to three of the Daughters of God. The whole action brings Peace—if there is peace there is no argument—who is omitted here, but Pees is the next speaker. That Jesus' righteousness is the ground of his mercy solves the debate. Compare Anselm: "Truly therefore you are merciful because you are supremely just" (*Proslogion* 9, ed. Schmitt 1968, 1:108, line 7).

432–36 (B.18.390–93) For holy writ wol . . . my haluebretherne: See 419n above. Though Scripture and his will (see 420–42n) incline Jesus to take vengeance on the sinful, he will show mercy. God's law commands punishment, but his mercy allows him to remit its full measure. The revisions in C (perhaps motivated in the first instance by corruption in L's exemplar of B—so R-KC, p. 73) distinctly expand the operation of mercy. C affirms that **holy writ wol** revenge, so that the countervailing **Ac ʒut** surprises, where B admits the conditional (**þouʒ holy writ wole**) at the outset. Both texts cite *nullum malum inpunitum*, a maxim (at least in its context in Innocent III) about the "just judge," *not* from Holy Writ unless that term is taken, as it seems to be in PP, to include extrabiblical authorities (Alford, *Quot.*; Gray 1986:55–56). The earlier context in which this maxim appears as personification is distinctly secular (4.140–41 [B.4.143–44, A.4.126–27]—see n); the use here measures the distance between human and divine justice. C omits the lines from B (391–92) that sup-

ply rational grounds for Jesus' mercy, the cleansing of Purgatory and the prayers for the dead (see below) that satisfy sin; the lines in B answer B.10.375–76 .
Ultimately it is simply God's nature to be merciful, as the daughter Mercy usually (but not in PP) argues (see 115–270n above). In his *Altercatio inter Deum
et diabolum*, Hugh of St. Victor had God argue "that he wished to have mercy
through his own kindness (*benignitatem propriam*)," cited in Marx 1995:60.

　　Jesus' **kynde**, his nature as of human kind, will constrain his authorized
and just desire for vengeance (whose scriptural basis is quoted in B.6.226a, etc.,
"Revenge is mine, I will repay"). Yet C adds the lection from the *Dirige* (see
420an above), **Domine ne in furore tuo**, "O Lord, rebuke me not in thy indignation" (Ps. 6:2, 37:2—the incipits of the first and third "penitential Psalms"),
a lection whose function is to alleviate purgatorial punishment. If the words
are parenthetical (see 438an below), the sense is that Jesus will respond to our
plea. If the words are construed as Jesus' utterance about himself they have
another meaning: he begs forgiveness from the just Father for his mercifulness.
C's omission here of any but such indirect reference to Purgatory (see the next
note and 430n above) strikingly promotes the efficacy of kind-ness, bloody
brotherhood.

B.18.392 parce: Alford (1972) finds the source of this word, from Job 17:16, in
the incipit of the first *lectio* of the *Dirige, Parce mihi, domine,* "Spare me, Lord"
(see 420a above), quoted at C.21/B.19.295; compare also B.10.376. As often in
PP, the incipit is taken for the whole, and the Latin phrase is personified. As
used here, and in a number of lyrics cited by Alford, where the word is likewise
personified, it means "mercy given in response to a sinner's plea," for the benefit of souls in Purgatory. In the context of a **prisone** the phrase likewise
alludes to the common formula in legal sentencings, so-and-so shall remain in
confinement "until he shall have made satisfaction," etc. (Alford, *Gloss.* s.v.
Parce).

　　C omits this line with its reference to Purgatory, perhaps to emphasize,
in this context, divine rather than human work, grace rather than merit (see
443–44n below, 420–42n above).

436 (B.18.393) monye: As Schmidt observes, this word excludes the doctrine
of universal salvation of the pre-Christians (1980:103); see 414n and 420–42n
above and 449n below. On **haluebretherne** see 419n above.

437–38 (B.18.394–95) bloed may suffre bloed . . . bote hym rewe: The
repeated stave **bloed** of these lines suggests play like that on "bote" in 4.88–89
(B.4.92–93) and "lyf" in 386–87 above (see n), or the rhythm of a charm.

Healing charms, especially for the staunching of hemorrhage, widespread and at least as old as the tenth century (*Die Merseburger Zaubersprüche*), often have phrases like "bone to bone, blood to blood" (ed. Ebermann 1903:1, 4, 8, 20, 23). The strange but homely auditory magic of these phrases anticipates the last lines of the passus.

438a (B.18.395a) *Audiui arcana verba*: "I heard secret words [which it is not granted to man to utter]." This citation (2 Cor. 12:4, varied from third to first person), and those in 435a above and 442a (B 399a) below, seem inappropriate to Jesus as speaker, as Pearsall notes, and may be taken as parenthetical, a "marginal gloss" (Barr 1986) by Will or L; the speaker "certainly cannot be Christ" (so Emmerson 1993:111–13). As such the phrases recall (and may reflect) Bernard's remark when about to tell the story of the Four Daughters of God, "Forte inenarrabilia sunt, et non licet homini loqui" (Perhaps these things cannot be told, and it is not permitted for a human to speak them—ed. Leclercq and Rochais 1968:24).

Yet in Jesus' role here as our "kyn," they may be felt as his words, too. In 435a, Jesus wishes to allay God's fury and to constrain his own (consequent) will; see 420–42n. Here Jesus, caught up in the mystery of mercy he utters, cannot speak the "secret words" to us fully; in 442a Jesus yearns, as Suffering Servant, not to enter into retributive judgment.

The quotation of Paul's amazed response to his vision as he was snatched up into the third heaven aptly expresses the wondrous temerity of this vision, especially in representing Jesus' words (and the whole extra-biblical account of the Harrowing) with such audacious novelty. If Jesus is indeed represented as extending salvation to any unbaptized sinners in the era following the Redemption, the words as heretical should be kept secret (Watson 1997b:159), but this application is not necessary. A Lollard sermon has it that "somme men wenon þat þes wordis weron ordenaunce of men to blisse, and these wordis [the *arcana verba*] schulde not be spoken for perel þat myȝte come þerof" (ed. Hudson 1983, 1:536). In the paradox, so familiar a notion as kinship's natural pity arouses the deepest visionary awe.

In the *Gospel of Nicodemus* the report of the Harrowing speaks of it as *mysteria* and *secreta* which the witnesses ask Jesus' special dispensation to report, *permitte nobis loqui mysteria* (permit us to speak of these mysteries); at the end of their report they say they are not permitted to tell "other mysteries of the Lord" (*cetera mysteria Domini*—18.1, 27.1). Following *Nicodemus*, the *Cursor mundi* reports that the sons of Simeon, after telling of the Harrowing, say "not dar we / Telle more of þat privitee / Seynt michaele forbode on vs leide" (ed. Mous 1986:40, lines 18453–55). An early sermon that treats the parley of the Four Daughters says the quarrel will be reconciled *in archano divini consilii,* "in the secret recess of divine counsel" (ed. Hunt 1982:298).

439 (B.18.396) rihtwysnesse and rihte: uses in this passage enable us nicely to distinguish Jesus' **ryhtwysnesse** (justice) from his **rihte** (power, privilege, possession); both virtues have dominion over the unredeemed in hell. See 168n above.

440 (B.18.397) mercy al mankynde: The sense is probably "mercy (shall reign over) all mankind," or possibly, as Pearsall suggests, "(my righteousness and right shall) impose a fine on all mankind" (2003:19, n3)—but "mercy" seems to parallel "righteousness" here.

441 (B.18.398) vnkynde kyng . . . kyn (B kynde): Schm reads **kyn** in B also, from manuscripts R and F. For play on these terms see Galloway 1994:373—a king should generally be gentle in its etymological sense (and see 417–44n above). A fine lyric from the mid-fourteenth century, "A Ihesu, þi swetnes," expresses many of the themes of this passus, and dwells on Jesus' setting aside his "noblelay" and assumption of our "wrecched kynde," and says that "If I for kyndnes suld luf my kyn" then surely I should love God (ed. Brown 1939:61–65, no. 48, lines 52–53, 17–20; quoted above in C.1.77–78n).

442a (B.18.399a) *Non intres*: "Enter not into judgment with thy servant: [for in thy sight no man living shall be justified]," the last quotation in this passage of the penitential Psalms (Ps. 142:2) from the *Dirige* (see 420an), also quoted in the Sarum burial service; the verse is also spoken toward the end of the Canon of the Mass in the Sarum rite (ed. Collins 1960:153, 97). See 438an above. It is as if Jesus' speech were a commentary on these texts—the very tools that Will labors with (5.45–46).

443–44 (B.18.400–401) by lawe . . . þat y louye and leued: Jesus concludes his foretelling of the Last Judgment (see 413–42n above), and returns now to the action of the Harrowing. The **lawe** is love: cp. the succinct statement of Wit, "he les his lyf for lawe sholde loue wexe" (C.10.196). The B archetype in line 401 may have read *me louede* for (manuscripts R and F) *I louede* (KD-B [I] lou[e]). The former reading would accord with Thomas Aquinas's requirements for the salvation of the patriarchs in limbo: love and faith in the Trinity (see Izydorczyk 1985:24; Turner 1966:175–90; 141n above). If C's **y louye** is L's revision and not scribal variance, it is theologically striking, and reinforces C's increased emphasis on grace rather than merit (see 303–40n, 414n, and B.18.392n above).

445–46 (B.18.402–3) for þe lesynge . . . bittere: ironically echoing Satan's rebuke of Lucifer, 345 (B.18.311) above. The devil must suffer righteousness without mercy (439 [B.18.396]); the economic terms of the Redemption as reciprocal justice (cp. 430 [B.18.388]) still apply in hell. Lucifer, the first sinner (1.107 [B.1.111]), and in PP specifically the seducer in Eden (313 [B.18.287]), enjoys Jesus' chief punishment, rather than Satan.

   bonde hym with chaynes: see 278 and C.1.121 . Jesus completes the Harrowing in the traditional way (Apoc. 20:2) with ease and speed. Devils, principles of evil, like personifications cannot be killed, only restrained.

447 (B.18.404) Astarot: a name derived from Judges 2:13, etc., a false god. See 281–94n.

448 (B.18.405) loke . . . the leste of hem alle: See 425n above. The sense presumably is that not even the least of the devils dared look at him; cp. "fendekynes" 415 (B.18.373) above. Schm (ed. 1995): "the *minor* devils would have *less* to fear."

449 (B.18.406) leue which hym likede: Not all the condemned from before the age of grace are yet, if ever, redeemed. See 414n, 420–42n, and 436n above. Neither the devils nor, terrifyingly, we ourselves know whom Jesus saves.

The Daughters reconciled

450–67 (B.18.407–24) Many hundret of Angels . . . thes damoyseles caroled: Precedent for the unusual return of the Daughters of God *after* the account of the redemptive events may be found in Guillaume de Deguileville's *Pèlerinage Jhesucrist*, in which the Daughters' music-making (responding to the Ascension; see next note) is likewise accompanied by angelic hosts, and the sound wakes the dreamer (ed. Stürzinger 1897, lines 10493–594; see Burrow 1993:118).

450a (B.18.407a) Culpat Caro: from the hymn *Æterne Rex altissime*, sung at vespers on the vigil of Ascension Day (Brev. I.dcccclviii), "The flesh sins, the flesh purges [of sin], the flesh of God reigns as God." Skeat, followed by Donaldson (1990), misconstrues the grammar and translates "the flesh reigns as God of God." In the preceding verses of this hymn, angels tremble at Jesus' ascension to the throne of God *Versa vice mortalium*, "with a reversal of the normal order of mortal things," namely the reigning of the flesh of God as God; the phrase suggests the scheme of contraries and inversions in this passus, which are resolved when God assumes flesh. L promotes, as it were, this hymn from later in the liturgical calendar, anticipating the Resurrection Christ seen in the next passus, to recognize the triumphant moment, and to continue the rhetorical *regressiones* characteristic of this passus (see Headnote): as a tree redeemed a tree, so flesh redeems flesh (see 388n). But the nice balance here generates an explanatory and unifying third term: the flesh that redeems is incarnate divinity, our flesh and blood.

451 (B.18.408) piped pees of poesie a note: Pees is naturally the state of things after the reconciliation of the Four Daughters. In most other versions of their story, when the sisters begin to argue Peace leaves the country. Pees was earlier described as "pleiynge" and dressed in the "gay garnements" (of Patience): 171, 178 (B.18.168, 175). She is the happy sister; the "merthe" (130 [B.18.127]) that she and Mercy foretell may be contrasted with the devils' buffoonery (see 171n).

The **poesie** (probably "classical, quantitative verse"; a poet for L is a sage of antiquity—see 11.118n) Pees pipes is one of the elegiac distichs collected in the *Liber parabolorum* attributed to Alain de Lille (PL 210.581–82; cp. C.9.265a), which is included in the widely used syllabus of elementary Latin readings called *Auctores octo* (Alford, *Quot.* 25–27). "Phoebus [the sun] is usually brighter after the greatest clouds, and love is brighter after enmities." For a translation by Lydgate see Whiting 1968:S797 (Pees's paraphrase, 452–55 [B.18.409–12], is superior). Skeat refers to the parallel sentiments of Tobias 3:22.

The distich differs in an important way from the earlier string of contraries adduced by the same Pees to prove that one cannot know a thing unless one knows its opposite (210–38 [B.18.205–39]). Whereas the former series presents timeless oppositions, the key word here is *post*: clarity comes *after* the dark, as salvation occurs in history—this is "wo *into* wele" (12.207–9).

In Repentance's account of salvation, which this and the next passus recall in several ways (see e.g. 364n and 419, 436n above, 21.200–12n below), the "seyntes" sing (see 366–67 [B.18.323–24] above), and "hope" blows a horn (7.151–54 [B.5.506–9]). As the sun at Jesus' death withdrew its rays (60 [B.18.60] above), now in simile, and a few lines later in fact, it returns: we have come to the dawn of Easter Sunday.

458 (B.18.415) pees thorw pacience: Peace's clothing is Patience (171 [B.18.168] above); the virtue is irresistibly associated with love as we begin to return to

the apparently unredeemed activity of the world. The personifications recapitulate history: peace through patience (< *patior*) is Jesus' love through the Passion (< *patior*), which has stopped the peril of damnation.

459–64 (B.18.416–21) 'Trewes,' quod treuthe . . . *osculate sunt*: a summation
marked by the common conclusion of a prayer, "for ever and ever," which
would elicit an automatic response, "Amen." See 3.433n. The *Te Deum* (see
465n below) includes the phrase *in seculum seculi*. Pees asks that her sisters
keep their former bickering private (see 206 [B.18.201] above)—they were
wrong to doubt. Perhaps because their quarrel and its resolution are too difficult for the **peple** to grasp with assurance, the summation refers merely to the
absolute power of God, and to the authority of the Psalm verse that generated
the Four Daughters, Ps. 84:11, here as usual not quoted until the end of the
Daughters' debate (see 115–467n).
     The grammar in 463–64 (B.18.420–21) is unusual, perhaps expressive in
its reciprocation of the mutuality of the personifications: "and reverently she
kissed her, / [that is,] Pees, and Pees [kissed] her, for ever and ever." The kiss,
from the Psalm verse, reflects as well the "kiss of peace" in the liturgy of the
Mass; as the common token of reconciliation see C.22/B.20.353 and the conclusion of Chaucer's Pardoner's end-link. Probably in imitation of PP, the
fifteenth-century play *The Castle of Perseverance* also concludes with the kiss
of the four daughters at its end. See next note.

465 (B.18.422) Treuth trompede: Pees "pipede" and "lutede loue"; that
Treuth trumpets continues the alliterative coupling, but her voice, presumably
pitched lower and louder, seems appropriate to her earlier grumbling (145
[B.18.142] above) and to her present rejoicing. Her great anthem of praise, the
hymn *Te Deum* (Brev. II.27–28), is sung at Matins on Sundays, but not in Lent
(Brev. I.ccccxciii; Hughes 1982:66, 365 n 44). Its return most forcefully at Easter
is striking. Trumpets traditionally are played in churches on Easter Sunday.
Medieval religious plays, including the Towneley and Chester plays of the Harrowing of Hell and *The Castle of Perseverance*, commonly concluded with the
singing of the *Te Deum* (Runnalls 1974:290)—it signals an action's consumma-
tion, as singing in itself may signal a happy resolution (as in Chaucer's *Parlement of Foules*). Medieval liturgists said that the Easter singing of the *Te Deum*
marked the moment when Jesus rose (Young 1933, 1:231, 573, 658).

466a (B.18.423a) *Ecce quam bonum*: "Behold how good and how pleasant it is
[*habitare fratres in unum*, for brethren to dwell together in unity]" (Ps. 132:1),
a common antiphon associated especially with the Last Supper (Alford,

Quot.:113; Vaughan 1980:136). Here we might imagine Love celebrating the unity of *sorores* rather than *fratres*; when L cites the same verse in A.11.191a he speaks of "breþeren & sustren." Love's **note** points forward to the dream of apostolic unity examined in the following two passūs, including the figure of the Church as "vnite" (see 21.328n and 17.128, **Alle kyne cristene cleuynge on o will**, i.e., *anima una*). Augustine associated *Ecce quam bonum* with the Pente-costal unity of the new Church as expressed in Acts 4:32, "And the multitude of believers had but one heart and one soul (*cor unum et anima una*)" (Gold-smith 1987:129). This must be the great hope for the polity of the Church; in light of the coming shattering of that unity the verse resounds with sad irony. The figure Love has just joined the sisters, or rather they have, in the allegory, become one in love, revealed as the enabling virtue of the Daughters of God. Pees had earlier called Love, the sender of the letters of mercy, her "lemman" (185 [B.18.182]; see 171–78n).

Will awake

467–75 (B.18.424–31) Til þe day dawed . . . hit shaddeweth: With the dawn (see 451n above) the pipe, trumpet, and lute of the dream merge into the bells of Easter Sunday. The bells are silent in churches from Maundy Thursday until the Gloria of the Easter vigil: Rupert, *De officiis*, ed. Haacke 1967, 5:29, lines 1489–1509; Tyrer 1932:71; St-Jacques 1977:131. See 22.59n below. With Will's waking we return from the celebration of the Harrowing to the **resureccion**, resuming the calendar sequence (see St-Jacques 1977). This auditory link between dream and waking experience underscores the link, enacted in Will's life, between Christian history and liturgical commemoration (see 6–112n, 15n above, and 18.178, not in B). The idea may derive from Guillaume de Deguile-ville—see 21.1–4n.

We learned of **kitte** in C.5.2; see note. "Kitte" is a type-name for a wife in 7.304; likewise **calote** is a type-name (Mustanoja 1970:72–74); in the fifteenth century it could mean "lewd woman," and by the sixteenth century a full type-name "Kit Calot" is recorded (OED s.v. *callet*; MED s.v. *callot*; see Prol.45n). In Hoccleve's 1415 poem attacking the Lollard leader Oldcastle he calls Lollard women who would dispute over holy writ "lewde calates" (ed. Seymour 1981:64, line 147; see Aston 1984:51 on "Lollard Woman Priests?"; Godden 1990:9–10). That these are type-names suggests inconclusively that they are merely fictional, and not names of L's family members. Less prestigious than a name like Eglantine, these names imply common status. In both places, at the opening of C.5 and here, the poem has just reached a kind of happy resolution—in the former, the king's decision to rule with Reason and Conscience as chief administrators. Tavormina notes that the passus concludes with several reunions: of God with humanity, of the four sisters, and of Will with his family (1995:201–2). In both places Will goes to church and behaves penitentially before a cross (5.105–7). And in both places the sad truth is, as Will again returns to the fair field of folk, that the apparent resolution of vexed issues turns out not to solve everything (see Emmerson 1993:113). In a forthcoming essay, Lawrence Warner argues that in fact the B Version of PP originally concluded at the end of this passus. Such a conclusion may well have seemed appropriate.

Will exhorts his nuclear family—introduced here in response to the themes of kinship in this passus, and in sharp contrast with his usual self-representation as a gyrovague loner (see 1–6n above)—to **reuerense godes resureccion** and **crepe to þe croes**, so they will not be like those who lose their joy "bote they reuerense his resurexioun and þe rode honoure" (267, similarly B.18.259). In contrast with the outset of the passus, Will is purposeful and active and for once an instructor, not a pupil. At least temporarily, having seen the form of redemption Will conforms himself to it (but cp. Vaughan 1991:78–83, arguing against the idea that Will here experiences "conversion"; see 22.201–13 and n). This familial gathering leads, as salvation history from Easter to Pentecost led, to the larger corporate enterprise of gathering the Church, the work of the next two passūs.

The family are to **crepe to þe croes on knees**, a ritual normally performed on Good Friday (*Dives and Pauper* I.4, ed. Barnum 1976:87–89; MED *creping* (a), *crepen* 2.(c); Maskell 1882, 3:391–92; Chambers 1903:17, 24). Some have proposed, with vague evidence, that such creeping also took place on Easter Sunday in the service of the Adoration of the Cross associated with its return from the "sepulchre" in which it had been placed on Good Friday (Vaughan 1980:146; Schmidt; St-Jacques 1977; Feasey 1897:114–28; Gasquet 1922:182; Duffy 1992:37). It is clear at least that the Adoration service involved much genuflection and kissing of the cross (Brev. I.dccvii, dcccix; Young 1910:905, 915; Wilkins 1737, 1:713; Harbert 1990:65–66).

In any case the cross has become a **relyk**, the memorial in present waking life of what Will has seen in his vision, our **bote** (see 9n above). Will's reverence for the cross dissociates him from a tenet of the Lollards, who avoided image-worship (Owst 1961:137–48; Aston 1988:96–159, esp. 107; see B.15.81n). One statement, issued under Archbishop William Courtney in 1389, alleges that Lollards hold "quod nulla crux est veneranda" (that no cross should be venerated—ed. Wilkins 1737, 3:208, and see 249, 255)—but some Lollards accepted veneration of a "poor cross" (Jones 1973:43). In 1400 William Sawtre

(Chartrys), abjuring his Lollardy, several times presumably under duress calls the cross a "precious relyke" (Wilkins 1737, 3:258), alluding to as he contravenes the Lollard doctrine that it was better to revere relics, at least true holy material, than the purely symbolic cross.

We have learned specifically how the cross **afereth the fende:** Jesus' death was hell's loss. But Will, here speaking as a pious Englishman, conceives of the cross's power as a talisman whose very shadow will here and now fend off evil spirits. A specific legend that the shadow of the cross wards off fiends has not been elsewhere identified, but the general power of the sign of the cross to rout devils is common opinion (Durandus 1568, 4.6.18; Morris 1871:95–96, 160, 169, 204–5; in the last of these passages the cross calls itself a "relyk choys," line 236; see likewise p. 140). In Acts 5:15, Peter's shadow may heal the sick. L may refer to the common notion that Jesus set up a cross of victory in hell at the Harrowing (MacCullogh 1930:167–69, 340–41). The speaker of *Meditation B* attributed to Richard Rolle uses the phrase; he wishes to follow the "shadow of þy cros" in his own life (ed. Ogilvie-Thomson 1988:81, line 474). The cross's virtue would be especially strong at dawn, when its lengthened shadow would appear and when ghosts, fearing daylight, stop walking the earth, as in *Hamlet.* The Easter morning hymn *Salva festa dies* has "expavitque chaos luminis ore premi" (And chaos/darkness fears to be overpowered by the face of light—St-Jacques 1977:135).

Goest is not used elsewhere in PP in the sense "evil spirit," nor is **grisly** used elsewhere in the poem; the phrase seems folksy (see MED s.v. *grisli*). This homely response to the vision measures human imagination against the unfathomable arcana of the Harrowing and Judgment.

C Passus 21; B Passus 19

Headnote

Because in Kane's Athlone edition the lineation and all substantive readings of the last two passūs are the same in B and C, the citation style adopted for these two passūs gives simply the line number.

Chambers proposed that, for whatever reason, the last two passūs of the poem are unrevised (1939:167; see also Russell 1969:48, RK-C, p. 82, 118–36). Donaldson had suggested emendations to Skeat's text that nearly equated the two passūs, and KD-B completed that work (Donaldson 1949: 234–44; KD-B 124–25). Skeat thought "the author has gone over them word by word" (2:xiv); Schmidt thinks C lightly revises B in the last two passūs (also Fowler 1977), and his lineation slightly differs from that of the Athlone edition. Countering Schmidt see RK-C 118–21. A few lines that look very much like authorial revision rather than scribal variance challenge the Athlone conclusion: see 21.243–53n and 22.37n, 128n, and 379n. But to distinguish author and scribe in detail is in fact impossible, and RK-C is at least fully rationalized. In his 1995 revised B-Text and parallel text editions Schm reverted to the Athlone editors' opinion of non-revision in at least two instances where his first B edition (1978) argued for revision: 21.298, 22.106.

In the rubrics of twenty-six manuscripts the last two passūs of PP constitute the "Vision of Dobest," and, like C.20/B.18, each passus contains a single vision, by one reckoning the seventh and eighth dreams (see C.20 Headnote). Yet the content of these two passūs in fact must seem not superlative (-best) but anticlimactic (see below) after the review of the life of Jesus and the description of the Redemption in the prior section rubricated "Dobet." Some have suggested that the rubrics can be read so as to begin "Dobest" proper at line 182 below (Coghill 1933:120–21, Chambers 1939:159), but the rubrics do not support this notion (Adams 1994:82–83).

R. W. Frank may be right when he argues that the grammatical degrees wel, bet, best in PP need not signal progressive grades of superiority in every case, but rather merely mark general instances of triadic division (1957:36–44). In this instance the marker Dobest may point to the third person of the Trinity, as Dobet had to the second (Frank 95–118). Yet to associate Dowel particularly with the first person of the Trinity strains interpretation; perhaps L came to the idea belatedly.

To divide the ages of history into a triad linked with the three persons was not novel (van der Pot 1951:46–51; e.g., Rupert of Deutz, PL 167:196), and in fact the Holy Spirit presides over much of the historical action of the last two passūs, especially the founding of the Church and the distribution of spiritual gifts, the "division of graces," among Christians (Pentecost), and the progress of the Church Militant. Since Mensendieck (1900:67) a number of scholars have explored the possibility that L was influenced by Joachim of Flora's conception, by no means a simple one, of the three ages of history, the third under the aegis of the Holy Spirit (Reeves 1969:16–27; see Wells 1938:349; Bloomfield 1961a:101, 207; Kerby-Fulton 1990:165). The idea of Joachimist influence has, however, been sharply criticized (Adams 1985b:200; Emmerson 1984:42, 46–47; riposte by Kerby-Fulton 1996:693–94; Clopper 1992). The effort to find precise correspondences of divisions of the poem to intellectual constructions, especially Joachimist ideas, will founder on L's resistance to system.

Since Wells's 1929 article, many readers have observed that the last two passūs in some ways recapitulate earlier segments of the poem, particularly the second vision, the half-acre scene (e.g. Coghill 1946:63–64; Kirk 1972:192–96; Martin 1979:122; Barney 1979:87–89, 99–100; Carruthers 1973:152–71, with further references; Lawlor 1962:175–76; Murtaugh 1978:59–60; with an elaborate chart, Bourquin 1978:303–9; Middleton 1997:269–70). Issues broached and explored in the first two visions of the poem are here viewed from the perspective of salvation history and of the history of the nascent Church.

The sequence of events from 182–334 echoes the sequence of the second vision: a move from penitence to pardon to a survey of society and division of labor in a new regime to plowing (with Piers as reeve), followed (367ff.) by backsliding, a turn toward spiritual sustenance, and finally (in the next passus) a new move toward penitence (see notes to 182–334, 194–98, 213–57, 227–28a, 229–51, 258–60, 335–480, 338, 361–71, 383–90, 396–408, 434–39). Within this sequence are specific reprises of the idea of Piers's pardon (182–98n, 182–90n), of the architecture of the Court of Truth (notes to 258–334, 317–34, 335–36), and the issue of a penitent's obligation to perform restitution (186–87n, 391–95n). L likewise recalls the second vision in a number of less sequential motifs in the final passus: the attack of hunger (notes to 22.1–51, 74–109, 183–200, 240–41), malicious agriculture (22.53–57n, cp. 21.338n), the return of vice after pardon (22.110–64n), ineffectual physicians (22.169–79n), generous admission to a building (22.242–45n), and the plea for grace (22.386n). But in the main the last vision broadly recalls the first one, especially the corrupt and venal world of Mede (see notes to 136–37, 156–64, 348–58). In the early part of the poem, after the preliminary statements of theme in the first two passūs, L displays the problems besetting humankind (Mede), and then a potential solution (the confessions, the Half Acre). At the end of the poem he displays the solution (the work of Christ, the institution of the Church), and then its dissolution.

Hanna (1993:12–13, 1996:233–34, 238), following Gwynn (1943), makes the likely proposal, on the basis of the dating of topical references, that L wrote the B-continuation (B.11–20) before returning to revise A into the earlier part of B (B.Prol.-10). This hypothesis can be corroborated by notice of a number of passages early in B that seem to have been inserted after and in light of materials here near the end of the poem. These tend to augment the broadly repetitive form of the poem, and to anticipate, sometimes prophetically, the final visions. For these see the following notes: 21.15–62, 182–334, 182–90, 309–16, 413–23, 428–48, 465–72 and 22.7–11, 52–53, 380–86. See also the important addition of C.7.120–57 (B.5.478–512), recollecting materials in B.18 (see notes at C.20.364, 419 and 436, 451). Further, a number of passages earlier in the C version reflect materials composed in the last two passūs of B: see notes to 21.186–87, 213–57, 219–26, 335–36, 355–56, 422–23, and 22.1–51 (the C.5 Apologia, references to "nede," and lines on finding, flattery, friars, and need at C.8.147–78), 74–109, 206–11 (several instances), 214–16, 235, 246, 313–15, 363–67.

The seventh dream (C21, B19) contains three movements bracketed by Will's very brief waking moments (1–4, 481). First is a continuation and recapitulation of the life of Jesus, divided into the vision of the resurrected Christ in Piers's arms (5–14) and Conscience's discussion of the names of Jesus (10–198), which contains the treatment of the names "Knight, King, Conqueror" (15–62) and the conqueror's Vita (63–198). The end of Conscience's speech begins the second movement, which recounts the founding of the Church (182–334). Within this part are accounts of the Petrine power (182–98), the coming of the Spirit (199–212), the division of graces (213–257), Piers's plowing and sowing, and the building of Holy Church (258–334). The third movement initiates the siege of the Church (335–480), with the attack of Pride (335–54), the defense of Conscience (355–390), and the reactions of a brewer, an unlearned vicar, a lord, and a king (391–480). Each of these divisions of the text is treated as a unit at the appropriate place in the notes that follow.

Passus 21/B.19 tells a more or less consecutive narrative, from the Resurrection through the founding of the Church, and apart from the Bible its structure derives mainly from earlier patterns set forth in the poem itself. Relatively little of it, as compared with Passus 20/B.18, derives from any other identifiable source. The siege of the Church depends on a tradition sketched in

335–54n below, perhaps especially on Huon de Meri's *Torneiment Anticrist*. The liturgy provides some material, but the passus is notable for its relative paucity of Latin, L's usual key to the liturgical and biblical subtexts. Apart from the repeated names of the cardinal virtues, Passus 21 presents a Latin phrase about every 17 lines; Passus 20, every 9 lines (and see Barr 1986). Like most of PP, nearly all the narrative motifs in Passus 21 appear to be original with Langland.

Passus 20/B.18 is organized as a series of antitheses and *regressiones* of plot, concept, and language, culminating in the synthesis of justice and mercy (see its Headnote). At first Passus 21/B.19 seems to be headed in the same direction: the work of Jesus that Conscience describes culminates in a pardon whose form is conditional, and the condition is expressed as a reciprocation, "pay what you owe," ***redde quod debes*** (see 186–97n below). The tit for tat of the divine order, the conflicts between the Daughters of God and between Jesus and the devils, now turn into a contract between God and humankind. It soon appears, of course, that the mutuality implicit in this contract is hugely imbalanced, and the covenant of merciful gift in return for perfected repentance develops into the one-sided series of grace's gifts. The passus focuses, then, on the idea of distribution, and a number of instances of divine giving (= grace) are represented as rhetorical distributions, divisions into enumerated parts of the crafts, of the Church's institutions, of the cardinal virtues. On these and other schemes of distribution in the passus see the notes to 1–4, 15–62, 83–95, 110–87, 182–334, 200–212, 213–17, 215, 229–51, 240–44, 258–334, 274–316, 317–34, 396–480. Humans are unable to accept grace, and the last distributive scheme of the passus (396–480; see n) begins another series of actions, marked by words for "take," and culminating in the sustained critique of wasting lords and grasping friars in the last passus. On the theme of taking see the notes to 396–408, 413–23, 428–48, 442, 459–64, 465–76, and C22/B.20.1–51, 7–11, 11–19, 20, 40–50 (a counter-example), 58, 90–92, 136–37, and the whole episode of the advent of the friars.

The plot of Passus 21/B.19 is the founding of the Church, the institution that mediates to humans what the pardon and grace have already conferred. We may take the keynote of Passus 20/B.18 as "The people that walked in darkness have seen a great light" (see 20.271n, 366–67n); the keynote of this passus then would be **thenne cam þer a kyng**, as the passus begins and ends with kings who define right and wrong kingship, and reverts insistently to such topics as royal titles, justice, communal responsibility, the governance of Conscience and Piers, and the limits of supreme power, both civil and ecclesiastic. As a vision of a polity the passus recalls the Mede episode, also featuring the figure Conscience and a king. But whereas the Mede episode responds to things as they are in L's time, the penultimate passus attempts to construct a polity *ab ovo*. The shift from the sublimely heroic narrative mode of the preceding passus to the baldly discursive mode of Conscience's speech comes as a shock. The effect is calculated: Conscience prepares us, by describing the well-doing king Christ, for the more narrative allegory of good governance in the founding of Unite, and then the pathetic dénouement, the sorry dissolution of unity as represented by the estates satire at the passus's end.

Will awake

1–4 Thus y waked . . . to offrynge: Will sets out, as usual in his waking state, but this time not to learn something, but rather to receive Communion, as Christians were especially required to do during the Easter season (see 383–90 and n below). Likewise, in the C text only, Will begins his second vision while he is in church (5.105–11, see note). Kerby-Fulton (1990:53) cites Lerner (1976b:118, 120) on the recurrent motif of a vision during Mass; e.g. Robert of Uzès had such a vision. In another article Lerner treats the widely known "Tripoli prophecy," an account of a vision seen by a Cistercian monk during Mass (1976a:12–17), and Rubin cites further instances, many used in defense of the orthodox doctrine of the Real Presence (1991:116–27). The poet of *Patience* similarly opens his poem with what he hears "at a hyʒe masse," line 9. The idea may ultimately derive from the story of the appearance of Christ to Gregory the Great as he celebrated Mass (see Bowers 1986:155–58), an appearance that, in turn, literalizes the Real Presence.

Will dresses himself **derely**, in his Sunday best, in contrast with the rougher clothing he had worn before, in "russet" and "wollewaerd" (C.10/B8.1, C.20/B18.1). As Robertson and Huppé note (1951:217), Will now wears a proper garment for the wedding feast (Matt.22:11).

Will **wrot what** he **hadde ydremed** in the preceding vision. Only here and at the end of this vision (line 481) does Will say he will write down his dreams (but see B.15.489 referred to below in this note)—perhaps thinking that only these two visions, the sixth and seventh, are worthy of report, the others being more quest than discovery. Will thus begins to fulfill Holy Church's injunction, "lere hit thus lewed men" (1.135 [B.1.136, A.1.125]) in writing as well as orally ("preche it in þin harpe"—A.1.137). By no means all medieval dream visions include assertions that the dreamer will write, but Chaucer and the French poets who influenced him made the topic common (Chaucer BD 1332, HF 1093, PF 678, LGW F579/G545). L seems here specifically to recall the end of the Guillaume de Deguileville's *Pilgrimage of the Life of*

Man (13502–4), where the dreamer wakes to hear the bell for Matins (see 20. 467–75n, 22.386n, and cp. Chaucer, BD 1322–24), thinks over his dream, and writes it down (ed. Stürzinger 1893:421–22; trans. Clasby 1992:185). Burrow collects resemblances between PP and Deguileville's poems (1993:17, 113–18, etc.)

L may allude to Apoc. 1:11, "What thou seest, write in a book," or Dan. 7:1. Emmerson remarks that generally prophets are called to speak, apocalyptic visionaries to write (1984:44). Will had represented himself as a copyist in A.8.43–44, and as a writer in B.12.16–28 (see n), chastised by Imaginatyf for meddling with makings, and by implication in C in a similar apologia where he claimed to be a clerk of the kind who "synge masses, or sitten and wryten" (5.63) and who "made of tho men" (5.5). Further, in B.15.489 Will asserts that priests "wol be wrooþ for I write þus"; elsewhere Leaute advises Will to berate sin in "retoryk" (12.36 [B.11.102]), but not specifically in writing. It appears that PP's "sporadic internal conceptualization of the poem as a written text" (Scase 1995:127) is usually motivated by the dreamer's awareness of adverse reaction or, as here, of his own quasi-prophetic stance. Will's making public of private experience parallels his turn from vagabond loner to churchgoer (again in parallel with the new C.5 proem).

Will falls asleep at the **offrynge**. The Offertory immediately follows the recital of the Creed (see 20.113–15n) and precedes the Canon of the Mass, when the bread and wine are consecrated, and when the events of the preceding passus—Crucifixion and Atonement—are symbolically reenacted. McGarry suggests that when Will says he will hear Mass **and be hoseled aftur** he means to take communion after the completion of the Mass proper, as was not uncommon (1936:39–40). The Eucharistic bread will be offered later in the passus (line 385). The bringing forward of the offerings (after the eleventh century, money—McGarry 1936:126) to the altar constitutes another of the many liturgical processions that take place on Easter morning, and triggers Will's vision, which begins with a kind of procession, as had the preceding vision, and is full of gifts—the gifts of the Magi, Jesus' enacting of the pardon, Grace's gifts to humankind, etc. (see Headnote). Weldon notes that the people's offering anticipates the later injunction, "pay what you owe" (1987:275; see 186–87n below). As at the beginning of Passus 20/B.18 (see 20.6–34n) the poem conflates the historical succession of events (there the Entry into Jerusalem, here the Resurrection) with its reenactment in the liturgy, but here the waking Will is actually in church. See also 5–14n below.

5–198 Y ful eftesones aslepe . . . withouten ende: The first part of the vision continues the Life of Jesus that began at 18.123, B.16.90 (see C.20 Headnote). Here the Life extends through the Resurrection appearances and the Ascension, and concludes with Christ's dwelling in heaven until the Second Coming and a forecasting of the Last Judgment. This account, mainly spoken by Conscience, includes the long disquisition on the names of Jesus (15–62—see note). L labels this segment at its end: "Thus Consience of Crist and of þe cros carpede" (199).

Jesus in Piers's arms

5–14 Y ful eftesones aslepe . . . conquerour of Cristene: For the last time Will sees Jesus. For him, as for all humans, the Ascension was the last time such vision was available. Will calls on Conscience to tell him whether the figure he sees is Jesus. Conscience appears here in the same instructional role at the outset of a passus that Faith/Abraham fills in the preceding passus, and that Holy Church and Imaginatyf fill earlier in the poem. He is to become the guiding figure for the remainder of the poem.

The figure Conscience first appears in C.Prol.95, B.2.139 (A.2.103) (see Prol.95–135n for discussion). General treatments include Schroeder 1970, Jenkins 1969 revised as Martin 1979:111–29, Whitworth 1972, Lawler 1995. Two interpretations help explain the figure's importance in PP, especially in these last passūs: Harwood's suggestion that Conscience "is suffering" among other things (1992:137), and Lawler's development of this, and the additional suggestion that Conscience may mean what the two morphemes compounded in his name can mean, "thorough (that is, not merely academic) knowledge" or even "perfect knowledge." His action in the last two passūs, as in the Mede episode, makes him as well an allegory of both individual and social/legal conscientiousness. Like Jesus (15–62n below) and Piers (258–60n below), Conscience has a number of offices: Liberum Arbitrium knows him well (C.16.159) and calls him God's "Clerk and his notarie" who refuses or consents (16.194, 201a [B.15.32, 39a]). In what may be among the last lines L wrote, he has Will speak of the function of Conscience: "For in my Consience y knowe what Crist wolde y wrouhte. / Preeyeres of a parfit man and penaunce discrete" (5.83–84). Conscience is the human knowledge of what humans should do in particular circumstances, and hence is the humble master of doing well and of the end of the poem, as he was the accuser of those doing ill in the first vision. See 22.72–74n.

Having just seen Jesus as light conquering the devil, Will is understandably uncertain about the identity of this bloody figure. But Jesus still bears the arms of Piers (20.21, B.18.22), and is recognizable as the **ioustare** of the Pas-

sion. The opening of this vision much resembles the opening of the last, with
Will questioning the identity of Jesus as warrior (see 20.8–12n, 16n).

That Jesus appears as a bloodied Piers, and as Christ clad in Piers's arms,
cannot yield to easy interpretation. A number of lines of understanding can
help approach this central mystery of the poem. First, as in 20.21–23 (see
notes), Piers's arms stand for human flesh, in which the godhead remains still
for a time incarnate in the post-Resurrection period. Again, the bloody person
of this vision must recall the blood of the Eucharist just now being created
from the Offertory wine, the blood of the Passion commemorated and reenacted. As Kirk observes, the host of the Mass is displayed for the first time
shortly after the Offertory (1972:184). The mysterious identity of Piers and
Jesus corresponds to the identity of human and God in the Incarnation and
the identity of wine and blood in the Eucharist.

Further, the bloodied Piers/Jesus recalls the suffering Pees with his
"panne blody," the victim of Wrong in the Meed episode, harmed "withouten
gult," who finally begs for mercy for the man who harmed him (4.45–98
[B.4.47–103, A.4.34–90]; see note). In this aspect Piers and Jesus represent suffering humanity, able to forgive (unlike Pees) without commutative repayment. Moreover, the terms of the identity of Piers and Jesus here, the **colours**
(red) and **cote armure**, are both heraldic, pointing to the chivalric Jesus of
Passus 20/B.18, and to the issue of Jesus' noble titles, enfances, and doughty
deeds treated below in Conscience's speech (see also 351n below). The red coat
of arms (the famous colors of suffering and heroic Parzival) also points (the
red is blood) to the suffering and nurturing Jesus who has fed with his "fresshe
blood our forfadres in helle" (7.133 [B.5.493]), as the wine still feeds Christians.

Further, the vision of Jesus here has him making a processional entry,
parallel to his Entry into Jerusalem at the outset of the preceding passus, and
reminiscent of a royal entry into a city. For the intricate connections between
Jesus' entries, royal ideologies, and the allegorical sieges of buildings in PP see
Mann 1994:200–205 and Kipling 1985, 1998:11–47 et passim. On the dominant
theme of kingship in this passus see the Headnote.

Repeated reference to the cross that Jesus carries (7, 14, 199) emphasizes
its significance as the "Resurrection cross," the slender cross, often bearing a
red-cross (St. George) banner, that is depicted in representations of the resurrected Jesus, and especially of the Ascension. Fowler (1961:147–53) treats the
links of this passus with the liturgy of Ascension Sunday. The figure here
recalls the Jesus of the *imago pietatis* scene, where he is often depicted as spat-
tered with blood and surrounded by the instruments of the Passion.

The blood-red Jesus of the post-Crucifixion period has a biblical basis in
Isa. 63:1–3 and Apoc. 19:13. The former includes questions like Will's, "Who is

this that cometh from Edom, with dyed garments. . . . Why then is thy apparel red, and thy garments like theirs that tread in the winepress?" On the common Christological interpretation of the Isaiah passage in Passion contexts see Bestul 1996:29, 31; for the connection with PP see Fowler 1961:148–50, St-Jacques 1967:149, Bourquin 1978:502–3, and Weldon 1989:58. Prsl notes that this passage was read on Wednesday of Holy Week (Sarum Missal, ed. Dickenson, 286); "he who comes from Edom" is also mentioned in the Palm Sunday hymn *En rex venit*, line 5 (Sarum *Processionale*, ed. Henderson 1882:50; see 20.6–34n).

The Apocalypse passage provides the Christian answer to Isaiah's question: "And he was clothed with a garment sprinkled with blood; and his name is called, THE WORD OF GOD"; and later, "And he hath on his garment, and on his thigh written: KING OF KINGS, AND LORD OF LORDS" (19:16). The Apocalypse figure, on horseback and with a sword proceeding from his mouth, may be called a jouster of the Word. His titles are written on him, as it were asking for Conscience's exposition (15–62n below). The episode concludes (19:19–21) with "the beast" and "the kings of the earth" making war on this swordsman, and with their defeat along with a "false prophet." The action provided a plot for the *Psychomachia*, and ultimately for the siege of Unite below. See 335–480n below.

Connecting the Isaiah imagery specifically to the Ascension, the *Golden Legend* in chapter 72, "De ascensione domini," says, "The Lord is said to have his garment, that is his body, red, that is dripping with blood, because he still had the scars on his body when he ascended" (ed. Graesse 1846:322). The Chester cycle refers thus to the bloody Jesus in its Ascension play: "Whye ys thy cloathinge nowe so reedd . . . like to pressars of wyne?" (ed. Lumiansky and Mills 1974, lines 121–24).

Bennett (1982:75–78) treats English versions of the Isaiah passage, and cites one that L may recall here, a poem by the Franciscan William Herebert (ob. 1333) that begins, "What ys he, þys lordling, that cometh vrom the vyht / With blod-rede wede . . . / . . . so douhti a knyht? / 'Ich hyt am, ich hyt am . . . / Chaunpyon to helen monkunde in vyht'" and goes on to speak of the must of the winepress (ed. Brown 1924:28, poem #25; see also Gray 1972:12–17); cp. 20.411–12n.

5 y ful eftesones aslepe: As Wittig wittily observes, "dream visions require dreams" (1997:179). No special significance attaches to Will's falling asleep here.

12 and knelede tho: On the repeated kneeling in this passus see 15–62n and 17n below. The congregation knelt at this point in the liturgy of the Mass: see 199–212n below.

13 conquerour of Cristene: On Christ as conqueror see 20.8–34n and the end of 20.8–12n, and Kroll 1932 passim.

Conscience expounds upon knight, king, conqueror

15–62 'Whi calle ȝe hym Crist' . . . **and that is Crist to mene**: The first part of Passus 21/B.19 continues the preceding passus's narrative treatment of the work of Jesus. Stirred by his vision of the bloodied jouster, Will poses a question, in the schoolish form of a *quaestio* (see 19n below), which Conscience graciously answers in a distributive scheme of the titles of Jesus. This distribution precedes others in Conscience's speech—the three gifts of the Magi, and another version of the Dowel triad (75–95 and 115–87)—that help him to organize his thought and to reflect on the meaning of Jesus in different modes. Simpson remarks, "To understand the names of Jesus Christ is to recount the whole life" (2001b:156). The discussion recalls other divisions of titles in PP: the names of Anima (16.182–201, B.15.22–39), and Will's consequent "bourdynge" about the "many names" of bishops (16.202–5, B.15.40–43). Compare also Scripture's observation of the God-man that "aftur his resureccoun *redemptor* was his name" (12.115; the words are Will's in B.11.207).

Conscience's analysis of Jesus' regal titles further extends to reflect on contemporary issues that emerge in the Prologue, in lines L probably added in revising A to B after completing the latter part of the B version (see Headnote). The issue is broached in the passage treating Peter's power to bind and unbind, and playing on the cardinal virtues and cardinals of the Church (Prol.128–37 [B.Prol.100–11]), subjects included in this passus (see 182–334n, 182–90, 413–23n below), and the passage treating the making and definition of a king (Prol.139–60 and esp. B.Prol.112–45). The former passage wonders that members of the papal curia "caught han such a name," a name of distinction like "cardinal." Picking up from this issue, the Prologue king-making passage, which surely alludes to the coronation of Richard II, scrutinizes the royal titles—*Sum Rex, sum Princeps*—and their relation to the appellated virtues of justice and mercy (*iustus, pius*), issues that inform the conceptions of Christ's kingship in Passūs 20 and 21 (B.18 and 19); see 83–95n below. We are to understand that Jesus perfectly exemplified these royal virtues; he is the mirror in which English kings should look, and the citizens of London carefully assimilated Richard II to Christ in their innovative civic pageants (see Kipling 1985, 1998:17–25 et passim). On the king as a figure of Christ, and vice versa, and on Christ and king as images of justice and equity, see Kantorowicz 1957:142–43, 156–57.

In B.Prol. the matter of a king's right name is pointed by the Goliardeis, who derives the name *rex* from "going straight" (*regere*) and warns about the possibility of bearing the name without the substance (*nomen . . . sine re*: B.Prol.141–42; see B.Prol.139–45n). What one calls the king matters: the royal titles honor the king and enunciate the scope of his power. Fourteenth-century documents are careful to address the king with comprehensive assertion of his titles. The triad knight, king, conqueror may also recall the formula that begins the *Laudes regiæ* liturgy: "Christus vincit, Christus regnat, Christus imperat (Christ conquers, reigns, has imperium)." English kings regularly subsidized the singing of this litany, and the formula appeared on English coinage. Although it may not actually have been sung then, the litany, called *Christus vincit*, was included in the coronation orders for Edward II and Richard II (Kantorowicz 1946:1, 3, 54, 172, 174–75).

Will's question refers explicitly (17–18, **alle kyn creatures sholde knelen . . . as men nemned þe name of god iesu**) to the text from which L quotes at 80a (see n), a Palm Sunday lection: "For which cause God also hath exalted him, and hath given him a name which is above all names: That in the name of Jesus every knee should bow, of those that are in heaven, on earth, and under the earth" (Philip. 2:9–10; see 20.21n above). The three regions correspond to the three titles knight (of heaven), king (of earth), and conqueror (of hell). This text and Acts 4:12 (quoted together by Chaucer's Parson, lines 597–98) were the basis of devotion to the name of Jesus Christ; see 19n, 137n below. The second Council of Lyon in 1274 adopted a constitution of Pope Gregory X "which encouraged kneeling and bowing of the head at the mention of the name, especially during Mass" (Renevy 1999:103). References to the titles of Jesus include Acts 2:36, "that God hath made both Lord and Christ, this same Jesus, whom you have crucified," and Isaiah 9:6, "and his name shall be called, Wonderful, Counsellor, God the Mighty, the Father of the world to come, the Prince of Peace." At Compline in Pentecost some fifty names of Jesus are listed (Brev. 2:236–37); Isidore lists more than fifty (*Etym.* 7.2, ed. Lindsay 1911:262–68).

L's point is not to define Jesus by these titles, but rather to define these offices by their ideal in Jesus. Hence this passage describes the doing-well of the first estate, and Conscience naturally describes Jesus' career in terms of the three do's (110–87 and n). Knights, kings, and conquerors should suffer; should act in accord with reason, justice, and mercy; should sue for grace; and should pardon offenders (see 63–68, 83–95, 120–21, and 182–98 and notes below, and 20.8–12n, last paragraph).

Skt and Prsl take line 62, **He may be wel called conquerour and that is Crist to mene**, as evidence that L thought "Christ" meant "conqueror," and conclude that this misconception underpins Conscience's argument. Bloomfield cites Nicholas of Lyra to the effect that "Christ" means "anointed" and hence "king and pontifex" (1961a:218, n7). Pelikan notes other instances of the same idea (1978:144), and Schm argues that L "merely associated" notions of anointing, kingship, and hence conqueror as the superlative degree of knight. The latter interpretation seems better; surely knowledge that 'Christ' means "anointed one," messiah (a kingly title), was rudimentary. On unction as the sign of kingship and imperium see Kantorowicz 1957:53.

The Gloss on Matt.1:1 and Mark 1:1 (citing Jerome) puts it succinctly: "Jhesus hebraice . sother græce . saluator latine. Christus grece . messias hebraice . vnctus latine" ("Jesus" in Hebrew, "savior" in Greek, "savior" in Latin; "Christus" in Greek, "messiah" in Hebrew, "anointed" in Latin) and "Christus nomen officii est; non naturae. quia unctus est in sacerdotem" ("'Christ' is a name of his office, not of his nature, for he was anointed into the priesthood"). The information is repeated, citing Isidore, in Trevisa's translation of Bartholomaeus, which adds that "he is ihiȝt [Messias] with priuylege of alle dignyte of prophecie, of presthode, and kynghode and realte; *Messias* is iseid 'anoynte'" (ed. Seymour 1975:56, Bk. 1, cap. 21). Wyclif observed that *Jesus* is a proper name meaning *Salvator*, and *Christus* an appellative name meaning *unctus* (*Sermons*, II, serm. 23, ed. Loserth 1888); similarly Isidore spoke of *Christus* (= *unctus*) as a common noun, and Jesus (= *salvator*) as proper (*Etym.* 7.2.2–9, ed. Lindsay 1911:263), and he says explicitly "'Christ' signifies a king" (7.2.8). Walter Hilton translates the name "Jesus" as "heler or hele" (Renevy 1999:120).

The sense of line 62 would be, "He may well be called 'conqueror'; indeed, this is the force of the term 'Christ,' the anointed king." Will's question, then, turns on the distinction of the terms "Christ" and "Jesus," as he says in line 15, and not on a misunderstanding on L's part of the word "Christ." Conscience takes up this question explicitly in lines 69–70 below.

Bloomfield (1961a:217, n 73) lists studies of the notion of Christ as king, an idea often repeated in the preceding passus (Harwood 1992:121). Kean (1969:96–108) treats Conscience's discussion here especially as filling out the idea of a just king introduced earlier by the figure Thought (10.100–106 [B.8.100–110, A.9.90–100]). L opposes the king at the end of this passus, a study in the unkingly, to Christ the king (see 465–76n).

16 Patriarkes & prophetes: L has Paul in mind (see preceding n) but knows that Paul alludes to the prophet Isaiah, "For every knee shall be bowed to me, and every tongue shall swear" (45:24). Hence the locution in 80 below, "was þat word fulfuld."

17 knelen and bowen: as in Philip. 2:10 and 80a below; see 15–62n above, and C.1.78n. On the repeated act of kneeling in this passus see Weldon 1989, 71–95n and 200–12n below.

19 *Ergo* is no name to þe name of iesus: because "Jesus" is specified in Philip. 2:10. See 15–62n above, 137n below. Will's *Ergo* signals that he is in the disputatious mood for which he is often chastised (see 20.388n); Conscience's reply begins with a quiet rebuke—"if you knew how to reason" (26), but on the whole exhibits the patience and courtesy that mark him. Schm finds here the influence of Richard Rolle on the name of the Lord as an object of devotion. For a prolonged example see the *Meditations on the Life and Passion of Christ*, lines 1035–1128 (ed. d'Evelyn 1921; see also Simpson 2001b). The phrase "hallowed be thy name" in the Lord's Prayer encouraged such devotion, as did Mark 16:17, Acts 4:12 and 16:18, and John 16:23, quoted with variation in 7.260 and 15.244, B.14.46, "Whatever you shall seek from the Father in my name shall be given to you."

The liturgical Feast of the Name of Jesus on August 7 was not formally established in England until 1488–89, but by the mid-fourteenth century the devotional cult of the Name had become partly liturgical; the Mass was devised as early as 1388 (Pfaff 1970:62–68, 77; Biasiotto 1943 passim; and Woolf 1968:172–79 on the Name in English poetry, Renevy 1996 in Anglo-Norman poetry). The Sarum liturgy for the feast is printed in Dickenson 1861–63, col. 846–47.

21 deueles aren drad: As the cross "afereth" the devil (20.475, B.18.431), so does Jesus' name, because "In my name they shall cast out devils" (Mark 16:17, quoted in B.13.249a). An Anglo-Norman poem "Le nun [name] Jhesu" speaks of the prophylactic power of Jesus' name (ed. Jeffrey and Levy 1990:174–80).

22 saued by þat name: because "Jesus" means "savior" (15–62n above), as is clear from Matt. 1:21, ". . . and thou shalt call his name Jesus. For he shall save his people from their sins." See 15–62n above.

27 knyht, kyng, conquerour: see A.11.219 and n (cp. B.10.336) where a puzzled Will asks whether "kinghed, & kniȝthed, & caiseris wiþ erlis" are Dowel, Dobet, and Dobest; Christ's kingship makes Will's question finally valid, as Christ's life is expounded in terms of the three Do's (110–87 below). See also 20.413n, and 13n above.

32–41 To make lordes of laddes . . . kyng of iewes: In language reminiscent of Faith's harangue (20.95–112, B.18.92–109; see notes), Conscience associates

Jesus' work with a conqueror's right to elevate servants to lordships and to enslave free men. (Will inveighed against such translations in C.5.70–80, but Jesus works in a different key.) The elevation would illustrate "hendenesse," and the enslaving "hardinesse." L insists that the definition of a conqueror includes not merely might, but generosity, the justice and mercy of Passus 20, and the two virtues continue to be linked through the following passage. A conquest legally overthrew all property rights of the conquered nation—as Lucifer lost his alleged rights in C.20/B.18. Lady Meed, of course, had argued that a conqueror should divide the conquest among his followers (3.242–68 [B.3.201–14]; cp. 3.31). Simpson cites instances of English kings in fact distributing lands and titles to their lieutenants, and reducing Jews to serfdom (1985:473–74; and see Baker 2000:57–60 on contemporary hopes for the conquest of France—though of course the Plantagenets claimed France not by conquest but by inherited right). Conscience's concept—redemption and faith as freedom (see 59 below)—is Pauline; L may be influenced by the persistent representation of sin as thraldom in *The Castle of Love* (see, e.g., 20.21n above). See 12.113n. These powers of a conqueror might recall the deeds of William of Normandy, already given the epithet "Conquerour" (see MED *conquerour* 1.(b)). Other alliterative poems turned to topics of world conquest and the conquering deeds of the Nine Worthies, notably the *Parliament of the Three Ages* and the *Morte Arthure*.

On Christians as free and **Ientel men** see 20.21n and 1.73. In baptism a Christian was manumitted from slavery to sin. On the accusation that Jews have become base in their denial of Christ see 20.106–10n. But observe that the Jewish leaders, the **gentel men** of line 34, were enthralled, whereas the Jews who accepted the Baptist's counsel became free **and Ientel men with iesu** (line 40). The antagonism shown here (and throughout PP) toward Jews is strictly theological (a matter of choice), and not racial (a matter of birth). **Tykes** means "churls," but may derive from a Welsh word meaning "bondman" (OED) rather than from the Norse word that lies behind modern "tyke" meaning "dog" (MED)—see Breeze 1993. L knew French and would know that **frankeleynes** etymologically means **fre men**, and here he pointedly defines English social classes in terms of Christian concepts of liberation (from sin).

42–43 Hit bicometh to a kyng to kepe . . . and his large: Conscience begins to assimilate the functions of king (toward his people) and conqueror (toward the conquered). With similar diction L speaks elsewhere of a king's duty to defend and to distribute largesse: see 442–48n below and 20:8–12n.

44–52 And so dede iesus . . . raueschede helle: The first of a series of summaries of the life of Jesus (and compare 18.123–77 [B.16.90–166]), here the teaching, healing, exorcism, Passion, Resurrection, and Harrowing. Conscience is about to distinguish in detail Jesus' given name from his title as conqueror. Here he is called **iesus** during his ministry, **kyng** with crown of thorns at the Passion (Matt. 27:29, etc.), and **conquerour noble** as redeemer on the cross and harrower of hell. The passage, like the whole of Conscience's speech, renders in expository discourse what the preceding passus realized dramatically. L may pun in **gentel profete** on "noble" and "gentile"—two senses of the same word. As **gentel** Jesus may be thought of as a "knyht," the first item in Conscience's triad (line 27 above).

51 deth hym fordo ne adown brynge: see 20.28–34n.

53 conquerour cald of quyke and of dede: One of the proof-texts of the Harrowing, 1 Peter 4:6, is immediately preceded by reference to Christ "who is ready to judge the living and the dead," a formula that lies behind a clause of the Creed.

57 And bonde hym: as in 20.446, B.18.403.

58 Ho was hardior: A conqueror must be hardy: line 31 above. For further definition see 96–107 below.

61 Places: "allotted spaces" (so MED *place* 4.(a)) or more pregnantly, "manor houses, mansions" (Alford, *Gloss.*, MED 6.(a); see C.5.159 and 22.1–4n), alluding to Jesus' words, "In my Father's house there are many mansions (*mansiones*)" (John 14.2), and to his bringing to heaven his "lele leges" in the Harrowing. Of courses national kings as well as international conquerors could, under certain conditions, set bondmen free or assign manors to their subjects, but these powers were more liberally acquired by conquest, e.g. the Norman Conquest.

62 Crist to mene: see 15–62n above.

The conqueror's vita

63–198 Ac the cause that he cometh . . . in wo withouten ende: Conscience continues his response to Will's question by weaving together a continuation of the Vita Christi to its conclusion at **domesday** (196), further discussion of the names of Jesus and the terms king and conqueror, an allegorization of the gifts of the Magi (71–95), and another schema of the triad dowel, dobet, dobest (110–87). Much of the speech reiterates the point that the God-man was both conqueror and suffering servant, somehow combining **godhede and manhede** (158).

63–68 Ac the cause . . . wilnen and soffren: Conscience explains why **he cometh thus with cros** with reference to Will's vision of the jouster with his cross (line 7). The explanation passes beyond Will's idea of the cross and the name of Jesus as talismans (20.474–75, 21.21 and n): the cross teaches us to avoid sin and to accept suffering **in this world** with patient poverty if we would have joy. We, too, must be conquerors and kings, fighting and defending, putting on the armor of God (Ephesians 6:11–17). The cross's power is moral, not magical. Fittingly, Conscience's explanation of the Atonement is like that of Abelard, as quoted in 20.400–12n; the moral faculty of conscience grasps the Crucifixion as first of all a moral instruction. The thinking parallels that of Resoun earlier, that God suffered "in ensaumple þat we sholde soffren alle" (13.199; cp. B.11.380–86, less specific).

69–198 Ac to carpe more of Crist . . . iesus . . . withouten ende: Conscience develops the distinction of the Son's two names (see 44–52n). As "Christ" is an appellative epithet or title and Jesus a given proper name (see 15–62n above), implicitly the name "Christ," as the title of king and conqueror, is earned by deeds rather than given at birth. Hence Jesus is **noþer kyng ne conquerour**, and hence not yet "Christ," until he grows up in human fashion, **in þe manere of a man** (97–98), but in his adult works there is **no man so worthy / To be Cayser or kyng** (137–38).

Confusingly, at line 117 Conscience seems to speak of **iesu** as a more advanced name than **Crist**, but with no special reference to "Jesus" as "salvator." See 117n for proposed solutions to this anomaly. It may simply be that here Conscience focuses on the **grace** (116) of God's becoming a human child, *filius Marie* (118) with a human given name, rather than on the earned quality of the title "Christ." Further, line 133 links the name **iesus** with the davidic, kingly line. In his analysis of Jesus' works as doing wel, bet, best (see 110–87n below) Conscience does not associate the grades of doing with the two names.

70 furste: in time, not in the order of names as praenomen and agnomen, as the context shows.

71–95 Tho he was bore . . . knelyng to iesu: With his account of the Magi Conscience offers the usual kind of allegorization of the three gifts, but his emphasis is rather on the worship of Jesus—that angels and kings **reuerensed hym riht fayre** (73)—as an acknowledgement of his incarnate divinity and coming kingship. Hence repeatedly they are described as **knelyng to iesu** (95, 91, and 74, 75, 81); see 17n above, 80n below. They acknowledge Jesus as sovereign of sand, sun, and sea (synecdochic for "the world" also at 13.135 [B.11.327]); compare Book's assertion that all the elements bore witness at his birth that Jesus was God, and that the heavenly beings kindled the comet to "reuerensen" his birth (20.246–49 [B.18.237–40]).

Kipling amply documents the interconnections of the gifts of the Magi, the ostentatious exchanges of gifts at royal progresses, and the idea of a king's entry as Augustan triumph and Christ-like advent and epiphany (1998:115–20, 130–34); see 83–95n below.

71 as þe boek telleth: the common formula appears word for word six other times in C. It occurs especially often in the alliterative romances, and may be among the chivalric touches in this Vita: see 108–23n below, 20.81n, and Duggan 1976:270–71. Here there may be specific reference to the speech of Book on the witnesses at the Nativity; see 71–95n above and 20.246n. Compare also "As holy writ telleth," line 109 below.

74a *Gloria in excelsis deo*: see B.3.328n.

79 by consail of Angelis: in Matt. 2:12 the Magi are warned "in sleep" to go directly home, and an angel appears to Joseph "in sleep" in the next verse.

80a *Omnia celestia . . . nomine iesu*: "All things heavenly and earthly bow down at this name of Jesus," Philip. 2:10 varied, perhaps influenced by the wording of the hymn *Æterne Rex altissimi*, also quoted at 20.450a, B.18.407a above (see note and Alford, *Quot.*:113): "Ut trina rerum machina / Cælestium, terrestrium, / Et infernorum condita / Flectant genu jam subdita." The *Myrour of Lewed Men* reads, "This name of Ihesus has so gret in him vertu and myȝt / That all in heuen, erth, and helle suld til him loute with riȝt" (ed. Sajavaara 1967:773–74). See 15–62n above.

83–95 Resoun and rihtwisnesse and reuthe thei offrede . . . knelyng to iesu: The three gifts correspond to frankincense, gold, and myrrh; righteousness is also called **lewetee** and ruth is called **pyte** and **mercy** and is associated with **mylde speche of tonge**. Of the many interpretations of the three gifts offered by medieval exegetes, none precisely corresponding to L's triad, another distribution (see Headnote), has been identified. The three qualities correspond to three of the Four Daughters of God who witnessed the Harrowing (see 20.115–270n above), respectively Truth, Justice, and Mercy (and omitting, perhaps ominously, Peace, the daughter who traditionally fled when the others quarreled). **Rihtwisnesse** is the common Middle English translation of *justitia*. Insofar as **resoun** corresponds to the virtue Truth (see, e.g., C.4.151), **rihtwisnesse** is properly **resones felawe**, because Truth and Justice pair off against Mercy and Peace among the Four Daughters.

As Schm and Prsl observe, these are virtues appropriate to a king and conqueror, and appropriately they are offered by kings. In fact, Richard II was formally asked, at his coronation, whether he would do justice (*iusticia*) in mercy and truth (*in misericordia et ueritate*—quoted Donaldson 1949:117). These three virtues, especially mercy, form the main theme of Psalm 88, chosen, surely with great deliberation, to be sung at Richard II's coronation (Saul 1997:25).

L seems to allude to contemporary concerns. William Thorne, in his chronicle of St. Augustine's Abbey at Canterbury, noting that Richard II was born on Epiphany day (6 January) in 1367, says that three kings, whom he calls Magi—namely the kings of Spain, Navarre, and Portugal—attended Richard's baptism (ed. Davis 1934:591). (Correcting the record, Saul and Barber report that among Richard's godparents were two aspirant kings, Jaime IV of Majorca and Richard of Armenia, and that the deposed Pedro of Castile may also have been present—1997:12, n14; 1978:193.) Thorne may recollect a similar legend told of St. Francis (Loomis 1948:16). The triad also resembles the three things that Conscience says the "comune" demands of a king: "lawe, loue and lewete" (3.378–79, not in A or B; see Kean 1964 on these royal virtues). Bloomfield argues that "Christ the King is the theme of the last three passūs" (1961a:129; see 15–62n above), and observes that "usually the gold represents royalty; the frankincense, godhead; and the myrrh, death" (p. 218, n 9).

85 *Magi* hem calde: Matthew calls them Magi (2:1); that they were three (doubtless from their three gifts) and kings are traditional accretions.

86, 88 ykyvered vnder, vnder: MED and OED do not notice L's use of **vnder** to mean "symbolized by"; cp. "bred yblessed and godes body þervnder," line 385 below and MED *under* prep. 4b.(b); OED *under* prep. III.c.

90 For it shal turne tresoun: so reads manuscript F of B. The archetype of B and C appears to read *And resoun to riche golde*–contradicting, as Skeat observed, line 86 and 88. Prsl and Schm independently divined the probable original, *And resoun to richel(e)s*, a reading accepted by Donaldson in his trans-

lation (1990) and in a personal communication of 1 Feb. 1980. More logical
would be "And richels to resoun," paralleling line 89 and smoother with the
b-verse of line 90. The (uncommon) word *rechels* ("incense," MED *rekels*)
occurs as a variant in line 76 in manuscript R of C. For counterargument see
KD-B p. 161 (different arguments in the first, 1975, and revised, 1988 ed.) and
RK-C p. 134. The latter argue that "Emending *riche golde* to *richels* unaccept-
ably differentiates *riht* and *treuthe* (90) from *lewetee* (89)." But **treuthe** at least
seems as close to **resoun** as to **lewetee** (see 83–95n above). Schm thinks the
phrase **to riht and to treuthe** refers to **lewetee** of 89 and *resoun* of archetypal
90a; because this construction requires ellipsis of something like "these offerings are likened," it seems syntactically improbable.

96–107 Ac for all this preciouse . . . þat he fore bledde: The emphasis is on
coming to be conqueror rather than the achieved state: **til he comsed wexe** in
deeds like a conqueror he was not one, and did not yet, even though kings
knelt to him, deserve the title king or Christ. Jesus' wiles and wit are most
evident in his repeated outsmarting of the "scribes and Pharisees," e.g. Matt.
9:3–6, 9:11–17, 12:1–13, 12:24–29, 12:38–40, 15:1–9, 16:1–4, 19:3–9, 21:23–27, 22:15–
22, 22:23–32, 22:34–46. This is the "lechecraeft" that Jesus learned from Liberum Arbitrium (18.137) or Piers (B.16.103–4). The guile with which Jesus
defeated the devil (20.327, etc.) culminates his strategy as a conqueror, as nar-
rated in C.20/B.18. He conquers by suffering and hiding: *patientes vincunt*.

Thomas Hill aptly finds in this passage allusion to the wily strategy of
David, especially in his younger guerilla warfare, and supports his argument
by citing an elaborate comparison, by Rupert of Deutz, of David's persecutions
with Jesus' (1976). L makes the association explicit in 132–39 below.

105 Lyf and lyme as hym luste he wrouhte: The Athlone editors and Prsl conclude line 104 with a semicolon (a period in KD-B) and punctuate this line to
make **lyf and lyme** the object of **wrouhte**. Prsl glosses **wrouhte** as "made
whole," a sense unattested elsewhere according to the editors of MED (personal communication, Nov. 1998). Probably it means "he brought life (e.g.,
Lazarus's) and limb (e.g., of those whom he miraculously healed) to the condition that pleased him," not far from MED *werken* v.(1), sense 4a.(d). Hence
line 105 glosses "graunted hele" of 104. With a comma ending line 104 and a
dash after **lyme**, Schm punctuates as if to make **lyf and lyme** appositive with
"hele" in 104. The line possibly means "With respect to life and limb he did as
he pleased," or with Schmidt's punctuation, "Whether life or limb—he did
as he pleased." Taking **he wrouhte** as rather beginning a new sentence would

make good sense but seems metrically unlikely unless we have to do with scribal mislineation and subsequent smoothing (see manuscript N² of C).

107 Til he hadde all hem, that is, those he redeemed (at first, those in the Limbo of the Fathers) when he defeated the devil, as well as, more specifically, those he won over in the course of his valiant and suffering ministry.

108–23 In his iuuentee this iesus . . . þer comsede he do wel: Conscience continues to emphasize the development rather than the finished achievement of Jesus (see 69–198n, 96–107n above). Here he introduces Jesus' **iuuentee,** as it were his enfances; both this term and **fauntekyn** (118) may suggest the youth of a romance knight, a child "prince" (96) in the sense of "royal heir apparent." Below Conscience speaks of Jesus as like David "douhtiest of dedes" in his time (134). See 71n above on chivalric motifs in this Vita.
   L selects a **iewene feste,** the miracle of the marriage at Cana (John 2:1–11), as the first sign of Jesus' future status as conqueror, and the most active, most obviously "doing," of the four Gospel epiphanies—manifestations of Jesus as divine: the others are the Nativity recognition of the Magi, Jesus' baptism, and the Nativity recognition of the shepherds. At Cana *bigan* **god of his grace to do wel** (110 and 116, and see 123). (The reference of **as y before tolde,** line 115, is to line 110 just above; the miracle of Cana does not appear earlier in PP.) Conscience interprets the miracle according to the idea implicit in Mark 2:22 et synop., "no man putteth new wine into old bottles," that is, the new wine is the new law of love, even to love one's enemy (Matt. 5:44, etc.). At Cana, we learn, Jesus gave **lawe,** and the granting and teaching of laws is the duty of kings and conquerors (42–45 above). Hence he earns the title "Christ."
   Conscience observes that Christ in his **iuuentee** is called Jesus, *filius Marie* (Mark 6:3), and that he worked the miracle before his mother. This contrasts his early, domestic deed with the later doings that earn him the title *filius dauid* (133 and n, 136 below; see 69–198n above). Burrow suggests that *filius Marie* is a knight's title [as it were, FitzMary], followed by *filius dauid* (a king's), and *Christus* (a conqueror's)—1986:143. Conscience notes that Jesus performed the miracle not by ingenuity (**wyt**) but **thorw word one,** just as he broke hell with a breath (see 20.364n) and did best with thought (182 below).

110–87 And þer bigan god . . . *Redde quod debes*: Conscience presents the ministry and Passion of Jesus in terms of a distribution (see Headnote), the grades dowel, dobet, dobest. Again the link between the three do's and Jesus' progress toward kingship and the titles Christ and conqueror is not clearly drawn (see 69–198n above), but connecting the topics is Conscience's interest in various appellations of Jesus from **iesu** to **Dominus meus & deus meus** (see 117, 128, 133, 137, 152, 172a, and notes). L wishes to tell a story of triumphant progress with its paradoxical supreme suffering, but this story is resisted by Christological reality. As the Son of God, Jesus was from the outset dobest and a conqueror, and in spite of statements like Luke 2:52, "And Jesus advanced in wisdom . . . ," any tale of Jesus' growth must be without substantial suspense (cp. Peter Lombard's elaboration of this question in *Sentences*, PL 192.782; Bourquin 1978:468–73).

What actually grows is the number of witnesses to Jesus' deeds. With dowel, it seems, only his mother grasped his miracle (119). With dobet, specifically **in his moder absence** (124), in **contreye** Jesus was recognized by þe **comune people** (132) who call him "son of David" and **nempned hym of nazareth** in þe contre þer iesu cam (136–37)—clearly the second arena of Jesus' deeds was the provincial region of Galilee. Finally the dobest of Jesus is acknowledged by the Jewish leaders in Jerusalem, by angels and archangels, by Roman knights and by **vch a companye þer he cam**—in short, by everyone þus cam hit out þat Crist ouerkam (160–61). As the witnesses multiply and increase in importance, so do Jesus' names. The pathos of the story, however, lies in the fact that despite all this witness Jesus is not yet universally acclaimed as conqueror—hence the struggle of these last two passūs.

Conscience's narrative shows the strain of conflicting imperatives, but the outline of the progress is discernible. The miracle worked at Cana was Jesus' doing well (110, 116, 123)—more precisely he **bigan** or **comsede he dowel**. Then he **cauhte a grettere name**, namely **dobet**, when **he was wexen more** (124–39). The work of dobet was specifically his healing ministry, when **he comforted carefole**. At this point Jesus is hailed as *fili dauid* (133, 136), "greater" than merely *filius Marie* (118), and in fact comparable to an actual military conqueror, who "killed ten thousand" (135a), King David (see 96–107n above). Thus at the height of his healing ministry Jesus was **worthy / To be Cayser or kyng**—ready for the title "Christ" but not quite finished.

Then, beginning with the envy of Caiaphas and the events of the Passion, Resurrection, and post-Resurrection appearances (of the kind with which this passus opened), **do best he thouhte** (182), as he grants forgiveness of sins. This finally is the saving deed, and L expresses it as the granting of pardon to and through Piers. Jesus' deeds seem not very active as he does best—his thinking is his doing—but we recall that the more palpable conquest took place out of sight of the Judeans, in the Harrowing—likewise a granting of pardon—of the preceding passus, the deed that earns him the title of conqueror (52–53 above). The principal actions here are three: of Jesus' body, **hit aroos . . . Verray man bifore hem alle** (152–53); he blessed Thomas and those who believe in spite of not seeing; and he granted pardon for sins. In short, he redeemed. As he "does best" Jesus is specifically recognized as Christ and king, as even angels sing **Christus rex resurgens** (152). His achievement is complete, and Will's question, "Whi calle ȝe hym Crist?" (15) is answered. Heaven and hell acknowledge Jesus as lord, but not all of humankind.

117 not only Crist but iesu: See 69–198n above. Three solutions to the logical problem of this phrase may be entertained. First is Kane's glossing of the difficult reading **only**, for which scribes offered various substitutes, as "unique, peerless," a well-attested sense especially of Christ, the "only (*unicus*) Son of God" (1993:141; MED *onli* adj. 2.(a)). Or possibly the sense is that Jesus' name as mere human *remains* with him as he assumes his more exalted titles. Or finally, simply emend: for **only** substitute the majority B reading **holy**, or read *not Crist but only iesu*.

118 ful of wyt, *filius Marie*: Mark 6:3—the Galileans wonder at the doctrine and wisdom (**wyt**) of the preaching of this local boy, the son of Mary. In fact, the word "Christ" is not used in Mark's gospel between the first verse and the confession of Peter in 8:29, "Thou art the Christ." See 110–87n above.

120–21 That she furste . . . sholde bileue / That he thorw grace was gete: Robertson and Huppé (1951:219–20) refer this idea of the purpose of the miracle to a traditional interpretation of Jesus' saying at Cana to his mother, "What is that to me and thee?" (John 2:4). Bede (PL 92.657) says that this signifies that Jesus did not receive his divinity from his mother, but that he had it eternally from the Father, and that it was not yet time to reveal it to others.

122–23 word one, / Aftur þe kynde þat he cam of: that is, according to his nature as the Word (John 1:1). The Word surpasses any "wyt" (118 above). See 20.364n.

128 a grettere name: Conscience now merges his explication of the names of Jesus with the dowel triad.

133, 136 [calde hym] *fili dauid*: Matt. 9:27, 20:30–31 et synop., and cp. *Hosanna filio David* and 20.13–14n above. Continuing his explication of the names of Jesus, Conscience alludes to the Gospel instances of blind men approaching Jesus and persistently begging for mercy, calling him "son of David"—they were physically blind, but could see that Jesus was Messiah, or at least a youthful version of the davidic conqueror. Hence Jesus earned this appellation when he "ȝaf liht to blynde" (125). L recalls here terms from the Passion sequence of the preceding passus; see also 134n, 139n below. But the meaning differs: in Passus 20/B.18 the Son of David was acclaimed in his king-like procession into Jerusalem; here the Son of David is appealed to as the king of mercy.

134 douhtiest of dedes: See 108–23n above. L may recall 20.36 (and see n), "To se how douhtyliche deth sholde do."

135 buyrdes tho songe . . . *decem milia*: Specifically women (**buyrdes**), *mulieres*, sang (*praecinebant*), "Saul slew his thousands, and David his ten thousands" (1 Kings 18.7 varied, and sung liturgically as an antiphon for first Vespers of the first Sunday after Trinity Sunday; see Alford, *Quot.* 114 and cp. 1 Kings 21:11). The point is David's attainment of the superlative degree, "dauid was douhtiest" (134), beyond the mere kingship of the proto-king Saul, as Jesus approaches the "dobest" of a conqueror.

137 nempned hym of nazareth: Conscience takes the title "Jesus of Nazareth" (Mark 1:24, etc.) as a mark of distinction, tantamount to a conqueror's title like "Bevis of Hampton" or "Godfrey of Bouillon," fit for a "Cayser or kyng" (138). The particular reference is to Acts 4:7–12: asked "by what name" he healed a lame man, Peter replied, "by the name of our Lord Jesus Christ of Nazareth. . . . For there is no other name under heaven given to men, whereby we must be saved." See 15–62n, 110–87n above.

140–60 Cayphas . . . *christus resurgens*: Langland mainly follows Matthew in this brief retelling of the Passion and Resurrection, and John for the post-Resurrection events. **Cayphas**, Matt. 26:3, etc., is one of the chief priests. The "chief priests and Pharisees" persuade Pilate to set a guard at the tomb "lest perhaps his disciples come and steal him away" (Matt. 27:62–66). The Jewish leaders are warned of the resurrection not by **profetes** (145) but by Jesus' own words (Matt. 26:61, etc.). Both an angel and Jesus tell the visitors to the sepulchre that Jesus was to **goen into Galilee** (Matt. 28:7, 10), and the guards, the **knyhtes þat kepten hit, biknewen** to the chief priests "all things that had been done" (Matt. 28:11) although the Gospels do not say that angels and archangels knelt at Jesus' corpse and sang (149–52).

Conscience also alters the Gospel account of the Sanhedrin's scheme to have the soldiers (*milites*, hence **knyhtes**; see 20.80n) **telle þe comune** (155) that Jesus' disciples "stole him away" at night, with no mention of bewitching (Matt. 28:13; also *Nicodemus* 13.2–3). Finally, in all the Vulgate Gospels **Marie Maudeleyne** is named as among the earliest witnesses of the risen Jesus, and

from Matthew's account it can be concluded that she **mette hym by þe weye /
Goynge toward galilee** (28:9–10). Although she reports (except in Mark) what
she has heard and seen (see 162n), in none of the Gospels does she specifically
cry *christus resurgens* (see 152n below).

142 Culden hym on cros wyse at Caluarie on fryday: The what, who, how,
where, and when, compressed into one line (cp. B.16.164). That we scarcely
need reminding of any of these facts oddly augments the effect. The account
of Jesus' death at 20.59 (see 20.51–59n, 59–62n) is similarly abrupt, brief, sub-
lime. See 197–99n below.

148 thus men bifore deuyned: Line 161a below indicates that L thinks here
specifically of the prophecies of Jesus referred to in Luke 24:25–27, 44–47.
Among the proof-texts of the Resurrection perhaps Osee (Hosea) 6:3 is most
striking; see 1 Cor. 15:4 and 140–60n above.

152, 160 Christus [rex] resurgens: Romans 6:9, "Knowing that *Christ* [*the
king*] *rising again* from the dead, dieth now no more, death shall no more have
dominion over him." The phrase (without **rex**) is part of an Eastertide antiphon (Alford, *Quot.* 114), and was used at the Elevation ceremony on Easter
Day (Sheingorn 1987:116, 130, 134, 249, etc.), hence "sung" (see 135n above).
Against the other editors, the Athlone editors accept **rex** in 152 with minority
C-Text support and against archetypal B, but surely rightly: the line's alliteration is weak without **rex**; its loss is a commonplace instance of scribal rever-
sion to the familiar wording of the Bible and the liturgy; the reading of
manuscript F of B indirectly supports **rex** (see RK-C, p. 124); L wrote **rex** here
continuing Conscience's discussion of the names of Jesus (see 110–87n above).
Further on the textual difficulties of 151–52 see Donaldson 1949:237–38.
    In a late fourteenth-century liturgical play produced at Barking nunnery,
Mary Magdalene sings this antiphon (Young 1933, I:381 -84).

155 companie: here in the legal sense, "band of conspirators" as in B.13.160
(Alford, *Gloss.* s.v. *Compaignie*).

156 woke: "kept watch."

161a Sic . . . intrare &c: "Thus it behooves Christ to suffer and to enter [into
his glory]," conflating Luke 24:46 and 24:26 (Alford, *Quot.* 114).

162 may nat wel be conseyl: Women can't keep a secret (cp. B.5.168). Prsl
observes that this "sly remark" is "very inappropriate in the context"—

especially, we might think, since Jesus told her to tell the others (Matt. 28:10, etc.). This is the first recorded use of the specific proverb, also found of course in Chaucer (Whiting 1968:W534), but the general sense of it is recorded much earlier. Conscience may be impersonating the apostles' skeptical (but not explicitly antifeminist) response, at first, to Mary Magdalene's news: in Luke her story is taken for madness, *deliramentum* (24:11). Elsewhere Conscience does exploit misogynist clichés: see 3.158–71 (B.3.121–33, A.3.110–22).

Richardson collects evidence that Mary Magdalene's priority in announcing the Resurrection made her *apostola apostolorum*, "apostle-ess of the apostles," in medieval tradition (see 7.136–37 (B.5.496–97); Graesse 1890:409), and traces to the *Lamentations of Matheolus* (twelfth century; French trans. fourteenth century) the widespread misogynist joke that the Lord first showed himself resurrected to the Magdalene because he knew that she would publish the news quickly "since it is the custom of women to reveal all" (2001:167–68, 166). In the Towneley play of Thomas of India the apostles scoff at Mary Magdalene as being a woman and therefore untrustworthy. Richardson puts the Matheolus tradition into the context of contemporary suspicions about women, especially Lollard women, usurping clerical and priestly functions. As if to counter such notions, Abbot Odo in his account of the Magdalene says, "For because death has been brought into the world through a woman, so that the female sex might not always be held in opprobrium, he wished to announce to men the joy of the resurrection through the female sex" (*Acta Sanctorum* 5.221E). In finding the motive for the slur in Conscience's "interest in centralizing ecclesiastical power" and retaining male clerical authority (165, 177–81), Richardson transgresses the text, in which L consistently represents the Church as embattled but beneficent, the means of grace, and Conscience as the frustrated supervisor of doing well.

163–81a Peter perseyued . . . & crediderunt: Again Conscience slightly deviates from the Gospels. In Luke and John, Peter witnesses the empty tomb after the women (Luke; Mary Magdalene alone in John); in John, Peter runs to the sepulchre, **pursuede aftur, iesu to seke**, along with "the other disciple whom Jesus loved," traditionally John—but not James and certainly not all eleven apostles. In Vulgate Mark, Luke, and John, Jesus appears to the eleven apostles (**Taddee and ten mo**) gathered in a room, and according to John with the doors shut (20:19), **here dore ybarred** (167). The doubting Thomas episode occurs in John 20:24–29.

If line 164 were closed with a period, and lines 165 and 166 transposed, the text would conform more closely to the Gospel account and make clearer sense.

168 closed: an absolute participle (Mustanoja 1960:114–16); many scribes supplied a clarifying verb. Construing **Crist** as subject of **closed** would make nonsense of the phrase opening line 169.

169 *pax vobis*: The common salutation, "Peace [be] unto you," here especially to allay the apostles' terror (Luke 24:36, John 20:19, etc.).

171 flescheliche herte: John 20:25, 27 has *latus*, "side," for **herte**, here **flescheliche** because Thomas had doubted the carnal presence of the risen Jesus.

172 with his tonge saide: *Dominus meus & deus meus*: John 20:28, translated in the next line, "My Lord, and my God." These appellations conclude most forcefully Conscience's exposition of the names of Jesus (see 110–87n above), as well as the "witnessing" theme of the preceding passus (see C.20 Headnote, final paragraph). The apparently otiose **with his tonge** is part of a series: "hoende," "grope," "fele with his fyngeres," "flescheliche herte," "touched hit." The issue, as in many of the Resurrection appearance accounts, is the connection of spiritual with palpable reality. So below Jesus speaks of those "That neuere shal se me *in sihte*" (180).

181a Beati . . . & crediderunt: John 20:29, "blessed are they that have not seen, and have believed," as paraphrased in 179–81.

The founding of the Church

182–334 And when this dede . . . the lawe of holi churche: The last events of the Life of Jesus (182–94) coincide with the founding of the Church. This middle section of the passus (see Headnote) broadly establishes an ideal society granted and directed by God's agent, Grace. Historically it allegorizes, primarily in terms of labor and agriculture, the initial outpouring of Spirit on the apostles and their successors.

This first act of grace in the Church was represented in Acts as the Pentecostal tongues of fire that sat on each of the twelve (Acts 2:1–12); this original distribution is reenacted in the several distributions of gifts in this part of the poem. (On Grace's gifts see Frank 1957:96–97, 102–5.) L also alludes to John 20:22, "Receive ye the Holy Ghost" (see 182–90n below). These gifts are: the gift of pardon, to all people, with Piers/Peter as agent (182–90); the Pentecostal gift of the Paraclete itself (200–206); the division of grace (as 215 puts it) proper, that is, of talents, skills, and vocations, **all craft and connyng** (so 253;

see 215–61); the provision to Piers of the instruments **to tulye treuthe** (261 and 333; see 260–334), including divisions of oxen, **stottes**, harrows, and seeds, of the elements of the barn **holy chirche**, and other necessities of farming.

The apportioning of gifts to humankind and the imposition of reciprocal obligations on the commune broadly reenact the second vision, with its narrative of pardon, division of labor, plowing, backsliding, and moves toward repentance (see Headnote).

Bourquin observes that the sequence a) granting of Petrine power, b) reference to the difference between cardinal virtues and unvirtuous cardinals (406–18 below), and c) the introduction of a king with the words "thenne cam þer a kyng" (465 below; see 465–76n) recapitulates the sequence of Prol.128–39, B.Prol.100–112 (not in A). See 15–62n above. The B Prologue lines were probably composed after this passage (Bourquin 1978:348; Hanna 1993:12–13; Hanna 1996:233, 238). See Headnote and 309–16n, 413–23n below.

The Petrine power

182–98 And when this dede . . . withouten ende: Conscience concludes the Life of Jesus with an account of his granting of conditional pardon to humankind and his Ascension, and a prediction of his final judgment to come. Having conquered, in the preceding passus, he now distributes largesse. Here the apostle Peter and the plowman Piers—who has received a pardon for all, similarly conditional upon their "doing well," in the second vision—are joined in a single continuous mission in human time. L thus returns to primary topics in PP: how one may be saved, and may obtain pardon. The work of salvation is Jesus', and Conscience specifies that the agent who will make pardon possible, Grace, is "Cristes messager" (207). See 258–334n below. In some sense Piers represents the papacy. The Commons in Parliament in 1376 speak generally of the pope as "Seint Pier(e)" regardless of the name of the present incumbent (Rot. Parl. 2.336, 337). Traditionally Peter is patron of the active, secular clergy, and John of the monastic contemplatives.

182–90 And when this dede . . . of dette one: Jesus' specific act of redemption, forgiveness, is the climax of Conscience's presentation, **do best** (see 110–87n above). For the theological import of this emphasis see 20.400–12n. This brief pardon scene should be compared with the larger and more vexed episode of A.8/B.7/C.9. Here the pardon is explicitly linked with "þe power that Peter hadde to kepe, / To bynde and vnbynde as þe boke telleth" (Prol.128–29

[B.Prol.100–101]; Matt. 16:19). The Latin of Matt. 16:19 is quoted at 9.327a (B.7.181a, A.8.159a), where Will worries over the pope's Petrine power.

This second pardon is a similar pardon presented more literally, but it differs in its allowance for repayment for sin (186–87 and n) and penance. Following as it does the account of the Redemption it is more deeply grounded, but of course its efficacy no more heals the world than the first pardon had, as the poem will unfold in its quasi-historical course. The action here, and the subsequent distribution of the cardinal virtues (274ff. below), recollect also Prol.128–33 (B.Prol.100–106; see n), an even more abrupt statement of God's gift and human inability to accept it.

With this act Piers begins to return to the poem conceptually (as in 260ff. below), though Will never interacts with him again. Obviously here Piers takes on the character of Peter, and particularly the capacity of Peter's successors, the priests, to absolve. Note that Grace gives Piers "power . . . to make" consecrated bread, the Host, an exclusively priestly power (385–87).

This Petrine commission aptly comes at this point in the Vita Christi, as L has been following the Gospel of John (see notes to 81, 171, 172, 181a, 182–334 above): when Jesus appeared to the apostles he breathed on them, filling them with the Holy Spirit, and said to them all, "Whose sins you shall forgive, they are forgiven them; and whose sins you shall retain, they are retained" (John 20:23; see. Matt. 18:18 for another apostolic but non-Petrine commission). Later Jesus singles out Peter for the thrice-repeated "Feed my lambs" (John 21:15–17). Hence John presents both a little Pentecost (cp. Acts 2 and 200–201 below) and another version of the Petrine commission as among Jesus' deeds in his post-resurrection appearances. John's Gospel thus authorizes the order of events in PP, providing for the pardon, the central act in L's theology, as Jesus' last act.

182–86 do best he thouhte / And ʒaf [peres pardoun] and [power] he graunted [hym], / <Myhte men to assoyle of alle manere synnes, / To alle manere men mercy and forʒeuenesse>/ In couenaunt: The angle brackets enclose lines that the Athlone editors transpose from the copy text. Complex scribal variation at this point renders the text uncertain. Schm finds the Athlone redivisions and transpositions unnecessarily elaborate, and reads:

> . . . Dobest he thouhte,　　(182)
> And ʒaf Peres power, and pardoun he graunted:
> To alle manere men, mercy and forʒeuenesse;
> [To] hym, myhte men to assoyle of alle manere synnes,
> In couenaunt. . . .

Prsl reads similarly, ending 183 with no punctuation and supplying (with several C manuscripts) ᵹaf rather than *To* before **hym** at the head of Schm/Prsl's 185. The probably archetypal text can be preserved by construing **hym** of Schm/Prsl's 185 as the elliptical (and difficult) indirect object parallel with **To . . . men** of 184; hence neither "To" nor "ᵹaf" is absolutely necessary at the head of 185. Defending the Athlone reading is RK-C, pp. 134–35, wrongly asserting that **Hym myhte** at the beginning of a line is simply ungrammatical. Roughly comparable ellipsis occurs at 20.463–64 (B.18.420–21).

The three editions finally mean the same: Jesus gave mercy and forgiveness to all people, and to Piers a special power, specified as a pardon at least in 187 and 188 below (and, to be sure, in 9.3 [B.7.3, A.8.3]), the (priestly) power to absolve people of sin, to act as agent of the forgiveness. Relevant to the textual problem is the locution at 17.224, B.15.561, "petres power"; see also 386 below, 9.325 (B.7.179, A.8.157), and the beginning of 182–90n above. Jesus *offers* forgiveness to all, but not all accept, and there is after all a condition—**in couenaunt** (see 193n below). L still emphasizes the breadth of grace; cp. C.20.414 and n.

Coghill and Chambers surmised that the "Dobest" section of the poem starts here; see Headnote.

185 alle manere men: a legal formula of inclusiveness (Alford, *Gloss.*), reinforcing "alle manere synnes" of the preceding line to emphasize the extent of Jesus' mercy.

186–87 knoleche to pay . . . *Redde quod debes*: Skt and Schm may rightly take **to pay** to mean "so as to please [God]." However, in context (*redde* means "pay"), and in light of the usage at 193–94 and C.22/B.20.308, and especially the unambiguous 389–90 below, Prsl and Donaldson 1990 have a more likely reading, taking "pay" as "give payment," another sense of the same verb. Possibly L intended a pun, as both meanings work: by pleasing one needn't pay in full, which is impossible in any case. Compare the wordplay in 8.115: as some work well on the Half Acre "Therwith was Perkyn apayed and payede wel here huyre."

The syntax is difficult; perhaps translate "acknowledge [their obligation] to give (as their side of the covenant) the payment 'Redde-quod-debes' as recompense for Piers Plowman's pardon." In this construction the Latin phrase, which means practically the same as what the whole sentence means, is treated as the object of pay, as in 259 below (so Prsl) and allegorized as the medium of payment. See 20.225n. *Redde quod debes* might also stand apart from the syntax of the sentence as a terse summation, as it were preceded by a dash, and with **pay** intransitive, "make payment" (MED *paien* 5.(a)). Or the Latin phrase in apposition glosses **pardoun**: the substance of this pardon is "meet your obligations, perform satisfaction," as the substance of the earlier one was "do well and you will be saved." In any case **pay** suggests and then emphatically rejects the idea that one can *buy* pardon in such forms as "indulgences . . . bionales and trionales" (9.320–21 [B.7.175–76, A.8.153–54]); we should pay **to**, not *for*, the pardon.

Redde quod debes, "Pay back what you owe." The phrase appears exactly in Matt. 18:28, in the mouth of the ungracious Wicked Servant as he throttles a lesser debtor—a context that colors its value—and in the liturgy. See Alford, *Quot.* 114 for reference to discussions of the concept of repayment by Augustine and in sermons, and for the general question of Pelagian trust in works and the issue of restitution see Douglas 1966:129–61, esp. 158. With this phrase the human side of the covenant abruptly enters the poem near the end of the sequence of Jesus' actions. The mandate "repay" recalls the hard law of reciprocal justice played out (and superseded) in C.20/B.18 (see Headnote)—"he shall render (*reddet*) life for life. Eye for eye . . ." (Exod. 21:23–24). Paul seems to echo Exodus as well as Roman law (see below) in his phrasing: "Render therefore to all men their dues (*Reddite ergo omnibus debita*). Tribute, to whom tribute is due: custom, to whom custom . . ." (Rom. 13:7; see 6.315, 321 [B.5.461, 467, A.5.233, 241]). L refers also to the *debita* of the Lord's Prayer, and to the notion that the basis of receiving forgiveness is offering it; see 383–90 and n below.

It turns out that restitution attenuates, rather than replicates, the severity of justice. This idea had been proposed clearly by the Samaritan, who said that the Holy Ghost's grace would melt the Trinity's might into mercy for whoever repents and makes restitution, to the extent that they can from their assets while alive (19.187–213 [B.17.221–47]; see 391–95n below). In an important article on the changing concept of debt in PP, Baldwin argues that restitution in Dobest comes to mean not mere commutation, but charity. She makes the point that the king's servant in Matt. 18, from which the phrase *redde quod debes* is taken, was ruined because he failed to be charitable (1994, esp. 46–48, 50; see also Bloomfield and Frank, below in this note). Likewise troubled by the Pelagian look of mere material restitution, Sheneman argues that what one "owes" is faith and penance; the debt is spiritual (1996). Conscience assures us that Jesus' conquering extends mercy to us, but that we remain morally obliged to act with justice. Jesus' work of Passus 20/B.18 relieved humankind of their infinite debt to God, but humans must still continually discharge their debts to one another before they can participate in the full pardon.

As 389–92 below make clear, the mandate is specifically to make good any indebtedness before receiving Communion. Christians were enjoined to "go to hosele" at least annually in Easter season (or monthly; see 388), and they were to do formal penance beforehand, including restitution and satisfaction. The requirement has a biblical basis: Lev. 6:1–5, Matt. 5:24–25. Scase observes that one manuscript has the notation "de restitucione" beside this passage (1989:30). Moreover, at issue in, for example, C.22/B.20.290–93 is the need to pay off, before or after death, one's unsatisfied lifelong debt of sin. Standard doctrine held that "Purgatory is the middle place of destination for people who die absolved of guilt but with an outstanding debt of temporal punishment" (Tentler 1977:318).

The phrase **Redde quod debes** echoes through the last passūs of PP, in 259, 390, 22.308, and varied in 193; see notes; see also B.Prol.122 and 208, C.5.32a and n, C.6.315, 321 (B.5.461, 467), A.5.233, 241). The principle proves ultimately ineffectual. Anticipating the failure of "repayment" at the end of this passus, L early on made the figure "Amends," restitution, the mother of Meed, unhappily married to False (2.123 [B.2.119, A.2.83]).

The principle of restitution as a preamble to penance was essential to the concept of satisfaction in the sacrament (see 6.256–57 [B.5.270–73] and 19.290 [B.17.310], and Alford 1993:12–17). Prsl draws attention to additions in the C version that indicate a "pervading concern" with themes of penance and restitution (his 10.51–55n); see the revisions at 10.51–55 and 16.25–38. Archbishop FitzRalph was especially concerned with the principle: "there is no contrition unless restitution go beforehand" (Walsh 1981:364). As such the question of restitution became part of antifraternal polemic associated with the friars' usurpation of the priestly right to confess and absolve, an issue in the next passus (see 22/B.20.232–41n, etc., and Scase 1989:23–32; Bloomfield 1961a:130–32, 219; Frank 1957:106–9). Here L firmly links the original gift of the power of absolution with the obligation of restitution. But as Bloomfield observes, too great an emphasis on restitution diminishes the role of grace, and cites Bradwardine who "calls those who say restitution is necessary for salvation 'Cainistae'" (p. 131).

Frank and Bloomfield extend the notion of restitution in PP to a general idea of justice, arguing that justice is a major concern of the last two passūs. The latter cites Thomas Aquinas's definition of justice as rendering to each his due (*reddere debitum unicuique—Summa contra gentiles* 1.93; see also ST 2.2.qu. 58,1), a commonplace of Roman law found, for example, at the opening of Justinian's *Institutes* (1.1), *Justicia est . . . suum cuique tribuens* (Justice is rendering to each person his own) and in Matt. 16:27, etc., where Jesus says that the Son of Man will "render to every man (*reddet unicuique*) according to his works" (see Alford, *Gloss.*, s.v. *His Own, Justice*; Alford *Quot.* 80, s.v. B.12.213a; Stokes 1984:3–9; Isidore, *Etym.* 2.24.6, ed. Lindsay 1911:1.105). The definition is evoked, possibly with irony, in the B.Prol. coronation oath (line 122; and see B.Prol. 208 and C.22.90–92n). Frank especially urges that the **redde quod debes** requires not mere "equitee" (19.290 [B.17.310]) but that one forgive sins and love one's neighbor (1957:108–9). Yunck cites the long article in Bromyard's *Summa praedicantium, Redditio*, on paying what one owes to God, neighbor, and self, and argues that the concept of repayment, the "dense network of personal obligations surrounding all individuals through their lives," is "the touchstone of L's satire" (in Alford 1988a:149–52).

Conscience says Piers can **assoile men of alle synnes saue of dette one** (189), "except for debt alone," that is, as Schm glosses it, "the binding obligation to make satisfaction." (In PP, **one** following a noun does not mean "a single.") The doctrine implied is striking, but see Stokes, who explains the **dette** of this passage as that part of human obligation not redeemed by Christ; a priest absolves from guilt (*culpa*) but not from satisfaction (*pena*) (1984:15).

193 that *reddit quod debet*: "who repays what he owes," now (cp. 187 above and 182–90n) making the Latin grammar conform to the syntax of the sentence in which it is embedded. Conscience's version of salvation is reciprocal, payment for payment; thrice he has included this condition on pardon (186–88, 193–98).

194–98 as puyr treuthe wolde . . . wo withouten ende: Pointed reference to the second vision continues: **as puyr treuthe wolde** means simply "in accordance with justice," but pregnantly, with reference to the earlier version of the pardon "purchasede" by "Treuthe" (C.9/B.7/A.8.1–3), here momentarily personified. So lines 197–98, as Hussey observes (1956:148), in effect repeat the "two lynes" from the Athanasian Creed written on the earlier pardon (9.285–88 [B.7.111–14, A.8.93–96]). Lawler shows that L constantly repeats this binary form of the pardon statement, setting the consequences of good and bad behavior in sharp antitheses (2001).

The coming of the Spirit

200–212 and thenne cam, me thouhte . . . helpe vs, Crist, of grace!: Will dreams that he sees the events of Pentecost (Acts 2:1–12): the coming of the Holy Spirit in the form of tongues of fire sitting on the apostles' heads, and the gift of tongues. L refers to the Third Person as **spiritus paraclitus**, the *paraclitus Spiritus Sanctus* spoken of in Jesus' final, Last Supper discourse in John (14:26; see also 14:16, 15:26, 16.7), "the Paraclete, the Holy Ghost." Jesus reiterates that when he must leave the apostles the "Paraclete," the Advocate or

Comforter, will come to them as protector, teacher, and witness of Jesus, and "when he is come, he will convince the world of sin, and of justice, and of judgment"—topics engaging the remainder of PP. The phrase *Spiritus paraclitus* occurs in a hymn sung at Vespers on Pentecost Sunday, *Beata nobis gaudia* (Alford, *Quot.* 115, Schm), as well as in an antiphon at the vigil of Pentecost (Brev. 2:236).

Burrow (1993:63–64) observes that to speak of the Holy Spirit at first as **oen** *spiritus paraclitus* seems an absurd use of the indefinite pronoun as part of the motif of veiled identity, and compares the earlier introduction of another new character into the poem, "oen Iesus" (18.125 [B.16.92]). Conscience immediately identifies the Pentecostal Spirit as **Cristes messager**, sent by God, and **grace is his name**.

At this point we return, as it were, to church. Conscience twice tells Will to kneel (200, 209; see 12n, 17n); as Kirk observes, the congregation kneels after the Offertory to hear the Canon of the Mass (1972:185). Conscience will soon be named king (256), and he kneels before the Spirit, thus replicating the kneeling before Jesus of angels and kings (see 71–95n). At this point of the Mass, too, is sung the hymn *Veni creator Spiritus*, "Come, Creator Spirit," which Will and Conscience sing with hundreds of others. At least in the York and Hereford (but not the Sarum) rites the hymn is always sung at the Offertory (McGarry 1936:110). In the Sarum rite it is sung before Mass as the priest vests himself (ed. Dickenson 1861–63, col. 577–78). L quotes from it at C19.140a.

The hymn refers to the association of the Spirit with grace and with gifts; it says, "Fill with supernal grace the hearts that you have created" (cp. line 212), and the Paraclete is called the "gift (Donum) of the highest God" and the "sevenfold gift (munus)" (ed. Dreves 1909, Part 1:80). The hymn is also sung at Terce on Pentecost Sunday (Alford, *Quot.* 115); the season of Will's dreams has moved from Easter to Pentecost. This allusion concludes the series of explicit references to the liturgical cycle begun at C.20/B.18.6 (but see 229–51n below). The narrative sequence here—an account of Jesus' mighty deeds, the presence of a fearful light, rejoicing hymn, and Will kneeling in worship—recapitulates the sequence of Passus 20/B.18.

Simpson refers to a record of a procession of London officials at which *Veni creator spiritus* is sung and examines the following scene, with its "division of crafts," in terms of the "often violent context of London city politics," including the rivalries of the craft guilds (1993:109 et passim; see 229–51n, 254n below). By "craft" L may mean either "vocational skill" or "craft guild."

On Pentecost the Church was founded. The remaining events in the poem enact, partly historically, partly contemporaneously, partly allegorically, the story of the Church Militant. After its Prologue, PP begins and ends with allegories of the Church. Will with Conscience and the whole Church community cries to **Crist** (Schm and Prsl, "God") to help of his grace (212), much as the "thousand of men" joined and "criede vpward to Crist . . . to haue grace" at the end of the confession of the sins (7.155–57 [B.5.510–12, A.5.251–54]; see 20.451n) in a joyful time of hope. Less optimistically, the action is repeated in the last line of the poem, when Conscience "gradde aftur grace." See 424–27n below and 22.76n.

The division of graces

213–57 Thenne bigan grace . . . clotheth ʒow and fedeth: The petition of line 212 is for a time successful, and Grace offers helpful gifts: **tresor to lyue by** and **wepne to fihte with** (217–18; see 228n below). These are no mean gifts: the ability to gain livelihood and to protect oneself. "The divinity of labor, the concept which creates the figure of Piers, is here expressed in the identification of the divisions of grace and the divisions of labor" (Frank 1957:102). To know a craft and thereby earn one's living is the antidote to the problem of mendicancy to which L ceaselessly recurs. Further, as Simpson argues, the work of penance, summarized in *redde quod debes*, is reinstated in the poem hand in hand with human work in general under a new scheme of justice (2001a, esp. p.67). Robert the rifler despairs of *reddere* because he knows no "craft" (6.321–22 [B.5.467–68, A.5.241–42]). The counter-figure, in the C version only, is Piers, who in response to a cry for grace appears as learned "in alle kyne craftes" (C.7.191). Indeed, Piers wears an allegorical garb of "alle kyn craftes" (C.8.58). L may have added these phrases, not in B/A, in light of the discussion here. See further on right craft 22.206–11n.

Warning Conscience of the evils that are to come, Grace gives each person, as a defense against vice, **a grace**, namely the arts and crafts, **all craft and connyng** (253). But Grace's division or distribution quickly begins to imply differentiation, as equal provision of sustenance and defense for all in common develops into a community of reciprocally interdependent virtues, a system that will invite strife. Hence the distribution to various vocations of their skills reintroduces to the poem humanity in its variety, the fair field of folk. The poem's pattern has been to introduce a world of people with their attendant problems, to come to some resolution of the problems, and to watch the resolution disintegrate when confronted with the world of people again. It is as if the very multiplicity of human behavior overwhelmed all virtue. See 215n, 229–51n below, 22.206–11n.

213–14 Thenne bigan grace . . . the comune to sompne: Grace, Piers, and
Conscience act together for a time, and summon **the comune** in a political
order comparable to that of the king, Reason, and Conscience in the first
vision. (MED indicates that Gower's *Confessio* is the first recorded English use
of "summon" of a king's convening Parliament.) This is the first of several
polities that L invokes in the last two visions and the first overt allusion to an
order like England's, with king and commons, since the speech of Liberum
Arbitrium (Anima in B) in 17.216–19 (B.15.553–56). Donaldson's remains the
most thorough examination of the meaning of **comune(s)** in PP (1949:85–116;
cp. Baldwin 1981b:12–20, and see also Middleton 1978; Alford, *Gloss.* s.v. *Commune*). Conscience and Piers are named as the summoners of the commune
perhaps because they represent private (conscientious) and public (priestly)
spiritual agency. The **comune** is at first the "many hundret" in church with
Will (211), then the whole social order first construed as the apostolic Church
with its various members.

215 dele . . . and deuyde grace: This division is the core of the theme of distribution that pervades this passus (see Headnote). Only with Grace's gifts can
humans "pay *Redde quod debes*." The notion derives from 1 Cor. 12:4–12 (see
228a below): *Divisiones vero graciarum sunt . . .* , "Now there are diversities of
graces, but the same Spirit; And there are diversities of ministries (*ministrati-
ones*), but the same Lord; and there are diversities of operations (*operationes*),
but the same God, who worketh (*operatur*) all in all. And the manifestation of
the Spirit is given to every man unto profit (*ad utilitatem*). To one, indeed, by
the Spirit, is given the word of wisdom: and to another, the word of knowledge
according to the same spirit; To another, faith . . . to another, the grace of
healing . . . prophecy . . . the discerning of spirits . . . diverse kinds of tongues
. . . interpretation of speeches. But all these things one and the same Spirit
worketh, dividing to every one according as he will. For as the body is one . . .
and all the members . . . are many, yet are one body, so also is Christ." As in
estates theory, the division implies unity, mutuality, and cooperation.
      Paul goes on to warn against thinking less of "those that seem to be more
feeble members," noting that we honor most those members of the body that
we think less honorable, and he urges "that there be no schism in the body,"
concluding that we are "the body of Christ," and that "God indeed hath set
some in the church; first apostles, secondly prophets, thirdly doctors . . . ," etc.
(I Cor. 12:22–31). From this description of the Church and its members Paul
moves on to the famous Chapter 13 on the nature of charity.
      In Romans 12, Paul likewise speaks of the members of the body of Christ
and our "different gifts," enumerating several—prophecy, administration,

doctrine, exhortation, simplicity, carefulness, cheerfulness—and of "loving one another with the charity of brotherhood." For the seven gifts of the Spirit enumerated in Isaiah 11:2–3 see 274–316n below.

Paul's linked concerns and his form of presentation are those of the succeeding lines in PP. The distributive grammar of Paul's Corinthians homily, *alii . . . alii . . . alteri . . . alii* ("To another . . . To another . . . To another"— eight times repeated) is mimicked with **and somme . . . and somme** (nine times repeated). Like Paul, Grace **lered** all to avoid disparaging one another, **þat noen lacke oþere** even though people's gifts differ, **bute loueth as bretherne** (254). See 229–51n, 254n, and 328n below.

217–18 Tresor . . . wepne: That Grace's charismata are called a treasure may recall, in this context of the founding of the Church, the emphasis, in Holy Church's sermon, on "treuthe and trewe loue" as the highest treasure (1.136, etc.). That they are weapons anticipates the struggle to come, "when Auntecrist ȝow assaileth" (227). The terms are repeated (as Holy Church repeated her theme) in 225–26 below. To these metaphors a third, the agricultural, will soon be added.

219–26 Auntecrist and hise . . . Auntecrist ȝow assaileth: L merges three common senses of Antichrist: the satanic antagonist whose destructive coming into the world will precede the Second Coming of Christ; the summation of vice; an appellation for a heretic or such a major enemy of the Church as a wicked pope. There are, then, theological-historical, moral, and political Antichrists— "even now there are become many Antichrists" (1 John 2:18). Representative Lollard conceptions of Antichrist both as a collective and as one preeminent figure are treated in Bostick 1998:51–75. On Antichrist and apocalypticism generally in PP see Frank 1957:111–12; Bloomfield 1961a, 1961b; Emmerson 1981:193– 203 and 1993; Adams 1985b; Kerby-Fulton 1990; Aers 1980:62–79).

Auntecrist is mentioned only seven times in PP, and never before here: C.21/B.19.219, 226, and C.22/B.20.53, 64, 69, 128, 216. In these first two instances he is defined by his followers, false prophets, hypocritical yes-men, and the vices pride, covetousness, and unkindness. When "Pryde" and other vices attack (335ff. below), Antichrist is not mentioned, but it is the same set of forces, with emphasis on falsehood. In the second attack of Antichrist, now named, falsehood and pride are again his chief signs (C.22/B.20.51–73; see 22.52–53n). In C.22/B.20.128, Antichrist is a mere figure of simony. Finally Antichrist is the leader of the "seuene grete geauntes," the seven sins (C.22/ B.20.215–16). Antichrist in PP sums up and personifies the communal corruption dealt with exhaustively through the poem, providing a retroactive and eschatological view of contemporary vice and decline.

If the Apocalypse reveals the last events before the end of the world, the last visions of PP and the activity of the poem's Antichrist are not strikingly apocalyptic. The destruction wreaked by the forces of Antichrist turns out to be moral viciousness. Missing are such themes of literary apocalyptic as the end of time, the trumpet of doom, beasts, angels, vials and seals, the darkening of heaven and other portents (except for pestilence), the earthquakes, famine, and fire of ultimate universal destruction, Gog and Magog, the coming, killing, and resurrection of the "two witnesses," Enoch and Elijah, the elaborate parody of the Vita Christi in the career of Antichrist, and the conversion of the Jews (but see 3.455–57, 480 [B.3.302–4, 327]). For contrast with PP see—besides the biblical book of the Apocalypse—Dan. 7–11; the "Little Apocalypse" of Matt. 24 et synop.; the influential tenth-century treatise of Adso of Montier-en-Der, the *Libellus de Antichristo* (ed. Verhelst 1976, trans. McGinn 1979; the same largely translated in *Cursor mundi*); and Emmerson 1981. A typical account of Antichrist appears in *The Pricke of Conscience* (ed. Morris 1863, lines 4047–4684).

L in fact stays mainly with our age, and deploys Antichrist rather as the emblem of social and moral decline than as the harbinger of cosmic doom. In PP, tropology trumps anagogy (see esp. 22.74–109n). "Indeed, the typical apocalyptic imagery and *personæ* are notable for their almost complete absence from the poem" (Kean 1969:109). Even Adso, following ancient tradition, speaks of Antichrist *both* as the eschatological antagonist *and* as a general term for anyone who now "lives contrary to justice and attacks the rule of his way of life and blasphemes what is good" (McGinn 1979:90, 82–83).

L's apocalypticism less resembles the eschatological speculation of medieval interpretation less than the prophetic analysis of the contemporary polity that motivated the original apocalyptic writings. For full discussion see Bloomfield 1961a, 1961b, 1981, and Steinberg 1991, and especially Kerby-Fulton 1990 passim, e.g., "There is a tension in Langland's writing between the preaching of eschatology and the preaching of a less universal and ultimate form of retribution" (p. 18). As she points out, if the eschaton were imminent at the end of PP, L would not propose that friars have a finding (p. 10). Emmerson finds that L juxtaposes the prophetic—with its optimism and its orientation toward the present, the social, and the national—with the apocalyptic, with its pessimism and its orientation toward the predicted future, the individual, and the universal (1984:44).

Agreeing with biblical apocalyptic (as well as biblical prophecy) is L's repeated connection of Antichrist with "false profetes fele" and falsehood generally: see e.g. 221 below, C.22/B.20.55, 131. Of course falsehood, broadly understood, has been L's most prominent representation of evil since its personification as Fals in A.2. Holy Church's theme is "treuthe is þe beste" (1.81, etc.); it follows that falsehood is the worst. Falsehood is the Duessa to the Church's Una. Hence C added the first dark note of the poem to the Prologue: "Of treuthe and tricherye, tresoun and gyle" (Prol.12). At the outset of antifraternal polemic, with William of St. Amour, falsehood (hypocrisy, duplicity) has been the main complaint against the friars (see 22.52–53n). It is a courtly and clerkly vice. After the Redemption, falsehood is the most dangerous human wrong, as only by twisting the truth of salvation, "sophistrie" (347 below), can anyone forestall the operation of grace (see Carruthers 1973:157–63; Szittya 1986:253–57). False prophets are soothers, "flateres and glosares" (221) typified by "frere flaterrere" (see C.22/B.20.313–15n); their archetype is the pseudoprophet "saying: Peace, peace: when there was no peace" (Jer. 6:14, 8:11). In the Little Apocalypse, Jesus specifically foretells the coming of the seductive false prophets, *pseudoprophetæ* (Matt. 24:11, Mark 13:22). Gower follows the tradition of naming friars pseudoprophets ("'Pseudo' is their prophet") in *Vox clamantis* 4.17, line 788 (trans. Stockton 1962).

L had already alluded to Apocalypse 19–20 (see 5–14n above), which associates the *pseudopropheta* with the apocalyptic events of the eschaton. There we learn of the war between "the beast, and with him the false prophet" and the Word, sprinkled with blood, who was King of Kings, together with the binding of the old serpent, the eternal torment of the false prophet, and the Last Judgment (Apoc. 19:11–20:15). See further 335n below, 22.230n.

221–24 And false profetes . . . Cardynales hym to lede: The activity of Antichrist, in effect his definition, is first of all falsity, and particularly the corruption of and by the clergy. Even as the Church is being founded, its officers become agents of misrule. The **curatours** who should administer penance, providing the grace that Jesus granted, instead give bad counsel—falsity, flattery, glozing—to magnates; of parallel rank with the redeless **kynges and Erles** are the pope Pride led by his cardinals Covetousness and Unkindness. The forces of Antichrist are an anti-Church that misleads a kingdom.

But the anti-Church seems to be implicit in the founding of the Church, as one learns from the speech of the unlearned vicar, a proper "curatour" (410 below), with its critique of pope and cardinals (413–50). In the second attack of Antichrist, friars are specified as his first followers, and immediately characterized by their falsity, in keeping with antifraternal tradition (see 22.58n). L clearly has friars in mind in this passage as well—see preceding note. Friars indeed were counselors of magnates, "chief to shryue lordes" (Prol.62

[B.Prol.64, A.Prol.61]). On royal confessors as learned counselors see 4.142–47 (B.4.145–50, A.4.128–33). Richard II's confessors were usually Dominicans, and two of them, Bashe and Rushook, were publicly criticized by contemporaries—the latter in the 1380s twice banished from court for harmful influence on the king (Saul 1997:320–21). Resoun had spelled out what a confessor should enjoin on a king (5.194–96). Lines 221–22, then, refer first of all to friars, and lines 223–24 to the secular clergy. Alternatively, might **curatours** refer to the coterie around Edward III in his dotage, or to the regency council during Richard II's minority?

227–28a And gaf vch man . . . *graciarum sunt*: See 215n above. The gifts of the Spirit particularly defend against idleness, envy, and pride: idleness because they are gifts that make possible productive work; envy and pride because "all craft and connyng come of my ʒefte" (253), hence no cause exists for pride in one's own ability or envy of another's (see 250–55 and, for envy of others' **grace** see B.5.98 [A.5.78]).

As he did in the second vision, L focuses on work as a form of right action until a breakdown occurs (367ff. below). Will's (and presumably L's) concern about his own vocational status, expressed most directly at the new opening of C.5 where he is asked whether he knows any "kynes craft" of service to the community, may well motivate the vocational slant of Grace's distribution. Grace's gifts defend against Antichrist, and it turns out that the defense amounts to a proper winning of sustenance (see 213–57n above, Simpson 1993:114), as it were a plowing of the half acre.

229–51 Som wyes he ʒaf . . . among hem alle: In imitation of the biblical enumerations of the gifts of the Spirit (see 215n above), L seizes the appropriate Pentecostal moment to survey once again the order of society (see 5.111–200n). The first half of the poem presents a number of these surveys; they return now (see also 367–80, 396–480, and C.22/B.20.101–5, 257–267 below) as L returns to a more social perspective, after Will's long quest for Dowel and the Vita Christi.

Comparison with the earlier surveys in PP helps us see what L does here (see Prol.19–21n). On these see Fletcher 1993; for the order of presentation of the estates in other poems see Mann 1973:203–6. Some seven briefer instances of these listings occur in PP. Longer surveys of the human classes are the Prologue, the confessions of the sins (C.6/B.5/A.5), the account of those enrolled in Truth's pardon (C.9/B.7/A.8), and the statements of representatives of the estates at the end of this passus.

Though the fair field of folk is hard to account for, some general features emerge. L, like Chaucer, tends to classify people first of all by their work. Sometimes L troubles to present the traditional three estates, but only once (in C, twice in B) in the "proper" order (nobility, clergy, laborers) and usually with a twist or two, and with many appendices. With deliberate perversity, indeed, L begins several of his reckonings, including the first survey, with laborers. Topics of special moment to L readily cause him to digress— especially bad administrative functionaries (clerks) and corrupt ecclesiastical figures (clerks), very likely people of his own "estate" who do not fit easily into the three-estates picture. Like many of L's set scenes, the visions of folk generally "peter out"; the pattern is that of a disruption of pattern (see Middleton 1982).

In contrast, the distribution of graces here is rational and, in spite of its complexity, achieves firm closure. The grammar, **somme . . . somme,** is maintained throughout, whereas in the Prologue the same distributive arrangement is forsaken after some dozen lines. No digressions occur. The controlled order of the survey befits its status, not a coursing over the human condition as it is, but a description of the origin of human crafts, in principle like the surveys of the invention of the arts (Jubal the father of music, etc.) in Godfrey of Viterbo's *Pantheon* and Gower's *Confessio amantis* (4.2363–2671). More precisely, Grace's gifts are not class affinities—estates (or, more properly, "orders")—or particular vocations—forms of work—but rather capacities for work— skills—a new principle of order that may reflect an emerging idea of identity as less a matter of blood or family patterns of vocation (such that a wine merchant's son still bears the name of a shoemaker: Chaucer) and more a product of native ability and education. On such shifting patterns of identity see Middleton 1997. The novelty of the idea helps account for the peculiar focus on the art of divination.

Further, the survey echoes the biblical lists (see 215n above). The items of **craft and connyng** granted by Grace are: **wyt with wordes** (for preachers, priests, lawyers); **konnynge of syhte,** as it were a sharp eye, in buying and selling; skill at manual labor generally; the art of agriculture; divination, with its arcane manipulations of numbers and other figures; the arts of carving, design, and painting; such arts of forecasting the future as astrology; the physical skill to recover ill-gotten goods (a knightly duty; see e.g. 8.26–27 [B.6.27–28, A.7.29–30]); those gifts of otherworldliness, poverty, patience, and prayer appropriate to a monk or other contemplative; and to all, the gifts of **leaute** and mutual love. This array of crafts may recall the interest in extra-university practical clerisy that Galloway finds in various English milieux, including Cistercian manuscripts (1992:89–107). Simpson argues that **craft** through this passage can allude to guilds, that a parish guild or fraternity, rather than a craft guild per se, might include the range of different crafts distributed here, and that such guilds' peacemaking function is reflected in 252–55 below (1990a: 225–27 and 1993:115 et passim).

As a development of the poem's (uneven) progression through the liturgical year, there may be allusion here to street processions in the towns from 1320 on (e.g., in York before 1376). Modeled on such Palm Sunday processions as we see at the opening of C.20/B.18, these processions involved guilds escorting the Host on the feast of Corpus Christi eleven days after Pentecost. Rubin treats the origin (in the 1250s) and development of this feast and notes that in 1389 a census found 471 fraternities, of which 44 were Corpus Christi fraternities (1991:164–287, esp. 234). L refers to this feast at 17.120 (B.15.388); see n. That feast's celebration of the institution of the Eucharist (see 383–90), and its association with the dramatization of sacred history in the cycle plays, make it a fit setting for the final actions of the poem. Aers further argues that L exposes as an empty fiction the "fraternity" of the unfraternally competitive and riotous craft "fraternities," which sometimes came to blows during the Corpus Christi processions themselves (1988:69–70; see also Aston 1993 for the association of Corpus Christi Day with the 1381 Rising).

Although the learned crafts of labor and of fighting are included, Grace emphasizes gifts of the practical intellect, like those in the lists of Paul and Isaiah 11:2–3 (215n above). Specifically, these are verbal skill (like the "word of wisdom" (*sapientia*) and "word of knowledge" (*scientia*) that head the Corinthians list; wisdom also heads Isaiah's list) and prophetic skill, as in both Paul's lists (and singled out by Paul as the chief gift). Hence this survey, unlike any others in PP, begins with preachers and priests and ends with religious, inserting the laboring and military classes in the middle. And like Paul's lists, this one concludes with an exhortation for the members of the Church to hold together and love one another (see 215n above, 254n below). The final lines (252–55) may refer especially to the clergy, who may claim to be **clenner then somme** (having vowed chastity), and who tend to **lacke opere** (see, e.g., B.11.214–15).

Thus, whereas everywhere in PP we find the effort to rationalize the social order practically overwhelming, here, in the view of Grace, it is a simple task to enumerate the gifts of skill that organize humankind. Further, the view of society is gracious, a "remarkably broad and tolerant vision, embracing workers of all kinds, even merchants and lawyers" (Godden 1984:151; cp. 9.22–57 [B.7.18–60, A.8.20–62]). Pearsall observes that the social order ordained at the Half Acre (8.5–79 [B.6.7–77, A.7.7–69]) is "inevitably, an agricultural one," whereas Grace's crafts include urban work, and hence the order is more complex and inclusive (1997:192–96).

The purpose of Grace's gifts is **to wynne with treuthe þat the world asketh** (230), just as the original folk of the fair field work "as þe world ascuth" (Prol.21 [B/A.Prol.19]). In the first vision "kynde wytt and þe comune contreued alle craftes," specifically a plow (Prol.145–46, cp. B.Prol.118–20). In some measure we have returned to where we began. The Prologue folk work and wander, and some "swonken ful harde / And wonne þat þis wastors with glotony destrueth" (21–24, B/A.Prol.19–22), and winning and wasting are prominent themes in the Half-Acre episode. Grace repeatedly speaks of "winning" (230, 235, 239, 245, 246), merging spiritual gifts with Realökonomie in L's (and not Paul's) characteristic way.

These gifts also recall the intellectual accomplishments that may be acquired under the tutelage of Dame Study (11.116–33 [B.10.176–221, A.11.128–64]). There Studie says "Of alle kyne craftyes y contreuede toles" and, like Paul and Grace, urges that the best lore is to love. See 22.206–11n, 230–31n.

L's including the arts of divination (see 240–44n below) seems strange. These are certainly intellectual skills, but, in a passage excised from C (B.10.212–21, A.11.155–64: did L become more tolerant of these arts as he aged?), Studie claims that she "ordeynede" such arts as Geomesie, Alkenamye, Nigromancie, and perimancie, but that they were first of all founded to deceive folk. These arts may be among the "sciences" and "sotil craftes" that Will wishes he knew, making him, in Liberum Arbitrium's judgment, one of Pride's knights (16.210–12 [B.15.48–50]). Further, in a passage added in C, Imaginatyf takes for granted that natal horoscopes, a matter of fortune, are determinative (14.30–34). Like Chaucer's Franklin and Canon's Yeoman, and one suspects like Chaucer himself, L seems to have entertained mixed feelings about the technological and magical arts. The loss, later in history, of these arts, according to Liberum Arbitrium (Anima in B) in a passage that should be compared with this, is caused by "werre and wrake and wikkede hefdes" (17.86–116, B.15.356–84). In any case, divination foretells the future, and Paul said prophecy, in part a matter of foretelling, is a gift of the Spirit. As Tester clarifies, the art of astrology, for example, was held by churchmen to be not mistaken, but merely not allowed when dealing with "contingent events, and those falling under free will"; hence "natural" astrology was accepted, but not "judicial" astrology (1987).

To think of Grace's exposition here as merely a description of a redeemed social order will involve problems; at this point in the narrative it is an order of hope rather than achievement.

231 prechours and prestes and prentises of lawe: People other than priests licensed, by pope or bishop, to preach include pardoners (see Prol.66

[B.Prol.68, A.Prol.65]) and friars like the Friars Preachers (Dominicans; see Prol.56–57 [B.Prol.58–59, A.Prol.55–56]). But "preachers and priests" may simply be a doublet for the latter: see B.15.95, 99, 114, 441 for examples. Apprentices of law were law students and barristers of less than sixteen years of practice (Alford, *Gloss.* s.v. *Apprentis*).

232 to lyue bi labour of tonge: the beginning of L's conflation of agricultural and intellectual or spiritual work. See 258–334n below. Lawler gathers references to the vocation of secular priests as labor (2003:94n11, 114). There is further reference to the general issue of payment for intellectual work; see 9.44–45 and n. **To lyue,** like "to harwen" in line 268 below, is an absolute or testamentary infinitive (Wittig 1986:230–31), unless in both instances the infinitive depends on the verb "gave."

236 a londe and a water: probably referring not specifically to agriculture and seamanship but to all manual labor; "on land and on water" is a legal formula of inclusiveness used several times in PP (Alford, *Gloss.* s.v. *Lond and Water*).

239 To wynne with . . . techynge: Schm and Prsl, allowing for revision from B to C, print the archetypal C reading, *As here wit wolde when þe tyme come;* the Athlone editors offer no comment on their preference for the B reading, in keeping with their rejection of the view that L revised his last two passūs (see Headnote and 243–53n below). The sense of "þe tyme" would be "the proper agricultural season."

240–44 And somme to deuyne . . . philosophres wyse: See the end of 229–51n above. The text is troubled in these lines. A *divinour* can simply be "a learned or wise man" (MED 2.(a)), and *divinacioun* can simply be the interpretation of dreams (MED 1.(b)) as in 9.306, B.7.158, A.8.141, a gift perhaps like Paul's "interpretation of speeches" (*interpretatio sermonum*—I Cor. 12:10). Possibly **to deuyne and deuyde** simply means "to take thought about things and to understand arithmetic." But more probably the divining and **astronomye** (= astronomy with astrology) here are arts that see and **saye what sholde bifalle,** as in B.15.589 and 148 above, that is, the gift of prophecy (1 Cor. 12:10). If **figures,** the Athlone editors' conjecture, is L's word, it may refer to geomancy (see MED *geomancie* and *figure* 7.(a)); the archetypal but unmetrical reading *noumbres* can refer to astronomy/astrology (Chaucer, *Boece* 1.m2.14–15). The association of numbers and divining seen here is replicated playfully in the Wife of Bath's Prologue 24–29.

    The sense of **deuyde** is also unclear, but seems to refer to the manipulation of numbers needed for what might be "calculed" in the heavens (B.15.371). Might L have thought that the stem of **deuyde** was Latin *videre*, "see," and hence that it means "foresee" as well as "divide"? Compare "deuyse wel þe ende" in 278 below. Of course Grace *divides* his gifts (215, 228a above). One might think a kind of dividing (see Headnote) is L's own gift, as is, Alford suggests, **to se and to saye what sholde bifalle** (1988a:61).

Those who **kerue and compace** ("fashion, contrive, construct") are less likely sculptors than stonemasons. At one point L associates "keruers" with "compas" the instrument (11.123), and at another point, "kerueres" with "Masons" (B.10.183), perhaps conceived as craftsmen and architects respectively. In B.17.172–73 "keruynge and compasynge" are further associated with "to portreye or peynten" as a "craft of þe fyngres," hence the association here with the craft of **coloures to make** (the usual verb; see MED *colour* 2c.(a) and 6., the craft-name "colour-maker"). These are the crafts most prominent in building great churches, whose carved stone interiors were painted all over. Master masons had to understand numbers and figures; a (jocular?) group-name for them in the fifteenth century was a *nombrynge of keruers* (MED *nombringe* (e)). It was in their interest to keep the arcane lore of their geometric **mester** (C.9/B.7/A.8.7) mysterious ("the masonic secret") as they enjoyed a reputation something like that of alchemists and astrologers (see Frankl 1960 passim).

The **philosopheres wyse** in this context are those defined under MED *philosophre* (c): "an alchemist; a magician, diviner, prognosticator, or an interpreter of dreams."

243–53 Bothe of wele . . . come of my ȝefte: In this passage fall three of the few more likely instances of small revisions in the last two passūs (see Headnote). Their bunching up here (see 239n above and 22.379n) may indicate that L returned to this passage, perhaps to improve B's meter. These are the apparently archetypal readings: 243, B *telle it er it felle*, C *and be ywaer bifore*; 251, B *And forbad hem alle debat þat noon were among hem*, C *Ne no boest ne debaet be among hem alle*; 253, B *Thynkeþ alle quod Grace þat grace comeþ*, C *That all craft and connyng come*. Schm adopts the archetypal readings, making emendations to smooth B's poor meter in each case; counter-argument is in RK-C, pp. 120–21 on lines 243 and 253, and KD-B, p. 95 on lines 243 and 251.

246 And fechen hit . . . thorw whitnesse of handes: Some families of B and C manuscripts read *wytnesse* ("knowledge," or "testimony"—or merely a spelling variant; see C.11.282 variants) for **whitnesse** (= *wihtnesse*, "strength, agility"). The sense may be "to recover stolen goods by judicial process": compurgators in trials were known by the technical term "hands" (*manus*), and **whitnesse of handes** would be "the witness of compurgators" (on *manus* see Helmholz 1983:14, 15, 17, 24). But strongly supporting the traditional interpretation, "agility and strength of hands," is L's usage "los of his handes" for a knight's reputation for prowess in 13.111 (B.11.297), and the use of the phrase *wyghtenes of hondus* with this meaning in *Anturs of Arther*, l. 263 (ed. Mills 1992).

247 fechen it fro false men with foleuiles lawes: The expression **foleuiles lawes** is not elsewhere recorded. The Folvilles were a homicidal criminal gang active in the 1320s to the 1340s (Stones 1957, Bowers 1961). Skeat proposed that "Folvilles' laws" were Lynch laws, an ironic use for extra-legal and violent justice—cp. *theues lauh*, MED *laue* 9.(a). Prsl finds that L "seems to admire such justice" even though the original Folvilles seem hardly admirable. Kane argued that **with foleuiles lawes** means "in despite of the rule of violence," citing OED for *with* meaning "against" (1993:141). Schm finds L's use "pungently ironic," and argues (1995), citing 8.161–66 (B.6.164–70, A.7.149–55) and 1.90–95 (B.1.94–97, A.1.92–95), that L believed that some lawbreakers require such "law" to be corrected, and that Kane's interpretation "renders the line commonplace." R. F. Green agrees with Stones that the Folvilles were regarded as Robin-Hood figures (1999:169–71).

But L nowhere defends the use of violence outside the law; he merely enjoins knights or other law-enforcers to help maintain the law. If "Folvilles' laws" indeed means "behavior like that of the Folville gang," a simpler solution than Kane's construes the phrase with **false men** rather than with **fechen**, to mean "false men with their Folvilles' laws," i.e., their banditry.

The Folvilles were involved in the murder in 1326 of Roger Bellers, baron of the exchequer and an adherent of the Despensers. Hugh Despenser, whose hanging the Dublin Annals record (Hanna 1993:25–26), pursued some of the conspirators (Stones 1957:119–20). Possibly L, son of the Despenser adherent Stacy de Rokayle (as the scribe of the Dublin Annals tells us), knew of the Folvilles through family memory. L's grandfather Peter de Rokayle was an adherent of the Despensers at least in 1326 (Bright 1928:35–36). The Bellers murder was still remembered by the chronicler Henry Knighton, who approved of it (Stones 133).

Barr (1994:22) notes that the Folvilles and Chichester (B.13.270) are the only fourteenth-century individuals whom L names. Striking in a work so engaged with social actuality, this omission may reflect L's stance of (feigned?) prudence.

248–49 And somme . . . preye for alle cristene: These lines might describe the vocation of any saintly or contemplative Christian, but the specification that they **preye** probably singles out the second of the three estates (militare, *orare*, laborare), the religious (here probably monastic) order—or hermits.

254 noen lacke oþere bute loueth: On L's developing antipathy toward "lak-kynge" see Lawler 1996:163–65 and Simpson 1990b, esp. 25–30, and see C.5.5n. On craft rivalry see Simpson 1993 and 200–212n, 229–51n above, and 22.206–11n. In an influential article, Mervyn James argues that the prime function of the Corpus Christi processions and drama was to express wholeness, unity, and concord, as symbolized by the Host of the Mass and the hierarchy of the processional order—but at the same time the day was often a time of civic conflict and rioting (1983). Owst quotes Wimbledon's sermon, ". . . and men of o craft shuld not despise ne hate men of none other craft, sith they be so nedefull everich to other . . ." (1961:551). In *Vox clamantis* 5.11, lines 663–70, Gower urges friendship between merchants and artisans. Guild ordinances commonly enjoined amity among the members. Positive and negative examples are printed in Krochalis and Peters 1975:214, 216, and Smith and Smith 1870:4, 79, 81, 84, 87, 92, etc.

256 crouneth Consience kyng . . . craft ȝoure styward: The head of Grace's society has not been identified until now—Conscience. We are to remember that Conscience and Reason were to be the king's chief advisors (in C, specifically Chief Justice and Chancellor) in the political order established at the end of Passus 4, all versions; in fact, Conscience does not assume the office. See 424–27n below. In the course of the poem we have seen Conscience rise from accuser (like a barrister) to knight to guide (like a homilist) to king (see 22.72–74n and 22.214–16n). A **styward** is the chief administrator of a manor or estate under its lord (Alford, *Gloss.* s.v. *Stiward*; Denholm-Young 1937:66–85; Oschinsky 1971:65); see 461 below. The bureaucratic terminology continues for a few lines, as the polity receives its functions and functionaries. The order Grace establishes is ruled by active knowledge of the good (Conscience) and administered and nourished by skilled labor (Craft personified). Conscience turns out to be a distinctly ineffectual king over this unruly polity (see Baldwin 1981b:75–80). The "comune" (line 214 above) whom Grace is addressing has the power to crown a king; compare B.Prol.113 and the issues raised there (see note).

Jesus and now Conscience are designated king, and later the vicar hopes that Piers will be "Emperour of al þe world" (427 below). What these three figures have in common (e.g., charity, sincerity, patience) defines the idea of heroism in PP, and what they lack (e.g., pedantry, hypocrisy, greed) defines what cumbers the world.

Piers's plowing and sowing

258–334 For y make Peres the plouhman . . . lawe of holi churche: Grace founds the Church now in another, allegorical mode. The action reprises at large the sketch of the benefits of the Court of Truth, where Grace admits people to find Truth in their hearts, and where Charity will make a church there that provides food for their souls (7.243–60, varied from AB). Having explicated "Piers" by way of the apostle Peter (182–98n above), L now explicates (fulfills, but does not destroy) the other half of his appellation, "plowman," by way of a commonplace exegetical topic: dissemination of God's word as agriculture (see Barney 1973; Wailes 1987:98; C.10.200; 21.232 and n above). As the *Northern Homily Cycle* puts it, "Obout midday and none also, / God ordand precheoures for to go, / Man-soul in erth for to till" (ed. Nevanlinna, 1973:11, lines 5811–13). The allegory is of the establishment of Church institutions: the priesthood, scripture, and doctrinal authority (the Fathers), which cultivate the field of the soul, and moral faculties, the cardinal virtues, which flourish in it. The Church is then gathered in its community, represented as a fortified barn.

   Presenting the foundation of the Church as an elaborated allegory seems to distance it conceptually as well as temporally from the Church of the brewer and the vicar that we encounter later. The action "is an obvious reprise of the pilgrimage to truth"—specifically of the Half-Acre episode (Alford 1988a:60; see Headnote)—and like that earlier episode it culminates in defiance by some of the folk, and collapse. The Half Acre had represented Piers's well-doing authority in secular society; here he represents well-doing authority in the Church (Raw 1969:146). Piers abandoned that earlier agriculture; this, too, will prove inadequate to the work of salvation.

258–60 For y make . . . ben on erthe: Grace assigns Piers five titles. Continuing his emphasis in this passus on the nature of good governance, L sorts through offices of manorial (and, in the allegory, Church) leadership by Piers in parallel with his study of natural leadership as exemplified in Jesus and in king. **Procuratour** (agent with, as it were, "power of attorney"); **reue** (manager of an estate below a steward—see 459–64n below); **Registrer** (any keeper of a register, specifically the clerk of an ecclesiastical court who among other duties records receipts, or the keeper of a bishop's register of licensed clergy;

see B.2.174, 22/B.20.271]); **prowour** (= purveyor, variously a procurer of supplies and provisions, a steward, an overseer, but in L's time with a specific
connotation—see below); and **plouhman**. For the first three of these see
Alford, *Gloss.*; for *purveiour* see MED and the references below.

A plowman could in fact be a reeve. The first four offices named all
require literacy and skill at management, but they are omitted from the vocations to whom Grace has given "craft and connyng." We are to imagine Piers
as something like an administative deacon under Grace as bishop, or a reeve
under Grace as lord of the manor, or a purveyor under Grace as king. In the
allegory, Piers would be the manager of the Church **on erthe** (260) and culti-
vator of the human heart, namely a priest. As Prsl notes, Piers has performed
the office of manorial reeve in the Half-Acre episode, e.g. at 8.112–21 "To
ouersey hem hymsulue," B.6.105–114 (A.7.97–106). There Piers calls himself
Truth's "hyne" (B.6.131 [A.7.123]), "servant, laborer." Parkes indicates that
reeves were servile, drawn from the local peasantry (1973:559; see also Oschinsky 1971:96, 291). For the reeve's accounting role see 459–64n below. This episode in effect expands the opening lines of Passus 9 (B.7/A.8): "Treuthe herde
telle herof and to Peres sente / To taken his teme and tilion þe erthe."

As the character of Chaucer's Reeve indicates, reeves were widely considered sly cheats. Yet L could speak positively of "resoun" [proper accounting]
"as a reue" (3.309, not in AB). To speak of Piers as a **prowour**, purveyor, is
likewise bold, as the "diabolical prerogative" of purveyance, the often abusive
and much hated exactions in England of taxes and provisions, nominally for
the king's troops or household, was bitterly resented in L's time (Given-
Wilson 1983, citing William of Pagula, p. 145; McKisack 1959:221, 362–63 et passim). The local officials charged with administering purveyance, usually drawn
from the minor gentry, were despised as extorters, embezzlers, and deadbeats
(Ormrod 1990:155, 158 et passim) and much legislation was directed toward
limiting the scope of purveyance. Under Edward III and Richard II the royal
household of 400 to 700 people required some thirty to fifty royal purveyors
to get provisions—this apart from military purveyance in time of active
war (Given-Wilson 1986:41–48). In 1362 the Great Statute of Purveyors was
enacted, to little effect. The Commons complained again of the purveyors of
the "grandes Seigneurs de Roialme" in the Good Parliament of 1376 (Rot. Parl.
2.342). Moreover, the title *Procuratour* had similarly a bad odor, as the term
(with *Exploratour*) used of papal collectors in England, who were likewise bitterly complained of in the Good Parliament (Rot. Parl. 2.338). Piers, as Grace's
purveyor, of course promises to be the antithesis of a corrupt purveyor like
the figure Wrong of the Mede episode (see 4.45–63n); still, L requires for his

perfected society a figure of administrative force, who eventually, in the vicar's wish, will be a world emperor (427 below).

For *Redde quod debes* see 182–90n above. The registrar keeps accounts of the payments made as restitution for sin—in the allegory, a priestly function.

261 to tulye treuthe a teme: punning on plow "team" and "theme," of a sermon, etc., as also in 8.20 (B.6.22, A.7.24); 8.141 (B.6.134); 9.2 (B.7.2); 20.358, B.19.271 (see 20.358n and Huppé 1950:168). The phrase "till truth" recurs at 333 below, the culmination of Grace's work.

262–65 foure grete oxen . . . gentill of all: L names Luke first because his traditional symbol was the ox; further to symbolize all the evangelists as oxen was common, from Jerome, "four oxen, that is, four evangelists" (PL 30.591, cited by Robertson and Huppé 1951:18). On the evangelists' symbols see 6.238n. Grace may think John the gentlest evangelist because of his Gospel's theological sophistication and its emphasis on love, or because he was thought to be "that disciple whom Jesus loved" (John 21:20), or with reference to his legendary beauty and virginity. Bloomfield points out that "to Joachim [of Flora], John is the symbol of the contemplative or monastic life, and is finally to replace Peter" (1961a:220, n29). Alliterative convenience may have induced the diction: cp. Job the gentle (11.21 [B.10.23, A.11.23], C13.15, 13.25), James the gentle (1.181 [B.1.185, A.1.159]), and Jesu the gentle (B.10.35).

267–73a foure stottes . . . *Id est vetus testamentum & nouum*: The four chief Fathers of the Church harrow the land with two rakes, the two Testaments. See 309–16n below. Only here is the word **aythe** "harrow" recorded in Middle English. Of "Austine, Ambrose, Gregore, and Jerom" the *Northern Homily Cycle* says "Þai ripid [reaped] the rotes of holy writ, / And vnto lawd men lerid itt. . . . In Goddes wine-ȝerd grubed þai"(ed. Nevanlinna 1973, lines 5797–800). Prsl and Alford (*Quot.* 115) observe that the *id est* imitates the language of biblical exegesis, of which these Fathers were masters (cp. B.15.212, *Petrus id est christus*). A *stot* is a draft animal, either bullock or horse. On the construction of **harwen** in line 268 see 232n above.

274–316 And grace gaf Peres graynes . . . the cardinal vertues: In another distributive scheme (see Headnote), Grace, having provided the means to survive (the crafts) and the resources to know the truth (Scripture and the institutional Church) now grants humans "tresor" and "wepne" (217–18) of another sort: the constitutional wherewithal to combat vice. These **cardinales vertues** counter the "cardynales," high vices, of Pride's forces (224 above), and they correspond as human virtues to the Four Daughters of God of C.20/B.18. The fourfold distribution here is complete and smoothly finished off, but when the topic returns below (393–474, esp. 463) the array is deliberately complicated. Tradition from Plato's *Republic* defined the four cardinal virtues, and Grace helpfully **toelde here names** (275): prudence, temperance, fortitude, and justice (see Prol.131–32n). The Prologue passage presents in brief the same sequence that we find here: Piers's receiving of the power to bind and unbind, and the flowing of that power into the gift of the cardinal virtues. Sadly, in the course of defining these virtues we immediately confront their opposing vices.

On sources for the conception of these seeds see Frank 1957:103–5, and Burrow 1993:68–70, citing Hugh of St. Victor, "The gifts [of the Spirit] are the first stirrings in the heart—certain seeds of the virtues, as it were (*quasi quaedam semina virtutum*), scattered over the earth of our heart. The virtues themselves grow up like a crop from these." The passage is also found in the anonymous *Summa sententiarum* and in both Peter Lombard and Thomas Aquinas (Horowitz 1998:51, 137). Bloomfield suggests that attaching the term *spiritus* to these virtues derives from the contested but received doctrine that the cardinal virtues were "infused," that is, a specific divine gift (1961a:134, 220n; also Goldsmith 1981:87; Wittig 1997:142–43). On the issue of infused vs. acquired virtues see Douglas 1966:120–25.

The Parable of the Sower and its interpretation (Matt. 13:3–23 et synop.) more or less directly assert that "the seed is the word of God" (Luke 8:11). L integrates this idea with the present granting of the gifts of the Spirit. Of the several biblical lists of these gifts (see 215n above), the one in Isaiah names seven that will rest upon the rod from the root of Jesse (i.e., Jesus): the spirits of wisdom, understanding (*intellectus*), counsel, fortitude (*fortitudinis*), knowledge, godliness, and fear of the Lord (Isa. 11:1–3). From *spiritus . . . fortitudinis* and *spiritus . . . intellectus* particularly, L drew his names for the four seeds (see 463n below).

Grace **sewe** the seeds **in mannes soule** (275), but L quickly complicates the allegory, conflating germination with ingestion: the seeds (metonymically, for their fruit) are eaten to activate their virtue (277, 282, 290, 299). The verb **shal/sholde** is repeated five or six times in the passage (see KD-B, p. 118 in defense of **Shal** in line 301) in the emphatically predictive sense (MED *shulen* v. (1), 6). These powers *will* be (and hence now are) ours to employ.

The world imagined here, in which these virtues operate, is a nasty one. Burnt fingers are the least of its sorrows: it is full of gluttony, vanity, jangling, and vile talk—lies, insults, guile. In the speeches of a lord and king at the end of this passus, and of Nede at the beginning of the next passus, these virtues, except perhaps for temperance, seem to collapse (455–74 and n below; C.22/

B.20.20–35). Alford argues that later the sins will appear in the guise of these virtues (see 455, 464, 473–74 below; Alford 1988a:60).

276–80 *Spiritus prudencie* . . . fatte aboue: As Schm notes, the Latin word *prudentia* derives from *providentia*, "foreseeing," and that is its force in L's conception. Humbler than the prognosticator's ability "to se . . . what sholde bifalle" (242 above), it is the practical ability to anticipate what will happen— for instance that a pot might boil over and spill its valuable fat, and that a short-handled spoon to stir such a pot will cause burnt fingers. The words **ymageny** and **caste** both refer to such ability, like the grandiose *heigh ymaginacioun forncast* of the fox in the Nun's Priest's Tale (3217). The homeliness of the example means that such prudence is well within our grasp if we would exercise this gift.

281–88 The seconde sede . . . iohann spyced: As L develops his account of the cardinal virtues he brings out their force as *virtues*, medicinal specifics against ailments, or talismans (MED *vertu* 6., 7.). Compare, for instance, Chaucer's Pardoner's relic that heals swelling (PardPro 353–60). A temperate person will not **swelle**—with fat or disease or hunger or flatulence or envy or pride—from intemperate eating (see MED *swellen* for all these senses, and 16.227 [B.12.57— swelling for pride], 8.225 [B.6.215, A.7.201—swelling for hunger; see Kane's note to A.7.201 on p. 449], 6.88 [B.5.12—swelling for envy]). Several senses of **meschief** are possible here: primarily "hunger, famine" (MED *mischief* 2.(a), C.10.202) as the privative of **mete**; "disease" (MED sense 3.) which intemperance may cause (see 8.269–95 [B.6.257–74, A.7.241–58]); "wrongdoing, fornication" (MED sense 4.). Any of these can cause swelling—Middle English describes the enlargement of pregnancy as swelling (see 18.99 [B.16.72]). This last sense is perhaps less likely because of the masculine pronoun **hym** in 283 and 284 (can male tumescence be in question?), but if it is possible it may account better, as bowdlerization rather than merely "easier substitution" (KD-B, p. 165), for the common B version substitution of *muchel drynke* for **meschief**.

Out of **skille** is an idiom meaning "immoderate, lacking self-control" (MED *skil* 2.(a)). The dignified **maistre iohann** is used mockingly of a cook; compare Chaucer's "sir John" for the humble Nun's Priest (VII.2810, 2820). Chaucer's Pardoner at his most feignedly puritanical preaches against "spicerie of leef, and bark, and roote" (VI.544). **Waste** (286) may be an adjective ("idle, vain": MED *waste* adj. 2.(b)), an adverb ("in vain," MED *waste* adv.), or an infinitive parallel with **meue**. The term is, as often, coupled with **wynnynge** (see Prol.24n), as L, as often, chastises vices of speech, jangling. Here both winning and wasting are seen as potential forms of intemperance.

289–96a The thridde seed . . . *dampnatus inique*: For L, both temperance and fortitude resemble his favorite virtue (after charity), patience, conventionally a part of fortitude. Orsten (1969:319) cites Augustine's naming of the "parts" of fortitude: magnificentia, fidentia, patientia, perseverantia (*De diversis quaest.* 31.1; PL 40.21). Hence fortitude is a defensive, inward virtue; twice it is **to soffre** (Latin *patior*), and to be **bold** is to be **abidynge**, "enduring, suffering" (MED *abiden* 11.(a)). L displays a bit of his rich diction of suffering: by **angeres** he means (as elsewhere) "distress, suffering, afflictions" (MED *anger* 1.); **mornynge**, "anxiety in general, distress" (MED *mornen* 1.(b)); **busmares**, "scorn, insults" (MED *bismare* 2.). In C.19.319–26 (B.17.339–46) the Samaritan tells us that even those without just this kind of fortitude against **seeknesse and angeres** will receive mercy.

295 pleieþ al with pacience and *parce michi domine*: Schmidt reads from one group of B manuscripts *plede* or *plete* for Athlone's **pleieþ**, and observes that "the man of fortitude 'goes to law' only by enduring mishaps and injustices." RK-C counters that **pleieþ** here in fact means "pleads," citing MED *pleien* v. (2) (a), not the verb "play" but a homophone derived from the noun "plea" (p. 123). Under *pleien* v. (1) 8.(b) MED lists this as the sole instance of a sense "to deal with (something), handle"; the dictionary editors might, considering **murye** above, have guessed "make light of" (close to sense 5.), but neither transitive use is likely; **al** is probably an adverb.

On ***parce michi domine***, "spare me, Lord," see B.18.392n. With wonted contrariness, L conceives of begging God for mercy, as it were falling on the mercy of the court, as an act of fortitude. The patient man is merry, and bravely endures contumely, because he knows his prayer to be spared is answered.

296 Caton . . . *dampnatus inique*: (Pseudo-) Cato's distich 2.14 (see 4.17n): "Be of stout heart even though [or, when] you are condemned unfairly, [for no one who wins by an unfair judgment is glad for long]." L's omission of the second half of the distich makes the counsel of patience more demanding, as the injustice is not relieved.

297–308 The ferthe seed . . . eueneforth his knowyng: Conscience will call "the Spirit of Justice" the "cheef seed þat Peres sewe" (406 below), and indeed the account of the four seeds rises to a climax with it, as the problem of justice in one form or another occupies the entire poem (see 182–90n above; but Nede asserts that temperance is foremost at 22.23—see n). Dowel (*benefacere*) is practically doing justice, according to Isaiah 1:17. Among the Four Daughters of God L had said Rihtwisnesse (= *justicia*) was eldest (see 20.169n). Picking up from the judicial terms at the end of the account of fortitude (295–96), L takes the concept of justice immediately as the principle of fairness in legal proceedings—the justice of justices, Trajan's particular virtue. It is as if the Latin name of the seed meant "the spirit of a justice."

Until the last line of the account, justice (like temperance and fortitude) is mainly expressed by its negatives—guilt, royal anger and its arbitrary power, undue influence by the likes of dukes or princes. Justice is here not simply the classical virtue of "giving to each his own" (see 182–90n above), but the property of incorruptibility in a world of extortion and bribery. We return to the world of Lady Meed, and find that Grace has granted protection, these seeds, against its venality, but history shows that humankind succumbs to its corruption.

298–99 euene trewe / With god: RK-C, p. 120 takes **euene** here to mean "uniformly, consistently" (MED *even* 15.); Donaldson 1990 translates "even-handed and true," perhaps thinking of MED sense 11., "impartially, justly." B archetype's *euere* is certainly easier. The phrase **With god** is perplexing, and aroused variation: manuscript F of B (*& of god*) and N² of C (*om.*). Manuscript F may catch the sense, "of God's party."

300–301 For gyle . . . *spiritus iusticie*: Guile sometimes keeps even the Spirit of Justice, as it were a justice's judgment, from discerning guile's opposite, good faith, in court. On the legalism **goed fayth**, *bona fides*, see Alford, *Gloss.* s.v. *Good Feith*, and C.22/ B.20.131, where Covetousness makes False supplant Good Faith.

302–7 *Spiritus iusticie* . . . prinses lettres: L returns to a repeated topic, the need for courageous figures, usually clergymen (esp. bishops) but here the Spirit of Justice itself, to chastise wrongdoers, even the nobility, when needed (see, e.g., 9.13–18, 10.93–99a, B.10.264–93a, and Kellogg 1965). A **domesman** is a judge or magistrate, the chief officer of a court (Alford, *Gloss.*). The **presente** here is a bribe like that of 4.91 (B.4.95, A.4.82); **preyere** a plea for special favor like that of 2.219 (B.2.207, A.2.168); and **prinses lettres** are pardons or letters of intercession like those in 9.280 and 22.325 (Alford, *Gloss.*, s.v. *Preiere, Letter*). On the whole L shows more concern about improper lenience than improper severity, and Friar Flatterer will epitomize such lenience (C.22/B.20.315–79).

The string of negatives makes 305–7 difficult. It means, "The Spirit of Justice was never afraid to make judgments as a magistrate; neither of duke nor of the threat of death [was he ever so afraid] that, because of bribery or special pleading or magnates' intercessions, he would not execute the law."

304 when he in Court sitteth: Here **he**, the Spirit of Justice, is the **domesman** or other court officer, standing for fair dealing in general, and not the king (though the king might actually preside over the "kinges bench"—A.Prol.95 and n; Alford, *Gloss.*).

308 equite: fairness, even in spite of the law, a special responsibility of the "English side" of the court of chancery. See 20.395n, Birnes 1975, Alford, *Gloss.* s.v. *Equite, Chauncelrie*.

309–316 Thise foure sedes . . . cardinal vertues: L takes the purpose of harrowing to be weeding. He deepens the agricultural allegory, saying that **loue myhte wexe / Among the foure vertues**. Henry compares Prol.130–31 (B.Prol.102–3), in which Peter's power works "with loue as oure lord wolde / Amonge foure vertues, most vertuous of vertues" (1990:42). See Prol.125–30n for discussion. Those Prologue lines were probably composed after the present passage (see C.21 Headnote).

The sense is that the cultivated soul or commune, defended by the classical virtues, can form the ground for the preeminent Christian virtue (1 Cor. 13:13)—as the tree "treweloue" grows in the heart (18.4–15). See also 15.275 (not in B), charity as chief virtue. In PP, love, like grace, is often a plant (see 20.400n; 1.148 [B.1.152, A.1.137]). The metaphor of **vices** as **wedes** derives from the parables of the Sower (Matt. 13:3–23 et synop.) and of the Tares among the Wheat (Matt. 13:24–30, 36–43; see Stock 1991, arguing that the parable's meaning, "patience," operates here). In the next passus the allegory is activated; see C.22/B.20.53–57 and n.

In his role as reeve, Piers commands **alle þat conneth kynde wit**, all sane people, to harrow and till the virtues in accordance with the counsel and teaching of **this doctours**, that is the four "stottes" named at 269–70 above. For the idiom *connen wit*, "possess intelligence," see MED *connen* 6.(h). Line 309 makes it clear that Piers causes the virtue-seeds to be harrowed; hence unlikely is Skeat's view, that **alle þat conneth kynde wit** are the object of **harweth**, whose implied subject then would be the laborers (priests?) on Piers's plowland. Also unlikely is Schmidt's view, translating "everyone who can should harrow their native understanding of Scripture . . ." (trans. 1992:236)— but understanding of Scripture is not **kynde**, native. A little less unlikely: "All who know how should harrow their native intelligence in accordance with the counsel. . . ."

The elements of the allegory are polysemous: the land tilled is truth (261), and Holy Scripture (272), and man's soul (275), and the cardinal virtues (309, 315–16); seed is sown in and fed to people (see 274–316n). Underlying this multiplicity of meaning is the dual application of the allegory to the individual soul and to the whole of humankind. So with some biblical parables: in the Sower, for example, the seed is first the Word, then the human beings who receive the Word (Matt. 13:19, 20–23; Mark 4:14–20; Luke 8:11–15). We should not be troubled to find that Holy Scripture is both the field and the roof of Unite (272, 327).

The building of Holy Church

317–34 Aȝeynes thy graynes . . . lawe of holi churche: The second movement of this vision (see 182–334n) concludes with the physical building of a **hous** named **vnite, holy chirche an englisch** (328) and the provision of a cart and a hayward for Piers's agriculture. Unite is the last and most overt expression of the series of Pentecostal distributions that begin with line 200 above, as it allegorizes the Church as an edifice of the work of Christ—in effect, his body (see 20.42n). The source of the allegory of barn as Church is obviously the numerous biblical metaphors of the gathering and sifting of people for divine judgment as the harvesting and storing of grain, e.g., Joel 3:12–15, Apoc. 14:14–15, Mark 4:29, John 4:35–38, Matt. 3:12.

Building allegories are common, and may be found in Grosseteste's *Château d'Amour* (see Passus 20 Headnote), *Cursor mundi*, *Le Pèlerinage de vie humaine*, and other works probably or possibly known to L (see Owen 1912 and Cornelius 1930 passim; Owst 1933:77–85; Cowling 1998:54–82; 362–66n below; Prol.15n). The third vision of *The Shepherd of Hermas* represents the Church as a tower, but other than PP no sustained allegorical fiction of the Church as a barn has been identified. In *De civili dominio*, c. 39, Wyclif concocts a brief allegory of this kind, building the Church from the three theological virtues. The Church has "pro fundamento fidem Christi, pro parietibus spem vite, et pro tecto caritatem (for its foundation faith in Christ, for its walls the hope of life, and for its roof charity)" (ed. Poole 1885:288–89).

Unite is the last of the series of allegorical buildings in PP, beginning with Truth's "tour" (Prol.15, A/B.Prol.14) and Wrong's "Castel of care" (1.57 [B.1.61, A.1.59]). The most elaborate of these are where Dowel and Anima dwell, the "Castel þat kynde maed," called *caro* in A and B and interpreted in A and B

as "man wiþ a Soule" (10.128–50, 171–74 [B.9.1–55, A.10.1–51])—a typical "Castle of Man" allegory (see Prsl 10.128n)—and the "Court" of Truth (7.232–82
[B.5.585–629, A.6.72–114]). The latter resembles Unite and should be compared
in detail; its constituents are the elements of Christianity. As with the allegory
of Unite, Grace is a crucial figure (the gateward); see 22.296–303n. It turns out
that the Court of Truth is likewise a kind of body allegory—because with
Grace one can see "treuthe sitte in thy sulue herte" (7.255; cp. I Cor. 3:16,
6:19)—and that Truth will charge Charity to make a church in one's heart "to
herborwe alle trewe," like Unite (7.258).

318–20 Ordeyne the an hous . . . ar ʒe hennes wende: Ordeyne simply means
"build," MED *ordeinen* 3.(a). Unite is a **hous** (any building), a "berne" (344,
357 below), and similar to a "pyle" (see 363n below). In *Pearl* heaven is called
a *proper pyle* (line 686). Compare the "grange," "barn," of 19.73 (B.17.75),
which is also an emblem of the Church (Smith 1966:78–79). *Grangia* and *hor-
reum* were the common Latin terms for "barn."

Brady points out that English barns of the period were sometimes huge
and ornate, of "cathedral-like proportions and layout" (1997:80), and function
in part as symbols of prestige useful to the lords for controlling a sometimes
unruly workforce. He interprets L's choice of a barn as a figure of the Church
as "a readily identifiable symbol of oppression in the landscape," and Conscience's demanding *redde quod debes* as meaning that he "has become the
symbol of an ecclesiastical lord" (100–104), but these interpretations have no
basis in the text.

L may allude to a deliberate architecture of humility adopted by friars
(Szittya 1986:53). Hinnebusch cites especially Dominic's and early Dominicans'
injunctions that priories should exhibit poverty and be modest and humble,
and records later criticism for their vanity (1951:124–30). Friars' churches were
often built without transepts and resembled barns (Clapham and Godfrey
n.d.:243; Knowles 1955, 2:152; Owst 1926:159). Conversely, aisled barns were
common in the period, and their interior space could roughly resemble the
nave and aisles of a church (Miller 1991:866–68). The traditional criticism of
friars for their vainly elaborate buildings extends at least as far back as Bonaventure and Pecham (Clopper 1997a:176, n19; Lambert 1998:173). Gower chastised more recent friars for building sumptuous churches (*Vox Clam.* Bk. 4,
ch. 23), and *Pierce the Ploughman's Crede* likewise attacks friars for falling away
from their earlier simplicity of building, particularly with reference to the
splendor of Blackfriars' house (ca. 1300) in London (ed. Barr 1993, lines 118–218
and notes, esp. 172–207n; see Hinnebusch 40–53). Skeat at his C.6.165n (= RK-
C.5.164) quotes a Wycliffite text from Arnold's edition: "Also freris bylden

mony grete chirchis and costily waste housis, and cloystris as hit were castels. . . ." See also 3.50–76 (B.3.47–75), and for further satire on friars' luxurious buildings, Aston 1984:47 and Mann 1973:232, n139.

Grace's request puts Piers in something of the role of a purveyor, exacting supplies from the neighborhood (see 258–60n above). Piers's reply (319–20) strikes also the tone of a steward or reeve, told by the lord of the manor to build a barn for the harvest—"I don't have any wood—*you* build it!"—of course the lord would have to give permission for his timber to be cut. Grace immediately converts to generosity the abuse characteristic of purveyance by providing the building materials himself, out of Christ's passion.

323 bapteme and bloed: liquids, appropriate for mixing mortar, and with reference to the two original and major sacraments, appropriate for the Church's foundation.

325 a goode foundement: That Christ is "the Church's one foundation" is commonplace; e.g., Peter the Chanter, *Distinctiones Abel*, s.v. *Ecclesia*, "The Church is the house of God, whose foundation (*fundamentum*) is Christ" (Reims, Bibl. Mun. Manuscript 508).

328 vnite, holy chirche an englisch: Trisyllabic **vnite** (like *charite, vilte, venemouste*, etc.) is still palpably French in form, and L makes as if to translate it.

The creed speaks of *una sancta catholica et apostolica ecclesia*: the first two adjectives appear in the barn's names here. St-Jacques shows that the liturgy for Pentecost dwells on the theme of ecclesiastical unity (1970:211–12). The name recalls, too, the Psalm verse cited at 20.466a (B.18.423—see n—and A.11.192a, "for brethren to dwell together in unity" (*habitare fratres in unum*—Ps. 132:1). See 22.246n. The verse may be read, with anticipating irony, as rejoicing in the presence of friars in Unite. As Stokes points out, the name points to the simplicity and integrity of the Church's original foundation, as opposed to the duplicity of the friars (1984:49). See also 355–56n below.

This name for the Church also recalls the only biblical occurrences of the word *unitas*, in a passage that seems to underlie much of the detail of this passus, Ephesians 4:1–13. Some well-known and relevant phrases (note the repeated verb "give"): ". . . that you walk worthy of the vocation in which you are called [see C.5.43a], With all humility and mildness, with patience, supporting one another in charity [see 249–55 above]. Careful to keep the unity (*unitas*) of the Spirit in the bond of peace (see 357 below). One body and one Spirit; as you are called in one hope of your calling. One Lord, one faith, one baptism. One God and Father of all. . . . But to every one of us is given grace, according to the measure of the giving of Christ. Wherefore he saith: *Ascending on high, he led captivity captive;* [see 7.130a, B.5.490a] *he gave gifts to men.* [See 215n above.] And he gave some apostles, and some prophets, and other some evangelists, and other some pastors and doctors [see 262–70, 315 above, 332 below], for the perfecting of the saints, for the work of the ministry, for the edifying (*ædificatio,* "building") of the body of Christ [= the Church; see 321–27 above]: Until we all meet into the unity (*unitas*) of faith. . . ." The Wycliffite Bible translates *unitas* as *vnite* here.

330–32 A Cart hihte Cristendoem . . . presthoed hayward: Cristendoem here is universal Christian polity, which contains and conveys toward God the harvested fruits of the seeds of the virtues. As a term distinct from "the Church in general" (= Unite) it may more precisely mean "the state of being Christian," or more specifically, baptism (OED *Christendom* 1., 4.). Such allegories are common; see 2.178–96n. A crude picture of a cart whose wheels are the symbols of the four evangelists, carrying a crowd of people and labeled "Þe cart of þe fayth" may be found on fol. 81ʳ of British Library Manuscript Addit. 37049 (ed. Doty 1969:448; reproduced in Salter 1988, Plate 5). An agricultural allegory in a (possibly) Lollard sermon has priests as drivers of the plow who goad the team (ed. Cigman 1989:211). *Cursor mundi* has an elaborated "weyn" of Christ, drawn by the four evangelists, etc. (ed. Mous 1986:130, lines 21263–304). Contrast the "lang cart" of Liar in the Mede episode (2.195 [B.2.182, A.2.143]).

   Contrissioun & confessioun, the sacrament of penance, actualize Christendom's work of salvation; their corruption is the problem at the end of the poem. The job of **hayward**—keeping hedges, guarding grain, overseeing the harvest, etc.—is among those Will said he was too weak to perform (5.16–17). As such **presthoed** is the succession from Peter and the surrogate for Piers, the chief steward of the manor, principal purveyor of that grace which is the power that founds and supervises priesthood.

332–35 the while hymsulue wente . . . Peres to the plouh: Having established Unite, Grace and Piers as well apparently travel abroad in missionary activity. Jesus charged the apostles to go "into the whole world (*mundum universum*), and preach the gospel to every creature" (Mark 16.15); the near translation, **As wyde as the world is with Peres to tulye treuthe** underscores the apostolic role of Piers. The action is in part a historical allegory of the early Church's growth. For L's interest in the Church's mission abroad see 17.315–21 (B.15.607–13) and esp. 10.190–200 with similar language, "as wyde as þe worlde" and "tulie þe erthe with tonge." Translate 333–34: "to sow truth and till the land with the doctrine, the law/religion of Holy Church." Hence Piers continues, or rather expands, the work he has been doing. The emphasis is not on his *leaving* Unite, but rather on his setting to work in an enlarged field. Twice the figure Conscience sets off on a comparable journey: after the banquet (15.183–88, much reduced from B.13.179–219) and at the end of the poem, with similar phrasing, "as wyde as þe world" (C.22/B.20.381).

Neither Piers nor Grace appears to Will for the remainder of the poem. Both are appealed to, as if they were still together, in the last lines of the poem (see 22.380–86n). Burrow takes L to mean that Piers significantly decamps, and compares Piers's sudden departure with the abrupt vanishing of Peter from the Book of Acts after Chapter 15 (1993:78–79). Closer to home in the C version, Piers abruptly vanishes (like Jesus at Emmaus—Luke 24:31) along with Reason in the banquet scene (15.148–50).

But Piers is "now" **to the plouh**, and the plowing has been at the manor of Unite. This means, simply but loosely, that the Church's work gets under way and then the vices attack. Alternatives: Piers tills truth elsewhere (so Prsl), and Pride attacks while he is away; or, he represents the absent apostle Peter, whose work was carried on by successors when he died; or, the manor or barn represents the geographical area of Roman Christendom, and Grace and Piers pass beyond its borders as missionaries; or, L imagines the arable of Unite as extensive and remote from the barn itself—"the field is the world" (Matt. 13:38)—or indeed all these meanings hold.

The siege of Unite

335–480 Pryde hit aspiede . . . toek his leue: Given human nature, the founding of the Church is followed immediately by the attack by sin. The third movement of this vision includes the attack of Pride (335–54), Conscience's defense (355–90), the rebellion of the commune (391–408), and the dissent of an unlearned vicar, a lord, and a king (409–80). Unite quickly disintegrates.

The siege of an allegorical dwelling has for precedent Prudentius's *Psychomachia*, a poem of vast influence, itself based in part on Apoc. 19 (see 21.5–14n above). As L develops the most elaborate and extended allegorical action in PP, he tips his hat to the arch-allegory of the soul-battle. Like PP, the *Psychomachia* presents the vices in combat, a walled edifice for the defense of the virtuous, overt reference to the Apocalypse, and finally a figure of discord who disrupts from within (see 22.313–15n). The elaborate attack on the allegorical castle of the Rose that concludes *The Romance of the Rose* may well have been known to L, as may the account of the attack on an allegorical castle (= BVM) by vices in Grosseteste's *Château* (ed. Murray 1918) and its translations (ed. Saja-vaara 1967) and in *Cursor mundi*, lines 9877–10094 (ed. Morris 1875); see Cornelius 1930:44–47.

But, as usual, L seems impatient with his own device. He introduces the attack on Unite twice, here and at 22.52–73 (see n). The latter attack is presented as a series of five assaults (see C.22/B.20 Headnote). But L neglects to satisfy any expectation that we will hear of a (potentially tedious) full-scale battle with neatly paired forces, Pride against Humility, etc., in the psychomachia tradition. The truncated description of the assault itself registers L's indifference to epic themes.

In his history of English poetry (1774–81) Warton noticed that some features of this battle resemble the *Torneiment Anticrist*, a French poem written probably soon after 1233 by Huon de Meri (quoted in Skt's note to 22 (his 23).53; see Owen 1912:81–82, 145–52; Cornelius 1930:81–82; Emmerson 1981: 188–93; Bestul 1996:37–39, 52; and 219–26n above). The poem describes the tournament (really a battle) of the forces of Antichrist, namely the vices, including Pride as a leading figure, against the forces of Jesus Christ—the virtues (ed. Bender 1976). As Skeat and Owen observe, no verbal resemblances show that L drew directly on Huon's poem, but it was well known in England and its general conception probably contributed to the descriptions of Pride's and Antichrist's attacks. The *Torneiment* and PP share a few motifs: the dwellings of God and demonic figures within sight of the narrator; the allegorical banquet in the tradition of Raoul de Houdenc (whom Huon names); reference to the Four Daughters of God (see 20.115–270n above); and the seeking of healing from figures representing penitence (see 22.304–72n below).

The twofold attack may also be compared with the twofold onslaught of Hunger in Passus 8 (171, 300 [B.6.174, 278, A.7.159, 262]). In both instances the repetition emphasizes the frustration of the agents for good (Piers, Conscience), the persistence of suffering, and the need for forgiveness (see 22.243–45n). Emmerson suggests that the first attack allegorizes an assault on the early Church, the second the besieged Church contemporary with L (1981:196).

Pride's and Antichrist's attacks are surprisingly bloodless affairs of agricultural disruption and allegorized weaponry, more talk than fight, e.g., 347 **oure sophistrie**; 351 **colours and queyntise**; C.22/B.20.115–18 "priue speche, paynted wordes, fayre biheste and many a fals treuthe" (see 22.111–20n; 22.121–39n; and 219–26n above). Similarly the fiend's attack on the Tree of Charity is mainly a matter of wiles and bad talk (18.43–46 [B.16.40–44]). Nature, disease, and death, called upon by Conscience, do the physical harm. The point of course is that the vices, especially the clerical vices of deceit and flattery, render humankind unable to muster the only effective militia in defense of the frail body—love and grace.

335–36 Now is Peres to þe plouh; Pryde hit aspiede . . . a grete oeste: The abrupt immediacy of the onslaught here (repeated in C.22/B.20.52–53) suggests the defenselessness of human nature. The infinitesimal gap of time between Grace's institution and its lapse allegorizes the inborn nature of original sin. Anticipating this action, at the Court of Truth that Piers described, Truth charged Charity "a churche to make" to harbor and provide for people (C only), but Wrath with Envy "poketh forth pruyde," and may keep a person out of the Court for a hundred years (all versions; 7.254–69 [B.5.609–15, A.6.95–101]). Piers's allegory was insistently psychological (Truth resided in the heart); here, like the *Psychomachia*, the allegory adds a social dimension, ultimately expressed in the next passus as the pride of the nobility and the attendant corruption of the friars.

Pride is of course the leader of the vices, and as Wyclif says, pride "never comes alone but with a great retinue" (ed. Loserth 1890:4.26). The early fourteenth-century poem "The Simonie" combines a similar figure of the vices' attack with a motif, Peace's flight from the land, from the usual version of the Four Daughters of God story (see 20.115–270n): "Pride priketh aboute, wid nithe and wid onde [discord and envy]; / Pes and love and charité hien hem out of londe . . . " (lines 459–60, ed. Dean 1996:209; see Salter 1988:166).

337 Consience . . . cristene and cardinale vertues: The collocation of Conscience and **cardinale vertues**, the latter treated as quasi-personifications, becomes frequent from here (337, 393, 407, 411–12, 452, C.22/B20.21, 73–74, 122, 303). The virtues are viewed in fact as particular powers of the faculty of conscience. Likewise from here on **cristene** is the repeated term for the inhabitants of Unite (see 22.61n).

338 Blowe hem doun and Breke hem and byte ato þe mores: The blowing and breaking, and perhaps the biting, recall the similarly unliteral but more violent warfare of Jesus in the Harrowing (e.g., see B.5.495, 20.34n, C.20.262 [B.18.253])—Anti-christ mimics his antithesis. But here the attack is allegorized as a militant georgic, in particular as crop-destroying wind and rodents. See 5.121n and further 22.53–57n. Piers is a plowman, grace a grass, virtue seed, humankind a crop: Pride's attack is figured as agricultural devastation rather than a military assault, though he adopts a quasi-military strategy and command.

339–50 And sente forth surquidous . . . with wrong or with vsure: Pride's emissaries, arrogance and backbiting—species respectively of pride and envy, for example in Chaucer's Parson's Tale—are sowers of discord, vices that might initiate a fellowship's destruction from within. With their epic battle-boast they make as if to fling down a gauntlet, but their threat almost farcically diminishes in violence as they talk. First they threaten loss of seed, forced entry into the barn, and exile, then confusion of the credal faith, then uncertainty about mercantile ethics, always a problem (see 9.22–42 [B.7.18–39, A.8.20–44]). In fact they threaten not an army but the institution of faith, not the body but the soul—they **spille loue** (340).

MS Ch of C reads *sir quydours* for **surquidous**, and we may indeed hear a (mocking) title of respect in the officer's name. Alford notes that sergeants of arms, enforcers for the nobility, were unpopular, and cites a statute, 13 Richard II, limiting their number to thirty "at the grievous complaint of the commons" (*Gloss.* s.v. *Sergeaunt of Armes*).

The threat to break and enter Piers's **berne** recalls Pees's complaint against the wealthy and violent bully Wrong, who "breketh vp my berne dores" (4.60 [B.4.57, A.4.44]), a figure like the "lord of lust" here (352, 382 below).

The vices specify (346) that the dray horses, the sacrament of penance, and the cart, **the bileue** (Christian faith, perhaps specifically the Creed, or, as in 330 above, "Cristendom"), will be twisted by sophistry. Falsity is L's idea of the final evil—see 219–26n above. A lively example of the ease with which right belief can be cunningly manipulated, "quaintly colored" (347) is the notorious finagling of what might seem to be the plain scriptural injunctions against usury (349–50 and n). Quibbling over doctrine, gnawing God with gorge (see 11.39n), likewise confuses, even for that most conscientious discriminator Conscience, the issue of who is Christian or heathen, the question of heresy (348). Whereas the malefactors in the Half-Acre episode are clearly identified, in this reprise they operate by guile.

Because a new speaker, Pride, is identified in line 354, the Athlone editors close Pride's emissaries' speech at line 350 and open Pride's at 353. Schm does likewise for the B version, and seems to have intended to do the same for C. Prsl notes the apparent change of speaker but still continues the speech from 344–54 (Athlone numbering).

349–50 Ne no manere Marchaunt . . . with wrong or with vsure: Chambers remarks that this is "a complaint against the growth of what we may roughly call capitalism" (1939:160). It certainly reflects the tortured scholastic quarrels about the legitimacy of usury (see Noonan 1957).

351 With such colours and queyntise cometh pruyde yArmed: Pride's progress parodies the entry of Christ, whose **colours** are blood red (13 above), whereas Pride's heraldic **colours and queyntise**, "(heraldic) colors and device (i.e., coat of arms)," are also sophistical "(rhetorical) colors (i.e., painted words) and cleverness" (see lines 347 and 458). Hence **yArmed** puns on the military and heraldic uses of the word.

352 the lord that lyueth aftur the lust of his body: This companion of Pride returns with Pride at C.22/B20.71, "a lord þat lyueth aftur likyng of body," and later (90) "the lord þat lyuede aftur lust." Dame Study speaks of wicked men who "louyen lond and lordschype and lykynge of body" (C.11.12), as L seems generally to associate lechery with lords, "al the lordschip of Leccherye" (2.93 [B.2.89, A.2.61]). See 382 below, and see 22.70–71n for comment. As Pride stands for the spiritual sins (pride, envy, wrath), Lust stands for the bodily (lust, sloth, avarice, gluttony). The lustful lord is a waster (353), whereas the merchant above is a winner (350); for the terms see Prol.22n . Compare the "proued prikeare of fraunce," the devil, who threatens the Castle of Kynde (10.135 [B.9.8, A.10.8]), and the laughing "lord" of 459 below.

354 '. . . Alle the world in a while thorw oure wit,' quod pruyde: As usually punctuated (see 339–50n above), **alle the world** is what the pleasure-seeking lord wastes. The line may also be punctuated to make it a single new speech by Pride, a kind of battle cry. For **oure wit** as a typically intellectual weapon of Pride see the end of 335–480n.

The defense of Unite

355–95 Quod Consience to alle cristene . . . sennes be hoseled: Conscience, instructed by **kynde wit** (see Prol.138n), here simply aptitude for building, commands the fortification of Unite, which becomes **as hit a pyle were** (363, see n). The fortification consists of a moat named **holinesse**, which is generated by contrition (weeping **for wikked werkes**, 377–78) and acts of satisfaction (prayers and pilgrimage and almsgiving and **oþer priue penaunse**, 375–76). In short, holiness, the defense of the Church, results from the sacrament of penance, which precedes the Eucharist.

355–56 Quod Consience . . . holde we vs there: These lines are nearly repeated at C.22/B.20.74–75 (and see C.22/B.20.246 and n, 204, 297), in response to the second attack of Antichrist's forces. There, instead of going on to pray for peace within the Church, Conscience prays for "kynde" to come to Unite's defense. In a passage added in C, Resoun exhorts the king and magnates to love the "comune" and "holde ʒow in vnite" with one another (5.189). The locution displays the generation of the idea of the Church out of the idea of community in general.

362–66 To deluen a dich . . . hem þat hit kepeth: The moat Holiness will be filled with tears of remorse (377–78 below; cp. 7.233 [B5.586, A.6.73], the moat Mercy). Wilkes (1965) draws attention to allegories in the *Ancrene Riwle* in which tears of repentance drive back the devil (see Ps. 73:13 on crushing the heads of the dragons in the water) and a moat of humility is watered by tears.

363 as hit a pyle were: See 318–20n above. **Pyle** appears to mean "castle, stronghold, fortified building" whether derived through French from Latin *pila*, "pillar, (architectural) pile," (MED *pile* n. (4), 2.(a); modern *pile*, "large building"), or (like *palis*; see MED) derived through French from Latin *palus*, "stake" (MED *pel* n. (1), (b); modern *peel*, "fortified house or tower")—the words were probably early confused (see OED *pile* sb.²). The *Catholicon Anglicanum* a century later defined "a Peille" by cross-reference to "a castelle."

367–71 Thenne alle kyne cristene . . . thei wisten hit: Digging the moat Holiness, it emerges, means repenting. The "shrewes" (373) who refuse to repent—prostitutes and two perjured court officials, an assizer and a summoner—recapitulate the action of those who refuse to take the way to Truth (7.283–304 [B.5.630–42—where in contrast "a comune womman" may ineptly turn toward Truth—A.6.115–18]) and the wasters who balk at plowing the half acre (8.122–64 [B.6.115–70, A.7.107–55]). For the offices of **sisour** and **sompnour** see 2.59n . With these figures we return in spirit to the world of the first two visions, of Mede in the city and Hunger in the country. Mede as "comune hore" is linked with a "sysour and a sumnour" in 4.160–63 (B.4.165–67). In Chaucer's Friar's Tale 1355–66 whores collude with summoners in an extortion racket.

375–80 Somme thorw bedes . . . in holinesse stande: Prayers, pilgrimage, and money offerings are usual acts of satisfaction in the sacrament of penance. The bitter tears are evidence of contrition, the onset of penitence. The distribution scheme **somme . . . somme . . . somme** recalls the division of graces (see 229–51n above), now sadly in need of remedy. By way of penance the commons and the clergy, cleansed of sin, can **in holinesse stande.**

382 The lord of lust: see 352n above. This **lord** now seems tantamount to Pride or Antichrist—defective desire, evil in general. The abstinence of Lent will not only abolish lust but also curb pride.

383–90 Cometh . . . *Redde quod debes*: The Eucharist naturally follows penance; see 355–95n above. Those who have **labored lelly**, done penance, now get **bred yblessed**; the action puts into sacramental form the interplay of labor, hunger, and food of the second vision, with its pardon pattern of repentance followed by grace, and alludes generally to the figuring of prayer as bread (5.84–88, etc.) and the Haukyn episode's interfolding of spiritual and physical bread. The labor has been performed **this lenten tyme**, the time just finished with the Easter appearance at the beginning of this passus, and the time when Christians performed their major annual penitential acts before the Eucharist of the Easter Season. The phrase **godes body þervnder** refers to the doctrine of transub- (-**vnder**) -stantiation.

Lines 386–87 echo 183–84 above, and line 390 exactly repeats line 187, as L returns to the idea of the gift given Piers, as the type of priesthood, to perform sacramental actions, there absolution and here consecration of the eucharistic elements.

Ones in a monthe: the canonical minimum since the Fourth Lateran Council of 1215 was to receive the Eucharist (and hence to make confession) at least annually, the period taken for granted at C.22/B.20.361. Some authorities recommended houseling at major feasts three times a year (Rubin 1991:70, 148); some laity took Communion up to fifteen times annually (McGarry 1936:36). L's advocacy of more frequent communion may presume a clerical audience (Vitto 1989:84, n76). Although the **bred yblessed** seems clearly, in light of **godes body þervnder, nede** in 389, and "hosele" in 392, to mean the eucharistic host, it may be that L also had in mind the "blessed bread" or "eulogia" that was blessed at the Mass and would be distributed to parishioners, as a "remedy" for the absence of Communion, after the Mass (McGarry 41–42, Rubin 73, Duffy 1992:125, Kelly 1993:8–9). See C.6.146 and n. Kelly quotes Mirk's *Instructions for Parish Priests* (lines 1345–46) to the effect that this bread was to be received every Sunday—that is, more often than monthly. The liturgy for the eulogia is found in the Sarum and other missals (ed. Dickenson 1861–63:33**-36**).

Here *Redde quod debes* means "complete the sacrament of penance, perform restitution and satisfaction"; see 186–87n above. More specifically it means to live in charity toward others, forgive their debts/trespasses (*debita*), as the "paternoster" says (394). For a comic misunderstanding of the injunction see 475–76 and n below. Conscience requires for the gift of the Eucharist what the Samaritan says is required in a royal court: "may no kynge mercy graunte til bothe men acorde / That eyþer haue equitee" (19.289–90).

391–95 'How?' quod alle þe comune . . . sennes be hoseled: The inhabitants of Unite wonder that *Redde quod debes* must precede taking Communion. Schm notes that the injunction derives from Jesus' counsel that one should "go first to be reconciled to thy brother" before offering a gift at the altar (Matt. 5:23–24).

Conscience and the cardinal virtues jointly counsel restitution or at least mutual forgiveness of debts (see 186–87n above). The people's chagrin, probably from their lacking the wherewithal to repay what they owe, repeats that of Robert the rifler "þat *reddere* ne haue" (6.315–22 [B.5.461–68, A.5.233–42]). Archbishop FitzRalph carefully specified that if one lacked the means for restitution, the will for restitution sufficed (cited Scase 1989:39; see Luke 7:42). The Samaritan has assured Will that "sorwe of herte is satisfaccioun for suche þat may nat paye" (19.300 [B.17.320]; see also 19.204–8 [B17.238–42]), and Repentaunce required for absolution only restitution "by thy myhte" ("in accordance with your ability"—6.295). On the requirement to forgive others as preliminary to penance see Frank 1957:108. Harwood suggests that Conscience has in mind the parable of the Wicked Servant, the source of the phrase *redde quod debes* (1992:125).

The reactions of the estates: brewer, vicar, lord, and king

396–480 'ȝe? bawe! . . . toek his leue: Conscience's offer of the Eucharist to those fit to receive it, essentially those who have undertaken penance with satisfaction of debts, has focused the meaning of the Church as the conduit of saving grace to needy humankind. L goes on to show in the end of this passus the grave disability of humankind to accept that grace. The episode is among the instances of the "dissenting voices" that, as Lawler observes, often occur at the end of a passus (2001:137). In a final distributive scheme (see Headnote), figures representing the three estates—a brewer, a vicar, and a lord and a king—in various ways display human refusal of grace (see 229–51n above). More precisely, the figures represent the four estates—king, prelates, magnates, and commons—in a scheme "frequently repeated in the rolls of parliament" (Giancarlo 2003:167).

The sequence begins and concludes (see 475–76n below) with specific response to Conscience's counsel toward absolution and the Eucharist (395). Further, the sequence opens and closes (402, 474) with reference to the *spiritus*

Iusticie, the chief virtue (406), and the whole passage may be read as an account of the systematic perversion of justice in society, of the failure of commons, clergy, and nobility to *reddere quod debent* (see 186–87n and 390n above, and 396–408n below) and to order themselves especially in their relations with one another.

The character of the critique differs from estate to estate, in that the brewer, lord, and king, representing the first and third estates, half wittingly assert their own vice, whereas the vicar thoroughly wittingly describes the failings especially of higher prelates—cardinals and pope. Generally L treats the vices of laborers with humor and regret, those of lords and clerks with anger.

The irony of the allegory is that while Holicherche is besieged by the vices, its members have already succumbed to vice. As for the historical allegory, the book of Acts makes clear that there is scarcely any interval between the foundation and the fall of the Church.

396–408 'ȝe? bawe!' . . . **lyf and soule:** Continuing the naysaying (see 367–71n above), a (male or female) brewer refuses specifically the **spiritus Iusticie,** the rendering to each his due that Conscience has just enjoined in the wording *Redde quod debes* (see 182–90n above). He or she will not **hacky aftur holinesse,** perform agricultural labor (with a "hak") like those at the Half-Acre scene or dig ditches like those digging the moat Holiness. The interjection recalls that of Trajan, "ȝe? bawe for bokes!" (12.75 [B.11.140]), both expressing, for radically different reasons, contempt for authoritative doctrine, and both initiating major turning points in the poem. See also the rough language of the naysayers who reject the pilgrimage to Truth (7.283–86 [B.5.630–33, A.6.115–18]).

The brewer cheats by a method like that of the alewife in Covetyse's confession (6.226 [B.5.218, A.5.134]), here simply by selling thin ale as if it were good stuff—drawn from the same barrel—and by selling the watered dregs as well. This crude transformation of good ale into bad parodies the transubstantiation of the Eucharist and its type, the transformation at Cana (see 108–9 above), as the bad ale opposes the "bred yblessed" offered by Conscience (385), and the brewer is therefore **vnblessed** (404). In the Chester play of the Harrowing, the first person to reject the Redemption and throw in her lot with Satan is an alewife. On the bad reputation of the ale trade and the brewers' methods of cheating see Bennett 1996:123–44.

The brewer's claim that avarice is his or her **kynde** directly contravenes the Christian concepts of hope and the grace that overrides nature; cp. 475–76n below and Prol.67n. Even now Conscience opens for him or her a loophole, **but yf god helpe** (see 20.413–46n). He or she swears profusely; such is a tavern vice, as we learn from Chaucer's Pardoner (PardT 472–75, 629–59; see C.2.100–101, C.6.361, etc.).

406 The cheef seed: See 297–308n above. Aristotle and his pupil Thomas Aquinas proposed that justice is the greatest of virtues, as comprehending all the virtues in relation to one's neighbor (Kean 1964:149).

407 Consience be thy comunes: Schm prints possibly archetypal "be thy comune fode," and Prsl conjectures "thy comune fynde," making straightforward sense; see KD-B, p. 208 and RK-C, p. 126 for defense of the Athlone conjecture, but see MED *commune* adj. 6.(c) for the sense "customary," which fits the possibly archetypal phrasing and would play on "commune" as commons, the class to which the brewer belongs (see 414n below). Making good sense too is the reading "thy comune fede," amply supported in both the B and C traditions.

In any reading the sense develops Conscience's offering of the Eucharistic bread to "lele" laborers (384 above), an alternative to the brewer's ale, itself also a mixed substance.

409–80 Thenne is many . . . and fayre toek his leue: Representing and criticizing the second estate, the **lewed vicory** is a contradiction in terms, an unlearned or lay clergyman (Gasse 1996:322–24). His point of view is that, we may imagine, of most English clergy—mildly royalist, and vigorously anti-foreign, especially opposed to rapacious foreign cardinals and to the (French-oriented) papacy. In his attack on prelates he comes close to Wyclif's position, for instance in a 1376 sermon against prelates (Scase 1989:13; Holmes 1975:165–78). His royalism likewise finds its counterpart in Wyclif, especially in his *Tractatus de officio regis* (ed. Pollard and Sayle, 1887). Special interests are clerical pacifism and the need for mission among the infidels and stability at home.

He is called **lewed** because it takes little Latin to see the evils he speaks of; he thus participates in PP's long debate on the uses of learning in the economy of salvation. He is briefly foreshadowed by the "burel clerkes" who need no advanced learning in theology (so "Clergie" implies!) to complain now of "Correctours" (bishops and other prelates) who keep silent in the face of iniquity (B.10.292 and n; see 302–7n above, 413–23n below). A "burel clerk" would be an "unlearned learned person" like a **lewed vicory** (MED *burel*); Gower calls himself a "burel clerk" in *Confessio Amantis*, Prologue 52 (see Kellogg 1965, esp. 31 and n19). In contrast is the cleric who flaunts his learning but lacks understanding, the priest in the pardon scene whom Piers calls "lewed lorel" (B.7.142 [A.8.124], not in C). L may also call the vicar **lewed** to distinguish him from the learned but hypocritical friars, with a nod toward contemporary disputes (see 22.230–31n). In 1380 an English friar spoke of secular clerks as know-nothings, *nichil scientes* (Scase 1989:41).

The vicar's speech begins cynically, and passes with increasing bitterness to prophetic satire, then to great hope, then back to the cynical view that all is hypocrisy. His views and his status as a minor cleric associate him with the Prologue's "lunatik" and "Goliardeis," with the "lunatyk lollares" of C.9.107, with Rechelesnesse and other socially marginalized figures in the poem who speak boldly with uncertain authority and who seem to impersonate aspects of L's own thinking, to be part-doubles of Will. See 477–79n, 479an, 480–81n below.

410–12 Ich am a Curatour . . . cokkes fether: As a **Curatour** (see also 451 below) charged with the cure of souls, the vicar is especially charged to administer penance (Fourth Lateran Council of 1215). This office would involve, as the many penitential manuals make evident, specific knowledge of the seven deadly sins and their remediating opposites, the virtues. Hence the vicar says that no ecclesiastical superior, bishop or cardinal, has ever come (cp. "cam" 413) to him with (real, actualized) knowledge of the rudiments of penitential work, **þat me couthe telle of cardinale vertues.** Further, none cares at all about the human ground of penance, conscience. The complaint resembles Will's remark that he never found charity in London (16.288–90 [B.15.152–53]). The same notion forms the plot of *Pierce the Ploughman's Crede*: the narrator searches in vain among the orders of friars for someone who can teach him the Creed.

413–23 Y knewe neuere cardinale . . . relikes to kepe: The vicar's shift from talk of virtues and Conscience, of penance, to criticism of cardinals is triggered by the pun on **cardinale** but motivated by the vicar's recognition of the sorry distance between the Church's responsibility for the cure of souls and the irresponsible behavior of the Church's cardinal priests, who should correct and inform curates. "Riht so oute of holy churche al euel spredeth / There inparfit preesthoed is" (16.246–7 [B.15.94–95]; cp. line 428 below). The same pun on "cardinal," in the context of the Petrine Commission (see 182–90n above), occurred at Prol.131–34 (B.Prol.103–107—see n), lines probably composed after these lines (see Headnote). The vicar chastises the pope, who should correct cardinals, but perhaps will not when cardinals "presumen" to make popes (Prol.135 [B.Prol.108]), and he chastises cardinals, who should correct bishops rather than burden the nation. This suggests another reason L makes his vicar "lewed": like all the clergy he has not received proper instruction from the prelates.

The critique has six elements: cardinal legates burden the clergy and the people for their keep when in country (while they gather unpopular taxes of clergy and people); they foster **lecherye**, conspicuous consumption and lechery; they travel too much; they associate with usurious Jews; they participate in the Babylonian Captivity of the papacy by the French; their titular churches in Rome are hollow fronts of which they are absentee curators. The passage reflects general English dissent, by king, clergy, and commons, from papal taxation and intrusion, as expressed in many forms, including statutes (1351–93) against papal provisions of benefices and against papal annulment of the king's judiciary authority (praemunire); see Pantin 1955:84–87 and Ch. 5; Holmes 1975 passim; Swanson 1989:69–72.

Specifically on English attitudes toward cardinals see Harvey 1999. She observes that Simon Langham, whom L must have in mind here, was made cardinal in 1368, the first English cardinal in fifty years, former treasurer of England, abbot of Westminster, archbishop of Canterbury, royal chancellor. He returned as *nuncius* from Avignon to England in 1371–72 and 1373 in a failed mission to broker peace between France and England. Gwynn proposed that Langham's 1372 visit prompted the vicar's complaint (1943:12–13). Harvey discusses his favors to English clergy, his great wealth, his English benefices, and his titular churches in Rome. She provides ample evidence that the chroniclers judged him severely, as ineffectual and burdensome. Edward III begrudged his 1371 entry into the country, and denied an effort in 1374 by the monks of Canterbury to have him made cardinal archbishop. Langham died in 1376. On finances in connection with Langham see Lunt 1962:662–63. For Wyclif's critique of cardinals see Leff 1967:535.

The royal government wavered in its papal policy. Usually opposed to any papal taxation, and thus in accord with popular anticlericalism, king and council in July 1375 agreed to a large papal subsidy (£9000) exacted from the English clergy, but reversed their position by late 1376 (Holmes 1975:33–62, 144–45, 159–94; see next n).

413–17 Y knewe neuere cardinale . . . cardinals cometh ynne: The papacy had exacted no direct taxes from the English people or king (apart from "Peter's Pence," some £200 annually) since 1333, but continued to tax the English clergy with income taxes called "subsidies" (1336, 1362, blocked by the government in 1372 but allowed again in 1375), "annates" (taxes on provisions to benefices), "services" (taxes on prelates' provision to their offices), and "procurations" (Lunt 1962 passim; 1968:xli-li). The vicar has the last particularly in mind, "a small tax levied on the clergy for the expenses of papal envoys and resident papal collectors, payment of which was normally allowed by the government," unlike the other assessments (McKisack 1959:284–86, quoting this passage; Lunt 1962:666, etc.; Swanson 1989:223–24). The procurations (an ecclesiastical version of royal "purveyance"—see 258–60n above, 415n below) exacted from 1373 to 1376 amounted to some £2000, and were the subject of complaint in the Good Parliament of 1376 (Rot. Parl. 2:336; Holmes 1975:148). Lunt reports that the papal collector Arnald Garnerius was to take in subsidies of 60,000 florins, some £8500, from the English clergy in 1375–76, and actually collected nearly £6000 (1968:xxxix; 1962:379). The Good Parliament exaggerated in complaining that 20,000 marks (£13,333) annually went to the papal curia from England (Rot. Parl. 2:339). See 428–48n below.

General English dissent finds expression in a Commons petition of 1376 opposing the farming of English benefices by absentee cardinals (Rot. Parl. 2:337–40; see Perroy 1933:59–60). A 1377 petition claimed (with great exaggeration) that the aliens holding English benefices, mostly allied with England's enemy France, drew £10,000 or more from the country (Rot. Parl. 3:19, Item 67). Lunt mentions other parliamentary protests (1968:xli; 1962 passim). Wyclif of course argued that the king should refuse to comply with papal taxation (Dahmus 1960:57–61). In the same period Gower likewise complains of cardinals with their expensive retinues, going about on horse and desirous of keeping "the subsidy of the clergy" under their control (*Miroir* 18,984–96). In an elaborate mummery-show staged before Prince Richard in January 1377, those disguised as papal legates "were cast as villains of the piece" (Saul 1997:21).

414 for here comunes paieth: The words **comunes,** (picked up from 407 above), and "comune" (from 391) work through the following lines (416, 420, 451), integrating notions of rightful sustenance, forced hospitality, and popular sentiment—the use of the commons's commons. The vicar continues to respond to the brewer as representative of the commons. Compare, e.g., Prol.142–48 (B.Prol.113–121), and see 213–14n above, 451 below.

415 For here pelure and palfrayes mete and pelours þat hem folweth: The vicar summons up the world of Lady Meed in a line. Both State and, now, the Church inflict the vices of purveyance. The Athlone editors (and Schm?) take the B reading **pilours** and the C reading **pelours** to be the same word. At B.18.40 they emend unanimously attested *pilour* to "p[e]lour" (see C.20.39n); presumably they think, with uncertain support from MED (s.v. *pilour, pelour*), that "accuser, appealer" is spelled *pelour* but "pillager, despoiler" can be spelled *pilour* or *pelour*. Hence here they take the word to mean "plunderer," an interpretation supported by "pileth," 442 below. More pregnantly it could be a pun: the cardinal legates' retinues include both despoilers of the clergy's hospitality and accusers of tax-evaders and other ecclesiastical wrongdoers.

416–17 clamat cotidie . . . cardinals cometh ynne: The formula "cries out daily" expresses the notoriety of a crime and was sometimes used to initiate criminal proceedings against a public enemy, as Alford notes (*Gloss.*). The public clamor parallels, from a cleric's point of view, the mouse's warning in the Prologue, woe to the land where a boy is king (Prol.206 [B.Prol.196]).

419–27 y wolde . . . were cristene: The verb **wolde** governs all the clauses that follow. The predicates of **Consience** and **grace** and **Peres** (424–26) are elided copulative verbs.

421 here holinesse: The vicar's increasingly bitter sarcasm now plays on a title, "your holiness," further playing on *sanctus* of line 422. For "your holiness" as a term of address (though of pope not of cardinals) see OED *holiness* 2., MED *holinesse* 3.(e). Contrast the "holinesse" in which Unite "stoede" (363, 380 above). He asks that cardinals practice the monastic virtue of *stabilitas*, in criticism of their constant and expensive travel as legates. Holding still is what the bustling world of satire and Meed cannot do.

422–23 At Auenon . . . relikes to kepe: In Avignon the popes and (after the Schism of September 1378) antipopes resided (among the despised French) from 1309 to 1408, except for the period from October 1367 to September 1370, and briefly from January 1377, before the Schism. According to Mossé, in 1357 there were 67 families of Jews in Avignon, and from 1342–70 they received special protection from the pope (1934:97, 78). Jewish merchants and artisans there supplied commodities to pope and curia, and loaned money to the pope's relatives (Grayzel 1940). Renouard's study of finance at Avignon speaks of an important Jewish district in Avignon, as in most cities in the Mediterranean ambit. He indicates that Jews had no part in papal banking at the time, but that Jews did lend money to the curia (1941:106).

L's silence about the Schism here, and the English presumption that the true pope resided in Rome from the time of the election of Urban VI in April 1378 (known in England by June), strongly suggest that he wrote this passage before the Schism, and that he did not return to it when he revised C, if C is post-Schism (see 428–48n below). Certainly an Englishman could speak with scorn of "la peccherouse Cité d'Avenon" before the Schism, as did a petition in the Good Parliament of 1376 (Jusserand 1894:130–31, quoting Rot. Parl.

2.337). The vicar quotes the phrase from Psalm 17:26, "with the holy, thou wilt be holy," with harsh irony, and tellingly omits the conclusion of the next verse, the "tail of þe text" (B.3.351): "and with the perverse thou wilt be perverted" (cp. 3.484–500 [B.3.331–53]). L quotes the phrase also at B.5.278 with the same irony.

þe relikes to kepe: cardinals, even those based at Avignon, had sinecure benefices in Rome (and elsewhere, including England—see Holmes 1975:19, Swanson 1989:53). The vicar thinks they should reside in their titular churches, maintaining the relics deposited in every cardinal church there, the "seyntes at Rome" that Resoun criticizes as objects of pilgrimage (5.197 [B.5.56, A.5.40]; see further Prol.48 and B.12.35–39). For L's anger at "ȝe prelates" for abuse of relics see C.Prol.95–104 (not in A or B). Compare the critique of titular bishops who were wont "in Ingelond to huppe aboute" (17.279–80), and the critique of cardinals who do not tend their flocks *in partibus infidelium* at 17.188–209 (B.15.491–547); see Justice 1994:156–58. What Gradon says of this last passage might be said of the vicar: "Anima perhaps stands out as much as an English patriot as a Wycliffite" (1982:188). The force of **as here reule wol** is unclear, although some cardinals were monks. Elsewhere in PP "rule" is used only of nonsecular (regular) clergy (e.g. 5.143, 9.222, 22.247, 22.265, B.13.285, B.15.87, B.15.317).

424–50 And thow, Consience . . . to welthe of soule: The vicar's prayer, as it were in the heat of the moment, generalizes to a prophetic hope for a perfected society before returning to the topics that began his speech, the cardinals and the commune's disinterest in Conscience and the cardinal virtues. Its main arguments are two: first that pope and king should hold to their proper spheres until a glorious time to come when all people are Christian and Piers is **emperour of al þe world**; and second more specifically that the pope should endeavor to save all humans, and not foster warfare against those he considers wicked. His prayer reasserts the prophetic wish of Patience in the banquet scene for peace and the reign of patience and charity, a hope immediately dashed by the doctor (15.152–73 [B.13.158–76]).

424–27 And thow, Consience . . . all men were cristene: The vicar wishes that Conscience would remain in the king's court, that Grace would remain as leader of the Church, and that Piers would become as it were the sovereign of both realms, the **world** and **cristene**. Again, the vicar envisions the world of the first vision, in which Conscience's role as chief counselor to the king gives some respite from the dominance of Meed (end of Passus 4, all versions).

Where the first vision concluded with Conscience and Reason jointly forming the king's council, the vicar's more clerical interest turns to Grace as a co-counselor, specifically **gyour of all Clerkes**. Grace will assume the role of a good prelate, who knows how to tell the vicar about the cardinal virtues. Conscience will *greden* after grace in the last line of the poem; see 200–12n above.

In wishing that Piers would be **emperour of al þe world** the vicar may reflect any of several medieval strains of thought about a future earthly savior king, a Christian messiah. Among these was the expectation in Joachimist and later Franciscan thought of an "angelic pope" (Bloomfield 1961a:52, 121, 126; Baethgen 1933 passim, esp. 81–97; Reeves 1961 and 1969:401–15; Leff 1967:73, 174–75, 185–90; McGinn 1978; Adams 1985b: 199–200 et passim; Kerby-Fulton 1990:98–99, 170, 177–80; for skeptical views see Erzgräber 1988:246–50; Emmerson 1993:41–49; Clopper 1997b:278–87; see Headnote); the idea of the Last Emperor from Pseudo-Methodius and Adso (Kampers 1896; McGinn 1978 and 1979:85, 93; Bostick 1998:22–34; Verhelst 1976:26); of course the idea of the Second Coming of Christ the (davidic) King; or simply the hope for a new emperor or reformed papacy to come (Lerner 1976a:15 et passim). Franciscan Spirituals had hoped that Celestine V (1294) was to be the angelic pope (Lambert 1998:176).

Of particular interest are the apocalyptic prophecies of the Franciscan Johannes de Rupescissa (Jean de Roquetaillade), who wrote *Vade mecum in tribulatione* at Avignon in 1356. It was widely known; an English translation of extracts was made in the fifteenth century (British Library Addit. Manuscript 24663, fol. 1ʳ-13ʳ). Jean foretold general disasters to come in the 1360s, including the appearance of a western Antichrist, a heretical emperor. Christ, through an angel, would elect a sovereign pontiff, the *Reparator orbis* (Restorer of the World), who would be the angel of the Apocalypse (Apoc. 10, 18, 20). A new saintly king of France would join with this angelic pope to cleanse the Church and subject the whole world. The *Reparator* would come in the year 1367 (Bignami-Odier 1952:163–72). 1367 is the year of Richard II's birth. Compare Conscience's prediction that in Resoun's future reign a davidic protector will come, "o cristene kyng," and Resoun's (Clergie's in B) prophecy of a reforming "kyng" to come (3.441–42 [B.3.288–89, A.3.264–65]; 5.168–79 [B.10. 322–35]).

Kerby-Fulton cites in this connection a remarkable passage about a future reformer figure from Bridget of Sweden's *Revelations* 4.22: "a plowman will come . . . [who] does not fear the threats of princes, and is not a respecter of persons" (1990:106–9, esp. 108; see Reeves 1961:333–34). Cp. 302–7 above. But it has not been shown that L knew Bridget's work.

The vicar's emphasis may be felt to fall not on **emperour** but on **al þe** world; he longs for the completion of the Church's mission, **þat all men were cristene**, and that the pope would become like Piers, even-handed, interested in the salvation of all (cp. 17.248–321 [B.15.568–612] and B.13.206–10). Hence the world would be governed by biblical mandate, the **newe plouh and þe olde** (see 273, 310 above, 446 below).

428–48 Inparfit is þat pope . . . nauht of þe remenaunt: A vigorous attack on the papacy, along with royalist sentiment. Compare the similar themes, with verbal echoes, at 17.188–321 (B.15.492–612) and 5.191–93 (B.5.50–51); see 434–39n below. Generally on papalism and antipapalism in PP see Overstreet 1989–90:334.

The particular imperfection of **þat pope** (who becomes **þe** (current) **pope** in 442) is his warfare—against anyone, even sinners, or especially against Christians. In a passage in C only, Liberum Arbitrium had made the same complaint (17.233–35). Here L departs from the traditional ground of antipapal and anti-Rome satire, curial venality (Yunck 1963:82–117), although in fact the pope's demands for money were motivated by his need to pay his mercenaries (Holmes 1975:7–20). Lunt details the huge sums exacted from the English clergy by the pope for the prosecution of his mercenary campaigns against the Viscontis of Milan and later the Florentine League from 1361 to 1376. The two "subsidies" garnered over £24,000 (1962:95–112, 380); see Perroy 1933:29–40 and 413–17n above. Reason, in a passage probably written after this one, urged the pope to be a peacemaker (5.191–93), but the "doctour" at dinner had complained that no wit could make peace between the pope and his enemies (15.171–73, cp. B.13.173–76). On Cardinal Langham's failed efforts to make peace see 413–23n above. Generally on antiwar sentiment in PP see Baldwin 2002.

Contemporary English irritation at papal warfare was expressed by Gower, who complained in his *Miroir* (ca. 1376–79) that popes have underwritten war and used simony to pay for it (18565–76, and see 18673–84 and 16697–732), and in his *Vox clamantis*: "Peter preached, of course, but today's pope fights" (trans. Stockton 1962:125; Book III, ch. 5—see also chs. 7–10). At the end of ch. 10 Gower specifically attacks the antipope Clement VII (Oct. 1378-Sept. 1394), whom he calls not clement, in an old joke that John Erghome in 1361 used of Clement VI (May 1342-Dec. 1352—ed. Wright 1859:151). For Wyclif's attack on the civil warfare of the Church see *De civili dominio*, ed. Poole 1885:74, and Gradon 1980:190–91, citing Wyclif's *Opera minora* to the effect that giving money to the pope for fighting against Christians would be to sin mortally (ed. Loserth 1913:25).

The vicar's critique has been used as a dating point for the B version.

Huppé (1941:41–44) and Bennett (1943:60–63) thought the allusions, here and at 17.233–34 (not in B) were to wars engaged from April 1379 between pope and antipope after the Schism. But as Kane (1988:185), Bloomfield (1961a:220), and Prsl (C.17.234n) observe, popes had made war against Christians and been criticized for it well before the Schism.

Gwynn suggested that L alludes to the sack of Cesena in February to April, 1377, organized by Cardinal Roberto, Count of Geneva, who was to become the antipope Clement VII (so also Huppé 1941:42), but also observed that Urban V commissioned a series of campaigns in Italy in 1353–67 (1943:13). In fact Pope Gregory XI employed the English mercenary John Hawkwood for wars in Tuscany and Romagna from 1372 to April 1377, and he carried out the sack of Cesena, a horror that quickly became known throughout the West. Hawkwood, bankrolled from time to time by both the pope and the Visconti, warred in Tuscany and Lombardy from 1364 on (Temple-Leader and Marcotti 1889:46–123 et passim). Chaucer's visit to Milan in the early summer of 1378 was in part motivated by letters, conveyed by a Franciscan, from Hawkwood to England about financing the wars (Riverside Chaucer, p. xxi; Perroy 1933:51, 137–38). Indeed the pope began the military campaign to recapture the Papal States of Romagna as early as 1353, under Cardinal Albernoz. The most thorough account of these wars, all fought by mercenaries, is Brucker 1962:172–83, 221–43, 265–335; see also Partner 1972:339–69.

Hudson argued that it is simplest to take the allusions to papal fighting as referring to the 1383 Despenser crusade, and Fowler (1996:4) concurs, citing an idea considered but rejected by Chambers, 1928:15. She adds that "the earlier territorial wars of the papacy did not involve England, and are unlikely to have struck the author or readers of PP sufficiently for such allusive reference to be likely" (1994:100; also 2001:210; so Gradon 1982:190). But Englishmen under their English leader Hawkwood fought in these earlier wars and, close to home, Commons in the Good Parliament (April to July 1376) drew up a petition attacking papal wars (Rot. Parl. 2.339): "Item, so soon as the Pope wants money to carry on his wars in Lombardy and elsewhere . . . he wants to get a subsidy from the clergy of England" (Rot. Parl. 2.339). The petition refers to papal requests for funds to pay for the recently concluded war, conducted under Pope Gregory XI, with the Viscontis of Milan (truce 4 June 1375) and the current papal war against the Florentine League, the "War of the Eight Saints" which broke out in the fall of 1375 (Holmes 1975:7–20, 124–26). Reference to the pope's hiring mercenaries (429 and n below) surely suits more aptly the Lombard and Tuscan wars than the Despenser crusade.

In short, nothing in the vicar's speech requires a date of composition as late as the Schism of 1378, known in England by October (Ullman 1948:102).

Because attacks on cardinal farming of benefices (413–17n and 413–23n above), on the wickedness of Avignon and papal farming of English revenues (422–23n above), and on papal warfare against Christians were all included in the petitions of the Good Parliament, the year 1376 was evidently a time when the vicar's complaints were bruited in England. See 422–23n above.

Many lines in this passage have metrical defects, either in the syllabification of the *b*-verse (by Duggan/Cable principles) or in the alliterative pattern. Perhaps L had not finished working the passage up, or more likely its exciting content aroused scribal participation—several of the defects are easily explicable and emendable. In line 428, **all**, and in 438, **also** or (less likely) **sore** may be scribal additions for emphasis or clarity; their omission corrects the lines. If 439 is unmetrical—if **alle** (plural) is invariably disyllabic in L's idiolect—the variant *lyke* (= "alike"), found in five manuscripts, for **ylyke** would yield good meter with a difficult form of the adverb (see 22.25–34n). Inversion of **wicke** and **gode** from their common order in 440 would emend the alliterative pattern. No obvious solution to the unmetrical syllabification of 443b appears. In 448, although the final stave and final lift of the line may fall on the first and last syllables of **remenaunt** (see KD-B p. 139, n 43 for this and other examples), the line is unmetrical by Cable's principle (which Schmidt accepts: 1995 ed., p. 506) that all lines end in an unstressed syllable.

Further, the repetition **Peres the Plouhman (þat) payneth hym to tulie** (434, 437) seems infelicitous, especially as the latter continues with another very awkward repetition, **And trauaileth *and tulieth*.** However, L often enough merely repeats a line or half-line; Donaldson gives a dozen examples (1949:61–62, 237), and Galloway proposes reasons for a number of them (1999:75–76). Possibly the fourfold repetition of forms of **tulie** and **tulthe** in lines 432–38 is artful; more likely, unless 437 is a rejected draft erroneously preserved, the rather difficult resumption of the main verb coordination after 436 induced a scribe to repeat 434 for clarity. Kane once thought line 437 spurious and found another, less plausible explanation for the scribe's motivation: he "doubtless wished to improve the text with a construction parallel to line [440], and failed to take in the fact that line [430] already corresponded to it. He lifted the second half of his line bodily from the preceding text; the first half was in all conscience easy enough to invent" (1948:18–19). Later Kane thought line 437's omission in archetypal B was "caused by homoteleuton" (KD-B p. 90).

428 Inparfit: this word and "parfit" are often used in PP of priests, prelates, and pope, who should aspire to perfection. In this use the word plays on the religious sense of *parfit* as "righteous," and specifically "observing religious vows" (MED, sense 6.).

429 soudeth: "employs as a mercenary," from the same root as the word "soldier." The verb "fyndeth" at 445 below repeats the notion.

430–33 Ac wel worth Peres . . . beste womman: The context of the Latin phrase, from the Sermon on the Mount, is relevant: "[Love your enemies: do good to them that hate you: and pray for them that persecute and calumniate you: / That you may be the children of your Father who is in heaven,] who [maketh his sun to rise upon the good, and the bad, and] raineth upon the just and the unjust" (Matt. 5:44–45). By pursuing God in doing, Piers is a child of the Father; the pope should love, rather than send mercenaries after, his enemies, in imitation of God who is equally benevolent toward the good and the bad (see 5.191–93).

The copy-text spelling **sente** 432 is for *sent* = 'sends,' Vulg. *Solem suum oriri facit,* present tense, as Skt notes, but leaves open the possibility of the common pun on **sonne.**

434–39 Rihte so . . . tymes ylyke: Piers cultivates such sinners as the "commune wommen" of 367 above and the one given "to waston on welfare and in wikked kepynge" of 353 above. In fact in the Half-Acre episode Piers had resisted helping such sinners and wasters, but came to realize, after witnessing the ravages of Hunger, that "Treuthe tauhte me ones to louye hem vchone" because they are "my blody bretherne" (8.216–17 [B.6.207–8, A.7.193–94]). Hunger goes on to advise Piers that he should love and not scorn "alle manere of men" (8.231) and (B only) "lat god take þe vengeaunce . . . *Michi vindictam & ego retribuam*" (B.6.225–26). The vicar quotes the same Latin phrase at C.21/B.19.446 below, indicating that L had the same passage (or train of thought) in mind, as he did in another quotation of it in a similar context at C.17.235a—see 428–48n above. In the Half-Acre episode and here and in the episode below where Conscience admits the friars into Unite (see 22.243–45 and n), the consequence of the advice—to love and let God deal with the wicked—is most vexed; neither L nor Christian tradition could be comfortable with the idea.

The force of **saue he is furste yserued** (436) is not obvious: why should the vicar say that Piers is first served from the produce of his tillage? Prsl points to the idea of "the hierarchy of heavenly reward" and refers to C.14.135 (see n), but the connection seems remote. The reference may be to the tithing of the first fruits. Or perhaps the vicar is thinking of the Eucharist as the reward for labor, as in 383–85 above. Priests first serve themselves the eucharistic elements before offering the bread to their parishioners, and so might Piers as, in part, a figure of a priestly prelate, whose **seruauntes** would be the clergy (so Troyer 1932:172).

442–48 And Peres amende . . . of þe remenaunt: The vicar holds that the king rather than the pope should be **kepare ouer cristene**; as Alford notes, **bifore þe kynge** means not "in the king's presence" but "having precedence over the king" (see Alford, *Gloss.* s.v. *Kepen and Defenden* and *Keper*). Here a **kepare** is not merely a custodian of a flock but specifically a defender, as in the repeated assertion that "Hit bicometh to a kyng to kepe and to defende" (42 and n above, C.22/B.20.257). PP frequently adverts to the commonplace that the first estate's duty is to "kepe" and defend, and especially to defend the other estates, the church and the commons: e.g., 467 and 477 below, and C.1.90–93 (B.1.94–97, A.1.92–95), C.3.442 (B.3.289, A.3.265), C.8.26–34 (B.6.27–36, A.7.29–37), C.8.156–57 (B.6.159–60, A.7.146–47), C.9.9 (B.7.9, A.8.9). As Liberum Arbitrium says, "þe kynde is of a knyhte or of a kynge . . . the comune to defende" whereas "þe kynde of a curatour" is to preach and sacrifice oneself to destroy sin, especially in heathen lands (C.17.287–92). The king who speaks below defines himself as one who rules and defends (466–67). The matter is of no small import: perhaps exaggerating, a petition of the Good Parliament of 1376 claims that the Church held more than one-third of England's territory (Rot. Parl. 2.337); Wyclif gives the same figure (Farr 1974:156). Swanson estimates that the Church in fact held a fifth or a quarter of England's agricultural land in the late Middle Ages (1989:196).

Much theory argued that the pope, as Vicar of Christ, must exercise Christ's lordship (*dominium*) over temporal as well as spiritual things—for example, William Woodford's 1376 treatise against Wyclif (Doyle 1973). Wyclif, of course, denied dominion to anyone in mortal sin (Wilks 1965:222, 231, 234; Holmes 1975:165–78). In *De civili dominio*, where he presents the argument in full, he specifies that prelates should rule only in spiritual, not in temporal affairs (I.xi, ed. Poole 1885:73–75, 194–95). In line 443 the vicar speaks, then, partly of "the doctrine of papal dominion" (Prsl n ad loc.) but also of the commonplace division of functions of the estates: the nobility to defend, the clergy to care for souls. The warring popes' mingling of *militare* with *orare* is the issue; compare the doctor's cynical parting shot about unpacific popes (15.171–73).

442 And [Peres] amende þe pope þat pileth holi churche: Among the boldest of the Athlone conjectures, with regard to the sense if not to the principles of textual criticism, in the first place *causa metri*. All the manuscripts of B and C read *god* for **Peres**. The editors defend the reading with diffidence in KD-B, p. 208 and with confidence against Adams (1992:35) in RK-C, p. 132. Schm and Prsl print *god*; Schm inverts, *God [the Pope amende]*, to produce ax/ax alliteration (acceptable for Schm) as opposed to unacceptable xa/ax (see Schmidt 1987:33). The Athlone reading respects the context in which Piers is world emperor, but the parallel with line 449, "And Crist of his cortesye þe cardinals saue," argues for the archetypal line is spite of the metrical ideal (see Barney 1981:163–64).

The pope **pileth**; the vicar thus likens him to the "pelours," the cardinals' ravenous hangers-on (415 above).

446 olde lawe . . . vindictam &c: The vicar knows that Jesus brought the old law, "Thou shalt not kill" (Exod. 20:13, Deut. 5:17), into the new (Luke 18:20). *Michi vindictam* likewise occurs, in different wording, in both testaments; see B.6.226an, Alford, *Quot.* 52, and 434–39n above. Vengeance is not the pope's business, but God's.

447–48 Hit semeth . . . þe remenaunt: "it appears that as long as the pope has *his* way he doesn't care at all for the rest." Such recklessness leads to the sinfulness of the common people (451–55 below).

450 wit to wisdoem and to welthe of soule: The cardinals are known for intellectual ingenuity and wealth; the vicar calls for true wisdom and wealth of soul.

451–58 For the comune . . . clene lyuynge: That each trade has its tricks is the basis of many fabliaux and of such estates satire as Chaucer's General Prologue (see Lawler 1980:36–47).

453 Bote hit sowne . . . wynnynge: RK-C pp. 126–27 translates, "Unless it [the conseyl] has to do, in their perception, with financial gain."

455–74 spiritus prudencie . . . spiritus iusticie: Carruthers notes that in this passage we find a "sophistical redefinition given to the cardinal virtues by the adherents of Pride" (1973:158–60). Prudence **among þe peple is gyle / And al tho fayre vertues as vises thei semeth**, fortitude is criminal violence (464), and justice is despotism. With **coloureth** 458 compare Pride's **colours,** 351 and n above. See 219–26n, 274–316n, 335–480n above.

459–64 Thenne lowh ther a lord . . . wolle he, null he: Representing the first estate (see 396–480n above) a lord claims (like Lucifer!) **riht and resoun,** a

formula for justice and equity (see 20.300 [B.18.278] and 20.395n), for extract-
ing all he can—whether the auditor, steward, and clerk make honest reckonings or not—from his reeve with his manorial account books, the **rolles**; see
Alford, *Gloss.* s.v. *Reves Rolles* and 258–60n above. Abundant materials on the
accounting functions of steward, bailiff, auditor, and reeve are printed in
Oschinsky 1971; on efforts to control fraud see pp. 232, 341. See also Alford
Gloss. under the names of these four offices, Denholm-Young 1937:66–85, 131–
51, and 256n above. A very clear account of manorial estate management is
Harvey 1976:12–83. Harvey makes the point that by the time of PP most pro-
prietors leased land for a fixed rent rather than worrying about the annual
Michaelmas accounting and the cycles of production and service (p. 12). Hence
PP refers to old-fashioned practice.

The lord falls short of doing well in Thought's definition, being one who
is "trewe of his tayl, taketh but his owne" (10.80 [B.8.83, A.9.74]). Compare
the other vicious lords in this part of the poem (see 352n above). His laughing
is in itself suspect: Jesus never laughed (see C.2.31–35n, Luke 6:25, and C.22.111–
20n). But there is a good laughter in PP; e.g., happy children (C.16.302), Liberum Arbitrium (18.3), and Conscience (22.242). The lord's behavior parodies
that of the "puyr ordre that apendeth to knyghtes," namely "treweliche to take
and treweliche to fyghte" (1.96–97; cp. B.1.99–100 [A.1.97–98]).

The regular practice in L's youth made the bailiff and reeve jointly
responsible for the estate accounts (or later, the bailiff or reeve alone), and the
auditor was to review the accounts as an independent expert in the lord's
employ. The steward was not to be involved in the audit. L does not make it
clear whether the reeve is a victim or a co-conspirator in the auditor's and
steward's corrupt reckonings. Mann takes the reeve as the victim here
(1973:164); Prsl, perhaps more shrewdly, thinks the lord takes for granted the
reeve's dishonesty, and winks at it, exculpating himself by relying on his mid-
dlemen, the steward and auditor. The books are cooked, in any case, for the
lord's benefit and his tenants' loss. This is *redde quod debes* gone bad. The
animus against the misuse of written documents here may be compared with
the assaults on documentary records and their managers during the 1381
Uprising (Crane 1992:204–5; Bowers 1992:8–9; Justice 1994 passim).

Skeat's 1877 note to 459–64 quotes a relevant passage from Robert Man-
ning's *Handlyng Synne* on the usual collusion of lord and steward in fraud:
"And þys ys a custummable þyng / Now wyþ eury lordyng, / Þat ȝyf hys steward hym oght wynne, / Be hyt wyþ ryht or wyþ synne, / Hym wyle he holde
most pryue / Of alle þo þat wyþ hym be. / But as he takþ þer of þe frame
["proceeds, profit"], / He shal haue part of synne & shame" (ed. Sullens

1983:112, lines 4417–24). Compare the reeve who outwits the auditor and skims off more than his lord in Chaucer's GP 594–612.

The lord's behavior compares unfavorably with that of the lords in the Gospel stewardship parables (see 5.22–25n), and strikingly opposes Piers's relation to his workers in the field. **Conseileth** here with its implication of conspiratorial cunning echoes sadly against "the conseyl of Consience" (452 above).

Kane glosses **toke** (463) as "find fault with," citing OED *tuck* vb.¹, 2. (1993:141–42). The OED and MED citations s.v. *tuken* feebly support this earlier sense in L's time; then the very rare word seems to mean "revile, verbally abuse" rather than "chastise, discover a need for correction." MED *taken* 23.(a) "consider" supplies apt sense, or **toke** simply means "seized," which with **take** (line 460) forms part of the "give and take" theme of the last two passūs (see Headnote and 465–76n below). Possibly *taken* is a technical term for auditing an account: see Denholm-Young 1937:132. MED guesses "review, examine," *taken* 29.(a).

463–64 *spiritus intellectus . . . spiritus fortitudinis*: Langland substitutes "the spirit of understanding," from Isaiah (see 274–316n above), for "the spirit of prudence," one of the cardinal virtues. Here of course the prophetic spirit of understanding becomes extortionate shrewdness. Perhaps the reeve acts with the spirit of prudence (guile), the auditors respond with the spirit of intellect (knowing what was going on), and the lord's agents act with the spirit of fortitude (enforcement of decreed rights). Possibly the archetypal scribe (or L, nodding) erroneously wrote ***intellectus*** here thinking of the phrase in Isaiah, which there is associated with the ***spiritus fortitudinis*** as well.

465–76 thenne cam þer a kyng . . . as my kynde asketh: Continuing the response of the first estate, its head the king asserts his duty to rule and defend (see 442–48n above) and his lawful (**þe lawe wol**) and natural (**as my kynde asketh**) right to **take** what he needs **to lyue by**. Compare 3.374–77 (not in A/B). Baldwin takes this passage, along with the Prologue passages it echoes (see below in this note), as representative of L's absolutist but not theocratic idea of kingship (1981b:7–20), but it appears rather to support, with irony, constitutional monarchy. This king takes the *spiritus iusticie* to be his license to exploit (473–74), whereas we have been told that the *spiritus iusticie* doesn't spare "to corecte the kyng and the kyng falle in gulte" (303 above). In Harwood's formulation, the king confuses his authority with his justice (1992:216, n53). We should contrast this king with the longed-for "emperour" of 427 above, and of course with Christ the King at the beginning of the passus. Conscience elsewhere concisely sets forth the proper relationship between king and people (C.3.374–82, not in B/A). Likewise Reason "consailed þe kyng his comine to louie" (5.180 [B.5.48]). But here thrice recurring **take** (468, 473), picked up from 460 and 463 above, signals the rapacious interest of this king's speech; where Jesus, Grace, and Conscience are givers, the lord and the king are takers (see Headnote and 22.1–51n). On *take* as "appropriate property unlawfully" see MED *taken* 3a.(a).

What the king takes is taxes, especially to support warfare, **to defende**. The context specifies that what the king is charged to defend is **holy kyrke** (467), as his coronation oath requires of him. Hence the immediate topic is the controversial question of the king's right to support his wars by taxing the clergy—the counterpart of the vicar's antipathy toward papal taxation of the clergy (see 413–17n above). Baldwin cites the argument of two Austin friars before Parliament in 1371, and of Wyclif, that all possessions, including those of the clergy, were subject to taxation in such cases of necessity as war (1981b:10–11; see 22.276n). For the friars' articles see Galbraith 1919, and for Wyclif's view that the clergy should pay taxes see, e.g., *De civili dominio* I.xxviii, ed. Poole 1885:200–203. The issue was an old one in England, and Ockham had forcefully argued the royalist position in *An Princeps* of ca. 1337 (Nederman 1986). In his treatment of the Austins, Gwynn brings the same argument to bear on 5.163–79 (B.10.317–35) and 17.208–32 (B.15.546–67) (1940:222–23, 212–15). Middleton suggests that the friars' presentation "gave Langland the idea of ending the penultimate vision of the poem with the king's claim of his right to unlimited appropriation under cover of a cynically redefined *spiritus justicie*, and to present Will's subsequent dream . . . as brought on by Need's slippery application of the friars' favorite tenet as a warrant for appropriation at will" (1992:234).

The phrase **thenne cam þer a kyng** repeats C.Prol.139 (B.Prol.112), likewise in the context of papal power and cardinals and cardinal virtues (see 182–334n above), and it echoes as well, in a similar context of dispossessioning of the Church, the prophetic phrase "Ac þer shal come a kyng" (5.168 [B.10.322]). For the transitional formula "Then came . . ." see 3.27–37n and lines 200, 360 above. The Prologue passage was probably composed after this one (see Headnote). In both Prologue and here the king seems at once to appear on the poem's stage and to be defined, as it were to be instituted as king, and in both places the assertion of royal power is followed immediately by an assertion of its limits, here expressed much more aggressively (see 477–79n below). This king dashes the hope invested in the Prologue king.

That the king is **heed of lawe** is of course commonplace (it can mean merely "lawful head"), but the king's way of expressing his principality subtly qualifies it before Conscience does in the following lines. First he speaks of himself as **heed**, and of the rest as **membres**, in the old figure of the body politic, but inevitably recalling the true king, as the earlier part of this passus defines him, *Christus rex*, who is head of that Church whose constituents are members in the familiar metaphor from the epistles (Col. 1:18, Rom. 12:4–5, etc.; see 215n above). The implied comparison belittles this **kyng**. Second, **hastilokest** (469) contradicts the circumspect deliberation we would expect of a wise king. Third, the abundant use of **y** and the phrasing **ʒe ben bote membres and y aboue alle**, especially the superfluous **bote**, smack of self-centered arrogance. Fourth, the continued presumptuous tone of the next line, **and sethe y am ʒoure alere heued y am ʒoure alere hele**, permits us to find a pun in **hele**, "well-being" of the commonwealth but also "heel" as well as head of the realm, the lowest of the members, parodying Jesus' injunctions to let the first be last. (The former **hele** has an open, the latter a close *e*, but Chaucer's occasional rhyming of the two sounds shows that they were not very far apart in the London dialect.) Finally, the king's claim that he may **boldely** receive the Eucharist counters the humility proper to a congregant at Communion.

The king's absolute dominion over the law was not English policy as the Great Charter and the coronation oaths formalized it. Strohm cites articles drawn up after Richard II's deposition that indignantly report, "He seyd opynly, with a sterne chere and ouertwert ["angrily" or "perversely"], that his lawes were in his mouthe, and other while in his breste, And that he allone myht chaunge the lawes off his Rewme" (1992:29; see also the Lancastrian "Record and Process," art. 16, ed. Given-Wilson 1993:177–78). Richard swore at his coronation, and again after the Merciless Parliament of 1388, to uphold the laws of the realm, including those that the people "justly and reasonably" would choose (Saul 1997:25, 195).

465–66 bi his corone . . . with croune: Skt and Prsl take **bi his corone** to mean "with reference to his crown" (see MED *bi* prep. 9a.), but Schm takes it merely as an oath. In either case the repetition of "crown" draws attention to the king's office as opposed to his person, a distinction the king will blur.

472 holy churche: churche is genitive.

475–76 be hoseled . . . my kynde asketh: The king thinks he may properly take the Communion Conscience has offered, and that he has met Conscience's condition *redde quod debes* (383–90 and n above) because, never having borrowed, he owes (*debet*) nothing. The claims here are comic: the king does not **borwe** because he intends no repayment; he appropriates. Of course English kings did borrow, often and largely, from bankers, London burgesses, and magnates. And the king would never **craue of [his] comune** except as is consistent with a king's nature, that is, ceaselessly. On **asketh** see next n. His appeal to **kynde** echoes wickedly with the brewer's cynical sense of his own "kynde," his petty rapaciousness (400 above), and echoes sadly against the self-sacrificing "kynde" of a king in Anima's view (17.287–89). See the end of 20.8–12n, 20.417–41n, and 21.396–408n. For a similar farcical misunderstanding about restitution see Covetise's confession, 6.234–37 (B.5.230–33).

477–79 In condicioun . . . thy lawe asketh: Conscience pointedly but tactfully (Prsl: "a little apprehensive") hedges the king's rights with conditions. He was similarly careful when he hedged the king's power in 4.176–78: "withoute þe comune helpe"; stronger in B, 'but þe commune wole assente" (B.4.182–84; cp. A.4.146–47). His remarks resemble those of both the "lunatik" ("kynde witt" in C) and the "Goliardeis" (omitted from C) in deftly counseling the king (Prol.148–51 [B.Prol.123–27], 139–42)—see 479an below.

First the king is to **defende** the commons as well as the clergy (467) in the contract made in the coronation oath. He is to rule **in resoun as riht wol** (in the Athlone reading; cp. Prsl, Schm *in resoun riht wel and in treuthe* and RK-C p. 134), not with the corrupt "riht and resoun" the laughing lord had espoused (460; see 459–64n). And Conscience plays, as RK-C note (p. 127), on the king's word "asketh" in 476: there it meant "requires"; here **thyn askyng** is "what you desire," constrained by what *thy* lawe asketh, "requires" (cp. Chaucer, Melibee 1443, "as the lawe axeth and requireth"), with further play on subjective (the law you are head of) and objective (the law to which you are subject) senses of **thy**.

479a Omnia tua sunt . . . ad deprehendendum: "Everything is yours to defend, but not to despoil." The wording has not been identified elsewhere, but Prsl found a close analogue in Peraldus's *Summa de vitiis*: "Item si bona servorum dicantur bona dominorum, hoc intelligitur ad defendendum et non ad depredendum"—"Again, if the goods of slaves may be called the goods of their masters, this means for defending, not for despoiling" (see Alford, *Quot.* 116). Conscience may have put a current notion into his own Latin formula partly, again, out of tact: the Latin seems less bald and would appear to be the quotation of an authority, not Conscience's own idea. The Wife of Bath shows that then, as now, foreign languages could have a coyly euphemistic use (*bele chose, quoniam*: WB Prol.447, 608). Compare the similarly motivated movement into Latin at Prol.153–59 (B.Prol.132–38) (explained in B.Prol.129–31), and especially the Goliardeis's Latin of B.Prol.141–42, of similar import (see preceding note).

480–81 The vicory . . . as me mette: The vicar still holds the stage, and is the only one to exit, perhaps indicating his governing role in the estates sequence and his similarity to the dreamer. That his home is remote, **fer,** from the courtly precincts of lord and king has granted him the rustic provincial's privilege of plain speech, a privilege available likewise to such types as lunatics and goliards and eccentric Cornhill poets. Simpson links the name "William Langland" (the surname is a "common field-name": Hanna 2001:186) with the satiric speaker "Jack Upland" of the later poem of that name, who assumes this privilege (Simpson 2001b:162–63, and see C.5.44var., "opeland"). The vicar seems to be an uplandish alter ego of Will. Fowler suggests that these lines are "the poet's humorous reference to himself": when the vicar goes home, the dreamer wakes (1961:159). For the second time and last time L has Will say he wrote down what he dreamed; see 1–4n above.

C Passus 22; B Passus 20

Headnote

See the Headnotes to the preceding two passūs for comment on some features of this one, particularly on recapitulations of earlier parts of the poem and on B and C revisions in earlier parts of the poem that follow from episodes introduced in the last two passūs of B. After the waking episode (1–51), the last dream of PP consists of a series of attacks on Unite followed by a series of efforts at defense, with one brief aside: Kynde's instruction of the dreamer (201–13). Antichrist attacks (52–73), and Conscience calls on Kynde (74–109). The sins renew the attack (110–64), and Eld counterattacks (165–200). The sins attack again (214–29), and the friars are marshaled in defense (230–96). In effect personifying the friars, Hypocrisy and others attack (297–303), and Friar Flatterer makes as if to defend (304–72). Finally the attack is renewed and Conscience seeks for help (373–86). Counting the initial assault described in the previous passus (21/B.19.335–53), the forces of Antichrist storm Unite six times.

As L persistently deploys chivalric and romance conventions and formulas parodically, so in presenting these assaults he makes as if to invoke another favorite matter of alliterative poetry, descriptions of battle (cp. 20.281–94 and n). But, as often, he frustrates such generic expectations: the warfare is a psychomachia, and at risk are souls, not bodies (see 21.335–480n). Hence the assaults are generally bloodless, immaterial affairs, with few and unimpressive exceptions in lines 130 (?—see note), 137 (with wordplay), the physical but not martial onslaught of old age (167–68, 175, 189–92, 192), and Hypocrisy's obviously allegorical wounding of the soul (300–302, 335). The weapons used in these attacks are repeatedly described as unmilitary reifications of vices, deceptive speech, and disreputable activities (114, 116–19, 123–25, 132, 135, 144, 164, 174, 184, 225–26, 296–303).

The last passus falls into two parts, each containing near its beginning a speech from the figure Nede (Szittya 1986:276, 287): need motivates the whole action, with regard first to the dreamer, then to the friars. The first part (1–213) focuses on the Pride of Life, the sense of exuberant well-being that, in blind vainglory, inhibits penitence and the pursuit of grace. It alludes broadly to the state of Will's youth as expressed in the Land of Longing episode (see 183–200n below), and surveys vices particularly of the nobility: luxury, trust in good fortune, the seeking of revelry and comfort. The threats of old age, disease, and death cannot rein in these vices.

The second part (214–386) more overtly treats defective penitence, but now as a result of the Church's failure to administer the sacrament of penance properly, especially in the hands of the friars. The principal vices in this critique are vain learning, sloth, covetise, and hypocritical guile—the vices of clerisy. The metaphor of penance as healing is here enlarged, such that the main problem of the secular half of the passus is the transience of good health—the patient's problem—and that of the ecclesiastical half, bad therapy—the physician's problem. Hence the chief human failing is a false sense of security, an imperfect sense of need, generated on the one hand by individual pride, and on the other by corrupted and flattering ministry. The vision persistently draws the analogy between individual and social conditions, a scheme older than Plato's *Republic*. For particulars see notes 70–71, 95, 110–64, 110, 111–20, 143–51, 165–200, 169–79, 183–200, 201–5, 214–29, 373–86.

The dreamer meets with Nede

1–51 Thenne as y wente . . . y ful aslepe: Two other long passages in PP present Will awake: C.5.1–108, Will's Apologia, and C.10.1–67 [B.8.1–67, A.9.1–58], his meeting with a pair of friars in his quest for Dowel. L draws these three passages together with a pattern: in each the formula "(with) X I met" adjoins a reference to time: "with resoun y mette / In an hot heruest" (C.5.6–7); "on a fryday two freres y mette" (C.10.8 [B.8.8, A.9.8]); "neyh þe noen and with nede y mette" (C.22/B.20.4). (Compare also Will's dreaming encounter with Abraham: "mette y with a man a myddelenton sonenday"—18.181 [B.16.172].) Each waking episode opens a passus and, of course, a vision, and all three concern Will's behavior, whether he does well. Otherwise the C.10/B.8/A.9 passage has little to do with this one, unless one accepts the view that Nede speaks as a friar (Frank 1957:113–14; Szittya 1986:278; Clopper 1990:64–66). However, the C.5 Apologia, surely composed after the Nede episode, should be closely compared with it. It appears that, toward the end of his composition of the B version, L decided to explore more fully the vocation and status of his alter ego Will.

Middleton suggests that, as the Nede episode falls between the last two visions, L fit the Apologia between the first two visions, which themselves are imitated in reverse by the last two in a grand structural chiasmus (1997:269–70; see Headnote to C.21). In each interstice Will meets personified figures (the only ones to act outside the dreams; L may have conceived this bold move only as he composed the last passus of B) who challenge him vigorously ("apposede," "aratede," **afrounted**) about his way of life and his means of sustenance. Each episode probably alludes to the parable of the Unjust Steward (Luke 16; see 48n below). In each the suggestion is made that Will is a **faytour**, a deceitful beggar (see 5n below). In each Will's condition individualizes and personalizes the more general and social issues raised by the preceding vision

The differences between the episodes are telling. In the Apologia, the setting is urban, Will is at home in his "cote," the season is harvest, the challengers, in part, are faculties of Will's own mind, he defends his (as always ambiguous, unauthorized, and marginal) form of life, and at the end he responds to the challenge with a distinct act. Perhaps most important, though Will's status is profoundly obscure, the grounds of the action in Gospel parable and parliamentary statute are clear and stable (see C.5 notes). In the present episode Will walks **by the way** in an undefined (exurban?) setting, the time is noon but the season unspecified, the challenger is a condition not a faculty, Will is silent and no response appears to follow upon the challenge—and the theological and legal grounds of the discourse are notoriously unfixed and, among L's contemporaries and modern students, controversial. The C.5 Apologia may be the last passage that L composed, and it complicates but finally resolves, in Piers-like prayers and penance (B.7.124, etc.), issues broached in the Nede episode, likewise resolved in 201–13 below.

Immediately after the Nede episode the theme of the wickedness of friars re-enters the poem (line 58), and we argue below that Nede's speech is in part a subtle exercise in antifraternalism. Possibly L composed and inserted it, about one folio in length (see Middleton 1997:315 n83), after composing—and as a prelude to—the overt critique of friars that follows it.

The main issues are: what is Nede? and how reliable are his views? (We assume that Nede's gender is masculine for convenience; the "he" of line 232 below is ambiguous, and Latin *necessitas* [as in C.13.44] is feminine.) Middleton poses the debate: "whether Need's sudden appearance . . . represents an especially dangerous last temptation to willful self-deception, in encouraging the subject to represent his cupidity, even to himself, under a vocabulary of probity . . . or whether . . . it reasserts . . . a last glimpse of the fragile and elusive ideal . . . of holy simplicity and sufficiency." Though she "would slightly favor the former over the latter" interpretation, she concludes that both the Nede episode and the C.5 Apologia are "ultimately irresolvable enigmas" (1997:271). In an earlier essay she had observed that "L is also capable of both flaying and reconstituting Franciscan arguments for the exemplary value of radical need—and sometimes in the same scene, as for example in the final passus" (1987:39, n14). Hence she seconds Scase's remark (1989:66) that Nede's speech "remains at the end of the poem [i.e., unrevised in the C version] more as a dramatic illustration of the problem rather than any solution." The ambivalence of the episode may result from L's own irresolution.

[Since this note was drafted I have seen, just published, Jill Mann's essay, "The Nature of Need Revisited," based on her talk at the Langland Conference in Birmingham, England, 2003, in vol. 18 (2005 for 2004) of *The Yearbook of Langland Studies*. With this excellent essay I agree in almost all details, and finally disagree with its conclusion, which supports, as Professor Mann says, the "pro-Need camp"—I continue to think that Nede offers rather a temptation than a move toward a solution. I commend it highly as a vigorous alternative view to that presented below, and as especially rewarding in its setting of the Nede episode in a larger theological and economic context within the poem and contemporary thought. Some materials in this note and Mann's essay are coincidental duplications.]

Abundant medieval argument, some reviewed below, posits that extremity justifies stealing of the necessities, that temperance is a good thing, that thoughtful people and Jesus himself were, in some sense, willingly needy. Behind Nede's words are the shadows of positive ideas: the apostolic life, Franciscan humility, patient poverty. But L's speakers often present wrong views wittily, plausibly, and vigorously, and while much of what Nede says can be read as true, nevertheless the speech is a tissue of subtle temptation, plausible but faulty inference, and generally shifty reasoning and deceit. Not necessity, but grace, must be the basis of a just society. Hence we mainly follow Szittya (1986:268–73), who with Frank (1950:310–12 and 1957:113–16), the inventor of this interpretation, and Adams (1978; see also Carruthers 1973:160–61, Fowler 1980:238, Simpson 1990a:232–34, Harwood 1992:133, Burrow 1993:95–100) have argued most forcibly the view that Nede is not trustworthy, as opposed to Bloomfield (1961a:135–37), Schmidt (1983:188–92), Bowers (1986:158–60), and most influentially Clopper (1990:64–66, 1997b:82–85, 93–97) and Aers (1988:62–65). Adams, Szittya, and Hewett-Smith (2001a) provide useful surveys of scholarship on Nede.

The word *nede* can mean logical or material necessity in general, or such dearth as famine, or an immediate exigency or emergency, or extreme poverty. The latter two senses first operate here: the dreamer represents himself as simply without food at the time of the midday meal—Will's personal reprise of the collective physical Hunger of the Half Acre as well as the spiritual hunger, represented literally in the allegory, of those who, not having paid what they owe, lack blessed bread (21.383–90 and n). L generalizes Will's condition and projects it onto a personification who now can address large and hotly contested issues of the right acquisition of sustenance, of temperance, and of poverty. Nominally constituted as merely a material condition, and hence amoral (Adams) or "ethically neutral" (Harwood), an experience or a reality rather than an authority (Hewett-Smith 2001a; Prsl's 22.37n; Burrow 1993:98), an "objective physical condition" (Kim 2003:165), Nede quickly comes to seem a persuasive interior voice as well as the spokesman for contested values (who speaks in the third person of the condition *nede* as a separate entity—9, 17, 20, 35, 37) that call for judgment.

It is the nature of temptation to make what is wrong to look right. While any of Nede's assertions can be taken innocently, their subtle catenation and their context give them the lie. The speech's topics (what to eat, the avoidance of death [11, 19], shame [48]) and its allegorical form (inner extenuation represented as outer seduction) reproduce the original temptation of Adam and Eve. Both the Genesis and the Nede episodes begin with the tempter asking a question and going on to suggest a way to improve the victim's life. Here, however, the seducer is the condition of material privation, driving from outside in, rather than the spiritual inclination to sin, to emulate God, driving from inside out.

The episode reveals its significance in the design of the poem in its own argument and form, and further in light of a number of contexts: its immediate placement, as one of the responses to Conscience's mandate, after the king's speech and before the assault of Antichrist; its relation to the later speech of Nede (232–41 below) and to the conceptualization of *nede* in PP generally; its place in the social order established by Grace and overseen by Conscience; its relation to a web of contemporary issues and authorities—fraternal ideology and the mendicants-possessioners controversies; the biblical, theological, and legal touchstones of those controversies as they resound here; and especially its echoing of other statements in the poem about solicitude, begging, poverty, and providential supply.

In itself the speech gives evidence of defective argument. Nede **afrounted me foule** (5); the foulness might suggest the quality of Nede's arguments, not only their manner of delivery (cp. B.11.215). First of all Nede protests too much, spraying reasons and insistently repeating the words **nede, nedy** as if compiling a *distinctio* without distinctions. Szittya observes that the term *nede* is ambiguous like *mede, tresor, clergye* (or *treuthe* and *kynde*; see 1.81–204n), but that Will and we have yet to discriminate its moral meanings (269). As Simpson puts it, using the example of Conscience's discrimination of the meanings of *mede*, "Analysis of name is the prelude to and premise of therapy"

(2001b:150). At the outset Nede blames Will for being a deceitful beggar (5), and hence immediately a "taker." But why does he go on to say that Will should excuse his taking (or conversely, why should taking be blamed if it is excusable)? Excusing oneself implies prior misbehavior; Nede urges that the behavior was virtuous, regulated by temperance. Making excuses for oneself seldom elicits approbation (see 6n below). Though in certain conditions need has no law, it does not follow that it never falls into debt (10). Singling out deceit (**sleithe**, 14) as the manner of the needy person's legitimate "taking" besmirches the taking, and seems unhappily to recall Nede's first remark, that Will is a **faytour**.

Again, exculpating "taking" apart from the counsel of Conscience and the cardinal virtues except temperance (21) seems gratuitous—if the taking is good, why should these agents of good object?—and patently dangerous. Hence the argument promoting temperance over the other virtues (23–34) is itself superfluous. Further, it is clearly wrong: the fortitude and justice and prudence referred to are not virtues in the usual sense, aptitudes for good, but rather are instances of failed exercises of those virtues. Presumably the exercise of temperance could likewise be presented as failing. Nede concludes this part of his argument with a non sequitur that accidentally posits (in the shortest possible line) the truth: **God gouerneth all gode vertues**. This maxim-like postulate cannot mean that God makes the virtues (aside from temperance) ineffectual, as Nede's argument has it, but rather that God supports and directs them to the good. Nede also seems to identify **nede** and temperance (see Bloomfield 1961a:137), yielding two absurdities, that need teaches one to "take" temperately (9), and that need is next to God for its humility (35–36; the latter proposition is set right in 37—see 35n below).

Louh herted-ness (which means "humility" and not "dispiritedness" in L's time, as is evident from the citations in OED s.v. *low*) may indeed be the closest human way and analog to kenotic divinity (35–37). Augustine said that "the way to obtain Truth is first, humility; second, humility; third, humility" (*Epist.* 118, PL 33.442, cited by Gradon 1980:198). But humility driven by need (rather than for example by reason or obedience as an expression of charitable patience) seems a fugitive and cloistered virtue, an enforced good. We have been warned of those who "loken louhliche to lache men Almesse" (9.141, not in A/B). Further, as Szittya points out, the need that is desperate and near death, the only need that has no law, has now mutated into a temperate poverty (1986:270–71).

Nede represents Jesus on the cross as saying, **in his sorwe**, that **nede hath ynome me** (46), yet he goes on to represent Jesus as, actively, **willefolliche nedy** (49). But it does not follow, without further argument, from Jesus' voluntary neediness that Will should endure (or beg) and be needy (48). And finally, the argument has lost its way: Nede first urged Will to take, by sleight if necessary, and at last he urges him to remain in a state of need. It is as if Nede had second thoughts, strange thoughts for a figure who, in the logic of the allegory, expresses the imperatives (and exculpations) of the state of being hungry.

Again, all of Nede's propositions can be read *in bono*. His speech's contexts within and without PP corroborate the thesis that Nede is shifty. First, in treating of issues of human (mis-) behavior as it were post-Pentecostally, and in treating of the four *spiritus*, in a self-contained speech, the episode forms a continuum with and explicitly refers back to (6) the speeches of brewer, vicar, lord, and king that immediately precede it. The reference to the **consail of Consience or cardinale vertues** (21) further ties the speech to that repeated formula of the previous passus (see 21.337n). Nede implies that the **kyng and o**þ**ere** excused themselves by appeal to the *spiritus temperancie* (6–8); in fact, however, they had appealed to the spirits of justice, prudence, and fortitude (21.405, 455, 463–64, 474).

Shepherd (1983:187) suggests that the topic of temperance in Nede's speech, the necessary virtue for a new kind of society, fills out the pattern of the king's concern with justice and the lord's with fortitude—and less obviously, the clergy's (vicar's?—see C.21/B.19.455) concern with prudence (1983:187). The lord's and king's speeches prepare us to take Nede's speech as likewise wrong-headed and self-serving, with the best face put on it because after all it represents Will's own effort to excuse himself. (Adams would include the vicar's speech as among these examples of guile, 1978:278.)

More specifically, Nede's assertion that **nede . . . neuere shal falle in dette** (10) responds, as brewer, lord, and king responded, to Conscience's and the cardinal virtues' "conseil" that the "cristene" must pay to Piers's pardon *redde quod debes* before partaking of the blessed bread (21.389–93). Nede expresses Will's own discomfort with and evasion of this counsel. "Taking" what one needs is as feeble a redemption of this debt as the king's claim that "y borwe neuere" (see 21.475–76n, 7–11n below). Repentaunce had explained to Covetyse that as long as he lives off ill-gotten gains "þou ʒeldest nat bote borwest" (6.343 [B.5.288]). Perhaps the most striking index of the error of Nede's speech also continues a pattern established by the lord and king, the repeated "favorite verb" *take* itself, with its fellows *cacchen, wynnen, comen to*, and (handily alliterating with *nede*), *nimen* (lines 7, 9, 11, 14, 15, 16, 17, 20, 41, 46; see 21.465–76n, Szittya 1986:272, Burrow 1993:97). At the conclusion of Nede's speech the dreamer uses the strikingly apt verb *undernimen* ("rebuke," as always in PP, a meaning developed from a sense like "*take up* [a disputed matter with someone]'') to describe Nede's action: **whenne nede hadde vndernome me thus** . . . (51). The root sense of the verb wittily catches up Jesus' own words a few lines before, **Ther nede hath ynome me** (46).

A second context for Nede's speech is his later advice to Conscience (232–41 below; see n) and the uses of the term *nede* elsewhere in PP. In his advice to Conscience Nede presents the argument that friars should labor manually rather than receive endowments or exercise cure of souls. With a comic twist at the end, Nede commends the friars to poverty. The advice in itself conforms to the persistent critique of latter-day friars, eager "to fare well" (235), in PP. The question is, why is it Nede who says this—or for that matter why is it Nede who at the beginning of the passus counsels Will, also with a twist, to live in temperate poverty? In both cases it seems that need (dearth) may indeed properly motivate the question. However, Nede is not obviously the proper agent of the counsel rendered—remain in need—unless we take the allegory in a joking way: dearth drives people to avoid dearth (take), but also personified Dearth wants Dearth to stay alive. This prestidigitation is more obvious (and humorous) in the advice-to-Conscience passage because there the shifts in the argument take place in fewer lines. In either passage, the nature of need has little bearing on the quality of Nede's advice. Nothing precludes Nede's speaking truly in one place and falsely in another. Here Nede tempts Will to exculpate his "taking," and later Nede represents himself as likewise tempting friars to do wrong, "for thei aren pore" (234).

Uses of the term **nede** elsewhere in the poem bear on the Nede interstice. Apart from the last passus need is personified only once in PP, briefly by Imaginatyf: a drunk, fallen into a ditch (an image perhaps recollected in C.22/B.20.19), is immune to reason, "Ac when nede nymeth hym vp anoen he is ashamed" and becomes able to blame himself (13.234–40 [B.11.427–34]; the B version also briefly personifies shame). Likewise Nede *undernimeth* the dreamer here (51), but contrariwise he argues that Will should **be not abasched to byde and to be nedy** (48), thus removing a possible motive for him to repent. Shame is generally a good thing, a spur to contrition, in Christian thought (see 284 below, Parson's Tale 152, etc.).

In the sense of "dearth," a number of the more pregnant instances of the term *nede*, as noted below, were added in the C version, presumably after L composed Nede's two speeches in the last passus, in keeping with C's increased emphasis on issues of poverty. Need as inability to survive: In C only, old and helpless people who are "nedy" are in the pardon (9.176, not in B/A); God might have made humans wise "and lyue withoute nede" (16.20, not in B). Those who "most neden aren oure neyhebores" (9.71, not in B/A), and providing for "ho hath moest nede" (17.63, not in B) is "helpe-hym-þat-nedeth"

(18.13, not in B), a part of *Caritas* which is "Cristes oune fode." Hence the idea of need involves the controversial questions about rightful begging and rightful alms with which L wrestles at greater length in C (Pearsall 1988; Aers 1983; see below in this note). Dame Study finds it outrageous that harlots are helped before the "nedy pore," whereas men should help those who have nothing rather than "tho that haen no nede" (11.26, 28, the terms not in B). In the last passus Nede sidesteps this issue by neglecting to consider the state of those from whom Will may "take."

These last uses of the term **nede** adopt the point of view of the almsgiver. Other occurrences focus on the recipient of alms, and chastise those who beg though they are in no real need. Excluded from the "bulle" of Truth's pardon are those who beg or bid "but yf they haue nede" (9.161, again not in B/A). Nede at the outset calls Will such a **faytour** (5), and as such we may think he cannot *reddere quod debet* and participate in the pardon, no matter how temperately he "takes."

Will's worry about providing for himself, "to clothe me and to fede" (line 209 below), persists and involves him in another controversial question, the provision—"fyndynge"—for various classes of potentially needy ecclesiastics. Hearing that Charity has no dread "of deth ne of derthe," Will asks Patience "ho fynt hym his fode . . . at his nede" and learns who the friend is who "fynt" him: *aperis-tu-manum* and *Fiat voluntas tua* (16.316–21 [B.15.176–80]), less substantial-looking providers, we may imagine, than the friends and relatives who "foende" Will in his youth (C.5.36, 49). Near the end of the poem Conscience wishes "þat freres hadde a fyndynge þat for nede flateren" (383; see n). This somewhat defeatist proposal responds to Piers's promise at the Half Acre to "freres þat flateren nat" that he will "fynde hem what þat hem nedeth" (C.8.147–48). The terms "friars," "flatter," "find," and "need" do not occur in the parallel places in the A and B versions, where Piers instead promises his "almesse" (B.6.146 [A.7.134]); the C version surely reflects the earlier composition of B Passus 20.

Need in PP can summon up the remediating sense of shame and the conditions of a charitable life, but more often it provokes "faitery" and flattery. Overmuch concern with need, in fact, belies the poem's insistent themes, be not solicitous and God will provide (Szittya 1986:262–64, 272): "That loueþ god lelly his liflode is ful esy" (B.7.128 [A.8.110]). Nede seems, like a friar, to "flateren" (= "palliate the solicitude of") Will, to give him an excuse, rather than to prod him to harsh penance.

In the context of the general action of the last two visions—the Pentecostal founding of the Church and the social order under Grace and Conscience, and the assault on those institutions by Antichrist—the Nede episode amounts to a wake-up call, so to speak, a reality check for our semblable, Will. Nede seems to cause, even as he recounts (23–34), the disintegration of those mainstays of individual and social well-doing, the cardinal virtues. The first, sudden onslaught of Pride's forces upon the Church (21.335) was abstractly motivated; we must know that postlapsarian humans are given to pride. The second assault, immediately after the Nede episode, is more materially motivated by Nede itself, and takes the form of two kinds of avarice. Nede arouses on the one hand friars and other false religious (58–61, etc.), and on the other a concupiscent lord (71, etc.), the former denying dearth with hypocrisy and sleight, the latter with wasting and oppression, revelry and "comfort." Friars and their wealthy patrons are two sides of the corrupt absolution system, pardon for pay. The fact of need cannot, and the figure Nede does not, know the solutions to the problem of material necessity that the poem offers: first what is given, Grace the giver and the crafts that permit survival (and that explicitly defend against Antichrist: 21.215–26), and second the craft Kynde commends, unsolicitous love (208–11). The solution is not taking, but giving.

Thus the Nede episode in relation to its context in PP (see also 55n below). Further and more compelling evidence of Nede's errancy comes from the episode's external context. Immediately after it we find that Antichrist's first followers are friars (58). Nede raises the issue of Jesus' voluntary poverty (40–50). He calls Will a deceitful beggar (**faytour**, 5), and he urges him **to byde and to be nedy**, to beg and assume voluntary poverty (see 48n below). These issues inevitably evoke the contemporary polemics of friars, antimendicants, and anticlericals, issues that unfold more openly in the second half of this passus with Nede's second speech (see further 58n below).

In lines 40–50 Nede refers to the contemporary debate about the nature of Christ's (and the apostles') poverty and the obligation his poverty imposes on his followers. That Jesus was of the "secte" of the poor scarcely anyone would deny (16.99 [B.14.259], but see 14.90–91 [B.12.146–47]). Wit says that Jesus had only three cloths, and lost even those before his death (C.10.194–95; see also 12.101, 120–28 [B.11.186]). The questions are: should we enter into such poverty intentionally, be **willefolliche nedy** (49)? Was Jesus' poverty in any sense absolute or "perfect" (as the Spiritual Franciscans argued)? Does the voluntary assumption of Christlike poverty justify begging? Was Jesus a beggar? To simplify: the friars (at least the Franciscans) and Nede would answer yes to these questions, and the possessioners (monks and secular clergy), the followers of Wyclif, and (we argue) L would answer no. A further question emerges: does the friars' "theoretical" or "notional" poverty, their voluntary neediness, drive them, given human nature, to sin in the form of taking easy money for easy penance and other abuses? In the voice of Conscience, PP answers, yes:

friars "for nede flateren" (line 383 below). Dolan summarizes: "The problem was the notional poverty practiced by the friars, as contrasted with the patient poverty of the real poor which resisted all forms of temptation" (1988:40). On the controversies about the theory of poverty and the friars see especially Leff 1967, Mathes 1968–69, Lambert 1961, 1998, and Coleman 1988.

At stake are the question of the spiritual and ethical validity of Will's own unsettled form of life and the larger, parallel question, treated in the second half of this passus, of the effectiveness of the Church's administration of penance as the way to salvation. Neither question is resolved in PP. L casts Will himself as somewhat like a friar: a mendicant, a wanderer, hermit-like (like the Austins, the Friars Hermits), sophistical and proud of learning, a minstrel (Szittya 1986:265–67, Kerby-Fulton 1990:144). For discussion of these matters see Pantin 1955:123–24, Bloomfield 1961a:220–21 n32, 225, Gradon 1980:203 n6, Schmidt 1983:192, and especially Szittya 1986, Scase 1989, Dolan 1988, and Clopper 1997b, passim, esp. 93–97 where he argues that Nede is a friar.

Among the many participants in the debates on these issues in the fourteenth century are the spokesmen for the Spiritual Franciscans before and after the condemnations of their doctrines by Pope John XXII in 1322 and 1323, the English antimendicant Archbishop Richard FitzRalph (especially in the 1350s), and the English anticlerical Wyclif and his adherents and opponents (especially in the 1370s). The issues of poverty and mendicancy involved issues of dominion, ownership of material goods.

Spiritual Franciscans believed in the apostolic example of absolute poverty (citing, e.g., Mark 10:21, "go, sell whatsoever thou hast"; see B.11.271–78) and hence in the renunciation of all dominion, and their Rule noted that Francis himself lived *sine proprio*, without personal belongings. On Franciscan emphasis on the issue of need see the "Earlier Rule" in Armstrong et al. 1999, I:71. The papal constitution *Exiit qui seminat* of 1279 agrees that Franciscans may have the use of but not dominion over worldly goods (*Sexti Decretalium* 5.12.3, ed. Richter and Friedberg 1879:col. 1109–21). The other orders, monastic and fraternal, permitted the holding of goods in common (citing, e.g., Acts 2:44, the original Christians *habebant omnia communia*, "had all things common"; see 276n below and Dolan 1988:35–37). The Austin rule's first chapter says, "And let you not call anything your own, but let all things be in common among you" (Mathes 1968:62). Yet the Dominicans, for example, were not technically possessionate until 1475 (Hinnebusch 1951:232). John XXII declared it heresy to teach that Christ and the apostles were without dominion *in proprio et in communi*, "with respect both to personal and to common ownership" (Clopper 1990:60–61). He further disallowed the Franciscan legal fiction whereby ownership of their houses was technically vested in the pope.

The poem, and contemporary antifraternal and anticlerical polemicists, make a number of distinctions that, when blurred, produce confusion of the kind that Nede dazzlingly exploits. The systematic, deliberate, careful, hoarding begging of the mendicant orders is not like the begging of the disabled, or of Will who begs without thought of the morrow, "withoute bagge or botel" (C.5.52). A secular priest's accepting his parish's "spiritualities," tithes and other offerings, is not begging. The Wife of Bath repeats the common understanding that God "In wilful poverte chees to lyve his lyf" (WBT 1179), but Jesus had, as FitzRalph argued, "natural" or "original" dominion over the necessities and therefore no need to beg (Walsh 1981:386–406; see Frank 1950:311, Szittya 1986:125–28, Scase 1989:19, 55, 58, 67). Piers puts it baldly: "the boek banneth beggarie" (C.9.162 [B.7.88]; see also C.9.61–65 [B.7.65–69, A.8.67–71], C.9.121, C.16.350–52, 372–74 [B.15.225–27, 256]). The chronicler Knighton reports as Lollard views that Christ did not order anyone to beg, that for sturdy men to beg was against both civil law and the Gospel, that religious should not beg, and that friars should work with their hands and not beg (ed. Martin 1995:282–93)—these are certainly the views of Wyclif. When L's speakers adopt the point of view of wretched and helpless beggars, he favors their activity. The admirable figure Patience begs (C.15.32–35 [B.13.29–30]), but he is perforce in great need, as his name says. PP stoutly holds, with FitzRalph and the other antimendicants, that deliberate begging robs the helpless poor of their alms: "For he that beggeth or biddeth, but yf he haue nede, / He is fals and faytour and defraudeth the nedy" (C.9.63–64 [B.7.67–68, A.8.69–70]).

1–4 Thenne as y wente . . . y mette: As at the opening of the preceding two passūs, Will's waking mood responds directly to the last moments of the preceding vision, and his physical condition (wetshod, dearly clothed, hungry) correlates with his mood. Conscience has asked the commune to repay its debts and to receive blessed bread; the waking Will does not acknowledge debt, "knoleche to pay . . . *Redde quod debes*" (C.21/B.19.186–87), and Nede encourages him in this at line 10.

The time **neyh þe noen** in the context of self-exculpation recalls the "hot heruest" of Will's Apologia (C.5.7), where he is similarly braced by interrogators. Middleton proposes an allusion to the obligation of a lord to provide the noon meal for harvest workers (1997:274; see C.8.196, 288). No harvest "werkeman" (C.5.25)—no Piers Plowman!—Will eschews manual labor and is consequently hungry, as he was at the end of the second vision, C.9.296 (B.7.147, A.8.129). Since Will has presented himself as clerk, hermit, vagabond, and beggar, the question of how various orders of ecclesiastics may acquire the necessities of life presents itself immediately. Nede's answer—take what you need by sleight and without blushing—would satisfy none of the current opinions on this question, but would parody most closely the friars' position: see 5n, 48n, 58n below.

Will doesn't know **at what place** he might eat; here **place**, if not merely a doublet of **where**, may mean "manor house, mansion" (see 21.61n) as in 181 below and C.7.184, 15.274, etc. If so it refers to Will's practice of singing for souls and begging at various houses in town and country, "now with hym, now with here" (C.5.44–52).

5 faytour: An "impostor," but surely "a deceptively needy beggar" here, because as far as we know Will has practiced no deceit (if it is such) other than begging while able-bodied. The word and its cognates usually refer to begging in PP, as they do in the petitions of the Good Parliament of 1376 against *faiterie* by *ribauds mendinent* and *faux faitours* (Rot. Parl. 2:332; see also 340 and C.Prol.41–46n above). Faitery is often linked with the activity of friars, like "frere faitour," excluded from the community that Piers provides for (8.73 [B.6.72]; also C.9.209, C.11.52 [B.10.72, A.I1.58], B.13.242), and the use of the term here suggests an immediate adversion to the issue of the propriety of mendicancy. Scase argues that PP is the first to use the term in connection with such issues (1989:69–71; see also Clopper 1997b:83, 147–48). For evidence of a growing fear in England of false beggars see Middleton 1997:240–44. Whether Will's practice is in fact faitery (of which he is accused by Resoun at C.5.30) is of course the overwhelming question.

Nede berates Will for faitery but goes on to recommend that he steal what he needs by sleight. The ethical slippage expresses a common psychological maneuver of self-defense.

6 excuse the as dede the kyng and oþere: That is, excuse yourself factitiously (see 21.465–76n). Further, since the royal government regularly "excused" its taxation policies by appeal to need—namely, to pay for national defense (which consumed more than half of the Exchequer's budget in such times of war as 1374–75; Holmes 1975:11)—Will's grounds for excuse would indeed be the same as the king's (so Baldwin 1994:48). The pope likewise excused his demands, in the early and mid-1370s, for large subsidies from the English clergy on the basis of need for his wars (see 21.428–48n). Scase points out that the Austin friar Geoffrey Hardeby in 1385 used this argument to defend mendicancy: "religious might beg on the basis of necessity if a king might seize temporalities [the yield of ecclesiastical endowments] on this basis" (1989:68).

In the C Apologia Will is asked whereby he "myhte be excused" for his apparently idle life (5.34; similarly B.12:20). In B, he offers a feeble effort "me to excuse" to Imaginatyf (B.12.20). Others who give a bad odor to the term "excuse" are Meed (3.219 [B.3.173, A.3.160]), those who beg off the journey to Truth (C.7.298, not in B/A, from Luke 14:18–20), and idle parsons and priests (B.15.486).

7–11 That thow toke . . . lyf for to saue: Craftily unloading the ethical baggage of the idea of "mesure" from the first vision (e.g. 1.33 [B.1.35, A.I.33]) and such passages as B.14.71–81 and 254 below, Nede contorts the idea of the virtue of temperance to bring it to bear on the situation of last-ditch survival, producing the strange advice to seize what you desperately need . . . moderately! Contrast the usual idea of temperance (voluntary restraint, sophrosyne) in C.21/B.19.282–88. With sly irony, Jean de Meun has the friar Fals Semblant invoke a favorite antifraternal text, Proverbs 30:8–9 ("Give me neither beggary nor riches . . ."), to espouse temperate moderation—"the mene is cleped suffisaunce"—while admitting that Christ and the apostles "were never seen her bred beggyng" (Riverside Chaucer, *Romaunt of the Rose* 6521–50).

The verbs **toke** and **was** appear to indicate Will's prior conduct, parallel to the prior conduct of "the kyng and oþere" (line 6), but **toke** may be a potential subjunctive: "Couldn't you (didn't you know how to) excuse yourself (by saying): whatever you might take . . . ."

The maxim "Need has no law," quoted also at 13.44a, is widespread, proverbial in English and Latin, preserved in canon and common law, and theologically correct, a tenet of natural law, the "lawe of kynde" (line 18; see Gregory IX's *Decretals* 5.41.4, ed. Richter and Friedberg 1879, col. 927, and Alford, *Quot.* 76, Dunning 1937:33, Carruthers 1973:161, Stokes 1984:51, Szittya 1986:270 [citing Gratian and Sext.] and 277–78, Clopper 1990:66 and 1997b:93, and 20n, 276n below). The jurists' commonplace was *tempore extremae necessitatis omnia sunt communia*, "in case of extreme necessity all property is in common" (Couvrer 1961:2, 152; quoted in English in *Dives and Pauper*, ed. Barnum 1976, 2:41, citing Matt. 12:1–8), or in Huguccio's formulation, "By natural right all property is in common; that is, in case of necessity it should be shared with the poor" (Couvrer 1961:99 and 147; Tierney 1959:32–39). Often applied to the national as well as the individual condition, the maxim that need has no law justified, for Wyclif and others, England's taxation of the clergy and confiscation of church endowments (Farr 1974:139–60). Yet as Simpson observes, the maxim's assertion in a poem so taken with law is suspect (1990a:233–34).

Insofar as need legitimizes begging, even deceitful begging (faitery), the maxim touches on current controversies about mendicancy and community property (see 1–51n above, 48n, 276n below). The "Earlier Rule" of St. Francis (ch. 9) quotes the commonplace that need has no law (ed. Armstrong et al. 1999, 1:71); Nede's restatement of the maxim here is the clearest sign that Nede speaks as a friar (Szittya 1986:277–78). The maxim can justly apply only to extreme exigency, and certainly not to the voluntary poverty (like the friars') that Nede urges on Will. The antimendicants were quick to argue that an *assumed* neediness was no dire indigence. Otherwise the logic would be that one could deliberately enter poverty and then with justice act lawlessly. Nede couples the maxim with a similarly dubious proposition that **nede**—that is, taking when in need—**neuere shal falle in dette** (cp. C.21/B.19.475). In a sense this is true, as Schm holds, if **dette** means "sin" and the "taking" is *in extremis*. But surely one should repay what one steals (or even begs) in need as soon as one can: Truth's pardon says "he þat biddeþ borweþ and bryngeþ hymself in dette" (B.7.81). It comes to seem that **nede hath no lawe** means that Nede is an outlaw.

    And (line 9), glossed "If, Provided that" by the Athlone editors (RK-C, p. 123), is a harder and sharper reading (from one of the B version families) than archetypal C (and Schm/Prsl) *And that*.

11–19 For thre thynges . . . deye for furste: Holy Church also names the "three thynges" that are "nidefole: fode, vesture, drynke," and urges that they be used in "mesure," and (unlike Nede) that God will provide them (1.17–35 [B.1.17–37, A.I.17–35]). Jesus' text on the subject demands that we be not solicitous for food, drink, and clothing and specifies that "your Father knoweth that you have need (*indigetis*) of all these things" (Matt. 6:31–33; so Luke 12:22–30). Both scriptural passages conclude: seek (*quærite*; cp. "sewe," line 22) first the kingdom of God *and his justice*, not his temperance.

    Nede seems to operate more comfortably in rational—here commercial and legal—rather than spiritual terms: **borwe, wed** (13), **cheuesaunce** (16), **maynprise** (17). Nede **nymeth . . . vnder maynprise** the needy person who steals clothing, that is, goes bail for him, excuses him (Alford, *Gloss.* 93–94).

20 nyme as for his owne: Nede anticipates the objection that the Ten Commandments say that one should not covet a neighbor's belongings (Exodus 20:17; see 279a below), adopting the standard argument used by FitzRalph that in cases of need property is held in common, so that what one takes is one's own, not another's (Szittya 1986:269–70, Rubin 1987:61–62). See 7–11n above, 276n below.

23 For is no vertue by fer to *spiritus temperancie*: The claim that temperance is superior to the other three cardinal virtues is explicitly contradicted by Conscience, who said that justice was the chief virtue (C.21/B.19.406 and n; see 21.297–308n). Adams observes that Thomas Aquinas followed one tradition in reckoning temperance the lowest of the four cardinal and three theological virtues (1978:286–87; so Bloomfield 1961a:137). However, as Mann notes (2005:7), at least one well-known treatise, the *Moralium dogma philosophorum*, does place temperance above the other three cardinal virtues. Others placed prudence highest.

25–34 For *spiritus fortitudinis* . . . all gode vertues: Nede brings to a climax the demolition of the meanings of the cardinal virtues by way of the sophistries and colors that constitute Antichrist's attack (C.21/B.19.339–50 and n). The virtues are criticized in terms of their operation in governance and law, as opposed to their more private application in the preceding passus (276–308). The simple reply to Nede's argument is that if these virtues do wrong— discipline intemperately, or judge partially, or predict wrongly—then they are not virtues.

    Forfeteth (25) means simply "transgresses" (Alford, *Gloss.* 62). The meaning of **Aftur þe kynges conseyl and þe comune lyke** is ambiguous: 1) "According as it pleases the king's council/counsel and the commons" (Schm); 2) "According to the king's counsel [or council] if it pleases the commons" (the most likely: Donaldson 1990); 3) "According to the king's counsel [or council] and similarly the counsel of the commons" (Prsl). Agreeing with one of the first two constructions are three scribes of C who wrote *likeþ*. Uncommon **lyke** for *yliche* ("similarly") and the grammar of **comune** without an -*s* ending (adjectival rather than genitive? cp. C.3.473) render the third interpretation difficult. For such uses of *lyke* see the Athlone variants at A.I.48, and B.14.167, C.7.128, 16.20, 18.20, 18.62, and C.21.428–48n.

    Conseyl in this context more likely refers to the Great Council of the king rather than the king's advice in general. Since king, council, and commune were major constituents of England's legislature, it appears that Nede would derive justice from a higher law. But a justice that is a respecter of persons is not justice.

    Lines 31–32 may be paraphrased, "And the Spirit of Prudence in a man shall fail in many respects with regard to what he supposes would happen if he didn't exercise foresight." We have been told (C.21/B.19.276–80) that prudence gives one the power to "imageny" the consequences of things, and hence to forestall catastrophe. This power was one of the gifts of Grace, "to se and to saye what sholde bifalle" (C.21/B.19.242–44). Denying this capability,

Nede invokes the proverb "Man proposes and God disposes" (see 11.303–4 [B.11.37–38n]), adding that God has control over the virtues. But the inference is faulty: if the exercise of prudence is indeed virtuous, then God's governance assures that it will not fail.

35 Ac nede is nexst hym: The sense is uncertain, though taking **hym** as temperance, picked up from line 23 (so Skt, Prsl) seems less likely than **hym** as God from the preceding line (Schm, Bloomfield). The locution, and perhaps the sense, parallel 19.272 (B.17.291), "Innocence is next god" and B.1.204, "Loue is leche of lif and next oure lord selue." Humility, innocence, and love sort well together. But even here Nede's argument is contorted: one might say that either temperance (if **nede** means temperance in line 35) or humility (being "louh herted," line 37) is next to God, but saying that necessity or dearth is next to God strains the capacity of even figurative language. Nede deftly tries to assimilate himself to the virtue of temperance.

36 as louh as a lamb: so Piers describes Treuthe at 7.197 (B.5.553, A.6.40).

37 For nede maketh neede fele nedes louh herted: The line, preserved in C and only the RF family of B, explains the preceding two lines; it could be a late addition. Disyllabic *neede* here means "a needy person" and **nedes** means "necessarily." Donaldson (2000) translates: "For Need by necessity makes needy men feel humble." The jaunty *traductio* on **nede** may seem to undercut the idea of humility, but see 20.386–87 and n, 20.437–38 (B.18.394–95) and n above, Salter 1962:39.

Prsl here grants that "the argument, that it is necessity that forces men to be humble (and not patience that teaches them to be so), seems specious," but draws attention to Patience's praise of poverty (15.279–16.157 [B.14.104–322]; for a survey of other passages in praise of poverty see Clopper 1997a:148). In response to Prsl, Fowler cites Patience's espousal of carelessness about the necessities of life, and willingness to die if it please God (1980:266; see 15.254–59 [B.14.55–60]).

40–50 And god al his grete ioye . . . ne porore deyede: Nede follows the friars in arguing that pursuit of a life of need imitates the life of Jesus. The phrasing **toek mankynde** (a right "taking," at last) specifically recalls the **boek** at Philippians 2:7, Jesus "emptied himself, taking (*accipiens*) the form of a servant . . ." (see C.20/B.18.21n). Among the **sondry places** telling of Jesus' poverty is 2 Cor. 8:9: "For you know the grace of our Lord Jesus Christ, that being rich he became poor (*egenus*), for your sakes; that through his poverty (*inopia*) you might be rich." See 12.120–44 (B.11.233–58), 16.98–99 (B.14.258–59).

Skeat was troubled by L's "singular mistake" in saying that another favorite proof of Jesus' poverty, Matt. 8:20/Luke 9:58, was spoken by Jesus on þe **sulue rode** (44–45; lines 46–47 are not biblical, perhaps added by Nede to inflate **nede**'s importance—Szittya 1986:272). The general association of the "foxes have holes" passage with the Passion was in fact common (see Marrow 1979:167–70). Schmidt finds the words as spoken from the cross in a number of fourteenth-century English works, and adduces as the source of the idea the Franciscan Bonaventure's *Vitis mystica* 8.161, where Matt. 8:20, quoted as Jesus' own witness to his poverty, is followed closely by the remark that Jesus was "poor in his birth, poorer in his life, poorest on the cross" (1983:189–90). The actual "Seven Words of the Cross" from the Gospels, the common theme of Good Friday homilies, were well known (e.g. Ernaldus, PL 189:1677–1724). A number of earlier sources that associate the "foxes have holes" passage with the Passion are gathered by Foster (1916, Part 2:67); see the *Northern Passion*, Harleian Manuscript 1804g-j and 1637–40, ed. Foster 1913, Part 1:211, and Rawlinson Manuscript 3008–16, ed. Heuser and Foster 1930:127–28. Adams observes that both the York and the Wakefield plays present the same venue for the **fox and foule** passage (1978:283), and Alford suggests that its basis is the liturgy of Passion Sunday (*Quot.* 23). Clopper shows that the radical friars took the Matthew 8 passage as evidence that Jesus and the apostles had no dominion, individual or communal (1990:64, 66; 1997b:94), and argues that L has the words spoken from the cross to present Jesus at his most needy.

L's poetic compression is sometimes interpreted as his ignorance (see 21.15–62n); elsewhere he similarly conflates Gospel materials (e.g. 18.145 [B.16.115] and 18.170–74a [B.16.153–57a]). Less likely is Szittya's proposal that the wrong attribution is another indication of Nede's error.

The second **nede** of line 46 may be an adverb (usually *nedes*, but see C.3.281 [B.3.226, A.3.213], C.13.37), as Donaldson takes it (1990), or more interestingly the object of **abyde**, "poverty" as distinct from the first **nede** of the line, "necessity."

48 Forthy be nat abasched to byde and to be nedy: At issue is **byde**: it means either "endure, be constant, suffer," or "entreat, pray, (or especially) beg." Will's neediness and his admission that he begs (explicitly in C.5.51, 90, presumably composed after this passage, and a little less explicitly in 15.3 [B.13.3]), and Nede's calling him "faytour" (line 5), fit the meaning "beg," but the term "abyde" in line 46 may suggest the meaning "endure." But the immediate context, raising the issue of voluntary poverty, invokes the issue of mendicancy (see 1–51n, 40–50n above).

The verbs that many scribes normally spelled *bidden* "beg" (short *i*) and *biden* (transitive or intransitive) "endure" (long *i*, but with a short *i* in many preterite forms) were, along with *beden* "command, offer," so often confused in Middle (and Old) English that spelling only feebly distinguishes them. See for examples of *biden* for *bidden* Kane's apparatus of variants at A.5.218, 6.71, 6.88, and 11.151. Manuscript families of B and C here at line 48 variously offer both *bide* (? < *biden*) and *bid* (? < *bidden*), though the modern editors' copy-texts of both versions read **byde/bide**. Eight manuscripts of B and thirteen manuscripts of C, more than half the manuscripts that include this line, read forms of *bid*. In C.6.345 the copy-text, followed by the modern editors, reads **bide** where the meaning is clearly "entreat, pray"; the B copy-text there reads **bid** (5.290).

If the original here is a form of *bidden* it more likely means "beg" than "entreat" (which requires an object) or "pray" (because the concept of prayer has not appeared before in the speech). *Bidden* quite commonly means "beg" in PP, and the collocations "beggars and bidders," "begging and bidding," etc., are frequent (examples from B: Prol.41, 6.203, 6.237, 13.241, 15.205, 15.227). L plays on the senses: "Beggeres for hir biddynge (the prayers they offer) bidden (beg) of men Mede" (B.3.219 [A.3.206]; cp. the parallel C.3.275 "Bothe Beggeres and bedemen crauen mede for here preyeres"). Donaldson took **byde** (48) to mean "abide" (1990); other critics' views conform to their reading of the entire episode (Schmidt 1983:191; 1987:129; Clopper 1990:65; 1997b:95; Scase 1989:68–69; Wittig 1997:147). The consequences of taking the word with the fuller sense "beg," which seems more probable, are examined above (1–51n), as if what Will "toke" (line 7) was by beggary not thievery.

The association of begging and shame evokes the remark of the Unjust Steward, "To beg I am ashamed" (Luke 16:3), and links Nede's speech with Will's Apologia (C.5.23–25, see n and 1–51n above). Szittya suggests that the line also echoes the statement in the Franciscan Rule (cap. 6) that one should not be ashamed to accept alms (1986:278; cp. Clopper 1990:65). On the other hand, Rubin shows that the "shame-faced poor" (*pauperes verecundi*) were considered especially worthy of alms (1987:72–77; also Coleman 1988:627–28, 631; and see C.9.86).

52–386 And mette ful merueylousely . . . y gan awake: See Headnote on the divisions of the remainder of the poem.

Antichrist attacks

52–73 And mette . . . and cardinale vertues: After the quiet waking interlude
Will experiences his last vision, the battle around Unite resumes, and the
remainder of the action is conducted with unrelieved frenzy. The repetition of
the attack on the Church affords us a "binocular view," like the repetitions of
the survey of the field full of folk and the assaults of Hunger in the first two
visions (Middleton 1997:212; see C.21/B.19.335–54 and 21.355–480n). The first
attack is led by "Pryde" with "a grete oeste"; the second by Antichrist, with
pryde carrying his banner (69–70, and see Headnote and 215 below). For the
more detailed renewal of Antichrist's attack see 110–64n below. Both initial
attacks break out suddenly, both are cast as agricultural destruction, both
armies include a lustful lord (see 90 below and 70–71n), both attacks multiply
figures of guile and falsehood, both initial assaults conclude with Conscience
offering "consayl" (C.21/B.19.355; 74 below). It appears that Pride and Antichrist differ little (see 21.219–26n). The main difference at first is the presence
in Antichrist's van of friars and monks, but even these can be compared with
Pride's two lieutenants "surquidous" and "spille-loue" (21.339–40), the arrogance and backbiting that characterize the regular clergy, as in the portrait of
Envy and Wrath (C.6.63–163 [B.5.75–181]). In both attacks the knightly and
clerical orders, but not laborers, appear among the evil troops (see 70–71n
below). In the responses to the initial assaults larger differences emerge.

52–53 in mannes fourme / Auntecrist: Adams argues that Antichrist follows
immediately on Nede because L recalls Job 41:13, concerning Leviathan, "In his
neck strength shall dwell, and want goeth before his face" ("Et faciem eius
praecedit egestas"—the Wycliffite translator has *nede* for *egestas*). Since the
Leviathan is commonly interpreted as Satan, and Satan as the Antichrist, Need
precedes Antichrist, and it was commonly believed that famine would precede
the Antichrist tribulation (1978:282–83). The connection seems strained and
unnecessary, and Adams in fact produces no account that explicitly associates
Job 41:13 with the idea of famine preceding Antichrist.

Still, the belief that Antichrist will bring famine is widespread (Bousset
1896:195–200), and the texts that support the idea (Matt. 24:7, Luke 21:11)
emphasize the apocalyptic onset of seducers and false prophets, the "fals" and
"gyle" of this passage finally personified as friars (line 58). No antifraternal jibe
was more common, from William of St. Amour and Jean de Meun to Wyclif,
Gower, and Chaucer, than that friars personify hypocrisy, whose name is Antichrist (see 21.219–26n). See Emmerson 1981:71, 264 n108; Szittya 1986:34, 212–21;

Kerby-Fulton 1990:12, 133–61; The Summoner's Tale; the figure Fals Semblant in the *Romaunt of the Rose* ("Of Antecristes men am I," Riverside Chaucer, line 7009, and see 7155–56); Gower, *Vox clamantis* Bk. 4, cap. 16–24, lines 677–1232; *Miroir* 21,229–432, 21,625–48, trans. Wilson 1992:284–86, 289; see 21.219–26n and 21.221–24n above. Miniatures in the fourteenth-century *Jour du Jugement* depict Antichrist in Franciscan garb (Emmerson and Hult 1998:25, line 586n).

Following a common tradition, Wimbledon in his famous sermon of 1388 interpreted the fourth seal of the Apocalypse as the last state of the Church before Antichrist, that is, the reign of hypocrites (ed. Knight 1967:119–20, lines 954–67). Hanna argues that the onslaught here fulfills the prophecy of B.10.334–35 (altered in C): "Ac er þat kyng come Caym shal awake," with "Caym" the well-known antifraternal acronym for the four major orders of friars (1998b:153–56; on Cain and friars Szittya 1986:229–30; see next note).

In parody of the Incarnation (and cp. "Peres armes," 21.5–14n), Antichrist comes **in mannes fourme**, in keeping with the belief that he will be a real historical figure (Emmerson 1981:197).

53–57 al the crop of treuthe . . . as he a god were: Though of human form, Antichrist (= Belial below, line 79) parodies the divine power of increase of plant life, and Piers's role as the plowman who oversaw the planting of the crop of truth (C.21/B.19.309–16; see 21.338n). On Antichrist as conqueror see Emmerson 1981:74. The bad growths of **fals** and **gyle** sadly undercut PP's theme of the greening of grace (see 20.400n), and invert Jesus' work, "And now bygynneth thy gyle agayne the to turne / And my grace to growe ay gretter" (C.20.399–400 [B.18.361–62]), "þat grace gile destruye" (B.18.347). See for relevant examples of the agricultural metaphor A.10.123–30, C.13.23–24, C.17.242–55 (B.15.92–102), all with the phrase "spring and spread." The source of the notion here is the parable of the Tares among the Wheat: "And the cockle, are the children of the wicked one" (Matt. 13:24–30, 36–43; see 21.309–16n above).

Crop can mean "produce of the field" in the fourteenth century, but the expression **vp so down and ouertulde þe rote** points to the more common meaning, "top of a tree or other plant." One of the "Fifteen Signs Before Doomsday," in a tradition found in England, e.g. in *Cursor mundi* (ed. Morris 1877:22549), was that "the trees turn upside down and grow with their roots in the air" (Heist 1952:29, 178–82, 189–90). The "Quindecim Signa Ante Diem Iudicii" has "The vi [usually seventh] day schall down Falle / The treys with þe croppys alle, / And toward þe erthe the croppys schalle be" (ed. Furnivall, *Hymns* 1867:20, line 67–69). The image conforms to the topic of evil and

degenerate times as topsy-turvy (see Curtius 1953:94–98), as in Gower's Prologue to the *Confessio amantis*: "Now stant the crop under the rote / The world
is changed overal" (ed. Macaulay 1900, lines 118–19). It likewise fulfills the
famous southwest-wind prophecy: for pride "Beches and brode okes were
blowe to þe grounde / And turned vpward here tayl in tokenynge of drede /
That dedly synne ar domesday shal fordon hem alle" (C.5.120–22 [A/B.5.
18–20]).

The Chester *Coming of Antichrist* represents Antichrist promising a miracle (in parody of the Rod of Jesse), to turn trees upside down and make fruit
grow from their roots (Lee 1971:8). Manuscript Morgan 524, fol. 7r, illustrating
an Anglo-Norman apocalypse, has a picture of Antichrist making a tree's roots
bloom (reproduced Emmerson 1981, figure 4 after p. 118; see also p. 198).

55 spede menne nedes: At first glance, "to provide for men's needs," that is,
"satisfy men's desires (for the things of the world)" (Prsl; see Kaske 1963:207),
a parody of the divine provision of sustenance that preempts solicitude. As
Carruthers and Szittya note, that **fals** allays dearth comments harshly on
Nede's argument (1973:162, 1986:271). Adams argues that the phrase can also
be construed as "to make men's needs prosper, increase," "to promote, further men's needs"; the ambiguity would exploit "the difference between the
appearance of prosperity brought on by Antichrist and the spiritual indigence
that actually results from his promotion of men's needs" (1978:284). Mann
rightly observes, however, that the phrase "spede (one's) needs" is in fact a set
phrase meaning "to satisfy one's desires" (2005:6).

58 Freres folewed þat fende for he ȝaf hem copes: The figure of Fals (55) inevitably brings to mind the friars; see 2.223 (B.2.213, A.2.172) . For the association
of friars with Antichrist see 52–53n above, and the latter half of this passus.
Szittya shows how L represents friars specifically as opposites of Piers and
Conscience (1986:284–85). Grace gives the means of salvation; the fiend gives
copes. The **copes** that entice the friars to vice continue a persistent theme in
PP, where copes are regularly the identifying garb of friars, less often hermits,
except for one indeterminate use at C.3.181 (B.3.143, A.3.132). Copes were in
fact often very valuable, weighed down with gold thread. Hence in PP copes
always symbolize venality, usually the grasping of friars; they are emblems of
pride, surfeit, and improper holding of office by ecclesiastics, from the Prologue on (C 59 [B 61, A 58]; see Prol.57–61n). Copes surpass any subsistence-
minimum "cloth" to which all needy have a right (16–17 above). The first
concrete image of vice in the poem, in the Prologue, exploits this same conflation of clothing as the sign of pride and as both maker and concealer of iden-

tity and status: "And summe putte hem to pruyde, aparayled hem þeraftir / In continance of clothyng in many kyne gise" (C.25–26 [B.23–24, A 23–24]).

59 rongen here belles: Monasteries were required to ring their bells at the *joyeuse entrée* of a prince or prelate. Failure to ring the bells upon the visitation of a bishop was a disciplinary offence.

60, 64, 67 tyraunt, regnede, kyng: Antichrist is emphatically the King of Guile, and as such parodies the kingly Christ of the preceding passus (see C.21 Headnote and 5–14n).

61 foles: guileless ordinary Christians. The term is glossed earlier: "lewed folk, goddes foles" (C.11.248). "Lewed" would nicely translate Paul's Greek *idiotes*, "layman, ignoramus" (I Cor. 14:16, 23, 24), Vulgate Latin *idiota*, glossed in Lewis and Short's dictionary "an uneducated, ignorant, inexperienced, common person" (see 11.287n). The first reference to Christians as fools is 1 Cor. 4:10, Greek *moros*, Vulgate *stultus*; compare PP's lunatic lollers. Franciscans spoke of "apostolic people" as *idiotæ* (Clopper 1997b:291). Repeated thrice below (62, 74, 77), the term momentarily supplants "cristene," the usual term for Unite's people (see 21.337n), distinguishing the simple, "mylde men and holy" (65) from the sophisticated religious regulars.

70–71 And pryde baer hit . . . likyng of body: Pride, as chief of the sins, led the initial attack (C.21/B.19.335–36 and n); here he is Antichrist's banner-bearer. L may briefly allude to the satirical use of martial banners in *Winner and Waster* (see also 96 below). It was "for pruyde" that the southwest wind did its damage (C.5.117 [A/B.5.15]; see 53–57n above). In both attacks Pride is accompanied by—and particularly represents the vice of—a member of the nobility, a "lord þat lyueth aftur the lust of his body" or "lord of lust" (C.21/B.19.352, 382, and notes; 90 below; see also 3.57 and 10.96), the laughing lord of C.21/B.19.459–64. Skt suggested that he is the personification of lechery, as in 111–120 below— note Lechery's "lauhyng chere," line 114 (see 111–20n). As Prsl observes, the lord represents one of the Three Temptations, the Pride of Life (*superbia vitæ*) of I John 2:16, the figure Lyf who "priked forth with pruyde" below (143–82; see 11.174 and n and C.22/B.20 Headnote). The lord, Pride, Lechery, and Lyf all represent the arrogance that results from bountiful well-being, overexuberant health, "hele . . . and heynesse of herte" (153 below), a sense of good fortune, a vain "glorie" (157) that defies death: the intemperate opposite of Nede.

L may recall the play *The Pride of Life* which, its editor thinks, may be as early as mid-fourteenth century. Its title figure, the "King of Lif," has a wonderful arrogance and delight in his strength and health: "In pride and likinge his lif he ledith, / Lordlich he lokith with eye . . . . He hath a lady louelich al at likinge" (lines 25–26, 29, ed. Davis 1970:90–91).

The lord of lust is first of a series of villains in the passus that includes—with Lechery and Lyf—Revel, Sloth, and Physic, all havens, as Harwood terms them, "the personified refuges from remorse" (1992:135). They seek the false "conforte" (91) that flattering Fortune or friars provide. The only non-allegorical figure in the first attacking army of C.21/B.19 is this lord; in Antichrist's army friars are first, soon accompanied by the same lord of lust. Antichrist marshals plenty of ecclesiastics of all orders, and plenty of the nobility, but none specifically of the laboring class, except perhaps for "wanhope, a wenche of þe stuyves" (160 below).

72–74 kepar was and gyour . . . 'Y consail': Conscience continues in his regal role as keeper of the Christians (see C.21/B19.256 and n, 442–48n; see 214–16n below). His repeated offer of counsel (21.200, 355, 393, 452, 22.21, 74) may allude to his role as Chief Justice (4.186), hence a member of the Great Council and a chief advisor to the king (see 21.256, 442–48n above, 129–30 below). In 147 below Conscience and counsel are practically identified. The counsel, that the fools should take refuge in Unite, repeats 21.355–56.

Conscience calls on Kynde

74–109 'Y consail' . . . peple amende: In a reprise of the attack, relenting, and then renewed attack of Hunger (C.8.168–340 [B.6.172–320, A.7.157–301]), Conscience, paralleling Piers's call for Hunger against "wastors," calls for Kynde to defend against Antichrist, then (106–8) asks him to relent, and finally (384 below) asks him for vengeance. Conscience may have intended to invoke Kynde in the general sense, common in PP, "God," and hence would be surprised by the ravages of Kynde in the specific sense of physical nature, *natura naturata* as opposed to *naturans* (see White 1988:66, 78–83). One should be careful about what one prays for. Disease, age, and the prospect of death may well induce the remedy for sin, repentance, the allegory says, but only temporarily. (Note that Antichrist here is an allegory of sin and not the eschatological figure, who would be allied with rather than battling against pestilence.) Thus some theologians distinguished "attrition," repentance motivated by fear, from the more perfect "contrition," repentance motivated by love (Lea 1896, 2:11, but see Tentler 1977:250–63).

Kynde's assault is first disease, then old age, then the diseases that naturally follow old age, then death. In context we inevitably think of the four horsemen of the Apocalypse (Apoc. 6:2–8; see Carruthers 1973:164), and of course of the horrors of the Black Death of 1348–49 and 1368, **pokkes and pestilences** (98) with its characteristic **boches** (84), buboes; it did not bring all England to repentance. The onslaught (with famine; see 52–53n above) fulfills the prophecy of Matt. 24:7, and closer to hand the prophecy that followed the attack of Hunger, "Pruyde and pestilences shal moche peple feche" (C.8.347, not in A/B). This assault, fierce, deadly, and corporeal, contrasts with the rather verbal, intellectual, but all too insidious assault of Fortune and its allies (110–64).

76 crye we: From the preceding passus (see 21.200–212n) to the end of the poem Conscience and the dreamer repeatedly cry out for help: see below lines 78, 140, 165, 201, 228, 375, 386.

77 fendes lymes: Antichrist and his forces parody the Church as Body of Christ.

80–89 Kynde Consience tho herde . . . vndoen vs alle: The gifts of nature, diseases, come **oute of the planetes**, as Skt says, because "diseases were supposed to be due to planetary influences" (see Curry 1960:3–36). The frenzied list of diseases makes a grim parody of the list-making of alliterative battle poetry (cp. 20.281–94n); here nature's abundance is not happy. The diseases are foragers, **forreours** and **forageres**, the mere forerunners of the heavier troops of old age and **deth** (89).

86 ypriked and preyede polles of peple: "Rode and preyed on people's heads." Although Donaldson translates the first verb "pricked," i.e. "stabbed," it more likely means "rode"; the forces are represented as on horseback (see 134, 149, 181), and apart from Lechery's arrows (117) the (allegorical) weaponry is not specified—the figures generally bash one another. But possibly the reference is to Death's lance, or to St. Sebastian, martyred with arrows, whom one invoked against plague. This line foreshadows the form of Will's more comic discomfiture below (183- 84).

90–92 The lord þat lyuede . . . kepe his owene!: The lecherous lord seeks the knight Comfort for his standard bearer (see 70–71n above), rather than Contrition. His still-reprobate state issues in his selfish *sauve qui peut*, with **kepe** meaning "protect" but also "hoard," and **his owene** echoing ironically with the idea of justice (to each his own) and its parody in the B Prologue (122 and 208, "wite wel his owene"; see 21.442–48n and 21.186–87n). **Lyf** is a common word for "person," but here, in combat against death (cp. 20.28–34 [B.18.29–35]), and in the context of the Pride of Life (see 70–71n above), it has a special charge—each life is to keep his own life, to maintain his own vice.

93–95 Thenne mette thise men . . . in þe Vawwarde: On heralds of arms see 20.13–14n. We are in a rush, and as Prsl observes: "This is a battle in earnest, not a chivalric exercise." Fowler doubts the punctuation here, and plausibly places a full stop after 94, admitting **he** of 95 as a pleonasm, or omitting it with many manuscripts of B and C (1977:23, n2). In this reading, in an obvious allegory, Eld is Death's standard bearer.

95 Elde þe hore: grizzled, he looks like what he is. Old age, with its nearer view of death and its diminution of libidinous vigor, counters sin. See generally Tavormina 1995b:205–13 and references gathered there. The idea picks up from the similar view of Eld in the Land of Longing (C.11.186–97, 12.1–14 [B.11.27–62]; see Headnote above), where Eld is the dreamer's own old age—as it will be again below (183–200; see note). In the Tree of Charity scene in C, Eld is simply the cause of death (18.105–27, not in B). As Szittya points out, this earlier "biography" of Will has many of the same characters as those whom we meet in Antichrist's army: the Three Temptations (see 70–71n above), Fortune, and the friars (1986:274; see L's summary, 15.5–9 [B.13.5–7]). See 143–51n, 165–200n, 183–200n below.

96 deth; bi riht: As Prsl notes, "perhaps we should imagine a skeleton astride a horse," a common illustration of the fourth rider of Apoc. 6:8 (see 74–109n above). The allegory resembles that of Gower's *Miroir de l'Omme*, perhaps written about the same time as the B version (1376–79). There a personified Flesh, led by Fear, sees Death and wants to repent. Fear sends Flesh to Conscience, who escorts him to Reason. Flesh manages to separate himself from the Devil (as in the World/Flesh/Devil triad) but later relapses (ed. Macauley 1899, I, lines 697–744; trans. Wilson 1992:13).

Elde claims the right to bear Kynde's banner as the natural precursor of death (cp. 70 above).

100–105 Deth cam dryuyng . . . dethus duntes: Richard Rolle in one of his lyrics speaks likewise of death's omnivorous charge: "Dede dynges al sa sare, þat nane may defende . . ." (ed. Allen 1931:39, line 9). Skt calls this "one of the finest passages in the poem"; John But remembers it at A.12.104. The quick allusion to the values of chivalric romance, the lovely ladies and their sweetheart knights, both arouses pathos and instructs us about the vanity of ephemeral pride of life—compare Dante's Paolo and Francesca, and Imaginatyf's rueful remarks about Felice and Rosamounde (B.12.46–48). Compare 20.8–12n toward the end, and see 111–20n below.

106 Concience of his cortesye: see 243–45n below. Conscience is always courtly: see for example C.3.152, 15.119 (B.13.112), 22.243 and 355, B.13.31, 46, 179, 198, 458, and Lawler 1995:97.

108 Leue pruyde priueyliche: The force of **priueyliche**, "secretly, quietly," is not obvious: "of their own accord"? "without further ado"? Perhaps best, "without (prideful) public display (of virtue)." Lechery's "priue speche" below (115) has clear import: secret nothings, in the seduction sense, and underhanded dealings, in the affairs sense (see 111–20n).

109 to se þe peple amende: as Schm notes, Skt needlessly takes this as ironic; the sense is "in order to see whether the people would correct themselves."

The sins' attack renewed

110–64 Fortune gan flateren . . . doysayne myle aboute: The prospect of disease and death fails to bring about repentance (see 155n below). Singled out among Antichrist's forces in the renewed attack are Fortune, Lechery, Idleness, Haughtiness (**hey berynge**, 116, 153), Falsity of various kinds (119–20, 131), Covetise, Avarice, Guile (124–25), Simony, Life, Liar, Pride, Health, Sloth, and Despair (**wanhope**, 160, 164), the prostituted daughter of a perjured assizer (160–62). Omitted from the seven deadly sins are only Gluttony, Wrath, and Envy. The list, something of a bustling hodgepodge like the participants in the Mede episode (with some of the same characters, and see 95n above), emphasizes two realms of sin, the foolish gloating consequent on one's sense of good fortune and good health, and the Mede-sins of urban venality and deceit.

The activity of the sins here may be compared with their repentance under the guidance of Reason and Conscience in the second vision. This last passus presents the two obstacles to saving contrition as flourishing good health (pride of life), and feeble administration of confession (flattering friars)—"refuges from remorse" (70–71n above).

110 Fortune: The gifts of Fortune (like friars—235 below) flatter the people with a deceptive sense of well-being ("long lyf," 111), in L's strong portrayal of "hele" and "wele" as pride of life and hindrances to due contrition. There may be reference to the temporary economic improvement in the lives of many craftsmen and laborers consequent on the labor shortage caused by the Black Death. We are far from Will's state of need at the opening of the passus (as if we recede in time to his exuberant youth, which Lyf in part personifies; see 95n above, 143–51n below); either condition conduces to sin. Bourquin notes several resemblances of the figure of Fortune to Mede (1978:312–13). **Fortune** seems to be masculine here (though "he" of 111 could represent L's feminine pronoun) but is feminine at 156–57 (see Cooper 1991:32).

111–20 lecherye he sente . . . þe techares: *Luxuria* in Latin, Lechery includes generally the sins of the body's pleasure, "lycames gultes" (C.6.176; see 16.90–93 [B.14.250–53], 16.256 [B.15.103] "lecherye of clothyng," and 311 below), a gift of Fortune the opposite of disease. Lechery appears when men's needs are "sped" (55 above). Cooper observes that the personification of lechery as a male is very unusual (1991:36–37); L has in mind male forms of the vice. Lechery is presented ambiguously here, as sexual seducer with wily speech and fair behests (115, 118; see next note), and more generally as a figure of falsehood of the kind we find in Mede's retinue, as if a corrupt official or merchant, a man of affairs. Lechery has a **lauhyng chere** like the laughing lord at the end of the preceding passus (see 21.459–64n) and the "lyf" who "lowh" in 143 below; the three figures are practically the same (see 70–71n). Expressive of the Pride of Life, their laughter ominously evokes the image of the rictus of Death. L elsewhere ascribes lechery particularly to lords (e.g., 2.96 [B.2.89, A.2.61]).

The allegorical arrows of Lechery recall the set of "fair" arrows of the God of Love in the *Romance of the Rose*: in the English version Beaute, Symplesse, Fraunchise (or Curtesie), Compaignye, and Faire-Semblaunt (Riverside Chaucer, *Romaunt* 949–65, 1749–1926). Lechery's arrow **fayre biheste** may be compared with the deceiving "faire biheeste" of Hope in the *Romaunt* (4446). Both instances suggest a world of courtly levity and falsehood—the world of "lemmanes knyhtes" (104), the lecherous lords. The allusion is corroborated by Lechery's arms, **ydelnesse** and **hey berynge** (cp. 153 below), corresponding to two prominent personifications in the *Romance of the Rose*, Ydelnesse and Daunger in the English version. Lechery's arms reify the darker side, the **vntidy**, of these courtly qualities; see 101–105n above. Now Conscience's allies are specifically **of holy kirke þe techares**, presumably the secular clergy (see Lawler 2003:86n2, 115–16)—or the cardinal virtues (122)?

121–39 Thenne cam couetyse . . . and deuors shupte: Covetise (with his twin Avarice as his arms) and his follower Simony attack with violence, but armed with money, **many a brihte noble**, and bad words: **wyles, glosynges and gab-bynges**, jousts in the ear (see 21.219–26n toward end, and 21.335–480n). See 296–303 and n below. His assault begins and ends with ecclesiastical crimes, and all the wrongdoings are those of learned officialdom. The world of Mede has expanded to include the papal curia.

125 glosynges and gabbynges: Elsewhere glossers are linked with flatterers, false prophets, and Antichrist (C.21/B.19.221), and in the Prologue with friars (C 58 [B 60, A 57]), a common association (see 368–72n below). "Gabbing" seems to have become a term in Lollard sect vocabulary (Hudson 1981:20 and 28, n27).

126–28 Symonye hym suede . . . to saue: Simony, by means of such gifts as English seekers after benefices would bring to Rome or Avignon, importunes the pope. Covetise, Simony, and the pope **made** prelates, like the prelates whom "þe pope maketh" as rectors of the merely titular sees of Nazareth, Nineveh, etc. (C.17.188–89 [B.15.493–94]), in order to farm their endowments, **here temperaltees to saue** (see RK-C, pp. 121–22). Alternatively the reference is to the practice of papal "provisions" to benefices in England, a practice vigorously resisted by the government from 1343 on, including promulgation of the Statutes of Provisors (1351) and Præmunire (1353, 1393; see Swanson 1989:70–72, 184, 223, 327; Alford, *Gloss.* s.v. *Provisour, Temporalties*; 21.413–23n; and C.3.125–30 [B.4.128–33, A.4.111–16]).

127, 130 presed on þe pope; knokked Consience: For these two phrases archetypal B reads *preched to þe peple* and *kneled to Conscience*. Schm argues that C revised here, and accepts the archetypal readings of both versions (see also Fowler 1977:35). C's revision of the former phrase would constitute a bold new antipapalism (but see B.19.428–48). KD-B, p. 92, attribute the archetypal B reading to censorship, and note that **presed on** is the harder reading (RK-C, p. 120). In fact B's reading is pointless in context—why would Simony preach to the people?—and misses the point that Simony and the pope jointly **made** prelates. The explanation is simpler than an assumption of censorship: **presed** (perhaps spelled "preesed") was misread as *preched* by a scribe (as in manuscript D of C), with common *c/e* confusion, and *þe peple* was picked up from 125 above in an effort to smooth the sense.

Skeat took archetypal B's *kneled to* as an expression of hypocrisy. KD-B say B here is a misguided improvement (p. 92), and RK-C note that "the story here is unmistakably of a violent intrusion," and call B's variant a misreading (p. 120).

132–35 And baldeliche baer adoun . . . amendement: The bearing down and jugging refer to a charge on horseback. As OED s.v. *jug* v.[4] suggests, both **ioggede** "spurred" and **ouertulde** "tilt over" suggest jousting (tilting) language (see Donaldson 1983:75). Compare Jesus' joust in C.20/B.18. **Brihte noble** puns on **noble**, coin and baronial person. L points to the sorry distance between the nobility's charge to defend the community with martial force and the sub rosa bribery that corrupts royal justice: the language of chivalry crosses with the language of bureaucratic officialdom. The **Wyt and Wisdoem of Westmunstre halle** recall such Mede-figures as "wareyn wisman" and "wittyman," alias "wysdom and wyt" (4.27, 31, 72 [B.4.27, 67], etc.).

Taek this vp amendement means "Accept this (gift/money) in consideration of your reversing your judgment" (Kane 1993:142, citing Alford, *Gloss.* s.v. *Amendement, Amenden*, and OED *up* prep.[1] 7.a.), or as Prsl aptly puts it, take this to "see things right."

136–37 Arches . . . syuyle into symonye . . . toek þe official: Naturally paired with Westminster is the Archbishop of Canterbury's Court of Arches which met in St. Mary-le-Bow (i.e., "of the Arches") in Cheapside, London. See B/C.2.61n; in the same passage "symonye & cyuyle" are persistently paired (B.2.63, 67, 71–72, 114, 142, 168–69, 204, and A/C parallels). On **syuyle** see 2.65n, Gilbert 1981, Alford, *Gloss.* s.v. *Civile*. **Official** means specifically, as Alford observes, the presiding officer of the Court of Arches (*Gloss.* s.v. *Official*; OED *official* sb. I.2.; MED *official* n. (a)—also called the Official Principal). Although **toek** can mean "gave" in PP (see 3.47 [B.3.45, A.3.44], in a similar context of corruption, and Skt's note, his C.4.47), the use with elided object of the verb here (Skt, Prsl) would be unparalleled. RK-C correctly indicate that it means "took captive," continuing the martial metaphor: playing off "taek" in 135, L says Covetise hooked the court officer with his bribe, took him in with what he took him.

138–39 For a meneuer mantel . . . deuors shupte: At the Arches one could obtain an annulment (*divortium*, not a divorce in the modern sense; see Alford, *Gloss.* s.v. *Divorce*). At first it seems that the Official (or Simony) celebrates a marriage; enjambed **Departen** comes as a surprise. Skt noted that **Departen ar dethe come** alludes to the wording of the marriage service, "tyl dethe vs departe," as recorded in the Manuals of the various English rites (e.g. Sarum, ed. Collins 1960:48; York, ed. Henderson 1875:19*). One scribe composed a spurious line about unhappily married people: "Þei lyue here lif vnlouely til deth hem departe" (after C.10.270; RK-C, p. 183). The offer of a fur coat as the bribe deploys the idea expressed in 58 above; see n. As records from the period abundantly demonstrate, fine clothing was the favorite reward for services rendered.

142 while his bagge lasteth: A mercenary, Covetise will quit fighting when his pay runs out.

143–51 And thenne lowh lyf . . . Consience one: At first Lyf seems to laugh at Conscience's joke (cp. 242 below). On the Pride of Life see 70–71n, 111–20n above. Lyf joins Pride himself in 149, in a kind of allegorical hendiadys. He is the same figure as the lord of lust (see 70–71n above), a vigorous but cynical dandy, foul-mouthed, impious, sneering at virtue, and above all reckless of his imminent death—he is Lyf, after all, but in a sadly different sense from the Lyf of 20.30 or 20.59. The plot and cast of characters replicate the image of Will's youth, the Land of Longing (C.11.171–95 [B.11.12–36]; see Headnote, 95n above). As Prsl notes, in both passages Wanhope (160 below) is "a consequence of following Fortune."

Only a **litel fortune** is enough to rally Lyf, and he forthwith takes her, his soul mate, as his mistress (see 110n above). The extravagant fashion of dagging garments, slashing their edges so as to leave elongated triangular jags of cloth, aroused the indignation of John Mirk (see 218–19n below) and Chaucer's Parson, as Skt observed (ParsT 418, 421; see Prol.22–26n). Vice continues to be largely verbal (**Armed . . . in harlotes wordes**); see 111–20n, 121–39n above. As Covetise wields guile "to wynnen" (124), Lyf holds graciousness **a wastour**. On **Consience and conseil** see 72–74n above.

151 saue Consience one: because at Doomsday, "þe laste" (150), one's conscience alone survives to answer judgment.

152 Lyf lepte asyde: that is, with good fortune evaded Kynde for a while.

153–55 Hele . . . ȝeve nouht: see 70–71n above. Apparently Pride is speaking (see 156). The Athlone emendations of 155 are brilliant (see KD-B p. 209, RK-C p. 132), but the inversion of the B/C archetypal off-verse, *ȝeue nat of synne*, is unlikely in ending the line with a stressed syllable. Archetypal C (and Schm in C) reads *ȝowthe* for B archetype's **sorwe**, a reading the Athlone editors think scribally derived from 12.12 (B.11.60). In context *ȝowthe* makes no sense. Some C manuscripts (and Prsl) read *þouȝt* here, a reading easily derived from erroneous *youthe*, so spelled, by common *y*/þ confusion—or conversely *þouȝt* (difficult sense) > *ȝowthe* (misreading and influence of 12.12) > *sorwe* (attempt to make sense and alliterate). **Sorwe** (or *þouȝt*, a harder reading developed from OED *thought* sense 5.a., MED 1a.(f), 5.(b)) here means "remorse"; lack of remorse is the main problem this passus addresses. Unless L revised the line he may have written *And to forȝete pouȝt and ȝeue nat of synne* (so Prsl), with less than ideal alliteration.

The comma supplied after **drede** in 154 should not mislead; **dethe** and **elde** are its objects. The antecedent of **the** in 154 is Lyf.

156–64 This likede . . . myle aboute: Lyf's forgetting (**forȝete** 155) is a characteristic of Sloth (see 7.13, 36 [B.5.397, 423]), represented as his illegitimate offspring: like Fortune and Lyf, Sloth is not "ryht sory for my synnes" (7.15 [B.5.399]; see 7.70, 78–79 [B.13.410, 418–19] and preceding note). On despair, **wanhope**, as the culmination (here, whore and wife: 160) of **sleuthe** see 2.105–106; 6.315–38; 7.58, 80.

The perjured assizer **Tomme two-tonge**, and the technique of using typenames as well, comes from the world of Mede (Alford, *Gloss.* s.v. *Sisour*; cp. Thomme trewe-tonge C/B.4.18). He is the natural ally of Civil and Simony (see 135–37n above; 2.65 [B.2.63], etc.). Why this particular form of vice is singled out as the parent of Wanhope is not obvious, unless it is the fact that Tom is already **ateynt**, convicted, of wrongdoing at the proceedings in which he serves, and hence despairs of redemption. An assizer and prostitutes were also singled out, along with a summoner, as unrepentant sinners at the building of Unite (C.21/B.19.367–71). See Alford, *Gloss.* s.v. *Atteinte, Enqueste.*

Sloth's projectile **drede of dispayr** is "despairing fear" (Schm) or perhaps "danger, the dreadfulness, of despair" (see MED *drede* 5.(a), referring to B.Prol.98, 152var); surely not "fear of despair," a good thing.

Eld counter-attacks

165–200 For care Consience . . . gan y quaken: As in the Land of Longing episode, Fortune and Wanhope are countered by Eld (11.166–96, 12.1–14 [B.11.7–62]); see Headnote and 95n above. The combat narrows its focus to the struggle between Life and Death, recalling with irony the different struggle in 20.28–34 (B.18.29–35), with parallel jousting terminology (**auntered** 175; **auntres** 20.14 [B.18.16]). Lyf sees that, ironically, not even the physician can heal himself. At 183, L suddenly converts the generalized story of personifications and vocational types into the story of Will's own experience, bringing this part of the passus full circle.

167 And elde hente gode hope and hastiliche he shifte hym: Eld grasped the best weapon against despair, hope, and bestirred himself. Skt took **gode hope**

here as not a weapon-name, in contrast with "wanhope" of the lines before and after, but it seems to be the name of the instrument with which Elde routs "wanhope"; in 180 below "goed herte" seems similarly to be the name of a weapon (or a horse?). The same opposition of Good Hope and Wanhope appears in 19.295 (B.17.315). Archetypal C reads *shroef* for **shifte**; RK-C accept the latter as harder (p. 122). The former reading is tempting, as refusal of penance is a dire result of despair (and sloth: 7.1–29 [B.5.385–414]).

169–79 fisyk . . . aȝen Elde: The figure **fisyk**, Medicine, turns into a specific **fisician with a forred hoed**, just as the Lyf whom Eld attacks turns into the specific person, the poem's "I." The **doctour** is like the equally ineffectual "fysik" who "shal his forred hode for his fode sulle" at the Half Acre (8.290 [B.6.269, A.7.253]). With the hood compare the "meneuer mantel" of 138 above, likewise a sign of venal clerisy. **Fisyk** is **lechecraft** (173, and cp. 18.137–40n, Jesus as physician, in the old figure of Christus Medicus), and its failure here foreshadows the failure of the effort to buy off the consequences of sin by way of the friar physician later in this passus; see 304–72n below. Neither physical health, the gift of nature, nor spiritual health, the gift of grace, can be bought. The jousting metaphor continues: Life thought that Medicine would **dryue awey deth** with his weapons, **dyaes and drogges**, and Eld **hitte** the physician.

172 And they gyuen hym agayne a glasene houe: The **they** are Medicine and Succor, who give in return for "goelde goed woen" (171), "a good quantity of gold," the vain protection of a proverbial glass coif or cap: see Whiting 1968:H218.

180–82 And in hope . . . The compeny of comfort: The apparent illogic of Lyf's hopefully plucking up his courage immediately on finding that medicine is worthless makes sense as we recall that the Pride of Life cannot do the sensible thing, fall into remorse. He resorts to the rich and merry **place** ("manor house, mansion"; see 1–4n above) called Revel and the Company of Comfort, ceaseless partying—the opposite of contrition—like the easy salves of Friar Flatterer below (see 371–72). See 70–71n.

183–200 And Elde aftur hym . . . for drede gan y quaken: The abrupt shift to Will's own growing old makes for poignant comedy. Tavormina describes the tone of this passage as affectionate, nostalgic, and comically self-deprecatory (1995b:210). Other instances of the surprising intrusion of the dreamer into the dream-narration where he is not a participant occur at B.5.186–87, where

Repentance absolves Will; C.6.2 (B.5.61, A.5.44), where Will weeps at Repentance's preaching; C.9.284 (B.7.110, A.8.92), where Will looks over Piers's and the priest's shoulders to see the writing on the pardon; and C.20.114 (B.18.111), where Will descends to Limbo. In each instance the issue is salvation, the dreamer's most compelling interest.

On Eld see 95n above. The idea of Eld's attack on the narrator has precedent in two poems that L may have known. At the end of *Le Pèlerinage de vie humaine* of Guillaume de Deguileville, the figures Elde and Infirmity attack the dreamer, after which Grace comes to comfort him, and he wakes (ed. Stürzinger 1893, lines 13,044–502; trans. Clasby 1992:179–85). In *The Parliament of the Three Ages* likewise Elde *vndir-ȝode* ("undermined"; cp. ȝede ouer 183, 185) the character named Elde, disfigures his face, makes him grow pale, whitens his beard and eyebrows, dulls his sight, makes him stoop, cramps his hands, and reduces him to needing a staff to stand (ed. Ginsberg 1992, lines 283–89).

Will's growing old has been addressed before, especially in the monitory passage in B (12.4–15) which C seems to have replaced with the Apologia of C.5, in which he likewise represents himself as "many ȝer" remote from his youth (C.5.35). In the B passage the theme was "amende þee while þow myȝt"; so it is here, but only implicitly: where Lyf turned to Revel when faced with disease, Will turns to Kynde for counsel and enters "contricion and confessioun" (213 below).

Hanna (1998b:156) suggests that the action here precisely fulfills 11.194–95 (B.11.35–36, see n), Rechelesnesse's proverbial advice in the Land of Longing episode (see 165–200n above): "Folowe forth þat fortune wole; þou has wel fer to elde. / A man may stoupe tyme ynowe when he shal tyne þe croune." If by "tyne þe croune" L means "grow bald" (rather than "be beheaded"—so Whiting, *Proverbs* M157), Rechelesnesse's counsel of despair ("wanhope was sib to hym") is pointedly converted here, as old age and the fear of death bring Will to penitence. Eld's assault also resembles that of Hunger, including the terms **boffatede** and **beet**, and follows a similar story, the assailant called on to counter vice (8.171–76 [B.6.174–80, A.7.159–70]).

Eld's attacking Will suggests that the dreamer is enveloped in the sin of the figure Lyf—as we would expect from the Land of Longing episode's description of what tempts him (see 70–71n, 95n above). That the dreamer is terrified by old age and the prospect of death at the end of the poem suggests the plot of a morality play (see 70–71n above), in which a character has a riotous Youth, comes to Old Age, and finally makes a deathbed confession (cp. 212–13 below).

186–90 'Syre euele ytauȝte Elde' . . . **vnnethe may ich here**: Will's imprecation (that of a crotchety old man?) and Eld's reply sound like what one might hear in the rough, comic dialogue of a mystery play like the York "Crucifixion." Eld responds rudely to Will's brief and ineffectual assumption of a haughty tone, challenging Eld's ill-breeding and discourteous manners.

193–98 And of þe wo . . . hit hadde forbete: Will experiences, willy-nilly, diminution of his own Pride of Life. About sexual matters L has the cleric's frankness, not the courtier's delicacy. Compare the blunt opening of one of the Kildare poems, "Elde makiþ me geld," cited in MED *geld* adj. (b), or the *Lamentationes Matheoli* 577: "My wife wants it, but I can't." The wife's **reuthe** turns out to be regret for her own loss rather than pity for Will's. Davlin observes that as Will loses the procreative power regularly associated with Kynde, Natura Naturans, he immediately turns to the figure Kynde, who advises him to learn to love! (1971:17).

199 y say how kynde passede: that is, I saw how natural things (like my own body) pass away.

Kynde instructs the dreamer

201–13 And cryede to kynde . . . til y cam to vnite: As Conscience had before (76 above), Will turns for help to Kynde, who tells him to go to Unite and to learn some craft before he leaves it (dies). The understanding of Kynde here is enriched; it is natural mortality, an effective teacher of penitential disciple. Counseled, in the famous line, to **lerne to loue**, and to be not solicitous, Will undertakes penance and enters Unite. This is the last we hear of the dreamer until he awakes in the last line of the poem. Although reading PP as Will's Bildungsroman will lead to confusion, it is hard to avoid concluding that he here attains the best state possible for fallen humanity, wherein, like Conscience at the end of the poem, he can at least sue for grace.

201–5 And cryede . . . sende for the: On the crying out see 76n above. Will specifically asks for vengeance (**awreke me**) on Eld; he has not exactly learned to love (cp. 17.4–5, B.15.258–62), and his reasoning for wanting vengeance, **for y wolde be hennes**, is ironic: he means he wishes to leave the site of the siege, but he *should* mean what Skeat takes him to mean, that he wishes to depart this life (so "hennes" in C.1.174, 9.53, 349, esp. 21.248, etc.)—as his wife wishes! (194 above). Will will miss the point of Kynde's **til y sende for the**, as he seems also not to understand that Kynde and Eld are on the same side. At the end of the poem Conscience likewise calls on Kynde to "avenge" him, this time upon the flattering friars (383–84 below), perhaps merely continuing the military allegory. Vengeance is the Lord's; see 21.434–39n.

206–11 And loke thow . . . while thy lif lasteth: Grace had granted crafts to humans as weapons against Antichrist (C.21/B.19.213–57 and n, 227–28an, 229–51n), but the dreamer seems to have been left out. In the C.5 Apologia Will is interrogated as to whether he knows how to do any of a number of jobs "or eny other kynes craft þat to þe comune nedeth" (C.5.20; see note, and cp. 15.191–92 [B.13.222–23]). He doesn't exactly know any, and only here do we learn what craft he really needs to know. Clergy reminds us that Piers had impugned "alle kyne craftes, / Saue loue and leute and lowenesse of herte" (C.15.131–32, the terms altered from B).

Alle kyne trewe craft (C.8.200, not in B/A) defends against Antichrist because it is, unlike begging, a vice-free means of livelihood (see, e.g., 9.58–65 [B.7.61–69, A.8.63–68]). The irony here, the most penetrating irony of the poem, is that the best craft of all, love, cannot "win," to use PP's term for productive acquisition (e.g., C.6.322), but merely bypasses the question of sustenance, the ever-present question with which the passus began (and see Prol.32n). As Prsl puts it, with his last words "the dreamer is uneasily conscious of what Need was saying earlier . . .: love is all very well, but surely a certain enlightened self-interest is proper?" Kynde firmly responds, **And thow loue lelly lacke shal the neuere / Wede ne worldly mete**. You will not be needy. Patience had made a similar promise to an equally worried Haukyn, 15.233–71 (B.14.29–70). In C.21/B.19.254 the crafts were enjoined to love one another (see n); now the craft itself is love. In *The Scale of Perfection* 2.19, Walter Hilton similarly speaks of the highest "craft" as the service of God (ed. Bestul 2000:170). At the conclusion of her homily, Will's first instruction, Holy Church tells him to love Treuthe: "lette may y no lengore / To lere the what loue is" (1.203–204; not in B/A).

The phrase **lerne to loue** may reflect the phrasing of some religious lyrics. In Lambeth Manuscript 853, edited under the title "The Love of Jesus": "Leerne to loue if þou wolt lyue / Whanne þou schalt hens fare . . ."—that is, to love Jesus (ed. Furnivall 1867:23, lines 33–34). Richard Rolle's lyric "Love is lif þat lesteth ay" has the line 17, "Lere to loue if þou will lyve when þou shal hethen [hence; see 203 above] fare," and "Thy ioy be euery dele" has the line 17, "Lerne to loue þi kynge [i.e., Jesus]" (ed. Ogilvie-Thomson 1988:42–44). The advice is not new in PP: see with similar wording C.11.132 (B.10.192), B.13.142; also C.15.131–32, C.22/B.20.250 below, and closely anticipating this passage Dame Study's summation, "Forþi loke þow louye as longe as þow durest" (B.10.210; see also Wit, C.10.201–2, quoting Psalm 33:11). On "learn to love" as an Augustinian byword see 15.140n. The friars are singled out for not knowing "eny craft," including love (231, 250, 342 below; see 21.229–51n).

212 Rome: "roam, travel"; in spite of the capital letter of the Athlone copy-text, obviously not the city.

The sins renew the attack

214–29 And there was Consience . . . of holy churche: At this point, as Szittya proposes, the action turns away from the kinds of sins characteristic of Will's youth (and of lecherous lords) and more generally toward the vices of clerisy, chiefly as embodied in the mendicant orders, "from the secular—both societal and personal—to the ecclesiastical" (1986:276, 287; see Headnote). At first come the sins, especially Sloth, the vice that avoids penance of the kind that Will has just undertaken (213; see 156–64n above), and also the vice of such negligent clerics as the **proute prestes** of this passage. Sloth himself is a priest in the confessions episode (C.7.30 [B.5.415]). In its common sense of lazy sluggishness, Sloth also characterizes the non-laboring friars (239 below). With Sloth comes—again (see 121 above)—Covetise, the other vice that inhibits the clergy from administering proper penance. Sloth and Pride are the last named attackers of Unite (see 373–86n below).

The figure Conscience undergoes shifts, or rather expansions, of meaning here. For some of his various roles see 72–74n above. First as constable (see next note) he continues in his role as keeper of Christendom. As the object of the proud priests' assault in 220 he is what they should be, the conscience of the Church, and is especially the faculty that enables saving contrition. The cursed priest who scorns Conscience in 222 spurns his own capacity for contrition, as conversely in 231 that capacity forsakes the friars.

214–16 Consience Constable . . . aȝeyn Consience: A **Constable** is the chief officer of a ruler's household or the warden of a stronghold; in 10.143–44 (B.9.17–18), Inwit is constable of the castle of the body as Conscience is constable of the Church (Alford, *Gloss.* s.v. *Constable*). Reflecting this passage in B, the C version has Mede say "sholde neuere Consience be my constable were y a king . . . Ne be Marschal ouer my men" (C.3.256–57). The **geauntes** of course are the deadly sins, routinely numbered seven, and as Emmerson indicates often associated with Antichrist and the seven-headed beast of Apoc. 13:1–8 (1981:52–53).

For the Athlone conjecture **sikerly** 215 read *soethly*, the reading of all the manuscripts, Prsl, and Schm as of 1995 (earlier *soorly*); the word here means not "in truth," implying a question of veracity, but merely "indeed," as often in PP (e.g. B.3.5, 3.190, 11.335, 17.58). See KD-B 117, RK-C 136, and MED s.v. *sothly* 1.(a), citing *William of Palerne* 379: "Sche wald haue sleie hire-self þere soþly . . . ."

218–19 Proute prestes . . . In paltokes and piked shoes, [purses and] longe knyues: Before his elaborate excoriation of the friars, L briefly takes on the secular priesthood. They are clothed pretentiously and inappropriately in the garb of the military class. The critique is common; e.g. Wimbledon's sermon of 1388, "It is to wondry how þe lif of prestis is chaunged. Þey beþ cloþed as knytes . . ." (ed. Knight 1967:78). Kerby-Fulton suggests that the idea of the priests' attack on Unite derives from the still-unpublished *Oculus sacerdotis* of William of Pagula, written in the 1320s. A late fourteenth-century copy contains a picture of "priests in worldly dress violently destroying a church" (Hatfield House Manuscript CP290, fol. 213; Kerby-Fulton 1999:528).

For the Athlone conjecture **purses and** most B and C manuscripts read *and pissares*, a striking, rather hard reading liable to censorship and very unlikely to be a scribal substitution. Probably censoring or merely clarifying, manuscript R of C reads, redundantly (but see below), *basalardes* for *pissares*. The Athlone editors defend their reading: KD-B, p. 184, were moved to conjecture because of the "extreme lexical difficulty" of *pissares*, and they arrive at **purses** as an alliterating synonym of the variant reading (manuscripts GC² of B) *gypsers*, "purse, pouch, wallet." Yet *pissares* cannot have been too difficult, as some thirty scribes, of whom a number probably thought it made sense, transmitted the reading. KD-B further argue, ingeniously, that a misreading of contractions could have generated the reading *pissares*—that is, presumably, a reading like *p'ses* (for *purses*) read as *ps'es* (*pseres*, then supplying an *i*—and an *s*?—for *pisseres*; but note that the *ur* sign generally differs from the *er* sign, and is rare in Middle English texts after an initial *p*). There is no need to adduce, with Skt, the biblical uses of the word "pisser" in the Wycliffite translation of Kings. The formation of the agent-noun from the common verb hardly needs a literary source.

Priests were not to bear weapons (see C.5.53–60n). (For that matter, Newton collects evidence of widespread criticism, in England, of the fashion of men in general (and women) wearing daggers—1980:9–11.) Gratian's *Decretum* says that not even the pope can authorize a cleric to take up arms (2.23.81, ed. Friedberg 1879, col. 953). The London Legatine Council's Constitutions of Ottobono in 1268 excommunicate clerics who bear arms and deprive of benefice those who recalcitrantly continue to bear them (4, ed. Powicke and

Cheney 1964, 2:751–52). It appears that clerics (e.g., Dominicans—Hinnebusch 1951:244) slipped around this ruling by wearing knives, which are not necessarily weapons and therefore licit, but sporting long ones girded on like swords, like the one reproduced in Newton 1980:71. Hence an edict of the London Council in 1342 attacks clerks for wearing "cultellis, ad modum gladiorum pendentibus," knives hanging down like swords (ed. Wilkins, *Concilia* 1737, II:703).

About the time the B version was composed, Gower in *Miroir* (ca. 1376–79) wrote, "I call upon you, O priest, why have you such a long knife hanging at your belt. . . . both the old and the new law forbid you to wage war" (ed. Macaulay 1899, lines 20653–64; trans. Wilson 1992:276). In his 1877 notes ad loc., Skeat cites Mirk's *Instructions for Parish Priests* (ca. 1400), lines 43–44, 48, precisely to the point: "Cuttede clothes [see 143 and 143–51n above] and pyked schone, / Thy gode fame þey wole for-done . . . . Baselard [dagger or short sword] ny bawdryke [shoulder-slung sword-belt] were þow non" (ed. Kristens-son 1974:69). Some lines from the Vernon "Dispute Between a Good Man and the Devil" attest to the swaggering bravado implied by wearing a long knife: "Now is non worþ a fart, / But he bere a baselart / I-honget bi his syde" (lines 270–72, cited MED s.v. *baselard*). A 1388 statute forbade members of the servant and laboring classes from wearing baselarts.

In a passage deleted from C, Anima speaks scornfully of priests who have "a baselard or a ballokknyf wiþ botons ouergilte" (B.15.124; see also A.I1.214). A ballock-knife, later euphemistically also called a kidney dagger, was worn at the belt upright in front of the body, and has testicle-shaped (or kidney-shaped) protrusions at the juncture of hilt and blade (described and illustrated in Strayer 1982–89, 11:550–51). The chronicler John of Reading inveighs against wearers of provocatively short paltoks (see Parson's Tale 422–29) who went "with long knives hanging between their legs" (*cultellis longeis inter tibias dependentibus*—ed. Tait 1914:166). Near-contemporary illustrations depict such knives in an obviously phallic display (Southworth 1989:66, a herald, and Newton 1980:57). The conception easily derives from its converse, speaking of one's penis as a "wepene kene" (C.10.286 [B.9.185]).

Either of two interpretations of the textual situation seems likely. Most simply, *pissares* could be the genitive plural of a term meaning something like bullyboys: cocky, menacing, lewd braggadocios. It would express indignation like that which provoked Waster to tell Piers to "go pisse with his plogh," a phrase of equally imprecise semantic use and equally clear force (8.151 [B.6.155, A.7.142]). Or Prsl might be right in both of two suggestions, that the word *pisser* "might suggest lechery; it might be a cant term for a long knife." If so, **longe knyues** glosses *pissares*, either epexegetically or possibly as L's or another person's gloss scribally intruded into the text. Thus the reading of manuscript R of C, *basalardes* for **pissares**, substitutes a synonym. A tempting reading on this basis is manuscript F of B's *& pisserys ful longe* (it is the sword-like length of the knives that infuriated the moralists), which would elicit a marginal gloss **knyues** and by deleting **ful** be smoothed to archetypal *and pissares longe knyues*. RK-C hold that the scribe of F took *pissares* "to mean penises" (135), whereas one would have thought long penises were a gift of nature and not a culpable appendage even of priests—and even less congruous with the preposition **in**.

221–27 a mansed prest, was of þe march of Ireland . . . holynesse adowne: If Irish priests were proverbially wicked, no other evidence has survived. Perhaps L had a particular cursed or excommunicated Irish priest in mind. As Pearsall observes, the Hiberno-English manuscript Douce 104, perhaps in defense of Irish sensibilities, alters **þe march of Ireland** to "þe march of wale" (Pearsall and Scott 1992:xiv). Compare the tight-fisted Welshman of C.6.308–9 and Holy Church's slyly tactful refusal to defame "northerne men" (1.115–16). As in this passage, when Clergie criticizes "mansede preestes" (B.10.284, not in C) he then turns his attention to religious and to friars: "Caym shal awake" (B.10.334; see 52–53n above). Likewise, but with different motives, when Covetise of Eyes tells Will like the mansed priest to "haue no conscience," she goes on to recommend that he confess to friars, who will be lenient as long as he has money (B.11.53–55).

    Bi so, "provided that, as long as," as often in PP (e.g. C.5.39, 6.332). As RK-C observe, **shoten aȝeyne** as simply "shot" was difficult enough to elicit variation (p. 127). L again presents allegorical weapons (see 111–20n etc.). Compare Chaucer's Parson, "ne swereth nat so synfully in dismembrynge of Crist by soule, herte, bones, and body" (591) and Pardoner, "of his othes is to outrageous. / 'By Goddes precious herte,' and 'By his nayles'" (650–51). The sequence repeats that of 6.357–61 (B.5.302–6, A.5.152–57), when ale leads Gluttony to the company of "grete othes"; the tavern vices reinforce one another.

    Holynesse is Unite's moat in C.21/B.19.363.

228–29 Consience cryede . . . prelates of holy churche: In calling on **Clergie** Conscience calls on an ideal clergy, and secondarily on the learning, clerisy, that helps priests do their job. He thus fulfills the prophecy of B.13.203–5. His cry will be repeated in line 375 below; see note. Conscience is similarly linked with his alliterating partner Clergy in C.Prol.152, C.15/B.13, and C.16.159; they are two kinds—more or less innate and acquired—of knowing. PP persistently urges, especially in its third vision, that the priesthood needs learning, and that

learning is liable to abuse. Clergy calls on clergy and is answered by friars: the
movement from the priests of 218–29 to the friars of 230 broadly repeats the
sequence from the Half Acre, with its defective priest, to the world of friars
and learning, the transition from C.9 to 10 (B.7 to 8, A.8 to 9). L, like the Lollards, often uses the term **prelates** disparagingly (Hudson 1981:22–23).

Friars come to Unite and Conscience instructs them

230–72 Freres herde hym crye . . . noþer mo ne lasse. Having displayed the
failures of the secular clergy, L shows that the friars cannot help. The allegory
briefly recapitulates as well an episode in the history of the Church: the secular
clergy being in need of reform, the friars (early in the thirteenth century)
came, as they allege, to help. The friars have been of the party of Antichrist (58
above), and now speciously ally themselves with Unite. From here to the end
of the poem the fraternal orders are the main object of L's criticism, and he
generally follows the tradition of antifraternal satire in attacking the friars'
greed, hypocrisy, flattery, improper administration of penance, superfluous
numbers, lechery, and intellectual vanity (see generally Szittya 1986; Mann
1973:37–54, 225 n65; Williams 1960; Prol.57–61n). They are epitomized in "oen
frere flaterrere," introduced at 315 below.

230–31 Freres herde . . . Consience forsoek hem: Friars respond to the cry to
Clergy because they have a zeal for learning, *clergie*. Conscience attributes their
zeal to envy and asks them to "leue logyk," synecdochal for both higher
schooling, of the kind that in L's time could lead to career advancement, and
the dangers of intricate theologizing (246–50, 273–79 below). The friars'
sophistical logic, for example, will enable the friar in the banquet scene to
rationalize "a freres lyuynge" (15.102 [B.13.95]; see n). On the inferiority of
"logyk and lawe" in comparison with "bileue" and "loue" see B.11.219–30. In
response Envy is roused all the more and orders friars to further schooling
(273–76 and 294–95 below). Mann documents criticism of the friars for their
pride in scholarship (preceding note); see 11.52–58 (B.10.72–78, A.l1.58–60) and
15.25–184n, 15.97–100n. Liberum Arbitrium/Anima tells Will that friars retail
logical tricks "for pompe and pruyde," to the detriment of faith (16.231–41
[B.15.70–81]). They even had papal sanction, in Nicholas III's constitution
Exiit qui seminat of 1279, for their ownership-in-common of books for study
because of their mission to preach the Gospel (ed. Richter and Friedberg 1879,
2:1114). Scase notes that friars defended themselves for putting their resources
into schooling by claiming that their large numbers were needed to supply the

deficiency of learning of the kind required of the clergy by the Fourth Lateran Council of 1215 (1989:40–41).

As the bad priest discounted Conscience (222 above), so Conscience forsakes the friars, who don't know their craft, a gift of grace (see 21.229–51n) specified below (250–52) as the special quality of Francis and Dominic, namely love, the same craft Will needs to learn (206–11 and n above). The friar-figure Fals Semblant in the *Roman de la Rose* says that if a man is so "bestial" that he "of no craft hath science," he may go begging until he learns a craft (Riverside Chaucer, *Romaunt* 6715–20). See 6.322 (B.5.468, A.5.242).

In line 231 Conscience forsakes the friars, but—perhaps in response to Nede's mockery, changes his mind by line 243.

232–41 Nede neyhede tho ner . . . angeles fode: Nede approaches because friars particularly claimed to embrace apostolic neediness, a stance that Nede himself derides. Nede's sardonic critique specifies how friars do not know their craft (231), which would be a loving **cure of soules** (normally the office of a parish priest). Instead, otherwise poor and unwilling to work for a living, they exploit **for Couetyse** their **cure**, their right to administer the sacrament of penance, granted by Nicholas III in *Exiit qui seminat* (see preceding note). They want to **fare wel**, ominously echoing Will's admission that he "louede wel fare" (C.5.8). FitzRalph's argument against the friars' right to cures is reviewed by Scase 1989:19–20. As Nede was the figure who expressed Will's effort to excuse himself at the beginning of the passus (see 1–51n), he here, with more transparent irony, commends the friars to beggary or saintly sustenance. In both passages Nede responds to, and makes as if to alleviate, a kind of need, and warns against the behavior he causes.

234 for patrimonye hem faileth: The friars lack endowments and benefices of the kind enjoyed by the possessionate clergy. PP several times expresses a prophetic hope that the problem of the friars will be solved when they acquire an assured living, e.g. C.5.173–74 (B.10.328–29), 8.147–48 (not in B/A), 248–49 below, and climactically 383 below (see 380–86n), "þat freres hadde a fyndynge þat for nede flateren." Clopper, as part of his unpersuasive argument that this passage is not critical of contemporary friars (1990:65), argues that in L's time friars, even Franciscans, did in fact have a patrimony, having accepted the principle of community property after 1323. Consequently Clopper prefers here the reading of two B manuscripts, *þei faille* for **hem faileth**—they fail because of their patrimony (1990:67, 1997b:97–98). In light of the other places in PP that speak of friars' lack of secure provision for their livelihood—they do beg, after all—this interpretation cannot be right, but the hard minority reading might nevertheless be right, taking *þei faille* as transitive "miss getting, fail to obtain" with **patrimonye** as object (MED *failen* 6.; OED *fail* 7., 11.c.—a common French sense) as (arguably) in C.2.162var., B.11.26.

235 Thei wol flatere: Friars conventionally flatter; among the first things Fals-Semblant, the friar-figure of *The Romance of the Rose*, son of Gile and Ipocrisy, says of himself is that he is "full of flatering" (Riverside Chaucer, *Romaunt* 6140). Here as throughout PP the word has more specific meaning than "feed one's vanity," and rather means "ease one's sense of guilt," a lucrative activity for a confessor (see 1–51n above). "Flatereres been the develes chapelleyns, that syngen evere *Placebo*" (Parson's Tale 617). Piers had promised to provide for "freres þat flateren nat" and (see 238–39 below) honest, disabled beggars (8.136–48; friars are not mentioned in corresponding B.6.129–47). See 313–15n below.

236 and Cheytyftee: The editors disagree on the reading of the off-verse of 236. Against the Athlone editors and Prsl, Schm adopts what appear to be the archetypal readings of B and C, *Cheytyftee pouerte*, and Hanna concurs on metrical grounds (1998a:180; see KD-B 117, RK-C 136). L may have intended to write *cheytyftee pouere*, with *t* added to *pouere* under influence of the preceding word. See C.12.128 and MED *caitif* adj. with ample support for the non-devaluative sense here of misery and poverty.

237–39 Late hem chewe as thei chose: repeats 20.206 (B.18.201), the human choice of sin. Since the friars are deliberately poor, says Nede, let them deliberately give up their gainful cure of souls. **He þat laboreth for lyflode** hints that friars might better do manual labor for a living, a position argued by many and condemned at the Blackfriars Council against Wyclif in 1382 (ed. Wilkins 1737, 3.158). Alternatively, the labor referred to here may be the parish priest's work in the cure of souls; for the idea see 21.232, 11.246–51, and Lawler 2003:94 and n11, 108.

240–41 And senne freres forsoke . . . by angeles fode: Nede's parting shot repeats the idea of letting friars chew as they chose, namely poverty—the condition of need itself! The solution proposed will fail as surely as the parallel solution tried on the wasters of the field—Hunger (8.167–344 [B.6.171–324, A.7.156–307]). Nede plays (as at C.15.300) on two senses of the term **beggares**: let them ask for alms, and let them be "wretched, destitute people" (OED *beggar* 2., MED *begger(e* 3., a sense found elsewhere in PP, e.g., B.10.85, altered to

pore in C.11.65, for clarity). A similar joke is cracked by Wrath (6.125 [B.5.149–50]). Scase calls it an old antimendicant joke (1989:101).

Nede's last joke lets friars live by **angeles fode**, rightly glossed by Prsl, "i.e., nothing"—angels have no need of physical sustenance. Such food parodies the troubling, physically un-nourishing spiritual food regularly offered in PP, as by *fiat voluntas tua* (15.249 [B.14.50]), or as *caritas*, "Cristes oune fode" (C.18.14), or the bread of tears (B.7.128). A secondary meaning at play is Schmidt's interpretation of the angels' food as the kind that angels provide to holy people, hence "God alone." He refers to Jesus' wilderness fast and Mary Magdalene's penitential sustenance of roots and dew and "moost þoruȝ meditacion and mynde of god almyghty" (B.15.294–95, cp. C.17.21; Schmidt 1983:191). See also the woman who fled into the wilderness, to be divinely fed (Apoc. 12:6). By living off such food the friars would rival the early desert fathers, including the alleged founder of the Austin friars, Paul the first hermit, fed by birds (17.10–16 [B.15.276–89]).

More precisely, Nede may refer mockingly to the angels' daily elevation of the fasting Magdalene to heaven, as reported in the *Golden Legend*, where she was "filled with this delightful repast" of angelic song (ed. Graesse 1890:413, trans. Ryan 1941:360–61). Following a further suggestion by Schm, Clopper refers also to Psalm 77:25, quoted by St. Francis in connection with mendicant poverty, where manna is called "the bread of angels" (1997b:98–99). Hence inevitably the eucharistic Host is commonly referred to as angelic bread, especially in Corpus Christi and Communion hymns (ed. Dreves 1909, 2:208–22 passim; Sarum Corpus Christi office, ed. Dickenson 1861–63:458; see McGarry 1936:96–97).

For another treatment of fraternal sanctimony as angelic see the *Decameron*, Fourth Day, Second Story—Frate Alberto as the angel Gabriel.

242–45 Consience of this consail . . . and holi churche: Conscience's response is complex: he laughs along with Nede's bitter and witty critique, and yet comforts the friars and invites them into Unite. The complexity arises from two considerations. First, Conscience is continuing the historical allegory (see 230–72n above), in which the saintly founders of the fraternal orders, whom he names in line 252, came to the rescue of the Church. But at the same time he responds to the contemporary state of the friars as Nede saw them.

Second, the character of Conscience in PP accounts for the paradox of his behavior. Schroeder observes that, in medieval psychology, the faculty of conscience can, unlike synderesis, err (see 20.339–50n and Potts 1980:132–33). In PP Conscience is consistently presented as a knight (3.147 [B.3.110, A.3.99]) of markedly courteous manners in his three major scenes—with Mede, as host at the banquet, and here (see 106 and n above). Both with the friar in the banquet scene and with the friars here, Schroeder argues, "he makes the mistake of being too gentle" (1970:28). Compare the "knyhte" who "courteisliche" tries to help Piers against the wasters—although even his threats of punishment (in C; milder threats in A/B) prove ineffectual (8.156–66 [B.6.159–170, A.7.146–55]). His defect recurs more obviously in 322–23 and esp. 348–61 below, where "hende speche" induces him to admit flattering friars to Unite.

But *cortesye* is not always a bad thing (see, e.g., 21.452). Piers advises a courteous knight that "Hit bicometh to the, knyhte, to be corteys and hende" (C.8.32, 47, not in A/B). Lawler disagrees with Schroeder, and finds Conscience's motive not in a misplaced gentlemanliness but in patience and hope (1995:97–103). As in the banquet scene, Conscience is willing to introduce divisive elements into his household, and finally has to leave it for an outdoor pilgrimage. Unlike the cynical Nede, Conscience has warmth of heart, and he honors the original impulse of Francis and Dominic (252 below), and has the "gentrice" of Jesus (see 20.21n). Compare the mercy shown by Piers (8.217) or in B by Hunger (B.6.225), to the idlers on the field. Lawler concludes, "Langland urges on us a reckless generosity." Hence Piers's advice on responding to one's enemy: "Caste coles on his heued of alle kynde speche" (15.142; the speaker is Love, quoted by Patience, in B.13.144). Schm (n to 311 below) points to Reason's homily on tolerance of others' faults: 13.194–212 (B.11.376–404). See 21.434–39 and n.

For an allegory of similarly generous admission into a building see 7.243–77 (B.5.595–624, A.6.82–109), the gatekeeper Grace and the seven porters of the Court of Truth, of whom "Largenesse þe lady lat in ful monye." Jenkins likewise compares Peace's offering forgiveness to Wrong in 4.94–95 (B.4.98–99, A.4.85–86)—and a figure Pees is the porter who, perhaps grudgingly, admits the villain in 348, 354 below (1969:139). Harwood agrees that it is because he can love his enemies that Conscience admits Friar Flatterer (1992:136 and 217, 61n).

246 Holdeth ʒow in vnite: that is, remain in the Church, and do not squabble with the other ecclesiastical orders (see Prol.64–65 [B.Prol.66–67, A.Prol.63–64])—but also, maintain a "syker nombre" (255 below), a unity as opposed to the disorderly multiplicity of present-day friars. The injunction "hold yourselves in unity" is elsewhere repeated: in a similar context (friars should hold to their rule, are to be endowed) Reason urges the rich and the commune to "holde ʒow in vnite" (C.5.189, not in AB; see 5.180–90n); see also C.21/B.19.355–56 and n, C.22/B.20.75. On Unite see 21.328n.

246–52 haueth noen enuye . . . for loue to be holy: Referring to envy of the possessionate clergy, especially the learned, as the friars' motive (see 11.54 [B.10.74]), Conscience prays that they will live according to the spirit of their rules. See 230–31n above. Their envy is personified in 273 below. In return for their renunciation of sophistical theologizing, Conscience, responding to Nede's remark that friars lack patrimony (234 and n above), will see that the friars have a living, the **necessaries** that allay need/Nede (see 380–86 and n below). The allegory continues that of 231 above: if friars practice their proper "crafte," love, their conscience will reunite them with Conscience and they will, as the poem insistently promises, gracefully be provided for (see 206–11n above). On **lerneth for to louye** see 206–11n above. Conscience will be the friars' **borwh** as God is the "borgh" of beggars in B.7.82.

To say of Francis and Dominic that **For loue lefte they lordschipe** refers to a disputed mendicant tenet (the refusal of dominion), while at the same time rebuking the friars for forgetting its principle, love. On the debates about the friars' claim to absolute poverty and their relinquishing of dominion see 1–51n above, toward the end, and Scase 1989:50–51.

253–72 And yf ʒe coueiteth cure . . . noþer mo ne lasse: Returning to Nede's accusation that friars covet the cures of secular clerks (233 above), Conscience recommends that the friars be mindful of the principle of **mesure**, a guiding principle of the first vision. But rather than "moderation" in their general conduct, Conscience specifies that the **mesure** God made is of the number of friars, which should be a fixed number, a **certeyne** (OED *certain* sb. 4.a., 5.a.). Wisdom 11:21: "Thou hast ordered all things in measure (*mensura*), and number, and weight." Adduced in antifraternal controversy were also Apoc.7:4–9 and 20:8–9, Job 10:22, and Ps. 146:4, quoted in 256a below. As Conscience develops his point it becomes clear that he associates stable provision for the friars with limits on their numbers. There are only so many stipends available.

The Wife of Bath voices the common complaint about over-numerous friars most sharply: they are "As thikke as motes in the sonne-beem," going about blessing everything in sight, and filling all the spaces that elves and incubi were wont to haunt (WBT 865–81; see also the prologue to the Summoner's Tale). Szittya amply treats attacks on friars' numbers by William of St. Amour, FitzRalph, and English poets (1986:47, 143–44, 146, 221–30; see also Bloomfield 1961a:146). Bishops were charged to maintain proper quotas of friars licensed to hear confessions or preach (see 271–72n below); on the problems involved see A. Williams 1960:24–39. Seculars like FitzRalph and Wyclif naturally exaggerated the numbers of friars, but according to Hinnebusch, in the early fourteenth century there were some 1800 Dominicans in England, in some 51 houses, and of these some 300 were lay brothers and perhaps 800 were preachers—in the same period there were perhaps a hundred more Franciscans than Dominicans (1951:275). Swanson estimates that there were about 2500–3000 mendicants in England in the period, down to about 2000 after the Black Death, and about 6000–6500 other regulars, along with some 24–25,000 secular clergy (1989:31, 83).

255 a serteyne: helpfully glossed as **a syker nombre**, a well-attested substantive use. Compare FitzRalph's complaint: "But sich multiplicacioun y-founded vppon beggyng & beggerye, as freres telleþ, may nouȝt ordeyne a *certeyn* noumbre of persones þat þei schulde fynde, noþer þei mowe of *certein* oon person fynde" (Trevisa's translation of *Defensio curatorum*, cited by Frank 1957:110 and Scase 1989:36–7; see 267 and n below). Like Conscience, FitzRalph (and Wyclif—see 257–72n below) couples ecclesiastical livings with fixed numbers.

256 And nempned hem names . . . *stellarum &c*: L translates Ps. 146:4, "Who telleth the number of the stars, [and calleth them all by their names]." Latin citations are rare in this passus; here L sets the Bible against the "logyk" of the friars.

257–72 Kynges and knyhtes . . . noþer mo ne lasse: Military officers not enlisted on the muster rolls but on the battlefield are not waged and are accounted thieves and illicit despoilers; likewise the regular clergy—except for friars—are registered in fixed numbers in keeping with a set number of findings (endowed livings). **Brybours** are simply thieves, especially imposters, not bribers (Alford, *Gloss.* s.v. *bribour*). Baldwin finds that Wyclif uses the same metaphor: "just as the captains of the corporeal army must certify to the king the quantity and quality of their soldiers, as they correspond to the given stipends, so much more should the bishops, captains of the spiritual army, be responsible to the king for the numbers and virtue of their spiritual soldiers" (1981b:79, quoting *De officio regis*, ed. Pollard and Sayle 1966:158–59). The generalships of Moses and David would exemplify the careful numbering of troops. On **kepen and defenden** see 21.442–49n. MED finds this the first recorded use of **officerys** in the military sense (*officer* 3.(b)).

Lines 260–65 contain some irregular meter; the passage may not have received finish.

267 A certeyne for a certeyne: Schm, Prsl, and Donaldson in his translation suggest "a certain number for a certain sort/category/job," but in context Szittya's rendering is better, "a fixed and assured living for a fixed number of Religious," with corroborating reference to B.6.151, "For it is an vnresonable Religion þat haþ riȝt noȝt of certain" (1986:282). Here "vnresonable" means "without *ratio*, of unfixed count." As Skt notes, the charters of religious foundations regularly specified the number to be housed.

270 Heuene haeth euene nombre . . . withoute nombre: The idea is embedded in the biblical texts cited in 253–72n above. Schm notes the play on nearly homophonic **heuene/euene**. **Euene** here means "of proper magnitude" (OED *even* a. 11.). **Withoute nombre** recalls the Latin phrase used by antimendicants, *sine numero*.

271–72 in þe register . . . vnder notarie sygne: Conscience wishes that the friars' numbers could be controlled by a **register** like a bishop's register with its ordination lists. See 253–72n above. Antimendicants were troubled by the fact that friars were not controlled by bishops, but answered to their local provincial, and ultimately to their vicar general and the pope. Conscience is called "goddess Clerk and his notarie" in 16.192 (B.15.32) and Piers is a "Registrer" (C.21/B.19.259). A notary's **sygne** is his official signatory mark, like a seal; see 2.159, 4.126, etc. See Alford, *Gloss.* s.v. *Registre, Registrer, Notarie, Signe*, and on bishops' registers see Swanson 1989:128–29, 31–36, and 1995:17–18. The first recorded English use of the former pair of words is in PP; it has often been suggested, since Skt's proposal, that L worked as a legal scribe or notary (Skt vol.II, xxxvi).

Envy corrupts the friars

273–96 Enuye herde this . . . Consience assailede: The friars' envy—specifically of the possessionate, "waged" clergy—is now personified, and drives them to superfluous learning (see 230–31n above), to administration of ineffectual penance, and to alliance with **Couetyse and vnkyndenesse**. They thus fulfill Nede's characterization of them, 232–41 above. Envy's injunction **lerne logyk** (274) directly contradicts Conscience's condition, "leue logyk" (250).

274 logyk and lawe and eke contemplacioun: Envy again contradicts Conscience, who observed that Francis and Dominic "lefte . . . scole" (251). Of course friars were in fact prominent in philosophical and legal studies. Alford, suggesting that the **lawe** in question is civil (Roman) law, refers to Gower's coupling of the two, *civilia iura et logicam* (*Gloss.* s.v. *Logik and Lawe; Vox Clamantis* 3.2105). But **contemplacioun** is not obviously a similar school-subject, whereas it is the subject of such fraternal literature as Bonaventure's *Itinerarium mentis ad Deum*. The hypocritical friar of Chaucer's *Summoner's Tale* assures Thomas that Elijah, putative founder of the Carmelite order, communed with God because "He fasted longe and was in contemplance" (line 1893). Possibly, then, L sarcastically refers to a mendicant claim that they were experts in contemplation. The term may refer, too, to theoretical as opposed to practical speculation. Although use of "contemplative" and "active" as versions of the ancient Greek opposition of "theoretical" and "practical" appears to be later in English (so OED, MED), Chaucer says the "Grekissch" P and T on Lady Philosophy's gown, which (as pi and theta) refer to the two divisions of philosophy, "practica" and "theorica," signify "the lif actif" and "the lif contemplative" (*Boece* 1.pr1.28–33). So friars claim expertise in contemplation and indulge in theorizing. Or **contemplacioun** may here simply mean "philosophy," as taught by the Plato and Seneca of the next line; cp. 295 below.

275 plato . . . seneca: Wyclif indeed thought that Socrates held that goods should be held in common (see next note), and that Aristotle disagreed on the grounds that this included wives (*De civili dominio* 1.14, ed. Poole 1885:99). Pantin suggests that in referring to **seneca** L may have in mind the Stoic doctrine that private property is a convention superimposed on the more natural condition of common ownership (1955:128–29).

276 That alle thynges vnder heuene ouhte to be in comune: Skt finds here the poet's "emphatic rejection" of such "principles of communism" as John Ball espoused, and hence "here plainly disavows all sympathy with unprincipled and thoughtless rioters." So Knighton reported as a Lollard tenet, "Among the clergy all things ought to be in common" (ed. Lumby 2:262), and Froissart said John Ball preached that all should be in common (Aers 1988:68). Indeed, Lollards did propose disendowment of the Church and community of property (Aston 1984:20–38, Gradon and Hudson 1996:162–68). In his diatribe of 1415 against the Lollard Oldcastle, Hoccleve imputes to Lollards a full secular communism: "Yee seyn eek: 'Goodes commune oghten be.'/ Þat ment is in tyme of necessity, / But nat by violence or by maistrie / My good to take of me or I of thee, / For þat is verray wrong and robberie" (ed. Seymour 1981:72, lines 452–56).

But this is not the issue here. Envy has taught the friars, as if by way of ancient philosophers, an important maxim justifying their doctrines of dominion and community property, in terms ultimately derived from Acts

2:44: the early Christians "had all things in common (*habebant omnia commu-nia*)"; L translates the last two words literally. As Wyclif argued in *De civili dominio*, 1 Cor. 13:5 says charity "seeketh not her own" (ed. Poole 1885:108). The point here, as Frank observes, is that the friars also hold that administering penance to parishioners is likewise a right in common, as the text goes on to indicate (1957:110–11). "What [the friars] particularly wish to hold in common are the privileges and income of the secular clergy" (Szittya 1986:282); they "coueiteth cure" (253). Wrath, in the B version a sometime friar, says "now persons han parceyued þat freres parte (divide the proceeds of confessions) wiþ hem" (B.5.144) because of the friars' lax confessions, and this leads to squabbling. On the controversy see the materials cited toward the end of 1–51n, and in 7–11n, 40–50n above, and especially Lambert 1961/1998, Couvrer 1961, Tierney 1959, Wilks 1965, Leff 1967, Mathes 1968–69, Rubin 1987, Coleman 1988, and with regard to PP, Szittya 1986, Dolan 1988, Scase 1989, Bishop 1996, Clopper 1990, 1997b.

The issue is large, but a few points of confusion and controversy may be noted. Until John XXII's condemnation of the radical Franciscan view, the Franciscans renounced both common (*in communi*) and individual (*in proprio*) ownership. The Franciscan Bonaventure held that Christ and the apostles rejected both common and individual ownership (Lambert 1961:136). But after 1323 orthodox Franciscans joined with the other fraternal and monastic orders in accepting community dominion over property (Clopper 1997a:150–51). Never resolved was a conflict of ideas in canon law as expressed by Gratian, following Isidore: in natural law all things are held in common, but in customary and statutory law individuals may have belongings (*Decretum* 1.dist.8.1, ed. Friedberg 1879:col. 12; *Etymologies* 5.4.1, ed. Lindsay 1911, 1.183). Divine (and, of course, civil and common) law permitted private property; see 279n below. Confused were the idea of the natural as the original and prelapsarian, and as the intellectual and spiritual quality in humans (Tierney 1959:30–31). As noted in 7–11n, 20n above, the idea that property was common only in case of dire need was the attempted solution. Further, FitzRalph against the friars makes another distinction, arguing that Jesus and the apostles were poor in "civil" but not "natural" or "original" dominion, and that Jesus willingly exercised restraint over his natural lordship (Scase 1989:55). Wyclif's complex antifraternalism held that all property should be held in common, indeed—but only by the just in the time of grace; for now all power and wealth are held in a Christian society's corporate person, namely God, and lay princes in this world are God's vicars (Wilks 233; *De civili dominio* 1.14, ed. Poole, esp. 96–103).

Such complexities are evident when a pair of Austin friars can argue before Parliament in 1371 that church property can be taxed in time of war (see

21.465–76n): "the law of God and of nature wills explicitly that all possessions, of the clergy as well as of others, are in common in all cases of necessity" (ed. Galbraith 1919:580; see Scase 1989:51, and for the wording see 7–11n above). Again, Patience, no advocate of mendicant ideology, can say "Forthy cristene sholde be in commune ryche, noon coueytous for hymselue" (16.42 [B.14.201]).

The friars, then, appear to the dreamer (and FitzRalph and Wyclif) to claim a lack of dominion, as their founders renounced it (251–52 above), but at the same to be covetous of property, held under various pretexts. Fals Semblant wittily sums up the possessioners' view of the friars' stance: "And alwey pore we [friars] us feyne; / But how so that we begge or pleyne, / We ben the folk, without lesyng, / That all thing have without having" (Riverside Chaucer, *Romaunt of the Rose* 6961–64). In *Vox clamantis* 3.11, lines 984–85, with reference to the mid-1370s dispute about whether the church could be taxed, Gower presents a solution that L might well accept: "If love were more common, then everything would be in common" (trans. Stockton 1962:138).

279a *Non concupisces rem proximi tui &c*: "Thou shalt not covet thy neighbour's property," the Tenth Commandment abbreviated, in a widespread form, from Exod. 20:17; see Alford , *Quot.* 117 and above, 20n. Szittya calls this FitzRalph's "favorite Commandment" used "against both the mendicants' conception of poverty and their procuring of privileges" (1986:282, 139).

280–93 And euele is this . . . day of dome: L turns to the issue of the friars' faulty administration of penance—in effect, their theft—the burden of the remainder of the poem. Friars come to represent everything that detracts from love, repentance, and the pursuit of grace—and hence from the possibility of salvation.

282 curatours cald to knowe and to hele: Linking curatorship—specifically the right to hear confessions—with healing, L may play here and in 326 below on the medical sense of *curen* as "to heal," common in Latin and recorded in English in Gower and Trevisa, although of course the idea that a priest specifically "heals" by hearing confession is of long standing. Alford argues that **knowe** here means "hear confession," a sense derived from *knowen* as "acknowledge, confess" as in A.I1.281 (*Gloss.* s.v. *Knowen*; cp. MED *knouen* 9., 14c.(a) and *knouinge* 8.(a)). But **to knowe** here may simply mean that a curate should "know" his flock and their sins in order to absolve them. Antimendicants urged people to go to their own parish priests—curates—for confession, rather than, for shame (see 284–85 below), to seek out friars who did not know them and would neglect probing their sins.

284 And be aschamed: "And (to enjoin them) to be ashamed." Mede makes an easy confession to a friar who asked for a seam of wheat in return, and she was "shameless y trowe" (3.46 [B.3.44, A.3.43]), hence not contrite. Penitential literature, e.g. Chaucer's Parson's Tale 833, regularly commends shame. See 48n above.

285–89 as fals folk to Westmynstre . . . oþere menne godes: The simile compares making ineffectual confession to friars, and hence avoiding the onerous repayment of the debt of sin (*redde quod debes*; see 21.186–87n), with taking sanctuary in the precincts of Westminster Abbey in order to escape financial debt. Chadwick first grasped the allusion to Westminster sanctuary (1922:22), and Baldwin, following a suggestion made by George Kane, explicated it (1982). A debtor would collude with friends or relatives to grant them the property that was collateral for the debt. The debtor would then retreat to Westminster, one of the chartered sanctuaries in which a felon could remain indefinitely, living luxuriously off the proceeds of the indebted property—as a sinner might live high if his penance were light. Any creditor would be unable to attach the debtor or the property, which now technically was not the debtor's property. Eventually the creditor would give in, accepting as repayment only a small part of the debt or granting an extension of the loan, "forȝeuenesse or lengore ȝeres lone," as better than nothing.

The issue of sanctuary for debtors was in the air in the late 1370s. Around 1376–79, Gower writes of the practice of a debtor fleeing to sanctuary, and "he refuses to leave the church before he gets a share of the other's wealth, until he is forgiven a third or even a half" (*Miroir* 25,849–72, trans. Wilson 1992:339). The Commons complained in detail of such collusion and flight to sanctuary in a writ before Parliament in the spring of 1377 and the answering statute of the same year (Rot. Parl. 2.369; *Statutes of the Realm* 50 Edward III, c. 6; 1.398; Alford, *Gloss.* s.v. *Westminstre*). The statute made it possible for creditors to attach fraudulently alienated collateral from the debtor's friends. L may have known the wording of this petition—see next note. On 11 August 1378, a breach of Westminster's sanctuary in a case of extortion led to a killing, and in response to an October petition the government then denied the right of indefinite sanctuary for debtors (Rot.Parl. 3.50–51; see also 3.276 and Trenholme 1903:26–27, 55–58, 81; Swanson 1989:153–58). Wyclif repeatedly defended the government's position against sanctuary (*De Officio Regis*, ed. Pollard and

Sayle 1887:157, 169; *De ecclesia*, ed. Loserth 1886:146–52, 243; Dahmus 1960: 61–63).

be bifore: "have the advantage" (MED *bifore(n* adv. 2.); the sense is missed by Schm and Donaldson (1990). In Chaucer's General Prologue 572 the Manciple is "Ay biforn and in good staat," always ahead and doing well.

290–93 And so hit fareth . . . to þe day of dome: L introduces another type of default of debt. A person wills, as was very common, for a part of his estate to be paid to some religious foundation in return for prayers for his departed soul. The executors (**secutours**) responsible for administering the estate, and the assizers or jurymen (**sisours**; see 156–64n above) who might participate in proving the will, make no provision for prayers for the deceased. They make their confession to friars (the parish priest would know of the decedent's will), give the friars a **parcel** of the bequest for prayers—for themselves!—and play with the **remenaunt**. The friars, we are to understand, absolve them without demanding restitution. The decedent's soul thus rots in purgatory, with a **dette** of sin unremitted, until Doomsday. Executors who fail to fulfill wills are similarly attacked by Imaginatyf (B.12.61 and n). See Alford, *Gloss.* s.v. *Executour*, *Sisour*; on the obligation of executors to discharge a testator's debts and oversee the offering of prayers to shorten purgatory see Duffy 1992:355–57.

Stokes (1984:22) draws attention to a parallel from *Winner and Waster*: "Forthi, Wynnere, with wronge thou wastes thi tyme; / For gode day ne glade getys thou never. / The devyll at thi dede-day schal delyn ["distribute"] thi gudis; / Tho [Those whom] thou woldest that it were, wyn ["obtain"] thay it never; / Thi skathill ["wicked"] sectours schal sever tham aboute, / And thou hafe helle full hotte for that thou here saved" (ed. Ginsberg 1992, lines 439–44). In the end, the winning is wasted. Compare also the issues of bequests and the need for proper restitution at 6.253–300, much expanded from B.5.260–78.

The word **parcel** here means "small amount" (MED *parcel* n. (g.); see B.10.64 [A.I1.50]), and **remenaunt** the residue of an estate after the material debts are paid (Alford, *Gloss.* s.v. *Remenaunt*). Possibly L remembered the wording of either the Commons' petition or the statute of 1377 about the sanctuary scam (see preceding note), in which "the said creditors are bound to take a small portion (*une petite parcelle*) of their debt and release the remnant (*remenaunt*)." Might he have had a hand in drafting these documents?

The attack on Unite renewed

296–303 The while Couetyse . . . cardinal vertues: Vices specifically attributed to the friars—covetise and hypocrisy—are joined by abusers of speech, gossips and idle chatterers. On friars as abusers of speech see Szittya 1986:251–57. The assault parallels that of covetise and "wiles" and "glosynges and gabbynges" before; see 121–39n, 125n above. Their victims are teachers; presumably these are the parish priests "þat couthe wel shryue" (304), whom the friars, in their **ypocrisie**, deprive of their right to hear confession. Possibly, however, the reference is to the academic infighting between mendicant and possessionate masters, a squabble with a history stretching back to he University of Paris in the mid-thirteenth century. Pees naturally bars the gate against such disturbers of the peace. We might expect Peace as porter to be lenient for the sake of peace, but he is surprisingly tough-minded in 341–47 below. His counterpart is Grace, gateward of the Court of Truth (7.243 [B.5.595, A.6.82]), whose servant is "amende-ȝow," a figure of penance sadly lacking here under the influence of the friars. See 21.317–34n.

The defense of Unite: Friar Flatterer

304–72 Consience calde a leche . . . synnes of kynde: Continuing his critique of friars and the defective contrition they foster, L exploits the metaphor of the sacrament of penance as medicine, introduced in 282 above, here for those wounded by the vices (302 above). Two physicians, the parson (359) Shrift and Friar Flatterer, attempt especially to heal Contrition, wounded by Hypocrisy and sick (334–35). The search for a **leche** recalls Lyf's vain trust in "fisyk" (169–74 above; see 311n below).

In the *Torneiment Anticrist* (see 21.335–480n) the figures Confession and Penitence and others tend to the wounded (ed. Bender 1976, lines 3026–92; see Owen 1912:151). Such an allegory was almost inevitable in the mendicant controversy, given the hackneyed shrift/medicine metaphor (see Szittya 1986:283–84). For instance, an unpublished antisecular sermon composed by the Dominican Richard Helmslay in 1379–80, described by Pantin 1955:164–65, contains this exemplum: a sick king (the people) had a skilled physician (the four orders of friars), but another physician (the secular clergy), jealous of the king's physician, wrote a letter (preachers, e.g. monks, hired to deceive the people) to the king warning against his rival's medicine. The king saw through the ruse, took his own physician's medicine, and recovered. An allegory of this type, if it were known to L, would help explain the **letteres** of line 309; see 325–28n below.

308 And þat Peres pardon were ypayd, *redde quod debes*: For the topic, the sense of **ypayd**, and the syntax see 21.186–87n. The **þat** clause may depend on "schupte" or "made" of 306, or (Prsl) may be elliptical: "and (to make sure) that."

310 sege that softur couthe plaster: The Samaritan tells Will that "the man" wounded by thieves cannot be saved without "þe bloed of a barn" and being "plastered with pacience" (19.84–91; B.17.94–98 has "plastred wiþ penaunce and passion of þat baby"). A plaster or poultice acts in part by "drawing out" infected matter, as a confessor draws out the sins of a confessing person. **Sege** means "the besieging force." Pees, Conscience, and Contrition seem naively unaware of the implication that the physician is an enemy. Conscience had already called friars into Unite (243 above), but consumed with Envy they keep the siege.

311 Sire leef-to-lyue-in-lecherye . . . wolde deye: For **leef** all but one C manu-script and the RF group along with other B manuscripts (and Schm in B, Prsl) read *lyf*. **Leef** means "willing, desirous" (OED *lief* adj. 2.). The easier reading, as RK-C observe, was induced by **lyue**—as well as by the lecherous Lyf of 148–182 above, the antecedent of this figure, who likewise sought the "company of comfort." The mild penance of fasting on Friday, commonly enjoined on all Christians, overcomes him.

313–15 'Ther is a surgien . . . fiscicien and surgien': An unspecified speaker (perhaps the quite fallible figure Contrition, with the punctuation adjusted) who shares the view of Sire-lief-to-live-in-luxury introduces Friar Flatterer as representative of too lenient penance. He is like the false prophet of Ezekiel 13:18–21 who traps souls by sewing "cushions under every elbow." Or like Chaucer's Friar, "He was an esy man to yeve penaunce / Ther as he wiste to have a good pitaunce" (GP 223–24; see Prsl n to his C.Prol.62). A friar-confes-sor tells Mede that for pay he will absolve her and "brynge adoun Consience" (3.42–43, and see 12.3–10 [B.11.53–58]). Three references to friars as flatterers were added in the C version after this passage was composed: see 12.25, 15.77, and 235n above. "The voluntary poverty of the friars—their institutionalized neediness—becomes a metonymy in *Dobest* for an attenuation of remorse" (Harwood 1992:132).

With this friar's name compare that of "frere faytour," among the wast-rels whom Piers will not provide for, in 8.73 (B.6.72). Compare also that type of hypocritical ingratiation, Favel, the civic aspect of what is here an ecclesias-tical vice (C/B/A.2.6, etc.). "Flatterer" has the sense outlined in 235n above, one offering soothing words—"lowe speche lordes to plese" (B.5.140)—or more precisely, one offering absolution without proper penance. Gower's antimendicant satire in *Miroir* (written ca. 1376–79) includes a friar-figure named Flaterie who goes about as a fraternal pair with Ipocresie and gives absolution without penance or punishment (ed. Macaulay 1899: I, lines 21227–58). L may respond specifically to what he would consider bad advice in *Le Pèlerinage de vie humaine*, in which Reason without irony urges the pope as confessor to be gentle in applying medicinal ointments in confession, and even to assume a false appearance (lines 571–689, trans. Clasby 1992:10).

In a tradition from the *Psychomachia* (see 21.335–480n), a deceitful, demonic figure, deriving from the Virgilian Fury and the biblical false prophet, intrudes into the final citadel of the narrative (Barney 1979:60, 73–78, 94–95). Friar Flatterer is this figure of discord in PP. Scripture warns of "lying teachers (*magistri mendaces*)" among the people (2 Peter 2:1, and see Apoc. 21:27), an epithet adopted by antimendicants against friars who presumed to call themselves masters (Szittya 1986:61, 149). Mere exposure normally defeats this *mendax* figure, but in PP, still caught up in history, he holds the fort to the end.

Two friars said to be physicians have been proposed, on very slender grounds, as models for Friar Flatterer. The Franciscan William Appleton, killed in the Rising of 1381, was John of Gaunt's physician. As Gaunt's liaison with Katherine Swynford was common knowledge, and as he aroused much enmity, he might be the lord, whom Green identifies with Sir-lief-to-live-in-lechery, who supports the friar (325 below; Green 1997). The Dominican Henry Daniel, who wrote treatises on the medical use of rosemary and on urinalysis, might be described as a maker of salves (336 below; Friedman 1994). Hanna points out that the (eighteenth-century?) tradition that Daniel was a physician before becoming a friar is unsupported (1994:187). More likely than either are the despised confessors of the king, Dominicans like Bashe and Rushook (see 21.221–24n), but indeed no particular friar need be in question, especially since the whole conception of confessor as physician is metaphorical.

316–17 Quod contricion . . . thorw ypocrisye: Contrition, the first movement of penance, can be deceived even more easily than his cousin Conscience (see 369–72, 357 below). To heal the wounds of hypocrisy he seeks help from the very emblem of hypocrisy.

318–21 We haen no need . . . dette lette hit: The wording, with **power** and **dette**, refers to the concepts broached at 21.182–90; see notes. The figure Shrift is a (secular) parson; 359 below. On friars' not requiring restitution of those confessing to them see Scase 1989:26–28. A **penytauncer** is "a priest appointed by a pope or bishop to administer the sacrament of penance, esp. in cases [like heresy] reserved to the bishop or pope" (Alford, *Gloss.* s.v. *Pentauncer*). The first records of the English word **indulgence,** remission of the punishment for sin still due after absolution of guilt, are in PP.

322–23 Y may wel soffre . . . fisyk ȝow seke: On Conscience's surprising sufferance, abruptly expressed, see 243–45n above. **Fisyk ȝow seke:** "heal you sick people."

325–27 To a lord for a lettre . . . his breef hadde: Instances of Lollard criticism of friars for striving to become confessors of the rich are gathered in Gradon and Hudson 1996:138; see 21.221–24n. The lord's letter induces a bishop to issue a **breef,** a letter of authority. In 1300 Pope Boniface VIII issued a bull that required friars to receive a bishop's formal license in order to hear confessions (Alford, *Gloss.* s.v. *Bref*). These are the last of the written documents so pervasive in PP; compare the "prinses lettres" that might thwart justice (C.21/ B.19.307; see 20.191–92n).

330 Pees vnpynned hyt: Peace unpins the little hatch in the gate so as to see and talk with whoever is outside.

332 for profyt and for helthe: Ostensibly for Contrition's **profyt,** benefit, but obviously for his own financial gain as well. Flatterer's hypocrisy nearly dissolves into bold-faced greed of the kind exhibited by Fals Semblaunt in the *Roman de la Rose* or by Chaucer's Pardoner.

340–47 sire *penetrans domos* . . . some were with childe: Friar Flatterer derives his alias from 2 Tim. 3:6, which warns of hypocrites "who creep into houses (*qui penetrant domos*), and lead captive silly women laden with sins, who are led away with divers desires" (cp. Galat. 2:4). The tag "penetrant of houses" became a common epithet in antimendicant satire from William of St. Amour on. Wyclif writes, "Few indeed are the houses or entrances so secluded that friars will not enter them forthwith, so that penetrating they may talk, in their mendacity, with the inhabitants—whence some assert that they are rabid dogs in their doings" (*Sermones,* ed. Loserth 1886, 1.289). Chaucer's Summoner's Tale exploits the epithet at large. In his *Collectiones* William defined the penetrated *domus* as both a material house and as the "spiritual house that can be called the conscience"—both an individual's conscience and the house of God, the Church (Szittya 1986:3, 58–61, 285). The biblical and early interpretation of the penetration as verbal and spiritual seduction developed into an attack on the friars for lechery as well, and Pees repeats the joke at 347; like Chaucer's Friar, Sir Penetrans-Domos seems to talk his way into sexual relationships (GP 210–14; see Mann 1973:40–41).

The criticism seems a mere sideswipe here, and as Scase argues the "old metaphor of lechery" was yielding in L's time to an emphasis on the "financial implications of the relationship between confessor and penitent" (1989:33; see also 80–81). Lollards could apply the epithet to secular priests as well. Knighton reports the articles of John Bukkynham, bishop of Lincoln, against the Lollard William de Swyndurby, accusing William of saying that "no priest enters any house except for badly treating the wife, daughter, or maidservant, and therefore he would ask husbands to beware of allowing any priest to enter their house" (ed. Lumby 1889, 2.197).

The friars lack **eny craft** (342); see 206–11n, 230–31n above. In this jocular context **salued**, "administered healing ointments," may be a sight pun on *salued, salewed*, "saluted, greeted" (OED *salue* v.); so Schm, 1995 ed., p. lii; in any case the implication is sexual. Friar Flatterer is accompanied by **his felawe** (340) because friars—at least Franciscans—were enjoined to travel in pairs.

348–58 Hende speche heet pees . . . to his sores: Hende speche personifies Conscience's affable nature (see 243–45n above), and here his hope for Lyf's conversion, for a good result of the penance administered by the friar. Schroeder compares his suggestion that Lyf and Conscience join in a kiss of peace with the king's equally unsavory command that Conscience kiss Meed (1970:29; C/B/A.4.3; cp. Chaucer's Pardoner's Tale, line 965). **Lyf** sums up both Sir-lief-to-live-in-luxury and the figure of the Pride of Life earlier in the passus (see 143–51n, 70–71n).

356–58 quod Consience: The thrice-repeated **quod Consience** seems to imitate some such repeated "hende" gesture as a welcoming bow.

359–62 The plasteres of the persoun . . . y schal amenden hit: The more severe and effective Parson Shrift is unwilling to remit the penance due between the sinner's annual Lenten confessions. A **lymitour** is a friar licensed to hear confession within a fixed area or limit.

363–67 And goeth gropeth . . . a litel suluer: The oily friar in the Summoner's Tale says, "Thise curatz been ful necligent and slowe / To grope tenderly a conscience / In shrift" (1816–18). The **plastre**'s name of some forty words may seem excessive even for PP (cp. 8.80–83, etc.), and Prsl punctuates to begin a semi-direct discourse, of a kind common in Middle English, with the words **y shal preye**. But the plaster is not merely the payment, but the whole vile contract. For similar allegorical medicaments in the *Torneiment Anticrist* see Owen 1912:151. The payment is **pryue** because its terms, money for prayer, are improper; such transactions are conducted by tactful implication only.

The editors offer varying solutions, all conceivable, to the crux at 366–67. The relevant manuscript variants in the B and C traditions are: *And make (of)(om.) ȝow (my ladye)(memory) in masse and in matynes* / *(As)(Of)(All þe) (&) freres.* . . . Manuscript F of B alone reads *of ȝow memory* for *ȝow my ladye.* Manuscript Ch of C reads *And minne ȝow in masse* . . . . Because manuscript R of B, F's congener, accords with the rest in reading *my ladye*, that reading is probably archetypal in both traditions, as KD-B acknowledge (p. 160). Hence, unless—as is possible; see KD-B, pp. 165–73—F's reading is a correction, the Athlone **of ȝow** *memoria* for *ȝow my ladye* is unsupported conjecture, relying on the guess that a contracted form of *memoria* was misread. Prsl reads *And make ȝow my Ladye in masse and in matynes* / *Of freres* . . . . , posing that *my Ladye* is "a particular object of my prayers as a member of our fraternity . . . with some hint that he will be equal to Our Lady in the zeal with which they pray for him." The sense seems unlikely (the figure Contrition is male). Schm reads *And make ȝow [and] my Ladye in masse and in matynes* / *As freres* . . . ; "Friar Flatterer is offering membership of the fraternity to both master and mistress." This reading would nicely characterize the friar's unctuous servility ("my lady") and wily salesmanship (two for the price of one). RK-C (p. 136 n65) object that the friar addresses Contrition alone (but in context, **hem** and **freres** suggest a plural recipient), and that the verb *maken . . . as* in this sense is not idiomatic (though they cite contradictory evidence).

A *memoria* in liturgical use is a commemoration, especially of the dead (Alford, *Quot.* 117; see 8.104 [B.6.95, A.7.87]). The Sarum Breviary specifies that such *memoriae* are to be said **in matynes** (ed. Proctor and Wordsworth 1882, 2.90). Corroborating the Athlone (and F of B) reading (though English **memorie** would be preferable to Latin *memoria*) is C.7.27, where Sloth says he can lie in bed "Til matynes and masse be ydo; thenne haue y a memorie at þe freres," a clarifying revision of B (with too many syllables in the off-verse) possibly with this passage in mind. An alternative that better explains the misreading *my ladye*, if such it be, would be *And make ȝow myldely, in masse and matynes,* / *As freres* . . . , expressing mendicant lenience and "hende speche." For similarly ironic uses of *myldeliche* see C.3.21 and 77.

On the admission of lay brothers and sisters as adjunct to fraternal orders by way of "letters of fraternity" see 3.54, 56n. The practice is criticized in 9.344 (B.7.198, A.8.176) and 12.8 (B.11.56). On silver to friars instead of proper restitution see also 12.15–17 (B.11.72–77).

368–72 Thus he goeth . . . for alle synnes of kynde: The confessor offering comfort (and gathering offerings) rather than chastising and urging repentance, the figure Contrition leaves contrition—has no need to feel contrite. For such "double allegorizations" see 20.30n. **Gloseth** means both "flatters" and "(mis-)interprets [Scripture]"; see Summoner's Tale 1793, 125n above, and 15.80–81 (B.13.74–75). The Athlone emendation of *kyne synnes* puts the *s*-stave in the normal position, but **for alle synnes of kynde** makes an unmetrical off-verse by Duggan/Cable principles. Monosyllabic or liaised **synne** would do—it would mean "sin rising from human nature"—or the archetypal line may be original. Likewise for metrical reasons **woned to do** should read **woned doone** or (as B) **wont to doone**.

The final attack

373–86 Sleuth seyh þat . . . tyl y gan awake: Sloth and Pride, vices particularly linked to defective repentance, mount the last attack on Unite, and the best defense, Contrition, is stupefied by the friar's ministrations. In this passus Sloth seems broadly to represent the vice of the clergy, and Pride the vice of the nobility (see 214–29n above). In exasperation Conscience vows to set out on a pilgrimage to seek Piers Plowman, who is the instrument of grace; compare 21.213 "Thenne bigan grace to go with Peres Plouhman."

375 cryede efte clergie: "called again upon Clergy," as the first time he so cried the friars came (228–29 above; see n). In becoming a pilgrim and crying after Clergy, Conscience fulfills the prediction at the end of the banquet scene, when Clergy tells him "þow shalt se þe tyme / Whan þow art wery forwalked; wille me to counseille." There we learn that a perfected Conscience ("Til Pacience haue preued þee") together with a duly patient Clergy ("If Pacience be oure partyng felawe") could amend any "wo in þis world" (B.13.203–14; see Lawler 1995a:96–97; Hanna 1998b:156); in effect, Friar Flatterer has obstructed the work of patience. The C version, more skeptical of the saving power of clerisy, omits these hopeful sentiments (15.177–183).

377 'He lyeth adreint and dremeth,' saide pees, 'and so doth mony oþere': The Athlone editors reconstruct the first part of the line from B's *He lyþ and dremeþ* and C's *He lyeth adreint*. Peverett argues that the line alliterates on *s*, because L never uses a form of the verb **saide** (vs. *quod*) as a speech marker except when it participates in the alliteration (as in the close parallel 334 above, and see C.6.93 vs. B.5.128), or follows its subject, or falls near the end of the line (1986:121). Alliteration on *s* would also correct the otherwise irregular prosody, by Duggan/Cable principles, of the off-verse. The line is two-stave; perhaps read *slepeth* for **dremeth**, the latter substituted by B in a misguided effort to improve alliteration.

379 And doth men drynke dwale; they drat no synne: The **dwale**, a stupefying opiate, especially belladonna, voids fear of sin. It counters the "poysen" given to Jesus on the cross, which helped bring salvation (20.52, 401–2 [B.18.52, 363–64]).

The archetypal variation in this line and 381 below looks like authorial revision; see Passus 21 Headnote. The C version here is certainly livelier as well as metrically correct—perhaps L glanced again at the last page of his poem. The B archetype reads *And plastred hem so esily þei drede no synne*; Schm emends *þei* to *hij* to produce three vowel-staves. RK-C argue that the very difficult **dwale** induced scribal variation to a phrase easily generated from the context (p. 121; KD-B, p. 95). They cite MED evidence that the medical use of **dwale** may be a neologism, but in fact *Cursor mundi* (along with Chaucer and Gower) reads *drinc duale* in a medical use (MED *dwale* n. 4.(a); OED *dwale* sb.[2] 1.). L may play on a homophone **dwale**, "deceit, fraud"—compare the idiom "drink shame." A disyllabic form of **drat** (many manuscripts) would yield normative meter.

380–86 'By Crist!' quod Consience . . . tyl y gan awake: In deploying in this passage the terms **Consience, pilgrime, Peres, pruyde, freres, nede, kynde, grace, awake**, with great compression L sums up much of the content of this passus, and indeed of the whole poem. Piers was last seen when Grace went "As wyde as the world is with Peres to tulye treuthe" (C.21/B.19.333; see 21.332–35n); the phrasing is recollected here, and recalls Wit's advice that priests should fearlessly undertake "to wende as wyde as þe worlde were" to preach love (C.10.198–200; see also Prol.4n, and for the biblical basis of the idea, 17.190–91 [B.15.490]). Piers is here "the means of grace, and the hope of glory," a true priesthood who might bring about a true Church. Conscience, too, becomes a pilgrim, "if god wol yeue [him] grace" (B.13.181), as he had at the end of the banquet scene, where likewise the discourse of a friar drove him to a new kind of undertaking (15.182–88 [B.13.181–82]; see 243–45n above). Jenkins finds the pathos in the fact that, whereas before Conscience had allies—Reason in the Mede episode and Patience in the banquet scene—he is here alone (1969:141). Conscience, like Will, is fallible and needs Piers Plowman.

Aers remarks that Conscience is driven "however reluctantly, outside the existing church" (1994:123; also 1986:71, 1988:66, 1996:75), and Harwood agrees:

"At the end, the simonists are left to their shell" (1992:132; cp. Simpson 2001a and Gradon 1980:200–201). If this means that L, more proto-Protestant than Wyclif, abandons hope in the Church, it reads the allegory too literally; recall that Piers and Grace likewise left Unite, but before it was besieged (see 21.332–35n). See also 201–13 and n, 246 and n above. The point of Conscience's pilgrimage is not the whence, but the whither. On allegorical pilgrimages generally see Prol.47–50n.

Conscience wants friars to have a **fyndynge** to allay their **nede** (see 1–51n above) and consequently their motive for flattery. See 1–51n, 7–11n, 232–41n, 234n, 235n, 237–39n, 276n, 280–93n, 313–15n above. The syntax of 382–84 is disputed. Emmerson, judging that merely providing sustenance for friars is too easy a solution to the problems raised in this passus, holds with Kaske, Adams, and Clopper (against all editors) that a semi-colon should follow **destruye**, and that the period or semi-colon following **Consience** in 384 should be a comma (1993:43–44). Kaske would translate, "And now may Nature avenge me [for the fact] that friars had a founding," i.e. were ever founded, citing MED *finding* 5(c)—but this stretches the sense of the MED citations too far; the word means "endowment." Alternatively, he proposes, **kynde** may be vocative; also **hadde a fyndynge** may mean "had a livelihood," that is, developed their begging into a comfortable livelihood. He grounds this construction in the idea that **hadde** as "subjunctive with future meaning, expressing a purpose not contrary to fact" is not good Middle English, which would use *haue* or *may haue* (1963:205). But both alternatives strain the persistent sense of "finding" in PP, the proposed constructions are contorted, and they miss the point of **for nede**. Kaske misconstrues the syntax: **hadde** is an optative subjunctive, like that in Chaucer's "I wolde I hadde thy coillons in myn hond" (PardT 952), whereas contrary-to-fact grammar applies to conditional clauses, not in question here. The clause **þat freres hadde** depends on **wol** in line 380, not a mere auxiliary verb, and not on **to seke** of 382. In his translation Donaldson simplifies by supplying a new verb: "And see that friars had funds . . ." (1990); Brewer would, without manuscript support, actually add this *see* to L's text (1983:200).

Conscience wishes that the friars had a stable provision, of precisely the kind he had promised, conditionally, in 248–50 above (see 246–52n), that is, "property and ecclesiastical livings like the rest of the church" (Szittya 1986:286), and the kind that Piers promised to friars who did not flatter (C.8.147–48). He wishes, indeed, what Reason prophesied in C.5.173–74: "Freres in here fraytour shall fynde þat tyme / Bred withouten beggynge to lyue by euere aftur," and what Clergie prophesied in B.10.328–29: "And þanne Freres in hir fraytour shul fynden a keye / Of Constantyns cofres þer þe catel

is Inne." In support of Kaske's reading Clopper argues that even Franciscan
friars held possessions in common after the edicts of John XXII and Benedict
XII, and especially after the 1354 Constitutions of Assisi under Innocent VI
(1990:69). But the poem repeatedly asserts that friars lack a dependable livelihood (see, e.g., C.8.147–48 and the texts quoted above, and Dolan 1988:35, 39,
who suggests that L had Franciscans particularly in mind)—they still beg, and
they depend on income from shriving, preaching, and burying, and contemporary documents regularly refer to them in opposition to possessioners.

Gwynn noted a relevant passage in the satiric poem and commentary, the
Vaticinia of pseudo-John of Bridlington, composed ca. 1361 by the Austin friar
John of Erghome (1940:136). The commentator wryly suggests that one of the
obscure prophecies in the poem may mean that one day "the friars will receive
prebends and ecclesiastical dignities from the Roman Church, and lands from
pious lords, as now monks do, and then they will no longer be bound to such
poverty that they beg door to door" (ed. Wright 1859, 1:210). The joke suggests
that contemporary friars could be of two minds about their own ideology and
conduct, and we may suspect that L was too, respecting the mendicants'
founding principles but scandalized by their conduct.

Like Will, Conscience calls on Kynde to avenge: see 201–5n above. The
Athlone editors prefer the conjecture **renneth** (381), "extends," to archetypal
B's *lasteþ* (F of B reads *askeþ*, probably recalling B.Prol.19) and archetypal C's
regneth, taking the former as a gloss and the latter as a homoeograph of
renneth (RK-C, p. 129). *Regneth*, if not L's revision (see 379n above), in a spa-
tial sense hard enough to provoke substitution by B, may be the original,
meaning "holds sway, continues, flourishes" (OED *reign* v. 2.b., c., 3.).

386 And sethe he gradde . . . tyl y gan awake: The cry for grace, the benevolent instrument of "kynde" (see 21.182–98n), repeats that of C.21/B.19.212, the
beginning of the sequence of which this is the conclusion: the story of the
Church Militant (see 21.200–12n and 76n above). It likewise recalls Will's cries
to Holy Church for grace (C.1.76 [B.1.79], C/B/A.2.1), the cry for grace by the
"thousand of men" after the confessions of the folk (7.155–57 [B.5.511,
A.5.253]), and Haukyn's cry for "mercy" at the end of his confession, at which
point Will likewise awakes (B.14.334–35). Carruthers proposes that the
sequence wandering, conversion, pilgrimage is "the essential salvational plot
of every Christian soul" (1982:178–79), and the conversions in PP are marked
by such cries. The noise wakes Will as had the Easter bells at the end of C.20/
B.18. At the end of the *Pèlerinage de la vie humaine* the figure Grace comes to
comfort the dreamer on his deathbed (see 21.1–4n). Here L may specifically
counterplead against its conclusion: "I thoughte it fooly for tasaille / Grace

dieu with questiouns / With demandes or resouns" (the Lydgate translation, ed. Furnivall and Locock 1904, lines 24822–24; see 313–15n above).

At the outset Will asked how he might save his soul. The only answer is continually to cry after grace.

List of Works Cited

Acta Sanctorum. Bollandist Society. Antwerp; Brussels: 1643–1940.

Adams, Marilyn McCord. *William Ockham.* 2 vols., continuous pagination. Notre Dame, Ind.: University of Notre Dame Press, 1987.

Adams, Robert. "Editing and the Limitations of *Durior Lectio.*" *Yearbook of Langland Studies* 5 (1991): 7–15.

———. "Editing *Piers Plowman* B: The Imperative of an Intermittently Critical Edition." *Studies in Bibliography* 45 (1992): 31–68.

———. "Langland and the Liturgy Revisited." *Studies in Philology* 73 (1976): 266–84.

———. "Langland's *Ordinatio*: The *Visio* and the *Vita* Once More." *Yearbook of Langland Studies* 8 (1994): 51–84.

———. "The Nature of Need in *Piers Plowman* XX." *Traditio* 34 (1978): 273–301.

———. "The Reliability of the Rubrics in the B-Text of *Piers Plowman.*" *Medium Ævum* 54 (1985): 208–31. =1985a.

———. "Some Versions of Apocalypse: Learned and Popular Eschatology in *Piers Plowman.*" In *The Popular Literature of Medieval England*, ed. Thomas J. Heffernan. Knoxville: University of Tennessee Press, 1985. 194–236. = 1985b.

Aers, David. *Chaucer, Langland, and the Creative Imagination.* London: Routledge and Kegan Paul, 1980.

———. "Christ's Humanity and *Piers Plowman*: Contexts and Political Implications." *Yearbook of Langland Studies* 8 (1994): 107–25.

———. *Community, Gender, and Individual Identity: English Writing, 1360–1430.* London: Routledge, 1988.

———. *Piers Plowman and Christian Allegory.* London: Edward Arnold, 1975.

———. "*Piers Plowman* and Problems in the Perception of Poverty: A Culture in Transition." *Leeds Studies in English* n.s. 14 (1983): 5–25.

———. "Reflections on the 'Allegory of the Theologians,' Ideology and *Piers Plowman.*" In *Medieval Literature: Criticism, Ideology and History*, ed. David Aers. Brighton: Harvester, 1986. 58–73.

Aers, David and Lynn Staley. *The Powers of the Holy: Religion, Politics, and Gender in Late Medieval English Culture.* University Park: Pennsylvania State University Press, 1996.

Alford, John A., ed. *A Companion to Piers Plowman.* Berkeley: University of California Press, 1988. = 1988a.

———. "The Figure of Repentance in *Piers Plowman.*" In *Suche Werkis to Werche: Essays on Piers Plowman in Honor of David C. Fowler*, ed. Míćeál Vaughan. East Lansing, Mich.: Colleagues Press, 1993. 3–28.

———. "The Idea of Reason in *Piers Plowman.*" In *Medieval English Studies Presented to George Kane*, ed. Edward Donald Kennedy, Ronald Waldron, and Joseph S. Wittig. Wolfeboro, N.H.: D.S. Brewer, 1988. 199–215. = 1988b.

————. "Literature and Law in Medieval England." *PMLA* 92 (1977): 941–51.

————. "A Note on *Piers Plowman* B.xviii.390: 'TIL *PARCE* IT HOTE.'" *Modern Philology* 69 (1972): 323–25.

————. *Piers Plowman: A Glossary of Legal Diction*. Cambridge: D.S. Brewer, 1988.

————. *Piers Plowman: A Guide to the Quotations*. Medieval and Renaissance Texts and Studies 77. Binghamton, N.Y.: Medieval and Renaissance Texts and Studies, 1992.

Alford, John A. and Dennis P. Seniff. *Literature and Law in the Middle Ages: A Bibliography of Scholarship*. New York: Garland, 1984.

Allen, David G. "The Dismas *Distinctio* and the Forms of *Piers Plowman* B.10–13." *Yearbook of Langland Studies* 3 (1989): 31–48.

Allen, Hope Emily, ed. *English Writings of Richard Rolle, Hermit of Hampole*. Oxford: Clarendon Press, 1931; repr. St. Clair Shores, Mich.: Scholarly Press, 1971.

Ames, Ruth M. *The Fulfillment of the Scriptures: Abraham, Moses, and Piers*. Evanston, Ill.: Northwestern University Press, 1970.

Andrew, Malcolm and Ronald Waldron, eds. *The Poems of the Pearl Manuscript*. Berkeley: University of California Press, 1978.

Andrieu, Michel, ed. *Le Pontifical romain au moyen-âge*. 4 vols. Vol. 3, *Le Pontifical de Guillaume Durand*. Vatican: Bibliotheca Apostolica Vaticana, 1938–41.

Anglo-Norman Dictionary. Ed. Louise Stone et al. London: Modern Humanities Research Association, 1981–92.

Armstrong, Regis J., J. A. Wayne Hellman, and William J. Short, eds. and trans. *Francis of Assisi: Early Documents*. Vol. 1, *The Saint*. New York: New City Press, 1999.

Arthur, Harold. "On a MS. Collection of Ordinances of Chivalry of the Fifteenth Century." *Archæologia* 57 (1901): 29–70, with a "Letter from Thomas . . . Constable of England to King Richard II. Concerning the Means of Conducting Judicial Duels," 61–66.

Astin, Isabel S. T., ed. *Anglo-Norman Political Songs*. Anglo-Norman Texts 11. Oxford: Blackwell, 1953.

Aston, Margaret. "'Caim's Castles': Poverty, Politics, and Disendowment." In *The Church, Politics and Patronage in the Fifteenth Century*, ed. Barrie Dobson. Gloucester: Alan Sutton, 1984. 45–81.

————. "Corpus Christi and Corpus Regni: Heresy and the Peasants' Revolt." *Past and Present* 143 (1993): 3–47.

————. *England's Iconoclasts*. Vol. 1. Oxford: Clarendon Press, 1988.

————. *Lollards and Reformers*. London: Hambledon, 1984.

Aulén, Gustaf. *Christus Victor: An Historical Study of the Three Main Types of the Idea of Atonement*. Trans. A. G. Hebert (from the German in *Zeitschr. f. systematische Theologie*, 1930, 501–38). New York: Macmillan, 1961.

Ayto, John and Alexandra Barratt, eds. *Aelred of Rievaulx's "De Institutione Inclusarum"*. Early English Text Society o.s. 287. London: Oxford University Press, 1984.

Baethgen, Friedrich. *Der Engelpapst*. Schriften der Königsberger Gelehrten Gesellschaft, Geisteswissenschaftliche Klasse 10:2. Halle: Max Niemeyer, 1933.

Bailey, Terence. *The Processions of Sarum and the Western Church*. Toronto: Pontifical Institute of Mediæval Studies, 1971.

Baker, Denise N. "Meed and the Economics of Chivalry in *Piers Plowman*." In *Inscrib-*

ing the Hundred Years' War in French and English Cultures, ed. Denise N. Baker. Albany: State University of New York Press, 2000. 55–72.

Balbus, Johannes. *Catholicon*. Lyon: Boniface, 1496.

Baldwin, Anna P. "The Debt Narrative in *Piers Plowman*." In *Art and Context in Late Medieval English Literature: Essays in Honor of Robert Worth Frank, Jr.*, ed. Robert R. Edwards. Cambridge: D.S. Brewer, 1994. 37–50.

———. "The Double Duel in *Piers Plowman* B xviii and C xxi." *Medium Ævum* 50 (1981): 64–78. = 1981a.

———. "Patient Politics in *Piers Plowman*." *Yearbook of Langland Studies* 15 (2002 for 2001): 99–108.

———. "A Reference in *Piers Plowman* to the Westminster Sanctuary." *Notes and Queries* 29 (April 1982): 106–8.

———. *The Theme of Government in Piers Plowman*. Woodbridge, Suffolk: D.S. Brewer, 1981. = 1981b.

Barber, Richard. *Edward, Prince of Wales and Aquitaine*. London: Allen Lane, 1978.

———. *The Knight and Chivalry*. New York: Scribner's, 1970.

Barber, Richard and Juliet Barker. *Tournaments: Jousts, Chivalry and Pageants in the Middle Ages*. Woodbridge, Suffolk: Boydell, 1989.

Barker, Juliet R. V. *The Tournament in England, 1100–1400*. Woodbridge, Suffolk: Boydell Press, 1986.

Barnes, Richard. "On Translating *Piers Plowman*, III." *Yearbook of Langland Studies* 3 (1989): 21–29.

Barney, Stephen A. *Allegories of History, Allegories of Love*. New Haven, Conn.: Archon, 1979.

———. "Langland's Prosody: The State of Study." In *The Endless Knot: Essays on Old and Middle English in Honor of Marie Borroff*, ed. M. Teresa Tavormina and R. F. Yeager. Cambridge: D.S. Brewer, 1995. 65–85.

———. "The Plowshare of the Tongue: The Progress of a Symbol from the Bible to *Piers Plowman*." *Mediæval Studies* 35 (1973): 261–93.

———. Review of Prsl and Schm 1978 Editions. *Speculum* 56 (1981): 161–65.

Barnum, Priscilla Heath, ed. *Dives and Pauper*. Part 1. Early English Text Society 275. London: Oxford University Press, 1976.

Barr, Helen. *The Piers Plowman Tradition*. Everyman's Library. London: J.M. Dent, 1993.

———. *Signes and Sothe: Language in the Piers Plowman Tradition*. Cambridge: D.S. Brewer, 1994.

———. "The Use of Latin Quotations in *Piers Plowman* with Special Reference to Passus XVIII of the 'B' Text." *Notes and Queries* n.s. 33 (Dec. 1986):440–48.

Bender, Margaret O., ed. *"Le Torneiment Anticrist" by Huon de Méri*. University, Miss.: Romance Monographs, 1976.

Bennett, J. A. W. "The Date of the B-Text of *Piers Plowman*." *Medium Ævum* 12 (1943): 55–64.

———. *Poetry of the Passion: Studies in Twelve Centuries of English Verse*. Oxford: Clarendon Press, 1982.

Bennett, Judith M. *Ale, Beer, and Brewsters in England: Women's Work in a Changing World, 1300–1600*. New York: Oxford University Press, 1996.

Benson, C. David. "What Then Does Langland Mean? Authorial and Textual Voices in *Piers Plowman*." *Yearbook of Langland Studies* 15 (2002 for 2001): 3–13.

Benson, Larry D. *Art and Tradition in "Sir Gawain and the Green Knight"*. New Brunswick, N.J.: Rutgers University Press, 1965.

Benson, Larry D. et al., eds. *The Riverside Chaucer*. Boston: Houghton Mifflin, 1987.

Benson, Larry D. and Siegfried Wenzel, eds. *The Wisdom of Poetry: Essays in Early English Literature in Honor of Morton W. Bloomfield*. Kalamazoo, Mich.: Medieval Institute Publications, 1982.

Berliner, Rudolf. "Arma Christi," *Münchner Jahrbuch der bildenden Kunst* 3rd ser. 6 (1955), 35–152.

Bestul, Thomas H. *Texts of the Passion: Latin Devotional Literature and Medieval Society*. Philadelphia: University of Pennsylvania Press, 1996.

———, ed. *Walter Hilton: The Scale of Perfection*. Kalamazoo, Mich.: Medieval Institute Publications, 2000.

Biasiotto, Peter R. *History of the Development of Devotion to the Holy Name*. St. Anthony's Athenæum dissertation. St. Bonaventure, N.Y.: St. Bonaventure College, 1943.

Bignami-Odier, Jeanne. *Études sur Jean de Roquetaillade (Johannes de Rupescissa)*. Paris: J. Vrins, 1952.

Birnes, William J. "Christ as Advocate: The Legal Metaphor of *Piers Plowman*." *Annuale Medievale* 16 (1975): 71–93.

Bishop, Louise M. "Will and the Law of Property in *Piers Plowman*." *Yearbook of Langland Studies* 10 (1996): 23–41.

Blanch, Robert J., ed. *Style and Symbolism in Piers Plowman: A Modern Critical Anthology*. Knoxville: University of Tennessee Press, 1969.

Block, K. S. *"Ludus Coventriæ", or The Plaie Called Corpus Christi*. Early English Text Society e.s. 120. London: Oxford University Press, 1922 (for 1917).

Bloomfield, Morton W. "The Allegories of *Dobest* (*Piers Plowman* B xix-xx)." *Medium Ævum* 50 (1981): 30–39.

———. *Piers Plowman as a Fourteenth-Century Apocalypse*. New Brunswick, N.J.: Rutgers University Press, 1961. = 1961a.

———. "*Piers Plowman* as a Fourteenth-Century Apocalypse." *Centennial Review of Arts and Sciences* 5 (1961): 281–95. = 1961b.

Blume, Clemens and Guido M. Dreves. *Analecta hymnica medii ævi*. Second series 50. Leipzig, 1907; repr. New York: Johnson Reprints, 1961.

Blythe, Joan Heiges. "Sins of the Tongue and Rhetorical Prudence in *Piers Plowman*." In *Literature and Religion in the Later Middle Ages: Philological Studies in Honor of Siegfried Wenzel*, ed. Richard J. Newhauser and John A. Alford. Medieval and Renaissance Texts and Studies 118. Binghamton, N.Y.: Medieval and Renaissance Texts and Studies, 1995. 119–42.

Bolard, A.-C., L.-M. Rigollot, and J. Carnandet, eds. *Ludolphus de Saxonia, "Vita Jesu Christi"*. Paris: Victor Palmé, 1865.

Bostick, Curtis V. *The Antichrist and the Lollards: Apocalypticism in Late Medieval and Reformation England*. Leiden: Brill, 1998.

Bourquin, Guy. *Piers Plowman: Études sur la genèse littéraire des trois versions*. Paris thesis, 2 vols. Paris: Honoré Champion, 1978.

Bousset, W. *The Antichrist Legend: A Chapter in Christian and Jewish Folklore*. Trans. A. H. Keane. London: Hutchinson, 1896.

Bowers, John M. *The Crisis of Will in Piers Plowman*. Washington, D.C.: Catholic University of America Press, 1986.

————. "*Piers Plowman* and the Police: Notes Toward a History of the Wycliffite Langland." *Yearbook of Langland Studies* 6 (1992): 1–50.

Bowers, R. H. "'Foleuyles Lawes' (*Piers Plowman*, C.xxii.247)." *Notes and Queries* 206 n.s. 8 (Sept. 1961): 327–28.

Bracton, Henry de. *De legibus et consuetudinibus Angliæ*. Ed. G. E. Woodbine. Vol. 2. New Haven, Conn.: Yale University Press, 1915.

Brady, Niall. "The Gothic Barn of England: Icon of Prestige and Authority." In *Technology and Resource Use in Medieval Europe: Cathedrals, Mills, and Mines*, ed. Elizabeth Bradford Smith and Michael Wolfe. Hampshire: Ashgate, 1997. 76–105.

Brandeis, Arthur, ed. *Jacob's Well*. Early English Text Society o.s. 115. London: Kegan Paul, Trench, Trübner, 1900.

Brantley, Jessica. "The Iconography of the Utrecht Psalter and the Old English *Descent into Hell*." *Anglo-Saxon England* 28 (1999): 43–63.

Breeze, Andrew. "'Tikes' at *Piers Plowman* B.xix.37: Welsh TAEOG 'serf, bondman'." *Notes and Queries* 238 (March, 1993): 443–45.

Brewer, Derek. *English Gothic Literature*. London: Macmillan, 1983.

Brewer, J. S., ed. *Monumenta Franciscana*. Rolls Series. London: Stationery Office, 1858; repr. Millwood, N.Y.: Kraus, 1965.

Brie, Friedrich W. D., ed. *The Brut*. Early English Text Society o.s. 131, 136. London: Oxford University Press, 1906, 1908.

Bright, Allan H. *New Light on Piers Plowman*. London: Oxford University Press, 1928.

Brock, Edmund, ed. *Morte Arthure*. Early English Text Society o.s. 8. 2nd ed. 1871; repr. London: Oxford University Press, 1961.

Brown, Beatrice Daw. *The Southern Passion*. Early English Text Society o.s. 169. London: Oxford University Press, 1927 (for 1925).

Brown, Carleton. *English Lyrics of the XIIIth Century*. Oxford: Clarendon Press, 1932.

————. *Religious Lyrics of the XIVth Century*. Oxford: Clarendon Press, 1924.

————. *Religious Lyrics of the XVth Century*. Oxford: Clarendon Press, 1939.

————. "*Poculum mortis* in Old English." *Speculum* 15 (1940): 389–99.

Brucker, Gene A. *Florentine Politics and Society, 1343–1378*. Princeton, N.J.: Princeton University Press, 1962.

Bryan, W. F. and Germaine Dempster, eds. *Sources and Analogues of Chaucer's Canterbury Tales*. Chicago: University of Chicago Press, 1941; repr. New York: Humanities Press, 1958.

Bullock-Davies, Constance. *Menestrellorum Multitudo: Minstrels at a Royal Feast*. Cardiff: University of Wales Press, 1978.

Burch, George Bosworth, ed. and trans. *Bernard of Clairvaux: The Steps of Humility*. Cambridge, Mass.: Harvard University Press, 1950.

Burgess, Anthony. *A Mouthful of Air: Language, Languages—Especially English*. New York: William Morrow, 1992.

Burlin, Robert B. *Chaucerian Fiction*. Princeton, N.J.: Princeton University Press, 1977.

Burns, J. Patout. "The Concept of Satisfaction in Medieval Redemption Theory." *Theological Studies* 36 (1975): 285–304.

Burrow, J. A. *The Ages of Man: A Study in Medieval Writing and Thought*. Oxford: Clarendon Press, 1986.

————. "Gestures and Looks in *Piers Plowman*." *Yearbook of Langland Studies* 14 (2001, for 2000): 75–83.

————. *Langland's Fictions*. Oxford: Clarendon Press, 1993.

Butler, H. E., ed. and trans. *The "Institutio Oratoria" of Quintilian*. 4 vols. Loeb Classical Library. Cambridge, Mass.: Harvard University Press, 1921–22.

Buytaert, Eligius M., O.F.M., ed. *Petri Abælardi Opera Theologica*. 2 vols. Corpus Christianorum, Continuatio Medievalis 11–12. Turnhout: Brepols, 1969.

Cable, Thomas. *The English Alliterative Tradition*. Philadelphia: University of Pennsylvania Press, 1991.

Cabrol, F. "Descente du Christ aux enfers d'après la liturgie." *Dictionnaire d'archéologie chrétienne et de liturgie*, vol. 4, cols. 682–93. Paris: Letouzet et Ane, 1920.

Campbell, Jackson J. "To Hell and Back: Latin Tradition and Literary Use of the 'Descensus ad Inferos' in Old English." *Viator* 13 (1982): 107–58.

Campbell, Gertrude H. "The Middle English *Evangelie*." *PMLA* 30 (1915): 529–613.

Carruthers, Mary. *The Search for St. Truth: A Study of Meaning in Piers Plowman*. Evanston, Ill.: Northwestern University Press, 1973.

————. "Time, Apocalypse, and the Plot of *Piers Plowman*." In *Acts of Interpretation: The Text in Its Contexts, 700–1600: Essays on Medieval and Renaissance Literature in Honor of E. Talbot Donaldson*, ed. Mary Carruthers and Elizabeth D. Kirk. Norman, Okla.: Pilgrim Books, 1982. 175–88.

————. See also Schroeder, Mary C.

Chadwick, D. *Social Life in the Days of Piers Plowman*. Cambridge: Cambridge University Press, 1922; repr. New York: Russell and Russell, 1969.

Chambers, E. K. *The Mediæval Stage*. 2 vols. Oxford: Oxford University Press, 1903.

Chambers, R. W. *Man's Unconquerable Mind*. London: Jonathan Cape, 1939.

————. "Preface" to Allen H. Bright, *New Light on Piers Plowman*. London: Oxford University Press, 1928. 9–26.

Chazan, Robert. *Church, State, and Jew in the Middle Ages*. New York: Behrman House, 1980.

Cigman, Gloria, ed. *Lollard Sermons*. Early English Text Society 294. Oxford: Oxford University Press, 1989.

Clapham, Alfred W. and Walter H. Godfrey. *Some Famous Buildings and Their Story*. Westminster: Technical Journals, Caxton House, n.d. [before 1913].

Clasby, Eugene, trans. *Guillaume de Deguileville: The Pilgrimage of Human Life*. New York: Garland, 1992.

Clifton, Nicole. "The Romance Convention of the Disguised Duel and the Climax of *Piers Plowman*." *Yearbook of Langland Studies* 7 (1993): 123–28.

Clopper, Lawrence M. "Langland's Franciscanism." *Chaucer Review* 25 (1990): 54–75.

————. "Langland's Markings for the Structure of *Piers Plowman*." *Modern Philology* 85 (1988): 245–55.

————. "Langland's Persona: An Anatomy of the Mendicant Orders." In *Written Work: Langland, Labor, and Authorship*, ed. Steven Justice and Kathryn Kerby-Fulton. Philadelphia: University of Pennsylvania Press, 1997. = 1997a.

————. "Langland's Trinitarian Analogies as Key to Meaning and Structure." *Medievalia et Humanistica* n.s. 9 (1979): 87–110.

————. "A Response to Robert Adams, 'Langland's *Ordinatio*'." *Yearbook of Langland Studies* 9 (1995): 141–46.

————. "Shifting Typologies in Langland's Theology of History." In *Typology and English Medieval Literature*, ed. Hugh T. Keenan. New York: AMS Press, 1992. 227–40.

———. *"Songes of Rechelesnesse": Langland and the Franciscans*. Ann Arbor: University of Michigan Press, 1997. = 1997b

Coghill, Nevill K. "The Character of *Piers Plowman* Considered from the B-Text." *Medium Ævum* 2 (1933): 108–35. Repr. in *Interpretations of Piers Plowman*, ed. Edward Vasta. Notre Dame, Ind.: University of Notre Dame Press, 1968. 54–86.

———. "God's Wenches and the Light That Spoke." In *English and Medieval Studies Presented to J. R. R. Tolkien*, ed. Norman Davis and C. L. Wrenn. London: Allen and Unwin, 1962. 200–218.

———. "The Pardon of *Piers Plowman*." *Proceedings of the British Academy* 30 (1946 for 1944): 303–57. Repr. in *Style and Symbolism in Piers Plowman: A Modern Critical Anthology*, ed. Robert J. Blanch. Knoxville: University of Tennessee Press, 1969. 40–86.

Coleman, Janet. *Piers Plowman and the "Moderni"*. Rome: Edizione di Storia e Letteratura, 1981.

———. "Property and Poverty." In *The Cambridge History of Medieval Political Thought*, ed. J. H. Burns. Cambridge: Cambridge University Press, 1988. 607–48.

Colish, Marcia L. *Peter Lombard*. 2 vols., continuously paginated. Leiden: Brill, 1994.

Collins, A. Jefferies, ed. *Manuale ad Vsum Percelebris ecclesie sarisburiensis*. Henry Bradshaw Society 91. Chichester: Moore and Tillyer, 1960 (for 1958).

Conlee, John. *Middle English Debate Poetry: A Critical Anthology*. East Lansing, Mich.: Colleagues Press, 1991.

Cooper, Helen. "Gender and Personification in *Piers Plowman*." *Yearbook of Langland Studies* 5 (1991): 31–4.

Cornelius, Roberta D. *The Figurative Castle: A Study of the Mediaeval Allegory of the Edifice with Especial Reference to Religious Writings*. Published dissertation. Bryn Mawr, Pa.: Bryn Mawr College, 1930.

Couvrer, Gilles. *Les pauvres ont-ils des droits? Recherches sur le vol en cas d'extrême nécessité*. Rome: Presses de l'Université Grégorienne, 1961.

Cowling, David. *Building the Text: Architecture as Metaphor in Late Medieval and Early Modern France*. Oxford: Clarendon Press, 1998.

Crane, Susan. "Knights in Disguise: Identity and Incognito in Fourteenth-Century Chivalry." In *The Stranger in Medieval Society*, ed. F. R. P. Akehurst and Stephanie Cain Van D'Elden. Minneapolis: University of Minnesota Press, 1997. 63–79.

———. "The Writing Lesson of 1381." In *Chaucer's England: Literature in Historical Context*, ed. Barbara Hanawalt. Minneapolis: University of Minnesota Press, 1992. 201–21.

Creek, Sister Mary Immaculate. "The Sources and Influence of Robert Grosseteste's *Le Chasteau d'Amour*." Dissertation, Yale University, 1941.

Curry, Walter Clyde. *Chaucer and the Mediæval Sciences*. Oxford: Oxford University Press, 1926. 2nd ed. New York: Barnes and Noble, 1960.

Curtius, Ernst Robert. *European Literature and the Latin Middle Ages*. 1948. Trans. Willard R. Trask. New York: Harper and Row, 1953.

Dahmus, Joseph H. "John Wyclif and the English Government." *Speculum* 35 (1960): 51–68.

Davis, A. H., ed. *William Thorne's Chronicle of Saint Augustine's Abbey, Canterbury*. Oxford: Blackwell, 1934.

Davis, Norman, ed. *Non-Cycle Plays and Fragments*. Early English Text Society Supplementary Text 1. London: Oxford University Press, 1970.

Davlin, Sister Mary Clemente, O.P. *A Game of Heaven: Word Play and the Meaning of Piers Plowman B.* Cambridge: D.S. Brewer, 1989.

———. "*Kynde Knowyng* as a Major Theme in *Piers Plowman B.*" *Review of English Studies* n.s. 22 (1971): 1–19.

———. "*Piers Plowman* and the Gospel and First Epistle of John." *Yearbook of Langland Studies* 10 (1996): 89–127.

Dean, James M., ed. *Medieval English Political Writings.* Kalamazoo, Mich.: Medieval Institute Publications, 1996.

———. *The World Grown Old in Later Medieval Literature.* Cambridge, Mass.: Medieval Academy of America, 1997.

de Clerk, D. E. "Droits de démon et necessité de la rédemption: Les écoles d'Abélard et de Pierre Lombard." *Recherches de théologie ancienne et médiévale* 14 (1947): 32–64.

———. "Questions de sotériologie médiévale." *Recherches de théologie ancienne et médiévale* 13 (1946): 150–84.

de Haas, Elsa and G. D. G. Hall, eds. *Early Registers of Writs.* Selden Society. London: Bernard Quaritch, 1970.

Delbouille, Maurice, ed. *Jacques Bretel: Le Tournoi de Chauvency.* Liège: Vaillant-Carmanne, 1932.

Denholm-Young, N. *Seignorial Administration in England.* London: Humphrey Milford, 1937.

D'Evelyn, Charlotte, ed. *Meditations on the Life and Passion of Christ.* Early English Text Society o.s. 158. London: Humphrey Milford, 1921 (for 1919).

Le Diable au moyen âge: Doctrine, problèmes moraux, représentations. Colloque CUERMA, 1978. Paris: H. Champion, 1979.

Dickinson, Francis H., ed. *Missale ad Usum Insignis et Praeclarae ecclesiæ Sarum.* Oxford: J. Parker, 1861–63.

Dobson, E. J. "The Etymology and Meaning of *Boy.*" *Medium Ævum* 9 (1940): 121–54.

Dolan, T. P. "Langland and FitzRalph: Two Solutions to the Mendicant Problem." *Yearbook of Langland Studies* 2 (1988): 35–45.

———. "Shame on Meed." In *Suche Werkis to Werche: Essays on Piers Plowman in Honor of David C. Fowler,* ed. Míceál Vaughan. East Lansing, Mich.: Colleagues Press, 1993. 81–88.

Dölger, F. J. "*Sol Salutis*": *Gebet und Gesang im christlichen Altertum.* Münster in Westfalen: Aschendorff, 1925; repr. 1972.

Donaldson, E. Talbot. "Apocalyptic Style in *Piers Plowman B* xix–xx." In *Essays in Memory of Elizabeth Salter,* ed. Derek Pearsall, *Leeds Studies in English* n.s. 14 (1983): 74–81.

———. "The Grammar of Book's Speech in *Piers Plowman.*" In *Studies in Language and Literature in Honour of Margaret Schlauch,* ed. Mieczyslaw Brahmer, Stanislaw Helszty'nski, and Julian Krzyzanowski. Warsaw: Polish Scientific Publishers, 1966. 103–9.

———. "Langland and Some Scriptural Quotations." In *The Wisdom of Poetry: Essays in Early English Literature in Honor of Morton W. Bloomfield,* ed. Larry D. Benson and Siegfried Wenzel. Kalamazoo, Mich.: Medieval Institute Publications, 1982. 67–82.

———. *Piers Plowman: The C-Text and Its Poet.* New Haven, Conn.: Yale University Press, 1949; repr. London: Frank Cass., 1966.

———. *William Langland, Piers Plowman: An Alliterative Verse Translation.* New York: Norton, 1990.

Donatelli, Joseph M. P., ed. *Death and Liffe.* Cambridge, Mass.: Medieval Academy of America, 1989.

Donna, Sister Rose Bernard. *Despair and Hope: A Study in Langland and Augustine.* Washington, D.C.: Catholic University of America Press, 1948.

Doty, Brant Lee. "An Edition of British Museum Manuscript *Additional 37049*: A Religious Miscellany." Dissertation, Michigan State University, 1969.

Douglas, E. Jane Dempsey. *Justification in Late Medieval Preaching: A Study of John Geiler of Keisersberg.* Leiden: Brill, 1966.

Douteil, Heriberto, ed. *Johannes Beleth "Summa de Ecclesiasticis Officiis".* Turnhout: Brepols, 1976.

Doyle, Eric. "William Woodford's 'De dominio civili clericorum' Against John Wyclif." *Archivum Franciscanum Historicum* 66 (1973): 49–109.

Dreves, Guido Maria. *Ein Jahrtausend lateinischer Hymnendichtung.* Parts 1 and 2. Leipzig, 1909; repr. Bologna: Forni, 1969.

Duffy, Eamon. *The Stripping of the Altars: Traditional Religion in England, c. 1400-c. 1580.* New Haven, Conn.: Yale University Press, 1992.

Duggan, Hoyt N. "The Role of Formulas in the Dissemination of a Middle English Alliterative Romance." *Studies in Bibliography* 29 (1976): 265–88.

———. "The Shape of the B-Verse in Middle English Alliterative Poetry." *Speculum* 61 (1986): 564–92.

du Méril, Edélestand, ed. *Poésies populaires latines antérieures au douzième siècle.* Paris: Brockhaus et Avenarius, 1843; repr. Bologna: Forni, 1969.

Dunning, T. P. "Langland and the Salvation of the Heathen." *Medium Ævum* 12 (1943): 45–54.

———. *Piers Plowman: An Interpretation of the A-Text.* London: Longmans, Green, 1937. 2nd ed. rev. T. P. Dolan. Oxford: Clarendon Press, 1980.

Durandus, Gulielmus. *Rationale divinorum officiorum.* Venice: Gratiosus Perchacinus, [1568].

Dustoor, P. E. "Legends of Lucifer in Early English and in Milton." *Anglia* 54 (1930): 213–68.

Ebermann, Oskar. *Blut- und Wundsegen.* Palaestra 24. Berlin: Mayer and Müller, 1903.

Eccles, Mark, ed. *The Macro Plays.* Early English Text Society o.s. 262. London: Oxford University Press, 1969.

Emmerson, Richard K. *Antichrist in the Middle Ages: A Study of Medieval Apocalypticism.* Seattle: University of Washington Press, 1981.

———. " 'Coveitise to Konne,' 'Goddes Pryvetee,' and Will's Ambiguous Dream Experience in *Piers Plowman*." In *Suche Werkis to Werche: Essays on Piers Plowman in Honor of David C. Fowler,* ed. Míceál Vaughan. East Lansing, Mich.: Colleagues Press, 1993. 89–121.

———. "The Prophetic, the Apocalyptic, and the Study of Medieval Literature." In *Poetic Prophecy in Western Literature,* ed. Jan Wojcik and Raymond-Jean Frontain. Rutherford, N.J.: Fairleigh Dickinson University Press, 1984. 40–54, 190–94.

———. " 'Yernen to Rede Redels?': *Piers Plowman* and Prophecy." *Yearbook of Langland Studies* 7 (1993b): 27–76.

Emmerson, Richard K. and David F. Hult, trans. *Antichrist and Judgment Day: The Middle French "Jour du Jugement".* Asheville, N.C.: Pegasus Press, 1998.

England, George and Alfred W. Pollard, eds. *The Towneley Plays*. Early English Text Society e.s. 71, 1897; repr. London: Oxford University Press, 1966.

Erzgräber, Willi. "Apokalypse und Antichrist in der englischen Literatur des 14. Jahrhunderts: William Langlands *Piers Plowman*, Joachim von Fiore und der Chiliasmus des Mittelalters." *Literaturwissenschaftliches Jahrbuch* n.f. 29 (1988): 233–51.

Evans, W. O. "Charity in *Piers Plowman*." In *Piers Plowman: Critical Approaches*, ed. S. S. Hussey. London: Methuen, 1969. 245–78.

Fairholt, F. W. *Costume in England*. Rev. H. A. Dillon. 2 vols. 3rd ed. London: G. Bell, 1885.

Fairweather, Eugene R. "'Iustitia Dei' as the 'Ratio' of the Incarnation." *Spicilegium Beccense*, 327–35. Congrès International du IXe Centenaire de l'Arrivée d'Anselm au Bec. Paris: J. Vrin, 1959.

———. *A Scholastic Miscellany: Anselm to Ockham*. Philadelphia: Westminster Press, 1956.

Farr, William. *John Wyclif as a Legal Reformer*. Leiden: Brill, 1974.

Feasey, Henry John. *Ancient English Holy Week Ceremonial*. London: Thomas Baker, 1897.

Fletcher, Alan J. *Preaching, Politics and Poetry in Late Medieval England*. Dublin: Four Courts Press, 1998.

———. "The Social Trinity of *Piers Plowman*." Cited from *Review of English Studies* 44 (1993): 343–61; revised in Fletcher 1998: 216–32 (see previous entry).

Ford, Alvin E., ed. *L'Evangile de Nicodème: Les versions courtes en ancien français et en prose*. Geneva: Droz, 1973.

Forshall, Josiah and Frederic Madden, eds. *The Holy Bible . . . by John Wycliffe and His Followers*. 4 vols. Oxford: Oxford University Press, 1850.

Foster, Frances A. *The Northern Passion*. Parts I and II, Early English Text Society o.s. 145, 147. London: Kegan Paul, 1913, 1916 (for 1912). Supplement, ed. Wilhelm Heuser and Frances A. Foster. Early English Text Society o.s. 183. London: Humphrey Milford, 1930.

Fowler, David C. "Editorial 'Jamming': Two New Editions of *Piers Plowman*." *Review* (University of Virginia) 2 (1980): 211–69.

———. "A New Edition of the B Text of *Piers Plowman*." *Yearbook of English Studies* 7 (1977): 23–42.

———. *Piers the Plowman: Literary Relations of the A and B Texts*. Seattle: University of Washington Press, 1961.

———. "Star Gazing: *Piers Plowman* and the Peasant's Revolt." *Review* (University of Virginia) 18 (1996): 1–30.

Fowler, Roger R. *The Southern Version of "Cursor Mundi"*. Vol. 2. Ottawa: University of Ottawa Press, 1990.

Francis, W. Nelson. "Chaucer Shortens a Tale." *PMLA* 68 (1953): 1126–41.

———, ed. *The Book of Vices and Virtues: A Fourteenth-Century English Translation of the Somme le Roi of Lorens d'Orléans*. Early English Text Society o.s. 217. London: Oxford University Press, 1942.

Frank, Robert W., Jr. "The Conclusion of *Piers Plowman*." *Journal of English and Germanic Philology* 49 (1950): 309–16.

———. "The Number of Visions in *Piers Plowman*." *Modern Language Notes* 66 (1951): 309–12.

————. *Piers Plowman and the Scheme of Salvation.* New Haven, Conn.: Yale University Press, 1957; repr. Hamden, Conn.: Archon Books, 1969.

Frankl, Paul. *The Gothic: Literary Sources and Interpretations Through Eight Centuries.* Princeton, N.J.: Princeton University Press, 1960.

Franks, Robert S. *The Work of Christ: A Historical Study of Christian Doctrine.* 2nd ed. London: Thomas Nelson, 1962.

French, Walter Hoyt and Charles Brockway Hale, eds. *Middle English Metrical Romances.* New York: Prentice-Hall, 1930.

Friedberg, Æmilius, ed. *Corpus Iuris Canonici. Pars Prima: Decretum Magistri Gratiani.* Leipzig: Tauchnitz, 1879; repr. Graz: Akademische Druck- und Verlagsanstatt, 1959. See also Richter.

Friedman, John B. "Figural Typology in the Middle English *Patience.*" In *The Alliterative Tradition in the Fourteenth Century,* ed. Bernard S. Levy and Paul E. Szarmack. Kent, Ohio: Kent State University Press, 1981. 99–129.

————. "The Friar Portrait in Bodleian Library MS. Douce 104: Contemporary Satire?" *Yearbook of Langland Studies* 8 (1994): 177–85.

Fry, Timothy. "The Unity of the *Ludus Coventriæ.*" *Studies in Philology* 48 (1951): 527–70.

Furnivall, Frederick J. *Hymns to the Virgin and Christ, The Parliament of Devils, and Other Religious Poems.* Early English Text Society o.s. 24. London: Trübner, 1867; repr. 1895.

Furnivall, Frederick J. and Katherine B. Locock, eds. *The Pilgrimage of the Life of Man, Englisht by John Lydgate.* Early English Text Society e.s. 77, 83, 92. London: Kegan Paul, Trench, Trübner, 1899–1904.

Furrow, Melissa M. "Latin and Affect." In *The Endless Knot: Essays on Old and Middle English in Honor of Marie Borroff,* ed. M. Teresa Tavormina and Robert F. Yeager. Cambridge: D.S. Brewer, 1995. 29–41.

Gaffney, Wilbur. "The Allegory of the Christ-Knight in *Piers Plowman.*" *PMLA* 46 (1931): 155–68.

Galbraith, V. H. "Articles Laid Before the Parliament of 1371." *English Historical Review* 34 (1919): 579–82.

Gallagher, Patrick J. "Imagination, Prudence, and the *Sensus Communis.*" *Yearbook of Langland Studies* 5 (1991): 49–64.

Galloway, Andrew. "Intellectual Pregnancy, Metaphysical Femininity, and the Social Doctrine of the Trinity in *Piers Plowman.*" *Yearbook of Langland Studies* 12 (1998): 118–52.

————. "The Making of a Social Ethic in Late-Medieval England: From *Gratitudo* to 'Kyndenesse'." *Journal of the History of Ideas* 55 (1994): 365–83.

————. "*Piers Plowman* and the Schools." *Yearbook of Langland Studies* 6 (1992): 89–107.

————. "Two Notes on Langland's Cato: *Piers Plowman* B I.88–91; IV.20–23." *English Language Notes* 25 (1987): 9–12.

————. "Uncharacterizable Entities: The Poetics of Middle English Scribal Culture and the Definitive *Piers Plowman.*" *Studies in Bibliography* 52 (1999): 59–87.

Gasquet, Cardinal. *Parish Life in Medieval England.* 5th ed. London: Methuen, 1922.

Gasse, Rosanne. "Langland's 'Lewed Vicory' Reconsidered." *Journal of English and Germanic Philology* 95 (1996): 322–35.

Georgianna, Linda. "Love So Dearly Bought: The Terms of Redemption in *The Canterbury Tales*." *Studies in the Age of Chaucer* 12 (1990): 85–116.

Giancarlo, Matthew. "*Piers Plowman*, Parliament, and the Public Voice." *Yearbook of Langland Studies* 17 (2003): 135–74.

Gilbert, Beverly Brian. "'Civil' and the Notaries in *Piers Plowman*." *Medium Ævum* 50 (1981): 49–63.

Ginsberg, Warren, ed. *Wynnere and Wastoure and The Parlement of the Three Ages*. Kalamazoo, Mich.: Medieval Institute Publications, 1992.

Given-Wilson, Chris, ed. and trans. *Chronicles of the Revolution 1379–1400: The Reign of Richard II*. Manchester: Manchester University Press, 1993.

———. "Purveyance for the Royal Household." *Bulletin of the Institute of Historical Research* 56 (1983): 145–63.

———. *The Royal Household and the King's Affinity: Service, Politics, and Finance, 1360–1413*. New Haven, Conn.: Yale University Press, 1986.

Glossa Ordinaria. Biblia Latina cum Glossa Ordinaria. Facsimile Reprint of the Editio Princeps. Adolph Rusch of Strassburg 1480/81. Intro. Karlfried Froelich and Margaret T. Gibson. 4 vols. Turnhout: Brepols, 1992.

Godden, Malcolm. *The Making of Piers Plowman*. London: Longman, 1990.

———. "Plowmen and Hermits in L's *Piers Plowman*." *Review of English Studies* 35 (1984): 129–63.

Goldsmith, Margaret E. *The Figure of Piers Plowman: The Image on the Coin*. Cambridge: D.S. Brewer, 1981.

———. "Piers' Apples: Some Bernardine Echoes in *Piers Plowman*." *Leeds Studies in English* n.s. 16 (1985): 309–25.

———. "Will's Pilgrimage in *Piers Plowman B*." In *Medieval Literature and Antiquities: Studies in Honour of Basil Cottle*, ed. Myra Stokes and T. L. Burton. Cambridge: D.S. Brewer, 1987. 119–32.

Goodman, Hadassah Posey. *Original Elements in the French and German Passion Plays*. Published dissertation. Bryn Mawr, Pa.: Bryn Mawr College, 1944.

Gradon, Pamela. "Langland and the Ideology of Dissent." *Proceedings of the British Academy* 66 (1982 for 1980): 179–205.

Gradon, Pamela and Anne Hudson, eds. *English Wycliffite Sermons*, vol. 4. Oxford: Clarendon Press, 1996.

Graesse, Th., ed. *Jacobi a Voragine: Legenda Aurea*. Dresden: Arnold, 1846. 3rd ed., 1890.

Gray, Douglas. *Themes and Images in the Medieval English Religious Lyric*. London: Routledge and Kegan Paul, 1972.

Gray, Nick. "Langland's Quotations from the Penitential Tradition." *Modern Philology* 84 (1986): 53–60.

Grayzel, Solomon. "The Avignon Popes and the Jews." *Historica Judaica* 2 (1940): 1–12.

Green, Richard Firth. "Changing Chaucer." *Studies in the Age of Chaucer* 25 (2003): 27–52.

———. *A Crisis of Truth: Literature and Law in Ricardian England*. Philadelphia: University of Pennsylvania Press, 1999.

———. "Friar William Appleton and the Date of Langland's B Text." *Yearbook of Langland Studies* 11 (1997): 87–96.

Gwynn, A. "The Date of the B-Text of *Piers Plowman*." *Review of English Studies* 19 (1943): 1–24.

————. *The English Austin Friars in the Time of Wyclif.* London: Humphrey Milford, 1940.

Haacke, Hrabanus, ed. *Ruperti Tuitensis Liber de divinis officiis.* Corpus Christianorum, Continuatio Medievalis 7. Turnhout: Brepols, 1967.

Hallman, Joseph M. *The Descent of God: Divine Suffering in History and Theology.* Minneapolis: Augsburg Fortress, 1991.

Hanawalt, Barbara, ed. *Chaucer's England: Literature in Historical Context.* Minneapolis: University of Minnesota Press, 1992.

Hanford, J. H. and J. M. Steadman, eds. "*Death and Liffe.*" *Studies in Philology* 15 (1918): 221–94.

Hanna, Ralph. "Emendations to a 1993 'Vita de Ne'erdowel'." *Yearbook of Langland Studies* 14 (2001 for 2000): 185–98.

————, ed. "Henry Daniel's *Liber Uricrisiarum* (Excerpt)." In *Popular and Practical Science of Medieval England,* ed. Lister M. Matheson. East Lansing, Mich.: Colleagues Press, 1994. 185–218.

————. "A New Edition of the C Version." *Yearbook of Langland Studies* 12 (1998): 175–88. = 1998a.

————. *Pursuing History: Middle English Manuscripts and Their Texts.* Stanford, Calif.: Stanford University Press, 1996.

————. "Reading Prophecy / Reading Piers." *Yearbook of Langland Studies* 12 (1998): 153–57. = 1998b.

————. *William Langland.* Aldershot, Hants.: Variorum, 1993.

————. "Will's Work." In *Written Work: Langland, Labor, and Authorship,* ed. Steven Justice and Kathryn Kerby-Fulton. Philadelphia: University of Pennsylvania Press, 1997. 23–66.

Hanna, Ralph and David Lawton, eds. *The Siege of Jerusalem.* Early English Text Society o.s. 320. Oxford: Oxford University Press, 2003.

Harbert, Bruce. "Langland's Easter." In *Langland, the Mystics, and the Medieval English Religious Tradition: Essays in Honor of S. S. Hussey,* ed. Helen Phillips. Cambridge: D.S. Brewer, 1990. 57–70.

Harnack, Adolf. "*Militia Christi*": *Die christliche Religion und der Soldatenstand in den ersten drei Jahrhunderten.* Tübingen: Mohr, 1905. Trans. David McInnes Gracie, *Militia Christi.* Philadelphia: Fortress Press, 1981.

Harvey, Margaret. "Simon Langham and the Reputation of Cardinals in England." Unpublished presentation at the Colloquium on Religious Orders in Pre-Reformation England, York, September 1999.

Harvey, P. D. A. *Manorial Records of Cuxham, Oxfordshire ca. 1200–1359.* London: Stationery Office, 1976.

Harwood, Britten J. *Piers Plowman and the Problem of Belief.* Toronto: University of Toronto Press, 1992.

Hector, L. C. and Barbara F. Harvey, eds. and trans. *The Westminster Chronicle 1381–94.* Oxford: Clarendon Press, 1982.

Heist, William. *The Fifteen Signs Before Doomsday.* East Lansing: Michigan State University Press, 1952.

Helmholz, R. H. "Crime, Compurgation and the Courts of the Medieval Church." *Law and History Review* 1 (1983): 1–26.

Henderson, W. G., ed. *Manuale et processionale ad usum insignis ecclesiæ Eboracensis.* Surtees Society 63. Durham: Andrews, 1875.

————, ed. *Processionale ad usum insignis et præclaræ ecclesiæ Sarum*. Leeds: M'Corquodale, 1882.

Henry, Avril, ed. *The Mirour of Mans Saluacioun: A Middle English Translation of Speculum Humanae Salvationis*. Philadelphia: University of Pennsylvania Press, 1987.

————. "Some Aspects of Biblical Imagery in *Piers Plowman*." In *Langland, the Mystics, and the Medieval English Religious Tradition: Essays in Honor of S. S. Hussey*, ed. Helen Phillips. Cambridge: D.S. Brewer, 1990. 39–55.

Heuser, Wilhelm. See Foster, Frances A.

Hewett-Smith, Kathleen M. "'Nede ne hath no lawe': Poverty and the De-stabilization of Allegory in the Final Visions of *Piers Plowman*." 233–53 in Hewett-Smith 2001b. = 2001a.

————, ed. *William Langland's Piers Plowman: A Book of Essays*. New York: Routledge, 2001. = 2001b.

Hickmann, Hans. *Das Portativ: Ein Beitrag zur Geschichte der Kleinorgel*. Kassel: Bärenreiter Verlag, 1936, 1972.

Hill, Betty, ed. "The Middle English Prose Version of the *Gospel of Nicodemus* from Washington, Library of Congress pre-Ac4." *Notes and Queries* 34 (232), no. 2 (June 1987): 156–75.

Hill, Thomas D. "Davidic Typology and the Characterization of Christ: *Piers Plowman* B.xix, 95–103." *Notes and Queries* n.s. 23 (January 1976): 291–94.

————. "Green and Filial Love: Two Notes on the Russell-Kane C Text: C.8.215 and C.17.48." *Yearbook of Langland Studies* 16 (2003 for 2002): 67–83.

————. "The Light That Blew the Saints to Heaven: *Piers Plowman* B, V.495–503." *Review of English Studies* n.s. 24 (1973): 444–49.

————. "Universal Salvation and Its Literary Context in *Piers Plowman* B.18." *Yearbook of Langland Studies* 5 (1991): 65–76.

Hinnebusch, William A. *The Early English Friars Preachers*. Rome: S. Sabina, 1951.

Hoffman, Richard L. "The Burning of 'Boke' in *Piers Plowman*." *Modern Language Quarterly* 25 (1964) 57–65.

Holmes, George. *The Good Parliament*. Oxford: Clarendon Press, 1975.

Holmstedt, Gustaf, ed. *"Speculum Christiani": A Middle English Treatise of the 14th Century*. Early English Text Society o.s. 182. London: Humphrey Milford, 1933 (for 1929).

Horowitz, Maryanne Cline. *Seeds of Virtue and Knowledge*. Princeton, N.J.: Princeton University Press, 1998.

Horstmann, Carl. *The Minor Poems of the Vernon MS*. Part I. Early English Text Society o.s. 98. London: Kegan Paul, Trench, Trübner, 1892.

Hort, Greta. *Piers Plowman and Contemporary Religious Thought*. London: Society for Promoting Christian Knowledge, 1938; repr. Folcroft, Pa.: Folcroft Library Classics, 1969.

Hoste, Anselm and C. H. Talbot, eds. *Aelred Rievallensis Opera Omnia*. Vol. 1, *Opera Ascetica*. Corpus Christianorum, Continuatio Mediævalis 1. Turnhout: Brepols, 1971.

Howlett, Richard. *Monumenta Franciscana*. 2nd vol. (Supplement). Rolls Series. London: Stationery Office, 1882; repr. Millwood, N.Y.: Kraus, 1965.

Hudson, Anne, ed. *English Wycliffite Sermons*. Vols. 1–3. Oxford: Clarendon Press, 1983–90.

————. "A Lollard Sect Vocabulary?" In *So meny people longages and tonges . . . Presented to Angus McIntosh*, ed. Michael Benskin and M. L. Samuels. Edinburgh: privately published by the editors, 1981. 15–30.

————. "*Piers Plowman* and the Peasants' Revolt: A Problem Revisited." *Yearbook of Langland Studies* 8 (1994): 85–106.

————. Review of David Wallace, ed., *The Cambridge History of Medieval English Literature. Yearbook of Langland Studies* 14 (2001 for 2000): 208–11.

Hughes, Andrew. *Medieval Manuscripts for Mass and Office: A Guide to Their Organization*. Toronto: University of Toronto Press, 1982.

Hulme, W. H., ed. *The Middle English Harrowing of Hell and Gospel of Nicodemus*. Early English Text Society e.s. 100. London: Oxford University Press, 1907.

Hunt, Tony. "'The Four Daughters of God': A Textual Contribution." *Archives d'Histoire Doctrinale et Littéraire du Moyen Âge* 56 (1982, for 1981): 287–316.

Huppé, Bernard F. "The Date of the B-Text of *Piers Plowman*." *Studies in Philology* 38 (1941): 34–44.

————. "*Petrus id est Christus*: Word Play in *Piers Plowman*." *English Literary History* 17 (1950): 163–90.

Hurnard, Naomi D. *The King's Pardon for Homicide Before A.D. 1307*. Oxford: Clarendon Press, 1969.

Hurst, D., ed. *In Lucae evangelium expositio*. Part 2, vol. 3 of *Bedae Venerabilis Opera*. Corpus Christianorum Series Latina 118–22. Turnhout: Brepols, 1955–80.

Hussey, S. S. "Langland, Hilton, and the Three Lives." *Review of English Studies* 7 (1956): 132–50.

————, ed. *Piers Plowman: Critical Approaches*. London: Methuen, 1969.

Izydorczyk, Zbigniew. "The Legend of the Harrowing of Hell in Middle English Literature." Dissertation, University of Toronto, 1985.

James, Mervyn. "Ritual, Drama and Social Body in the Late Medieval English Town." *Past and Present* 98 (1983): 3–29.

Jeffrey, David L. and Brian J. Levy. *The Anglo-Norman Lyric: An Anthology*. Studies and Texts 93. Toronto: Pontifical Institute of Mediæval Studies, 1990.

Jenkins, Priscilla. "Conscience: The Frustration of Allegory." In *Piers Plowman: Critical Approaches*, ed. S. S. Hussey. London: Methuen, 1969.

————. See also Martin, Priscilla.

Jodogne, Mer, ed. *Mystère de la Passion*. Brussels: Palais des Académies, 1965.

Jones, W. R. "Lollards and Images: The Defense of Religious Art in Later Medieval England." *Journal of the History of Ideas* 34 (1973): 27–50.

Jusserand, J. J. *Piers Plowman: A Contribution to the History of English Mysticism*. Trans. Marion Richards and Elise Richards. London: Unwin, 1894; repr. New York: Russell and Russell, 1965.

Justice, Steven. *Writing and Rebellion: England in 1381*. Berkeley: University of California Press, 1994.

Justice, Steven and Kathryn Kerby-Fulton, eds. *Written Work: Langland, Labor, and Authorship*. Philadelphia: University of Pennsylvania Press, 1997.

Kampers, Franz. *Die deutsche Kaiseridee in Prophetie und Sage*. Munich: Kaiser, 1896. Repr. Aalen: Scientia, 1969.

Kane, George. *Chaucer and Langland: Historical and Textual Approaches*. Berkeley: University of California Press, 1989.

———. "A New Translation of the B Text of *Piers Plowman*." *Yearbook of Langland Studies* 7 (1993): 129–56.

———. "The Perplexities of William Langland." In *The Wisdom of Poetry: Essays in Early English Literature in Honor of Morton W. Bloomfield*, ed. Larry D. Benson and Siegfried Wenzel. Kalamazoo, Mich.: Medieval Institute Publications, 1982. 73–89.

———. "*Piers Plowman*: Problems and Methods of Editing the B Text." *Modern Language Review* 43 (1948): 1–25.

———. "Poetry and Lexicography in the Tradition of *Piers Plowman*." *Medieval and Renaissance Studies* 9 (1982): 33–54; cited from Kane 1989 (see above).

———. "The Text." In *A Companion to Piers Plowman*, ed. John A. Alford. Berkeley: University of California Press, 1988. 175–200.

———. "Word Games: Glossing *Piers Plowman*." In *New Perspectives on Middle English Texts: A Festschrift for R. A. Waldron*, ed. Jeremy J. Smith and Susan Powell. Cambridge: Boydell and Brewer, 2000. 43–53.

Kantorowicz, Ernst H. *The King's Two Bodies: A Study of Medieval Political Theology*. Princeton, N.J.: Princeton University Press, 1957, 1997.

———. "*Laudes Regiæ*": A Study in Liturgical Acclamations and Medieval Ruler Worship*. Berkeley: University of California Press, 1946.

Kaske, Robert E. "The Defense." In *Critical Approaches to Medieval Literature: Selected Papers from the English Institute, 1958–59*, ed. Dorothy Bethurum. New York: Columbia University Press, 1960. 27–60.

———. "*Gigas* the Giant in *Piers Plowman*." *Journal of English and Germanic Philology* 56 (1957): 177–85.

———. "*Piers Plowman* and Local Iconography." *Journal of the Warburg and Courtauld Institutes* 51 (1988): 184–86.

———. Review of Morton W. Bloomfield, *Piers Plowman as a Fourteenth-Century Apocalypse*. *Journal of English and Germanic Philology* 62 (1963): 202–8.

———. "The Speech of 'Book' in *Piers Plowman*." *Anglia* 77 (1959): 117–44.

Kean, P. M. "Justice, Kingship and the Good Life in the Second Part of *Piers Plowman*." In *Piers Plowman: Critical Approaches*, ed. S. S. Hussey. London: Methuen, 1969. 76–110, 331–35.

———. "Love, Law, and *Lewte* in *Piers Plowman*." *Review of English Studies* n.s. 15 (1964): 241–61. Repr. in *Style and Symbolism in Piers Plowman: A Modern Critical Anthology*, ed. Robert J. Blanch. Knoxville: University of Tennessee Press, 1969. 156–73.

Keen, Maurice. *Chivalry*. New Haven, Conn.: Yale University Press, 1984.

———. "Brotherhood in Arms." *History* 47 (1962): 1–19.

Kellogg, Alfred L. "Langland and Two Scriptural Texts." *Traditio* 14 (1958): 385–98.

———. "Langland and the 'Canes Muti'." In *Essays in Literary History Presented to J. Milton French*, ed. Rudolf Kirk and C. F. Main. New York: Russell and Russell, 1965. 25–35.

Kelly, Henry Ansgar. "The Metamorphosis of the Eden Serpent During the Middle Ages and Renaissance." *Viator* 2 (1971): 301–27.

———. "Sacraments, Sacramentals, and Lay Piety in Chaucer's England." *Chaucer Review* 28 (1993): 5–23.

Kengen, J. H. L., ed. "*Memoriale Credencium*: A Late Middle English Manual of Theology for Lay People." Dissertation, Katholieke Universiteit Nijmegen, 1979.

Kennedy, Ruth, ed. "'A Bird in Bishopswood': Some Newly Discovered Lines of Alliterative Verse from the Late Fourteenth Century." In *Medieval Literature and Antiquities: Studies in Honour of Basil Cottle*, ed. Myra Stokes and T. L. Burton. Cambridge: D.S. Brewer, 1987. 71–87.

Kerby-Fulton, Kathryn. "*Piers Plowman.*" In *The Cambridge History of Medieval English Literature*, ed. David Wallace. Cambridge: Cambridge University Press, 1999. 513–38.

———. *Reformist Apocalypticism and Piers Plowman.* Cambridge: Cambridge University Press, 1990.

———. Review of *Yearbook of Langland Studies* 6 (1993) and Míčeál Vaughan, ed., *Suche Werkis to Werche: Essays on Piers Plowman in Honor of David C. Fowler. Modern Language Review* 91 (1996): 691–96.

Kerby-Fulton, Kathryn and Steven Justice. "Langlandian Reading Circles and the Civil Service in London and Dublin, 1380–1427." *New Medieval Literatures* 1 (1997): 59–83.

Kim, Hack Chin, ed. *The Gospel of Nicodemus.* Toronto: Pontifical Institute of Mediæval Studies, 1973.

Kim, Margaret. "Hunger, Need, and the Politics of Poverty in *Piers Plowman.*" *Yearbook of Langland Studies* 16 (2003 for 2002): 131–68.

———."The *Gospel of Nicodemus* Translated by John Trevisa." Dissertation, University of Washington, 1963.

Kipling, Gordon. *Enter the King: Theatre, Liturgy, and Ritual in the Medieval Civic Triumph.* Oxford: Clarendon Press, 1998.

———. "Richard II's 'Sumptuous Pageants' and the Idea of the Civic Triumph," In *Pageantry in the Shakespearean Theater*, ed. David M. Bergeron. Athens: University of Georgia Press, 1985. 83–103.

Kirk, Elizabeth D. *The Dream Thought of Piers Plowman.* New Haven, Conn.: Yale University Press, 1972.

Knight, Ione Kemp, ed. *Wimbledon's Sermon "Redde Rationem Villicationis Tue".* Pittsburgh: Duquesne University Press, 1967.

Knowles, Dom David. *The Religious Orders in England.* 3 vols. Cambridge: Cambridge University Press, 1948–59. Vol. 2, 1955.

Kölbing, Eugen and Mabel Day, eds. *The Siege of Jerusalem.* Early English Text Society o.s. 188. London: Humphrey Milford, 1932.

Kolve, V. A. *The Play Called Corpus Christi.* Stanford, Calif.: Stanford University Press, 1966.

Kristensson, Gillis, ed. *John Mirk's "Instructions for Parish Priests".* Lund: Gleerup, 1974.

Krochalis, Jeanne and Edward Peters, eds. and trans. *The World of Piers Plowman.* Philadelphia: University of Pennsylvania Press, 1975.

Kroll, Josef. *Gott und Hölle: Der Mythos vom Descensuskampfe.* Leipzig: Teubner, 1932.

Lambert, Malcolm D. *Franciscan Poverty: The Doctrine of the Absolute Poverty of Christ and the Apostles in the Franciscan Order, 1210–1323.* London: S.P.C.K., 1961. Rev. ed. St. Bonaventure, N.Y.: Franciscan Institute, 1998.

Lawler, Traugott. "Conscience's Dinner." In *The Endless Knot: Essays on Old and Middle English in Honor of Marie Borroff*, ed. M. Teresa Tavormina and Robert F. Yeager. Cambridge: D.S. Brewer, 1995. 87–103.

———. "The Gracious Imagining of Redemption in *Piers Plowman*." *English* 28 (1979): 203–16.

———. *The One and the Many in the Canterbury Tales*. Hamden, Conn.: Archon, 1980.

———. "The Pardon Formula in *Piers Plowman*: Its Ubiquity, Its Binary Shape, Its Silent Middle Term." *Yearbook of Langland Studies* 14 (2001 for 2000): 117–52.

———. "The Secular Clergy in *Piers Plowman*." *Yearbook of Langland Studies* 16 (2003 for 2002): 85–117.

———. "A Reply to Jill Mann, Reaffirming the Traditional Relation between the A and B Versions of *Piers Plowman*." *Yearbook of Langland Studies* 10 (1996): 145–80.

Lawlor, John. *Piers Plowman: An Essay in Criticism*. London: Edward Arnold, 1962.

Lawton, David A. "The Subject of *Piers Plowman*." *Yearbook of Langland Studies* 1 (1987): 1–30.

Lazar, Moshe. "Les Diables: Serviteurs et bouffons," *Tréteaux* 1 (1978): 51–69.

Lea, H. C. *A History of Auricular Confession and Indulgences in the Latin Church*. 3 vols. Philadelphia: Lea Brothers, 1896.

Leclercq, Jean and Henri Rochais, eds. *S. Bernardi Opera*. Vol. 5, *Sermones*, 2. Rome: Editiones Cistercienses, 1968.

Lee, B. S. "Antichrist and Allegory in Langland's Last Passus." *English Language Studies* (Capetown) (1971): 1–12.

Leff, Gordon. *Heresy in the Later Middle Ages*. 2 vols., continuously paginated. Manchester: Manchester University Press, 1967.

Le Goff, Jacques. *The Birth of Purgatory*. Trans. Arthur Goldhammer from *La naissance du Purgatoire*, Paris: Gallimard, 1981. Chicago: University of Chicago Press, 1984.

Le May, Sister Marie de Lourdes. *The Allegory of the Christ-Knight in English Literature*. Published dissertation. Washington, D.C.: Catholic University of America, 1932.

Lerner, Robert E. "Medieval Prophecies and Religious Dissent." *Past and Present* 72 (1976): 3–24. = 1976a.

———. "Refreshment of the Saints: The Time After Antichrist as a Station for Earthly Progress in Medieval Thought." *Traditio* 32 (1976): 97–144. = 1976b.

Lindsay, W. M., ed. *Isidori Hispalensis Episcopi Etymologiarum . . . Libri XX*. 2 vols., paginated separately in recent issues. Oxford: Clarendon Press, 1911.

Loomis, C. Grant. *White Magic: An Introduction to the Folklore of Christian Legend*. Cambridge, Mass.: Mediæval Academy of America, 1948.

Loserth, Iohann, ed. *Iohannis Wyclif Sermones*. 4 vols. Wyclif Society. London: Trübner, I, 1886; II, 1888; III, 1889; IV, 1890.

———, ed. *Iohannis Wyclif: Tractatus de Ecclesia*. London: Trübner, 1886; repr. New York: Johnson, 1966.

———. *Iohannis Wyclif: Opera Minora*. London: C.K. Paul, 1913; repr. New York: Johnson, 1966.

Lumby, Joseph R., ed. *Henry Knighton: Chronicon*. Rolls Series 92. London: Eyre and Spottiswoode, 1889–95.

Lumiansky, R. M. and David Mills, eds. *The Chester Mystery Cycle*. Early English Text Society suppl. ser. 3. London: Oxford University Press, 1974.

Lunt, William E. *Accounts Rendered by Papal Collectors in England, 1317–1378*. Ed. Edgar B. Graves. Philadelphia: American Philosophical Society, 1968.

———. *Financial Relations of the Papacy with England, 1327–1534*. Cambridge, Mass.: Mediæval Academy of America, 1962.

Lunz, Elizabeth. "The Valley of Jehoshaphat in *Piers Plowman.*" *Tulane Studies in English* 20 (1972): 1–10.

Luscombe, D. E. *The School of Peter Abelard: The Influence of Abelard's Thought in the Early Scholastic World.* Cambridge: Cambridge University Press, 1969.

Lyonnet, Stanislas and Léopold Sabourin. *Sin, Redemption, and Sacrifice: A Biblical and Patristic Study.* Rome: Biblical Institute, 1970.

Macaulay, G. C., ed. *The Works of John Gower.* Vol. 1 (*The French Works*); vol. 4 (*The Latin Works*). Oxford: Clarendon Press, 1899; 1902. *The English Works*, 2 vols. Early English Text Society e.s. 81, 82. Oxford: Oxford University Press, 1900–1901.

MacCullogh, J. A. *The Harrowing of Hell: A Comparative Study of Early Christian Doctrine.* Edinburgh: T. and T. Clark, 1930.

Mäder, Eduard Johann. *Der Streit "Töchter Gottes": Zur Geschichte eines allegorischen Motivs.* Bern: Herbert Lang, 1971.

Mâle, Emile. *L'Art religieux du XIIIᵉ siècle en France.* 9th ed. Paris: A. Colin, 1958.

Mann, Jill. "Allegorical Buildings in Mediæval Literature." *Medium Ævum* 63 (1994): 191–210.

———. *Chaucer and Medieval Estates Satire.* Cambridge: Cambridge University Press, 1973.

———. "The Nature of Need Revisited." *Yearbook of Langland Studies* 18 (2005 for 2004): 3–29.

Manual of Writings in Middle English. Ed. Albert E. Hartung. New Haven, Conn.: Connecticut Academy of Arts and Sciences, 1967-.

Marrow, James H. *Passion Iconography in Northern European Art of the Late Middle Ages and Early Renaissance.* Kortrijk, Belgium: Van Ghemmert, 1979.

Martin, A. R. *Franciscan Architecture in England.* Manchester: University Press, 1937. Repr. Farborough, Hants.: Gregg, 1966.

Martin, G. H., ed. and trans. *Knighton's Chronicle: 1337–1396.* Oxford: Clarendon Press, 1995.

Martin, Priscilla. *Piers Plowman: The Field and the Tower.* London: Macmillan, 1979.

———. "Response" to J. A. Burrow, "Gestures and Looks in *Piers Plowman,*" *Yearbook of Langland Studies* 14: 75–83. *Yearbook of Langland Studies* 14 (2001 for 2000): 84–89.

———. See also Jenkins, Priscilla.

Marx, C. William, ed. *"The Devils' Parliament" and "The Harrowing of Hell and Destruction of Jerusalem".* Middle English Texts 25. Heidelberg: Carl Winter, 1993.

———. *The Devil's Rights and the Redemption in the Literature of Medieval England.* Cambridge: D.S. Brewer, 1995.

Marx, C. William and Jeanne F. Drennan, eds. *The Middle English Prose Complaint of Our Lady and Gospel of Nicodemus.* Middle English Texts 19. Heidelberg: Carl Winter, 1987.

Maskell, William. *Monumenta Rituaba Ecclesiæ Anglicanæ.* 2nd ed. Oxford: Clarendon Press, 1882.

Mathes, Fulgence A. "The Poverty Movement and the Augustinian Hermits." *Analecta Augustiniana* 31 (1968): 5–154; 32 (1969): 5–116.

Matsuda, Takami. *Death and Purgatory in Middle English Didactic Poetry.* Cambridge: D.S. Brewer, 1997.

Mayo, Janet. *A History of Ecclesiastical Dress.* New York: Holmes and Meier, 1989.

Mazouer, Charles. *Le Théâtre français du moyen âge*. Paris: Sedes, 1998.

McAlindon, T. "The Emergence of a Comic Type in Medieval English Narrative: The Devil and Giant as Buffoon." *Anglia* 81 (1963): 365–71.

McGarry, Sister Loretta. *The Holy Eucharist in Middle English Homiletic and Devotional Verse*. Published dissertation. Washington, D.C.: Catholic University of America, 1936.

McGinn, Bernard, trans. "Angel Pope and Papal Antichrist." *Church History* 47 (1978): 155–73.

———. *Apocalyptic Spirituality: Treatises and Letters of Lactantius, Adso of Montier-en-Der, Joachim of Fiore, the Franciscan Spirituals, Savonarola*. New York: Paulist Press, 1979.

McKisack, May. *The Fourteenth Century: 1307–1399*. Oxford History of England. Oxford: Clarendon Press, 1959.

Meech, Sanford Brown and Hope Emily Allen, eds. *The Book of Margery Kempe*. Early English Text Society o.s. 212. London: Oxford University Press, 1940, repr. 1961.

Mensendieck, Otto. *Characterentwickelung und ethisch-theologische Anschauungen des Verfassers von Piers Plowman*. Inaugural dissertation, Giessen. London: Wohlleben, 1900.

Middle English Dictionary. Ed. Hans Kurath et al. Ann Arbor: University of Michigan Press, 1952–2001.

Middleton, Anne. "Acts of Vagrancy: The C Version 'Autobiography' and the Statute of 1388." In *Written Work: Langland, Labor, and Authorship*, ed. Steven Justice and Kathryn Kerby-Fulton. Philadelphia: University of Pennsylvania Press, 1997. 208–317.

———. "The Idea of Public Poetry in the Reign of Richard II." *Speculum* 53 (1978): 94–114.

———. "Langland's Lives: Reflections on Late-Medieval Religious and Literary Vocabulary." In *The Idea of Medieval Literature: New Essays in Early English Literature in Honor of Donald R. Howard*, ed. James M. Dean and Christian K. Zacher. Newark: University of Delaware Press, 1992. 227–42.

———. "Narration and the Invention of Experience: Episodic Form in *Piers Plowman*." In *The Wisdom of Poetry: Essays in Early English Literature in Honor of Morton W. Bloomfield*, ed. Larry D. Benson and Siegfried Wenzel. Kalamazoo, Mich.: Medieval Institute Publications, 1982. 91–122, 280–83.

———. "The Passion of Seint Averoys [B 13.91]: 'Deuynyng' and Divinity in the Banquet Scene." *Yearbook of Langland Studies* 1 (1987): 31–40.

Mills, Maldwyn, ed. *Ywain and Gawain; Sir Percyvell of Gales; The Anturs of Arther*. London: J.M. Dent, 1992.

Miller, Edward, ed. *The Agrarian History of England and Wales*. Vol. 3, *1348–1500*. Cambridge: Cambridge University Press, 1991.

Moore, R. I. *The Formation of a Persecuting Society: Power and Deviance in Western Europe, 950–1250*. Oxford: Blackwell, 1987.

Morris, Richard, ed. *Cursor Mundi*. Early English Text Society (London: Oxford University Press) o.s. 57: Part 1, ll. 1–4954, 1874, repr. 1961; o.s. 59: Part 2, ll. 4955–12558, 1875, repr. 1966; o.s. 62: Part 3, ll. 12559–19300, 1876, repr. 1966; o.s. 66: Part 4, ll. 19301–23826, 1877, repr. 1966; o.s. 68: Part 5, ll. 23827-end, 1878, repr. 1966; o.s. 99: Part 6, Pref., Notes, Gloss., 1892, repr. 1962; o.s. 101, essay by H. Hupe (disowned by Morris), Part 7, 1893, repr. 1962.

————, ed. *Legends of the Holy Rood*. Early English Text Society o.s. 46. London: Trübner, 1871.

————, ed. *The Pricke of Conscience*. Berlin: A. Asher, 1863.

Mossé, Armand. *Histoire des Juifs d'Avignon et du Comtat Venaissin*. Paris: Lipschutz, 1934; repr. Marseilles: Lafitte, 1976.

Mountain, W. J., ed. Augustine, *De Trinitate Libri XV*. Corpus Christianorum Series Latina 50–50A, continuous pagination. Turnhout: Brepols, 1968.

Mous, Peter H. J., ed. *The Southern Version of "Cursor Mundi"*. Vol. 4. Ottawa: University of Ottawa Press, 1986.

Mozley, J. K. *The Impassibility of God: A Survey of Christian Thought*. London: Cambridge University Press, 1926.

Murray, J., ed. *Le Château d'Amour de Robert Grosseteste*. Paris: Edouard Champion, 1918.

Murtaugh, Daniel Maher. *Piers Plowman and the Image of God*. Gainesville: University Presses of Florida, 1978.

Mustanoja, Tauno F. *A Middle English Syntax*. Part I. Helsinki: Société Néophilologique, 1960.

————. "The Suggestive Use of Christian Names in Middle English Poetry." In *Medieval Literature and Folklore Studies in Honor of Francis Lee Utley*, ed. Jerome Mandel and Bruce A. Rosenberg. New Brunswick, N.J.: Rutgers University Press, 1970. 51–76.

Narin van Court, Elisa. "The Hermeneutics of Supersession: The Revision of the Jews from the B to the C Text of *Piers Plowman*." *Yearbook of Langland Studies* 10 (1996): 43–87.

Nederman, Cary J. "Royal Taxation and the English Church: The Origins of William Ockham's *An princeps*." *Journal of Ecclesiastical History* 37 (1986): 377–88.

Neilson, George. *Trial by Combat*. Glasgow: Wm. Hodge, 1890.

Nelson, Alan H. "The Temptation of Christ; or, The Temptation of Satan." In *Medieval English Drama*, ed. Jerome Taylor and Alan H. Nelson. Chicago: University of Chicago Press, 1972. 218–29.

Nevanlinna, Saara. *The Northern Homily Cycle*. Vol. 2. Helsinki: Société Néophilologique, 1973.

Newhauser, Richard G. and John A. Alford, eds. *Literature and Religion in the Later Middle Ages: Philological Studies in Honor of Siegfried Wenzel*. Binghamton, N.Y.: Medieval and Renaissance Texts and Studies, 1995.

Newton, Stella May. *Fashion in the Age of the Black Prince*. Woodbridge, Suffolk: Boydell Press, 1980.

Noonan, John T. *The Scholastic Analysis of Usury*. Cambridge, Mass.: Harvard University Press, 1957.

Norton-Smith, John, ed. *John Lydgate: Poems*. Oxford: Clarendon Press, 1966.

————. *William Langland*. Medieval and Renaissance Authors 6. Leiden: Brill, 1983.

Oesterley, Hermann, ed. *Gesta Romanorum*. Berlin: Weidmann, 1872. Repr. Hildesheim: Georg Olms, 1963.

Ogilvie-Thomson, S. J., ed. *Richard Rolle: Prose and Verse*. Early English Text Society o.s. 293. Oxford: Oxford University Press, 1988.

Orme, Nicholas. *Education and Society in Medieval and Renaissance England*. London: Hambledon, 1989.

———. *English Schools in the Middle Ages.* London: Methuen, 1973.

Ormrod, W. M. *The Reign of Edward III.* New Haven, Conn.: Yale University Press, 1990.

Orsten, Elizabeth M. "*Patientia* in the B-Text of *Piers Plowman.*" *Mediæval Studies* 31 (1969): 317–33.

Oschinsky, Dorothea, ed. *Walter of Henley and Other Treatises on Estate Management and Accounting.* Oxford: Clarendon Press, 1971.

Overstreet, Samuel A. "Langland's Elusive Plowman." *Traditio* 45 (1989–90): 257–341.

Owen, D. D. R. *The Vision of Hell: Infernal Journeys in Medieval French Literature.* New York: Barnes and Noble, 1971.

Owen, Dorothy L. *Piers Plowman: A Comparison with Some Earlier and Contemporary French Allegories.* London: University of London Press (Hodder and Stoughton), 1912; repr. Folcroft, Pa.: Folcroft Library Editions, 1971.

Owst, G. R. *Literature and Pulpit in Medieval England.* Cambridge: Cambridge University Press, 1933. Rev. ed. Oxford: Blackwell, 1961.

———. *Preaching in Medieval England.* Cambridge: Cambridge University Press, 1926.

Oxford English Dictionary. 2nd ed., ed. J. A. Simpson and E. S. C. Weiner. Oxford: Clarendon Press, 1989. Cited from *The Compact Oxford English Dictionary.* Oxford: Oxford University Press, 1992.

Palmer, Robert C. *The Whilton Dispute, 1264–1380.* Princeton, N.J.: Princeton University Press, 1984.

Pantin, W. A. *The English Church in the Fourteenth Century.* London: Cambridge University Press, 1955.

Parkes, M. B. "The Literacy of the Laity." In *The Mediæval World*, ed. David Daiches and Anthony Thorlby. London: Aldus Books, 1973. 555–77.

Partner, Peter. *The Lands of St. Peter: The Papal State in the Middle Ages and Early Renaissance.* Berkeley: University of California Press, 1972.

Patrologia Latina. Ed. J.-P. Migne. *Patrologia Cursus Completus Series Latina.* 221 vols. Paris, 1844–64.

Pearsall, Derek. "Langland's London." In *Written Work: Langland, Labor, and Authorship*, ed. Steven Justice and Kathryn Kerby-Fulton. Philadelphia: University of Pennsylvania Press, 1997. 185–207.

———. "Poverty and Poor People in *Piers Plowman.*" In *Medieval English Studies Presented to George Kane*, ed. Donald Kennedy, Ronald Waldron, and Joseph S. Wittig. Woodbridge, Suffolk: D.S. Brewer, 1988.

———. *William Langland, William Blake, and the Poetry of Hope.* Bloomfield Lectures 5. Kalamazoo, Mich.: Medieval Institute Publications, 2003.

Pearsall, Derek and Kathleen Scott, eds. *Piers Plowman: A Facsimile of Bodleian Library, Oxford, MS Douce 104.* Cambridge: D.S. Brewer, 1992.

Peck, Russell A. "Social Conscience and the Poets." In *Social Unrest in the Late Middle Ages*, ed. Francis X. Newman. Binghamton, N.Y.: Medieval and Renaissance Textual Studies, 1986. 113–48.

Peebles, Rose Jeffries. *The Legend of Longinus in Ecclesiastical Tradition and in English Literature, and Its Connection with the Grail.* Bryn Mawr College Monographs 9. Baltimore: J.H. Furst, 1911.

Pelikan, Jaroslav. *The Growth of Medieval Theology (600–1300).* Chicago: University of Chicago Press, 1978.

Peltier, A. C., ed. *S. Bonaventuræ . . . opera omnia.* Vol. 12, 509–630, *Meditationes Vitæ Christi.* Paris: Ludovicus Vives, 1868.

Perroy, Edouard. *L'Angleterre et le grand schisme d'occident.* Paris: J. Monnier, 1933.

Perry, Anne Joubert Amari, ed. *La Passion des jongleurs.* Paris: Beauchesne, 1981.

Peverett, Michael. "'Quod' and 'Seide' in *Piers Plowman.*" *Neuphilologische Mitteil-ungen* 87 (1986): 117–27.

Pfaff, R. W. *New Liturgical Feasts in Later Medieval England.* Oxford: Clarendon Press, 1970.

Phillips, Helen, ed. *Langland, the Mystics, and the Medieval English Religious Tradition. Essays in Honor of S. S. Hussey.* Cambridge: D.S. Brewer, 1990.

Picciotto, Cyril M. "The Legal Position of the Jews in Pre-Expulsion England, as Shown by the Plea Rolls of the Jewish Exchequer." *Transactions of the Jewish Historical Society of England* 9 (1918–20): 67–84.

Pickering, O. S., ed. *The South English Ministry and Passion.* Middle English Texts 16. Heidelberg: Carl Winter, 1984.

Plucknett, Theodore F. T. *A Concise History of the Common Law.* Rochester, N.Y.: Lawyers' Cooperative, 1929. 5th ed. Boston: Little Brown, 1956.

Pollard, Alfred and Charles Sayle, eds. *Iohannis Wyclif: Tractatus de Officio Regis.* London: Trübner, 1887; repr. New York: Johnson, 1966.

Poole, Reginald Lane, ed. *Iohannis Wycliffe, Tractatus de Civili Dominio, Liber Primus.* Wyclif Society. London: Trübner, 1885.

Potts, Timothy C. *Conscience in Medieval Philosophy.* Cambridge: Cambridge University Press, 1980.

Powicke, F. M. and C. R. Cheney, eds. *Councils and Synods with Other Documents Relating to the English Church.* Vol. 2, Part 2, *1265–1313.* Oxford: Clarendon Press, 1964.

Proctor, F. and C. Wordsworth. *Breviarium ad usum insignis ecclesiæ Sarum.* 3 vols. Cambridge: Cambridge University Press, 1882–86.

Prost, Bernard, ed. *Traités du duel judiciaire, relations de pas d'armes et tournois.* Paris: Léon Willem, 1872.

Raby, F. J. E, ed. *The Poems of John Hoveden.* Durham: Andrews, 1939.

Rand, E. K. "Sermo de confusione diaboli." *Modern Philology* 2 (1904): 261–78.

Rashdall, Hastings. *The Idea of Atonement in Christian Theology.* London: Macmillan, 1920.

Raw, Barbara. "Piers and the Image of God in Man" In *Piers Plowman: Critical Approaches,* ed. S. S. Hussey. London: Methuen, 1969. 143–79.

Reeves, Marjorie K. *The Influence of Prophecy in the Later Middle Ages: A Study in Joachimism.* Oxford: Clarendon Press, 1969.

———. "Joachimist Influences on the Idea of a Last World Emperor." *Traditio* 17 (1961): 323–70.

Renevy, Denis. "Anglo-Norman and Middle English Translations and Adaptations of the Hymn *Dulcis Jesu Memoria.*" In *The Medieval Translator,* ed. Roger Ellis and René Tixier. Turnhout: Brepols, 1996. 264–83.

———. "Name Above Names: The Devotion to the Name of Jesus from Richard Rolle to Walter Hilton's *Scale of Perfection,* I." In *The Medieval Mystical Tradition,* ed. Marion Glasscoe. Cambridge: D.S. Brewer, 1999. 103–21.

Renouard, Yves. *Les Relations des papes d'Avignon et des compagnies commerciales et bancaires de 1316 à 1378.* Paris: E. de Boccard, 1941.

Richardson, Gavin. "Langland's Mary Magdalene: Proverbial Misogyny and the Problem of Authority." *Yearbook of Langland Studies* 14 (2001 for 2000): 163–84.

Richardson, H. G. *The English Jewry Under Angevin Kings*. London: Methuen, 1960.

Richter, Æmilius L. and Æmilius Friedberg, eds. *Corpus Iuris Canonici. Pars Secunda: Decretalium Collectiones*. 2nd ed. Leipzig: B. Tauchnitz, 1879–81. See also Friedberg.

Rickert, Edith. *Chaucer's World*. Ed. Clair C. Olson and Martin M. Crow. New York: Columbia University Press, 1948.

Rigg, J. M. *Select Pleas, Starrs, and Other Records from the Rolls of the Exchequer of the Jews: A.D. 1220–1284*. Selden Society. London: Bernard Quaritch, 1902.

Riley, Henry Thomas, ed. *Liber Albus. Munimenta Gildhallæ Londoniensis*. Vol. 1. London: Longman, Brown, 1859. Repr. Nendeln/Leichtenstein: Kraus, 1968.

———, ed. *Thomas Walsingham: Historia Anglicana*. 2 vols. Rolls Series, 1863, 1864.

Rivière, Jean. *Le Dogme de la rédemption au début du moyen âge*. Bibliothèque Thomiste, 19. Paris: J. Vrin, 1934.

Robbins, Rossell Hope, ed. *Historical Poems of the XIVth and XVth Centuries*. New York: Columbia University Press, 1959.

Robertson, D. W., Jr. and Bernard F. Huppé. *Piers Plowman and Scriptural Tradition*. Princeton, N.J.: Princeton University Press, 1951.

Ross, Woodburn O., ed. *Middle English Sermons*. Early English Text Society o.s. 149. London: Oxford University Press, 1940 (for 1938).

Roth, Cecil. *A History of the Jews in England*. Oxford: Clarendon Press, 1941. 3rd ed., 1964.

Rotuli Parliamentorum. Ed. J. Strachey. 6 vols. London: Stationery Office, 1767–77.

Rubin, Miri. *Charity and Community in Medieval Cambridge*. Cambridge: Cambridge University Press, 1987.

———. *Corpus Christi: The Eucharist in Late Medieval Culture*. Cambridge: Cambridge University Press, 1991.

Ruffing, John. "The Crucifixion Drink in *Piers Plowman* B.18 and C.20." *Yearbook of Langland Studies* 5 (1991): 99–109.

Runnalls, Graham A. *Le Mystère de la Passion Nostre Seignure*. Geneva: Droz, 1974.

Russell, George H. "Aspects of the Process of Revision in *Piers Plowman*." In *Piers Plowman: Critical Approaches*, ed. S. S. Hussey. London: Methuen, 1969. 27–49.

———. "The Salvation of the Heathen: The Exploration of a Theme in *Piers Plowman*." *Journal of the Warburg and Courtauld Institutes* 29 (1966): 101–16.

Russell, Jeffrey Burton. *Lucifer: The Devil in the Middle Ages*. Ithaca, N.Y.: Cornell University Press, 1984.

Russom, Geoffrey. "The Drink of Death in Old English and Germanic Literature." In *Germania: Comparative Studies in the Old Germanic Languages and Literatures*, ed. Daniel G. Calder and T. Craig Christy. Woodbridge, Suffolk: D.S. Brewer, 1988. 175–89.

Ryan, W. Granger and Helmut Ripperges, trans. *The Golden Legend of Jacobus de Voragine*. New York: Longmans, Green, 1941. Expanded ed., trans. Ryan. 2 vols. Princeton, N.J.: Princeton University Press, 1993.

Rymer, Thomas. *Foedera, conventiones, literæ, et cujuscunque generis acta publica*. 3rd ed. 10 vols. The Hague: Neulme, 1739–45.

Sadie, Stanley, ed. *The New Grove Dictionary of Music and Musicians*. 2nd ed. London: Macmillan, 2001.

St.-Jacques, Raymond. "Conscience's Final Pilgrimage in *Piers Plowman* and the Cyclical Structure of the Liturgy." *Revue de l'Université d'Ottawa* 40 (1970): 210–23.

———. "Langland's Christ-Knight and the Liturgy." *Revue de l'Université d'Ottawa* 37 (1967): 146–58.

———. "Langland's Bells of the Resurrection and the Easter Liturgy." *English Studies in Canada* 3 (1977): 129–35.

———. "Langland's *Christus Medicus* Image and the Structure of *Piers Plowman*." *Yearbook of Langland Studies* 5 (1991): 111–27.

Sajavaara, Kari, ed. *The Middle English Translations of Robert Grosseteste's "Chateau d'Amour"*. Helsinki: Société Néophilologique, 1967.

Salter, E. Gurney, trans. *The Coming of the Friars Minor to England and Germany*. London: J.M. Dent, 1926.

Salter, Elizabeth. "Langland and the Contexts of *Piers Plowman*." *Essays and Studies* 32 (1979): 19–25.

———. *Piers Plowman: An Introduction*. Oxford: Blackwell, 1962.

———. "*Piers Plowman* and *The Simonie*." In *English and International: Studies in the Literature, Art, and Patronage of Medieval England*, ed. Derek Pearsall and Nicolette Zeeman. Cambridge: Cambridge University Press, 1988. 158–69, 317–20.

———. "*Piers Plowman* and the Visual Arts." In *English and International* (see preceding entry). 256–71, 340–41.

Sargent, Michael G., ed. *Nicholas Love's "Mirror of the Blessed Life of Jesus Christ": A Critical Edition*. New York: Garland, 1992.

Saul, Nigel. *Richard II*. New Haven, Conn.: Yale University Press, 1997.

Sayles, George O. *Select Cases in the Court of King's Bench under Richard II, Henry IV and Henry V*, vol. 7. Selden Society. London: Bernard Quaritch, 1971.

Scase, Wendy. *Piers Plowman and the New Anticlericalism*. Cambridge: Cambridge University Press, 1989.

———. "Writing and the Plowman: Langland and Literacy." *Yearbook of Langland Studies* 9 (1995): 121–39.

Schmidt, A. V. C. *The Clerkly Maker: Langland's Poetic Art*. Cambridge: D.S. Brewer, 1987.

———. "The C-Version of *Piers Plowman*: A New Edition." *Notes and Queries* n.s. 27, 1 (Feb. 1980): 102–10.

———. "The Treatment of the Crucifixion in *Piers Plowman* and in Rolle's *Meditations on the Passion*." *Analecta Cartusiana* 35 (1983): 174–96.

———, trans. *William Langland: Piers Plowman. A New Translation of the B-Text*. Oxford: Oxford University Press, 1992.

———, ed. *William Langland: Piers Plowman. A Parallel-Text Edition*. Vol. I. London: Longman, 1995.

Schmitt, Franciscus Salesius. *S. Anselmi Cantuariensis Archepiscopi Opera Omnia*. Vol. 1. Stuttgart: Friedrich Fromman, 1968.

Schroeder, Mary C. "The Character of Conscience in *Piers Plowman*." *Studies in Philology* 67 (1970): 13–30.

———. See also Carruthers, Mary.

Seymour, M. C., ed. *Selections from Hoccleve*. Oxford: Clarendon Press, 1981.

———, gen. ed. *On the Properties of Things: John Trevisa's Translation of Bartholomæus Anglicus, "De proprietatibus rerum"*. 2 vols. Oxford: Clarendon Press, 1975.

Sheingorn, Pamela. *The Easter Sepulchre in England.* Kalamazoo, Mich.: Medieval Institute Publications, 1987.

Sheneman, Paul. "Debt and Its Double in *Piers Plowman.*" *Studia Neophilologica* 68 (1996): 185–94.

Shepherd, Geoffrey. "Poverty in *Piers Plowman.*" In *Social Relations and Ideas: Essays in Honour of R. H. Hilton,* ed. T. H. Aston et al. Cambridge: Cambridge University Press, 1983. 169–89.

Simpson, James. "'After Craftes Conseil clotheth yow and fede': Langland and London City Politics." In *England in the Fourteenth Century: Proceedings of the 1991 Harlaxton Symposium,* ed. Nicholas Rogers. Stamford, Eng.: Paul Watkins, 1993.

———. "The Constraints of Satire in *Piers Plowman* and *Mum and the Sothsegger.*" In *Langland, the Mystics, and the Medieval Religious Tradition: Essays in Honor of S. S. Hussey,* ed. Helen Phillips. Cambridge: D.S. Brewer, 1990. = 1990b.

———. "Desire and the Scriptural Text: Will as Reader in *Piers Plowman.*" In *Criticism and Dissent in the Middle Ages,* ed. Rita Copeland. Cambridge: Cambridge University Press, 1996. 215–43.

———. "Grace Abounding: Evangelical Centralization and the End of *Piers Plowman.*" *Yearbook of Langland Studies* 14 (2001, for 2000): 49–73. = 2001a.

———. *Piers Plowman: An Introduction to the B-Text.* London: Longman, 1990. = 1990a.

———. "The Power of Impropriety: Authorial Naming in *Piers Plowman.*" In *William Langland's Piers Plowman: A Book of Essays,* ed. Kathleen M. Hewett-Smith. New York: Routledge, 2001. = 2001b.

———. "Spiritual and Earthly Nobility in *Piers Plowman.*" *Neuphilologische Mitteilungen* 86 (1985): 467–81.

Skeat, Walter W. *A Student's Pastime, Being a Select Series of Articles from "Notes and Queries," Reprinted.* Oxford: Clarendon Press, 1896.

———, ed. *The Vision of William Concerning Piers Plowman.* Part IV, sect. 1, *Notes to Texts A, B, and C.* Early English Text Society o.s. 67. London: Trübner, 1877; repr. Millwood, N.Y.: Kraus, 1987.

Smith, Ben H. *Traditional Imagery of Charity in Piers Plowman.* The Hague: Mouton, 1966.

Smith, Toulmin and Lucy Toulmin Smith, eds. *English Gilds: The Original Ordinances of More Than One Hundred Early English Gilds.* Early English Text Society o.s. 40. London: Humphrey Milford, 1870; repr. 1924.

Smithers, G. V. "Five Notes on Old English Texts." *English and Germanic Studies* 4 (1951–52): 65–85.

Southworth, John. *The English Medieval Minstrel.* Woodbridge, Suffolk: Boydell Press, 1989.

Spalding, Mary Caroline. *The Middle English Charters of Christ.* Published dissertation. Bryn Mawr, Pa.: Bryn Mawr College, 1914.

Spector, Stephen. *The N-Town Play.* Vol. 1, *Introduction and Text.* Early English Text Society s.s. 11. Oxford: Oxford University Press, 1991.

Spencer, H. Leith. *English Preaching in the Late Middle Ages.* Oxford: Clarendon Press, 1993.

Stanesco, Michel. "Le Héraut d'armes et la tradition littéraire chevaleresque." *Romania* 106 (1985) 233–53.

Statutes of the Realm. Vol. 1. London: Eyre and Strahan, 1810; repr. London: Dawson's, 1963.

Stauffenberg, Henry J., ed. *The Southern Version of the Cursor Mundi.* Vol. 3. Ottawa: University of Ottawa Press, 1985.

Steinberg, Theodore L. *Piers Plowman and Prophecy: An Approach to the C-Text.* New York: Garland, 1991.

Stevens, Martin and A. C. Cawley, eds. *The Towneley Plays.* 2 vols. Early English Text Society s.s. 13. Oxford: Oxford University Press, 1994.

Stock, Lorraine Kochanske. "Parable, Allegory, History, and *Piers Plowman.*" *Yearbook of Langland Studies* 5 (1991): 143–64.

Stockton, Eric W., trans. *The Major Latin Works of John Gower.* Seattle: University of Washington Press, 1962.

Stokes, Myra. *Justice and Mercy in Piers Plowman: A Reading of the B Text Visio.* London: Croom Helm, 1984.

Stones, E. L. G. "The Folville's of Ashby-Folville, Leicestershire, and Their Associates in Crime, 1326–47." *Transactions of the Royal Historical Society* 5th ser. 7 (1957): 117–36.

Strayer, Joseph R. *Dictionary of the Middle Ages.* 13 vols. New York: Scribner's, 1982–89.

Strohm, Paul. "Saving the Appearances: Chaucer's *Purse* and the Fabrication of the Lancastrian Claim." In *Chaucer's England: Literature in Historical Context,* ed. Barbara Hanawalt. Minneapolis: University of Minnesota Press, 1992. 21–40.

Stürzinger, J. J., ed. *Le Pèlerinage Jhesucrist de Guillaume de Deguileville.* Roxburghe Club. London: Nichols and Sons, 1897.

———, ed. *Le Pèlerinage de Vie Humaine de Guillaume de Deguileville.* Roxburghe Club. London: Nichols and Sons, 1893.

Sullens, Idelle, ed. *Robert Mannynge of Brunne: Handlyng Synne.* Binghamton, N.Y.: Medieval and Renaissance Texts and Studies, 1983.

Sullivan, Francis A., S.J. *Salvation Outside the Church? Tracing the History of the Catholic Response.* New York: Paulist Press, 1992.

Swanson, R. N. *Church and Society in Late Medieval England.* Oxford: Blackwell, 1989.

———. "Passion and Practice: The Social and Ecclesiastical Implications of Passion Devotion in the Late Middle Ages." In *The Broken Body: Passion Devotion in Late-Medieval Culture,* ed. A. A. MacDonald, H. N. B. Ridderbos, and R. M. Schlusemann. Groningen: Egbert Forsten, 1998. 2–30.

———. "*Speculum ecclesie*? Sources for the Administrative History of the Late Medieval English Church." *Richerche di storia sociale e religiosa* n.s. 48 (1995): 13–32.

Szittya, Penn R. *The Antifraternal Tradition in Medieval Literature.* Princeton, N.J.: Princeton University Press, 1986.

Tait, James, ed. *Johannis de Reading et Anonymi Cantuariensis, 1346–67.* Manchester: Manchester University Press, 1914.

Tavormina, M. Teresa. "The Chilling of Charity: Eschatological Allusions and Revisions in *Piers Plowman* C.16–17." In *Art and Context in Late Medieval English Narrative: Essays in Honor of Robert Worth Frank, Jr.,* ed. Robert R. Edwards. Cambridge: D.S. Brewer, 1994. 51–77.

———. *Kindly Similitude: Marriage and Family in Piers Plowman.* Cambridge: D.S. Brewer, 1995. = 1995b

Tavormina, M. Teresa and Robert F. Yeager, eds. *The Endless Knot: Essays on Old and Middle English in Honor of Marie Borroff.* Cambridge: D.S. Brewer, 1995. = 1995a.

Temple-Leader, John and Giuseppe Marcotti. *Giovanni Acuto (Sir John Hawkwood): Storia d'un Condottiere*. Florence: G. Barbèra, 1889. Trans. Leader Scott, *Sir John Hawkwood (L'Acuto): Story of a Condottiere*. London: Unwin, 1889.

Tentler, Thomas N. *Sin and Confession on the Eve of the Reformation*. Princeton, N.J.: Princeton University Press, 1977.

Tester, S. J. *A History of Western Astrology*. Woodbridge, Suffolk: Boydell, 1987.

Theramo, Jacobus de. *Consolatio peccatorum, seu Processus Belial*. Augsburg: Schüssler, 1472.

Thomas, Arthur Hermann, ed. *Calendar of Select Pleas and Memoranda of the City of London . . . 1381–1412*. Cambridge: Cambridge University Press, 1932.

Thomas, J. A. C. *The Institutes of Justinian*. Capetown: Juta, 1975.

Thorne, Samuel E., ed. *Readings and Moots at the Inns of Court in the Fifteenth Century*. Vol. 1. Selden Society 61. London: Bernard Quaritch, 1954.

Tierney, Brian. *Medieval Poor Law*. Berkeley: University of California Press, 1959.

Tischendorf, Constantinus de. *Evangelia Apocrypha*. 2nd ed. Leipzig: Hermann Mendelssohn, 1876.

Traver, Hope. "The Four Daughters of God: A Mirror of Changing Doctrine." *PMLA* 40 (1925): 44–92.

———. *The Four Daughters of God: A Study of the Versions of This Allegory with Special Reference to Those in Latin, French, and English*. Bryn Mawr College Monographs 6. Bryn Mawr, Pa.: Bryn Mawr College, 1907.

Trenholme, Norman Maclaren. *The Right of Sanctuary in England*. Columbia: University of Missouri, 1903.

Troyer, Howard William. "Who Is Piers Plowman?" *PMLA* 47 (1932): 368–84. Repr. in *Style and Symbolism in Piers Plowman: A Modern Critical Anthology*, ed. Robert J. Blanch. Knoxville: University of Tennessee Press, 1969. 156–73.

Turner, Ralph V. "*Descendit ad Inferos*: Medieval Views on Christ's Descent into Hell and the Salvation of the Ancient Just." *Journal of the History of Ideas* 27 (1966): 173–94.

Tyrer, John Walton. *Historical Survey of Holy Week, Its Services and Ceremonial*. London: Oxford University Press, 1932.

Ullman, Walter. *The Origins of the Great Schism*. London: Burns Oates and Washbourne, 1948. Repr. Hamden, Conn.: Archon, 1967.

Vale, Malcolm. *War and Chivalry*. London: Duckworth, 1981.

van der Pot, J. H. J. *De Periodisering der Geschiedenis*. The Hague: van Stockum, 1951.

Vasta, Edward. *Interpretations of Piers Plowman*. Notre Dame, Ind.: University of Notre Dame Press, 1968.

———. *Middle English Survey: Critical Essays*. Notre Dame, Ind.: University of Notre Dame Press, 1965

Vaughan, Mícéál F. "The Liturgical Perspectives of *Piers Plowman* B, XVI-XIX." *Studies in Medieval and Renaissance History* 3 [o.s. 13] (1980): 87–155.

———, ed. *Suche Werkis to Werche: Essays on Piers Plowman in Honor of David C. Fowler*. East Lansing, Mich.: Colleagues Press, 1993.

———. "'Til I Gan Awake': The Conversion of Dreamer into Narrator in *Piers Plowman* B." *Yearbook of Langland Studies* 5 (1991): 175–92.

Verhelst, D., ed. *Adso Deruensis: De ortu et tempore antichristi*. Corpus Christianorum, Continuatio Mediævalis 45. Turnholt: Brepols, 1976.

Vinogradoff, Paul. *Roman Law in Medieval Europe*. Oxford: Clarendon Press, 1929. Repr. Cambridge: Speculum Historiale, 1968.

Vitto, Cindy L. *The Virtuous Pagan in Middle English Literature*. Transactions of the American Philosophical Society 79, part 5. Philadelphia: American Philosophical Society, 1989.

Vriend, Joannes. *The Blessed Virgin Mary in the Medieval Drama of England*. Dissertation, Amsterdam. Permerend, Netherlands: J. Muusses, 1928.

Wagner, Sir Anthony Richard. *Heralds of England: A History of the Office and College of Arms*. London: Stationery Office, 1967.

———. *Heralds and Heraldry in the Middle Ages*. London: Oxford University Press, 1956.

Wailes, Stephen L. *Medieval Allegories of Jesus' Parables*. Berkeley: University of California Press, 1987.

Waldron, R. A. "L's Originality: The Christ-Knight and the Harrowing of Hell." In *Medieval English Religious and Ethical Literature: Essays in Honour of G. H. Russell*, ed. Gregory Kratzmann and James Simpson. Cambridge: D.S. Brewer, 1986. 66–81.

Walsh, Katherine. *A Fourteenth-Century Scholar and Primate: Richard FitzRalph in Oxford, Avignon and Armagh*. Oxford: Clarendon Press, 1981.

Walther, H. *Das Streitgedicht in der lateinischen Literatur des Mittelalters*. München: Beck, 1920.

Warner, Lawrence. "Jesus the Jouster: The Christ-Knight and Medieval Theories of Atonement in *Piers Plowman* and the 'Round Table' Sermons." *Yearbook of Langland Studies* 10 (1996): 129–43.

Warton, Thomas. *The History of English Poetry*. Vol. 1. London: J. Dodsly, 1774.

Waterland, David. *A Critical History of the Athanasian Creed*. Ed. J. R. King, based on the 2nd ed. of 1727 (first pub. 1723). Oxford: James Parker, 1870.

Watson, Nicholas. "Conceptions of the Word: The Mother Tongue and the Incarnation of God." *New Medieval Literatures* 1 (1997): 85–124. = 1997a

———. "Visions of Inclusion: Universal Salvation and the Vernacular Theology of Pre-Reformation England." *Journal of Medieval and Early Modern Studies* 27 (1997): 145–87. = 1997b.

Way, Albertus, ed. *Promptorium Parvulorum*. Vol. 1. Camden Society 25. London: Camden Society, 1843.

Wee, David L. "The Temptation of Christ and the Motif of Divine Duplicity in the Corpus Christi Cycle Drama." *Modern Philology* 72 (1974): 1–16.

Weldon, James F. G. "Gesture of Perception: The Pattern of Kneeling in *Piers Plowman* B.18–19." *Yearbook of Langland Studies* 3 (1989): 49–66.

———. "The Structure of Dream Visions in *Piers Plowman*." *Medieval Studies* 49 (1987): 254–81.

Wells, Henry Willis. "The Construction of *Piers Plowman*." *PMLA* 44 (1929): 123–40. Repr. in *Interpretations of Piers Plowman*, ed. Edward Vasta. Notre Dame, Ind.: University of Notre Dame Press, 1968; *Middle English Survey: Critical Essays*, ed. Edward Vasta. Notre Dame, Ind.: University of Notre Dame Press, 1965. 147–68.

———. "The Philosophy of *Piers Plowman*." *PMLA* 53 (1938): 339–49. Repr. Vasta 1968: 115–29 (see preceding entry).

Wenzel, Siegfried, ed. and trans. *Fasciculus Morum: A Fourteenth-Century Preacher's Handbook*. University Park: Pennsylvania State University Press, 1989.

————, ed. *Summa virtutum de remediis anime*. Chaucer Library. Athens: University of Georgia Press, 1984.

Whatley, Gordon. "The Uses of Hagiography: The Legend of Pope Gregory and the Emperor Trajan in the Middle Ages." *Viator* 15 (1984): 25–63.

White, Hugh. *Nature and Salvation in Piers Plowman*. Cambridge: D.S. Brewer, 1988.

Whiting, Bartlett Jere, with Helen Wescott Whiting. *Proverbs, Sentences, and Proverbial Phrases from English Writings Mainly Before 1500*. Cambridge, Mass.: Harvard University Press, 1968.

Whittaker, William Joseph, ed. *The Mirror of Justices*. [By Andrew Horne.] Selden Society 7. London: Bernard Quaritch, 1895.

Whittridge, Ruth, ed. *La Nativité et Le Geu des Trois Roys*. Published dissertation. Bryn Mawr, Pa.: Bryn Mawr College, 1944.

Whitworth, Charles W., Jr. "Changes in the Roles of Reason and Conscience in the Revisions of *Piers Plowman*." *Notes and Queries* 217 n.s. 19 (January 1972): 4–7.

Wieck, Heinrich. *Die Teufel auf der mittelalterlichen Mysterienbühne Frankreichs*. Inaugural dissertation, Marburg. Leipzig: Hirschfeld, 1887.

Wilkes, G. L. "The Castle of Vnite in *Piers Plowman*." *Mediæval Studies* 27 (1965): 334–36.

Wilkins, David, ed. *Concilia Magnæ Britanniae et Hiberniae, A Synodo Verolamiensi A.D. CCCXLVI ad Londinensem A.D. MDCCXVII*. 4 vols. Vols. 2 and 3, London: R. Gosling et al., 1737. Repr. Brussels: Culture et Civilisation, 1964.

Wilks, Michael. "Predestination, Property, and Power: Wyclif's Theory of Dominion and Grace." *Studies in Church History* 2 (1965): 220–36.

Willems, R., ed. *Sancti Aurelii Augustini in Johannis Evangelium Tractatus CXXIV*. Corpus Christianorum Series Latina 36. Turnhout: Brepols, 1954.

Williams, Arnold. "Relations Between the Mendicant Friars and the Secular Clergy in England in the Later Fourteenth Century." *Annuale Medievale* 1 (1960): 22–95.

Williams, George Huntston. *Anselm: Communion and Atonement*. St. Louis.: Concordia, 1960.

Williams, Peter. *The Organ in Western Culture, 750–1250*. Cambridge: Cambridge University Press, 1993.

Wilson, William Burton, trans. *John Gower: Mirour de l'Omme*. Rev. Nancy Wilson Van Baak. East Lansing, Mich.: Colleagues Press, 1992.

Winn, Herbert E., ed. *Wyclif: Select English Writings*. London: Humphrey Milford, 1929.

Wirtjes, Hanneke. "*Piers Plowman* B.xviii.371: 'right ripe must'." In *Medieval Literature and Antiquities: Studies in Honour of Basil Cottle*, ed. Myra Stokes and T. L. Burton. Cambridge: D.S. Brewer, 1987. 133–43.

Wittig, Joseph S. "The Dramatic and Rhetorical Development of Long Will's Pilgrimage." *Neuphilologische Mitteilungen* 76 (1975): 52–76.

————. "The Middle English 'Absolute Infinitive' and 'The Speech of Book'." In *Magister Regis: Studies in Honor of Robert Earl Kaske*, ed. Arthur Groos et al. New York: Fordham University Press, 1986. 217–40.

————. *William Langland Revisited*. New York: Twayne, 1997.

Woolf, Rosemary. "Doctrinal Influences on *The Dream of the Rood*." *Medium Ævum* 27 (1958): 137–53.

————. *The English Religious Lyric in the Middle Ages*. Oxford: Clarendon Press, 1968.

———. "The Tearing of the Pardon." In *Piers Plowman: Critical Approaches*, ed. S. S. Hussey. London: Methuen, 1969. 50–75.

———. "The Theme of Christ the Lover-Knight in Medieval English Literature." *Review of English Studies* n.s. 13 (1962):1–16.

Wright, Thomas, ed. *The Chronicle of Pierre de Langtoft.* 2 vols. Rolls Series. London: Longman, 1866–68.

Wright, Thomas. *Political Poems and Songs Relating to English History.* 2 vols. Rolls Series. London: Longman, Green, Longman, and Roberts, 1859, 1861.

Young, Karl. *The Drama of the Medieval Church.* 2 vols. Oxford: Clarendon Press, 1933.

———. "The Harrowing of Hell in Liturgical Drama." *Transactions of the Wisconsin Academy of Sciences, Arts, and Letters* 16 (1910): 889–947.

Yunck, John A. *The Lineage of Lady Meed: The Development of Mediæval Venality Satire.* South Bend, Ind.: University of Notre Dame Press, 1963.

Index of Historical and Modern Works, Authors, Persons, and Topics mentioned in the commentary

Literary works by known authors are listed under the authors' names, anonymous works under the names of the works. References to characters and personages in *Piers Plowman*, and in the Bible, are included (but are not exhaustive for sections where those figures are continually present), but not those in other works. All modern scholars are included (except simply as editors or translators of primary texts), using initials only of first names; all other writers, early and modern, are given with full names. References to the commentaries in Pearsall (Prsl), Schmidt (Schm), the Athlone editions of *Piers Plowman*, and the two handbooks by John A. Alford (Alford, *Gloss.* and Alford, *Quot.*), are not included since they are ubiquitous, but references to other works by those scholars are included, as are references to comments by Skeat in his edition (Skt). The topics included are chiefly restricted to literary, historical, and social materials mentioned in the commentary, and some basic issues in the poem and its contexts (e.g., "dominion and common property"; "law"; "kingship"). Such references are meant to be suggestive and are certainly not comprehensive. References to discussion of editorial or textual issues are gathered under "textual cruces"; references to manuscripts under "manuscripts."

Index of Passages and Notes Mentioned in the Commentary

This list includes references to passages from *Piers Plowman* and notes in the Commentary, apart from reference to lines included in the lemma. Entries citing notes ("n") by passage refer to notes that often include discussion of the parallel versions. Such entries tacitly refer to the passages themselves as well. The references for lines in C.21 and C.22 will apply to the equivalent lines in B.19 and B.20.